The Making of Iran's Islamic Revolution

Second Edition

THE MAKING OF IRAN'S ISLAMIC REVOLUTION

From Monarchy to Islamic Republic

Mohsen M. Milani

Westview Press

BOULDER • SAN FRANCISCO • OXFORD

Copyright © 1988, 1994 by Westview Press, Inc.

Published in 1994 in the United States of America by Westview Press, Inc., 5500 Central Avenue, Boulder, Colorado 80301-2877, and in the United Kingdom by Westview Press, 36 Lonsdale Road, Summertown, Oxford OX2 7EW

Library of Congress Cataloging-in-Publication Data
Milani, Mohsen M.
The making of Iran's Islamic revolution : from monarchy to Islamic
 republic / Mohsen M. Milani. —2nd ed.
  p. cm.
 Includes bibliographical references and index.
 ISBN 0-8133-8475-3. — ISBN 0-8133-8476-1 (pbk.)
  1. Iran—History—Mohammed Reza Pahlavi, 1941–1979.   2. Iran—
History—1979– I. Title.
DS318.M495   1994
955.05'3—dc20   94-14600
                                                                          CIP

Printed and bound in the United States of America

The paper used in this publication meets the requirements
of the American National Standard for Permanence of Paper
for Printed Library Materials Z39.48-1984.

10   9   8   7   6   5   4   3   2   1

In the memory of my mother, I dedicate this book to those who preach and practice nonviolence.

Contents

Part Three: Preconditions of the Islamic Revolution

Part Four: The Mechanics of the Transfer of Power

Part Five: The Postrevolutionary Power Struggle

Tables

Preface to the Second Edition

This book presents a comprehensive analysis of the internal (political, economic, and ideological) and external (U.S. policy) causes and consequences of Iran's Islamic Revolution. It explains how and why an essentially nonviolent and popular movement overthrew Mohammad Reza Shah's apparently impregnable regime in 1979 and built upon its ashes a theocratic Islamic order, one that has changed both Iran's destiny and the political landscape of the Islamic world.

In the second edition, I have not changed the conceptual framework outlined in the first edition for explaining the Islamic Revolution. Nor have I altered my original assessment of why the Shi'i fundamentalists, under the leadership of Ayatollah Ruhollah Mussavi Khomeini, defeated their opponents and established their rule.

The new edition contains, however, some revisions and additions, which are often based on the newly released information and documents about Iran. Whereas a few sections have been totally rewritten, many others are now considerably shorter. In some sections, such as the ones on the Teheran hostage crisis and the Iranian involvement in the Kuwaiti crisis, I have included the information from the many interviews I conducted with the officials of the Islamic Republic of Iran during the past three years.

Two entirely new chapters have been added to inform readers of the latest developments in Iran's domestic and foreign policies. One deals with the challenges that the Islamic Republic faced in the 1980s, including the bloody Iraq-Iran war, which ended in 1988. The other is devoted to the domestic and foreign challenges that President Ali Akbar Hashemi Rafsanjani has confronted during the past five years, including a section about Iran's policy of active neutrality during the Kuwaiti crisis or the Second Persian Gulf War.

Since the dawn of the Islamic Revolution in 1979, Teheran and Washington have been engaged in what Professor R. K. Ramazani calls "mutual satanization" of each other. The essential ingredients of this campaign are excessive exaggeration of the perceived negative aspects of the other side plus dubious information, disinformation, mistrust, crude jingoism, and paranoia. The insatiable appetite of the mass media to sensationalize certain adventuristic actions by Iran, such as the Teheran hostage ordeal, has certainly helped perpetuate the prevalent atmosphere of mistrust. Given this inhospitable atmosphere, fiction and facts about Iran have often been confused in the United States. If we are to change this regrettable state of mistrust and paranoia, we must move in an entirely different path: the path of understanding what actually happened when the Shah was overthrown and what the Islamic Republic has done to make Iran Islamic. The ultimate goal of this book is to render the Islamic Revolution and its idiosyncrasies and peculiarities comprehensible to the U.S. reader.

I have tried to achieve this goal by presenting a fair analysis of the revolution, recognizing that total objectivity is a myth some of us take too seriously. In revising this book, I constantly reminded myself of my biases and genuinely tried to eliminate or minimize them. My hope was to produce a book that neither defends and glorifies nor defames and sensationalizes the Islamic Revolution. You will be the judge.

Mohsen M. Milani

Acknowledgments

Making appropriate revisions and updating this book was more time-consuming and challenging than what I first imagined when I agreed to undertake the task. However, the invaluable guidance, support, and encouragement I received from my colleagues and dear friends made the completion of this job possible and gratifying.

Unlimited gratitude goes to my beloved father, who has been the most important source of inspiration for all my education. I am grateful to my brothers, Hossein and Hassan, and to my sister, Farzaneh, for their constant encouragement.

I am indebted to the colleagues who used this book's first edition as required reading in their courses. They and some of my own students made thoughtful suggestions to improve its quality.

I feel blessed to have received the generous support of Bahman Bakhtiari, Hoshang Chehabi, Manocher Dorraj, Michael Gibbons, Thomas Greene, Jo-Anne Hart, Farhad Kazemi, Abbas Milani, R. K. Ramazani, and Reza Sheikholislam. I express my sincere gratitude to them all.

Special thanks go to Marianne Bell and Carole Rennick from the University of South Florida for completing the word processing of a good portion of the manuscript; to Zhand Shakibi, one of my best students, for helping with the Chronology; to Helen Snively for her proficient copyediting and suggestions about style; to Karl Nayeri for assistance with the cover design; to Barbara Ellington, senior acquisitions editor at Westview Press, for good-humoredly seeing to it that I completed the project as scheduled; to Sarah Tomasek for her excellent copyediting; to Libby Barstow, senior production editor, for her valuable help in the production of the book; and to the staff and owner, my friend Jeff Babcock, of Joffrey's Cafe, for allowing me to use the cafe, where I did some editing of the manuscript, as my second office.

Finally, I would like to thank my wife, Ramak, whose wisdom and love have enriched my life. She did much of the research for the last two chapters. Having completed her university education under the Islamic Republic, she made eloquent observations about life in Islamic Iran and thus strengthened the analysis presented in the second half of the book.

If there are any merits to this book, I share them with the individuals mentioned above. But I alone accept responsibility for its content and deficiencies.

M.M.M.

Glossary

The terms are defined here only in the context used in the book.

Asnaf   Guilds (sing.: *senf*)

Auqaf   Charitable-religious endowments (sing.: *vaqf*)

Ayatollah   Revered title in Shi'ism conferred on a recognized *mujtahed* with some following

Bazaar   Demarcated area recognized as the center of trade and commerce

Faqih   Expert jurisprudent (pl.: *foqaha*)

Fatva   Authoritative opinion pronounced by an ayatollah on religious and other matters

Feqh   Islamic jurisprudence

Hadith   Sayings attributed to the Prophet and to the Twelve Imams

Hey'at   Religious group

Hezbollah   Party of God; a group highly devoted to Ayatollah Khomeini; created in 1979 in Iran

Imam   Title that prior to the Islamic Revolution was used primarily in reference to the twelve leaders recognized by Twelver Shi'ites as the legitimate rulers of Islam between A.D. 630–874; implies infallibility; recently Khomeini also called the Imam

Khan   Tribal chief; major landowner

Komites   Ad hoc committees created after the Shah's fall to safeguard the Islamic Revolution

Majles   Iranian parliament created in 1906

Marja'-e taqlid Source of imitation; the highest living religious authority in Shi'ism (pl.: *muraja'-e taqlid*)

Mujtahed An Islamic expert sanctioned to make independent judgment (*ejtehad*) on religious matters

Pasdaran Guardians; militia created after the Islamic Revolution

Seyyed Direct descendants of Prophet Mohammad, Imam Ali, and the other eleven imams

Shari'a Islamic laws

Sheikholislam A rank below ayatollah in the Shi'i hierarchy

Ulama Experts on Islamic laws (sing.: 'Alem)

Velayat-e Faqih Rule of jurisconsult; the basis of governance in the Islamic Republic of Iran

Chronology of Significant Events

1501	Shah Isma'il founds the Safavid dynasty (1501–1747) and imposes Twelver Shi'ism as the state religion in Iran.
1811–1821	Iran loses two wars and some lands to Russia.
1882	Mohammad Mossadeq is born.
1892	Naser ad-Din Shah cancels a tobacco concession to a British company.
1901	William D'Arcy, a British subject, acquires a sixty-year oil concession.
1902	Ruhollah Khomeini is born.
1906–1907	Iran's first constitution is written and the Majles is created. In a secret treaty, England and Russia divide Iran into respective areas of influence.
1908	The Anglo-Persian Oil Company is founded.
1914–1921	Iran declares neutrality in World War I. Reza Khan and Seyyed Zia stage a coup and topple the government.
1919	Mohammad Reza Pahlavi is born.
1926	The Pahlavi dynasty replaces the Qajar dynasty. Khomeini completes his studies at Qom.
1926–1941	Reza Shah's modernization program unfolds. The government's compulsory unveiling of women begins.
1941	Despite Iran's neutrality in World War II, Allied forces occupy Iran and force Reza Shah to abdicate. His son, Mohammad Reza Shah, replaces him.
1944	Reza Shah Pahlavi dies in exile.

1951	Premier Haj Ali Razmara is assassinated by the Fada'iyun-e Islam. Premier Mossadeq nationalizes Iranian oil industry.
1953	In a British MI-6/CIA operation, Mosaddeq is overthrown. Iran signs a new treaty with Western oil companies.
1957	SAVAK, the Shah's secret service, is formed.
1962	Some of the ulama oppose a bill that grants suffrage to women and replaces the phrase "holy Quran" with "holy book" in the oath of office.
1963	The Shah launches his White Revolution. Khomeini declares an open war on the Shah, but not on the institution of the monarchy. Violent demonstrations are staged in major cities to protest Khomeini's detention (the June Uprising).
1965	Khomeini is exiled to Turkey and then to Iraq.
1967	Mohammad Mosaddeq dies.
1970	With the British withdrawal, Iran's military buildup in the Persian Gulf begins.
1971	Iran occupies three strategically located islands in the Strait of Hormuz. Sporadic guerrilla warfare against the Pahlavi regime begins. Communist China and Iran establish diplomatic relations. The Shah celebrates the 2,500-year anniversary of the Persian monarchy. Khomeini declares the incompatibility of Shi'ism with monarchism.
1972	At the request of Sultan Qabus, Iranian forces are introduced in the Dhofar province in Oman to fight the communists. The United States guarantees that the Shah can purchase the most sophisticated nonnuclear arsenal. The Mojahedin bomb the U.S. Information Center in Teheran and assassinate a U.S. military adviser.
1973	The Shah refuses to join the Arab oil embargo of the supporters of Israel. Oil prices increase substantially. King Zahir is overthrown in Afghanistan.
1975	Iran and Iraq sign a peace treaty. Two U.S. Air Force officers are assassinated in Teheran by guerrillas. To lower inflation, thousands of shopkeepers are fined and hundreds arrested.

1976   The Shah expresses doubt on the reliability of the United States as an ally.

Three more Americans are killed by guerrillas in Teheran.

The Imperial calendar replaces the Islamic calendar.

The Shah's liberalization policy begins.

National Front leaders submit an open letter to the Shah demanding that the Persian Constitution be observed.

Haj Aqa Mostafa, Khomeini's oldest son, dies in Iraq. His funeral is held in Teheran.

1978

Jan.   In Teheran, U.S. President Jimmy Carter praises the Shah for creating an "island of stability" in the region.

In a newspaper article, the government attacks Ayatollah Khomeini.

Riots by religious dissidents break out in Qom.

Feb.   Riots break out in Tabriz.

Aug.   Esfahan is placed under martial law.

Hundreds are burned to death when a theater is set ablaze in Abadan by arsonists.

Sept.   Martial law is imposed in Teheran.

Hundreds of protesters are killed by the police (Black Friday).

Oct.   Khomeini is forced to leave Iraq and goes to Paris.

U.S. ambassador Sullivan emphasizes that "our destiny is to work with the Shah."

Oil workers go on strike.

Nov.   General Azhari forms a military government.

From Paris, Khomeini states that an Islamic Republic will be formed in Iran.

Dec.   Millions participate in the anti-Shah demonstrations.

National Front's Shahpur Bakhtiyar agrees to form a cabinet.

1979

Jan.   In Guadeloupe, the leaders of the Western nations decide to ask the Shah to leave Iran.

The Shah leaves Iran.

Carter declares U.S. support for Bakhtiyar.

Feb.   After fifteen years in exile, Khomeini returns to Iran and appoints Mehdi Bazargan to head the Provisional Revolutionary Government.

Feb.	The Imperial Guard attacks the mutinous air force technicians in a Teheran garrison but is defeated by the revolutionaries who confiscate thousands of weapons.
	The armed forces declare their neutrality. Bakhtiar goes into hiding.
	Evin Prison, Iran's Bastille, is stormed. Summary executions of the officials of the Shah's regime by the Revolutionary Courts begin.
	The Fada'iyun attack the U.S. Embassy in Teheran.
March	Women demonstrate against government dress code regulations.
April	By referendum, the Islamic Republic is born.
May	The Pasdaran is officially created.
Oct.	The ailing Shah is admitted to the United States.
Nov.	The U.S. Embassy in Teheran is seized by Moslem students. Embassy personnel are taken hostage. Bazargan resigns.
Dec.	Shariatmadari's supporters stage an uprising in Tabriz and demand the annulment of the new constitution.
	The Red Army invades and occupies Afghanistan.

1980

Jan.	Abolhassan Bani Sadr is elected president.
April	The United States severs relations with Iran, imposes economic sanctions, and makes an abortive attempt to rescue the hostages.
May	The elections for the first Majles are completed.
June	In a failed coup against the Islamic Republic, hundreds are arrested. The universities are shut down and purges of educational institutions begin.
July	Mohammad Reza Shah Pahlavi dies. He is buried in Egypt.
Sept.	Iraq invades Iran.

1981

Jan.	The U.S. hostages are freed.
March	Bani Sadr is removed from power. He escapes to France.
	A bomb kills high-ranking officials. The government blames the Mojahedin.
July	In the second presidential elections, Raja'i wins.
Aug.	In another bomb explosion, Raja'i, Prime Minister Bahonar, and the chief of police are killed. The Mojahedin are again blamed by the government.

Oct.   Hojatolislam Ali Khamenei is elected president.

1982
Jan.   The Communist League takes over the city of Amol. The Pasdaran quickly puts down the rebellion and kills the rebels.

Feb.   A Mojahedin hideout is attacked by the government and Khiyabani, the Mojahedin's leader, and scores of others are killed.

April   Ayatollah Shariatmadari admits to having had prior knowledge of Sadeq Qotbzadeh's plan to stage a coup.

May   Iran recaptures the port city of Khoramshahr.

June   Kuzichkin, a Russian officer, defects to England and gives information about the Tudeh Party to the British.

Sept.   Qotbzadeh is executed.

1983
Feb.   Some sixty top Tudeh Party officials are arrested on charges of spying for the Soviet Union.

April   The government makes veiling of women compulsory.

Sept.   Universities reopen, many of them for the first time since 1980.

Dec.   The United States begins Operation Staunch to stop the flow of arms to Iran.

1984
March   Independent laboratory tests confirm that Iraq has been using mustard gas against Iranian troops.

Nov.   The Council of Experts declares Montazeri as Khomeini's successor. Amnesty International claims that 6,027 persons have been executed in Iran since 1979.

1985
March   President Khamenei escapes an assassination attempt.

Aug.   Khamenei is reelected president.

1986
June   Rajavi moves the Mojahedin's headquarters from Paris to Baghdad.

Nov.   A Lebanese newspaper reports that the United States had clandestinely delivered arms to Iran in exchange for Iranian assistance in the release of the U.S. hostages held in Lebanon.

1987

Jan. Senate Intelligence Committee reports that officials in the Reagan administration deceived one another and the Congress.

March House Resolution 216 warns that the continuation of the Iraq-Iran war could result in an "Iranian breakthrough" that would damage the strategic interests of the United States.

April Rafsanjani states that U.S.-Iranian relations need not remain hostile until "doomsday."

July Ayatollah Khomeini dissolves the Islamic Republican Party.

Oct. Mehdi Hashemi is executed. His supporters allegedly provided a Lebanese newspaper with information that unraveled the secret Iran-U.S. arms deal.
U.S. president Ronald Reagan announces a comprehensive embargo on U.S. imports from Iran.

1988

April The Reagan administration announces U.S. protection of all vessels in the Persian Gulf.

July USS *Vincennes* downs a commercial Iranian aircraft and kills all of its 290 passengers. Later it was revealed that the *Vincennes* was in Iranian territorial water and that the commercial aircraft was downed in Iranian airspace.

Aug. Iran and Iraq accept the UN-sponsored resolution for a cease-fire.

1989

Feb. The Islamic Republic claims that Ayatollah Khomeini issued a *fatva* sanctioning the killing of Salman Rushdie, the author of *The Satanic Verses*.

March Iran breaches diplomatic ties with England over the Rushdie affair.
Ayatollah Montazeri resigns as Khomeini's successor.

June Ayatollah Khomeini dies.
Hojatolislam Khamenei succeeds Khomeini as the new *faqih*.

July Rafsanjani is elected president.

1990

Aug. Rafsanjani promises to privatize some of the major industries.
Iraq invades and occupies Kuwait. Iran strongly condemns the Iraqi aggression but declares neutrality in the Second Persian Gulf War.

Oct. Iran resumes diplomatic relations with Iraq and England.

Nov.	U.S. president George Bush authorizes importation of Iranian oil and relaxes the 1987 ban on Iranian imports.

1991
March	The end of the Second Persian Gulf War. Bush states that Iran should not be "treated forever as an enemy."
April	Rafsanjani calls for closer cooperation with the West and with the Persian Gulf nations.
Aug.	Former prime minister Bakhtiyar is assassinated in Paris. The opponents of the Islamic Republic blame the Iranian government.

1992
Jan.	Some U.S. officials believe that Iran paid captors $1 million for the release of each American held hostage in Lebanon.
Feb.	Israel kills chief of the Lebanese Hezbollah in Lebanon. Rafsanjani urges restraint. The International Atomic Agency concludes that Iran's nuclear sites and activities are only for peaceful purposes.
March	Iran attempts to mediate between different fighting factions in the Islamic republics of the former USSR. Iran expels some "suspected" elements from the Abu Musa island. The United Arab Emirates protests the Iranian action. The parliamentary elections for the 4th Majles are completed.

1993
March	The World Bank approves a $157 million loan to Iran for agricultural projects and a $165 million loan to finance a power station in Iran.
April	Iran bombs the headquarters of the Mojahedin in Iraq.
May	Martin Indyk, National Security Council adviser, discusses the essence of a new U.S. policy of dual containment to isolate Iran and Iraq.
June	President Rafsanjani is reelected for a second four-year term.

The Making of Iran's Islamic Revolution

Introduction

Iran's Islamic Revolution of 1979 was one of the most fascinating and surprising events of the second half of this turbulent and bloody century. It bewildered experts and policymakers alike. Shortly before Mohammad Reza Shah Pahlavi (1919–1981) was overthrown, everything seemed to be in his favor. He enjoyed the support of the United States and other Western powers, the half-million-strong and well-equipped army, and SAVAK—the acronym in the Persian language for his secret intelligence agency that was perceived by most Iranians to be omnipotent and omnipresent. His government faced no dire financial crisis, nor had it come out of a devastating war or a humiliating military defeat, as had been the case in prerevolutionary France, Russia, and China. In fact, the Shah could take credit for making Iran an important force in the international arena and for managing Iran's stupendous economic growth in the first part of the 1970s, unprecedented in its modern history.

Moreover, the opposition to the Peacock Throne was checkmated by SAVAK. It was divided and confused. His sworn enemies, like most Iranians, could not even imagine overthrowing the powerful Shah, not to speak of his dynasty. In fact, the idea of his invincibility—the Supershah Syndrome—had become endemic in Iran and within the U.S. foreign policy establishment: President Jimmy Carter praised the Iranian monarch, exactly a year before he was toppled, for having created an "island of stability" in a troubled region of the world.

Then came the sudden tidal wave of revolution. It took the revolutionaries about one year to hammer the final nail into the coffin of the Shah's well-fortified regime and his dynasty.

That a popular revolution overthrew a repressive despot was neither strange nor unique: The history of revolutions is replete with such events. Truly startling, however, was the role Islam played in precipitating the Islamic Revolution and its emergence as the hegemonic ideology in postrevolutionary Iran. After all, modern revolutions have inspired societies free of ecclesiastical influence and based on new ideas and ideals. In France, for example, the revolutionaries confiscated the enormous properties of the Roman Catholic Church and changed its Gregorian calendar to the year zero, symbolic of their determination to begin something entirely new. The communists in Russia and China relied on a secular ideology that was inherently antagonistic to all religions. Once in power, the communists did what they could, albeit with little success, to suppress religion.

Prior to the revolution in Iran, the conventional wisdom portrayed religion as a dying and anachronistic force whose appropriate place was in history books. In utter defiance of that flawed paradigm, the Shi'i ulama, who were to have been crushed beneath the wheels of secularization and capitalist development of the Pahlavi era, became the "philosopher kings" of a new theocracy founded on the doctrine of the Velayat-e Faqih or the ulama's direct rule. Quickly Imperial Iran, "that island of stability," became Islamic Iran and the center of a new Islamic movement that has haunted much of the Islamic world during the past decade.

Why was the Shah's regime so easily defeated? Why did so many experts fail to see the coming of the Islamic Revolution? How and why did Islam become the dominant ideology of the revolution and how did the Shi'i ulama defeat their opponents and establish their rule? What are the failures and accomplishments of the Islamic Republic? This book is designed to answer these and other intriguing questions about the Islamic Revolution.

Specifically, I endeavor to explain the economic, political, and ideological preconditions that precipitated the revolution, some of the internal and external factors that facilitated the ulama's accession to power, and some of the profound consequences of Iran's Islamization on the fortunes of an old nation in hopes of a better future. In pursuit of these objectives, I focus on the nature and evolution of the Iranian state, for whose control the Islamic Revolution was launched. I discuss the changing patterns of the Iranian state's relations with the hegemonic foreign powers, particularly the United States, and with social groups that possessed considerable organizational and financial resources, namely the ulama, the bazaar merchants and shopkeepers, and the intelligentsia.

The arguments of this book are organized into five parts and eleven chapters. That experts failed to envision as late as 1978 the end of the monarchy and the ascendancy of the ulama was the product of their erroneous assumptions about Pahlavi Iran. Part 1 explains the roots of this conceptual crisis—what I call theoretical glaucoma in the study of Iran. In it, I propose a holistic conceptual framework for explaining the Islamic Revolution, one that is based on the synthesis and revision of and addition to various theories of revolution. It is assumed that the interaction of factors Niccoló Machiavelli called *fortuna* with both the idiosyncrasies of leaders and objective preconditions precludes the possibility of applying prepackaged and often ethnocentric theories of revolution.

Part 2 provides the historical background to the Islamic Revolution. Chapter 2 analyzes the Constitutional Movement of 1905–1911 and the reasons for the creation of the Pahlavi dynasty. Chapter 3 explains Mohammad Reza Shah's successful drive toward absolute power in the first two decades of his reign (1941–1979) and the challenges he faced from Dr. Mohammad Mossadeq and Ayatollah Ruhollah Khomeini. Included here is a detailed account of the June Uprising of

1963 (a dress rehearsal for the Islamic Revolution, as it has been called), which led to Khomeini's exile to Turkey and then to Iraq.

Why was Khomeini so easily defeated by the Shah in 1963 but able to come back in 1979 to dethrone him? An important part of the answer to that puzzle may be found in the transformation of Iranian society and polity in the 1960s and 1970s. Part 3, consisting of three chapters, focuses on the political, ideological, and economic preconditions of the Islamic Revolution.

Revolutions do not come; they are made. Part 4 deals with the art of making the Islamic Revolution and how power was transferred from the ancien régime to the Islamic revolutionaries. The popular movement that overthrew the Shah went through eight stages. For each stage, I explain the strategies of and interactions among the Shah's regime, the United States, and the revolutionaries, bringing to the surface such critical factors as the leadership abilities of both the Shah and Khomeini.

Part 5 explains how the Shi'i fundamentalist forces under Khomeini's leadership defeated their rivals and created an Islamic theocracy. Here I challenge the proposition that Shi'i fundamentalism was the principal cause of the revolution, a proposition based on reading history backward. I argue that Shi'i fundamentalism was more a consequence than a principal precondition of the revolution: Its ascendancy was neither predestined nor inevitable. Chapters 8 and 9 describe how the fundamentalists shrewdly outmaneuvered their rivals, mainly the Islamic nationalists, the secular nationalists, the Islamic socialists, and the leftists. This process began with the gradual strangling of Mehdi Bazargan's Provisional Revolutionary Government and ended with the ouster of President Abolhassan Bani Sadr. This section includes a detailed discussion of the Teheran hostage crisis.

It is one thing to win a revolution and an entirely different matter to govern a country. In the last section, I discuss the challenges the Shi'i fundamentalists have faced in the past fourteen years in trying to govern and Islamize Iran. Chapter 10 describes the nature and consequences of Iran's drive toward radicalism under Ayatollah Khomeini's rule, and Chapter 11 details the Islamic Republic's drive toward moderation and pragmatism under Ayatollah Seyyed Ali Khamenei and President Ali Akbar Hashemi Rafsanjani. Considerable attention is given to the Iraq-Iran war and to Iranian foreign policy during the Kuwaiti crisis.

Because there is no standardized system for transliterating Persian into Latin characters, I have opted for a simple system. Familiar nouns, like imam, are given in their common spelling. Other words are transliterated in agreement with Persian pronunciation. Consonants are written as pronounced; the short vowels are represented by *a, e,* and *o*; and the three long vowels by *a, i,* and *u*. To avoid diacritical marks, *a* represents both the Persian short and long vowels. Ezafeh is -*ye* after a vowel and -*e* for a consonant.

Unless otherwise stated, all translations from the Persian-language sources are by the author.

A review of the Chronology of Significant Events is recommended before reading the text.

Part One

Conceptual Framework

1

The Study of Revolution: Science of Anarchy or Anarchy of Science?

> Two young men came to me and started talking. One of them said: We have read your writings. "There should be a revolution in this country [Iran]." Before I could answer, the other said: "Yes, we have lagged behind, we must move fast." I told them, "Your talk is so vacuous that I do not know how to answer. If I ask you what revolution is, I bet you cannot answer. In any event, do you have a plan for it [revolution] and have you prepared the ground for it?" They said, "No. We only wanted to express our views. We have no plan [for revolution] as yet."
>
> *Ahmad Kasravi, Enqelab Chist? (What Is Revolution?), n.d.*

Revolution generates both intense enthusiasm and abhorrence. It is revered as a historical necessity: Victor Hugo regarded it as "the larva of civilization." It is also condemned as a cataclysmic event and "the most wasteful, the most expensive, the last to be chosen."[1] This is perhaps why, despite the abundance of analytical literature on revolution, there is little consensus about what revolution is and what produces it. There is, however, a unanimous agreement that revolutions are momentous events with long-lasting impact.

The Evolution of the Modern Concept and Myth of Revolution

In the past few centuries, the meaning of revolution has undergone radical changes.[2] In the late Middle Ages in northern Italy, revolution, *rivoluzione*, gained its own physiognomy as "a long-term movement of fortunes accompanied by sudden, sharp reversal."[3] This emphasis on fortune gave revolution a mysterious coloring and elevated it to an act beyond human control.

In the mid-sixteenth century, Copernicus popularized revolution in astronomy as the return of the stars to the point of origin. By the mid-seventeenth century, Copernicus's notion found its way into England's political literature.[4] Thus, the restoration of the monarchy under Charles II of the House of Stuart in 1660 and the confirmation of the supremacy of Parliament over the authority of the king in 1688 were both called revolution—the latter, the Glorious Revolution.

The French Revolution of 1787–1794 revolutionized the concept of revolution and gave it a new mystique and meaning, a romantic bent that has persisted to this day.[5] No longer was revolution conceptualized as the return to the point of origin or as an event beyond human control. The French revolutionaries, inspired by the enlightened thoughts of philosophers like Voltaire, Rousseau, and Diderot, insisted that once the shackles of superstitions and archaic institutions were removed through creative political engineering, the human mind would usher humanity to a promising future. The change of France's Gregorian calendar to one beginning at the year zero was symbolic of this new optimism. Soon, revolution, despite the terror of the French Revolution itself, became synonymous with liberty and progressive change, a belief only a few thinkers like Edmund Burke dared challenge.[6]

In the nineteenth century, the towering presence of Karl Marx became the apotheosis of the revolutionary. Marx perceived revolution as an inherently liberating necessity, the motor of historical progress. For him, the task of philosophy was not to interpret the world, but to change it, and to do so by revolution. And this is what one of his disciples, Vladimir Lenin, accomplished in Russia by orchestrating the Bolshevik Revolution in 1917.

Following the imposition of socialism in the former Soviet Union, the idea of revolution became quite attractive to the Third World. For most Third World intellectuals, who were often influenced by the philosophical underpinnings of Marxism, revolution became a political necessity, a convenient shortcut to progress, the only genuine method of terminating the Third World's dependent ties with the West, and the only road to political independence. This is perhaps why the twentieth century will be remembered as the century of revolution.

With the victory of the Bolsheviks in neighboring Russia followed by the creation of an Iranian communist party, both Marxist views and the idea of revolution gradually found their way into Iran's political discourse. Until the 1920s, revolution was neither sought nor discussed by most Iranian reformers because monarchy was a religiously sanctioned institution.[7] This is why during the Constitutional Movement of 1906–1911 reformers never spoke of revolution. It was years later that Iranian historians, influenced by Western and Russian historiography, began to refer to that event as a revolution, which it certainly was not.

As the Pahlavi state became more entrenched and as the Pahlavi shahs became more autocratic, the idea of revolution became ever more tantalizing to the educated Iranians who were disenchanted with the slow pace of progress in their native land. By the 1960s, it had become "chic" to be a revolutionary, so much so that even Mohammad Reza Shah, the very symbol of the status quo, labeled his reforms in 1963 as a "White Revolution."

Why was the idea of revolution so popular in Iran and in other Third World nations? One reason was the myth that revolution was the harbinger of individual freedom and civil liberties. Dictatorship and poverty, so prevalent in the Third World, made revolution a popular ideal: Revolution was synonymous with progressive change.

Hannah Arendt explained why this perception of revolution could be erroneous. She argued that revolutions often are launched with the objective of expanding democratic rights. Once the ancien régime is demolished, revolutionaries begin to consolidate their power and expand their popular base of support by adding a social dimension to revolution, which means advocating the herculean but popular goal of eradicating poverty and misery. But the revolutionaries often fail to achieve this goal. In order to perpetuate the myth of their "success," they must therefore suppress those who may expose the revolutionaries' utter failure to accomplish what they had promised. Soon, Arendt concluded, revolutions would rot and become even more repressive than the regimes they had replaced.[8] The fate of the twentieth-century revolutions seems to have vindicated Arendt's position.

Revolution Defined

Today few other words in the lexicon of social sciences are more ubiquitously and loosely used than the term "revolution," a reflection of the preparadigmatic stage of the study of revolution. For Raymond Tanter and Manus Midlarsky, revolution is an event in which a "group of insurgents illegally and or forcefully challenges the governmental elites."[9] For Charles Tilly, it is "the displacement of one set of power-holders by another."[10] For Hannah Arendt, only when "the liberation from oppression aims at least at the constitution of freedom, can we speak of revolution."[11] Samuel Huntington regards revolution as "a rapid, fundamental and violent domestic change in the dominant values and myths of a society, in its political institutions, social structure, leadership and government activity and politics."[12] Theda Skocpol refers to it as "a rapid, basic transformation of a society and state structure ... accompanied and in part carried through by class-based revolts from below."[13]

For the purpose of this study, I define revolution as a rapid, fundamental change in the social structures as well as in the state's personnel, institutions, and foundation of its legitimacy, accomplished from outside the legal channels and accompanied in part by a movement from below (the nongoverning classes).

This definition distinguishes revolutions from coups d'état (the forceful replacements of one faction of the elite by another), from rebellions (spontaneous mass uprisings against a specific government policy or event), and from "revolutions from above" (radical, elite-initiated change imposed on society). Further, the definition is neutral: It attaches no moral standards to outcomes of revolutions, which may be progressive or regressive. It also regards a revolution as a modern and rare phenomenon. Great civilizations of the past (Egypt, Babylon, Persia) experienced dynastic changes and slow societal transformations, but not revolutions.

According to our definition, the 1979 event was a revolution: The Shah's regime was overthrown in part by the participation of the lower classes; the state's personnel and its foundation of legitimacy were changed; and new structures and institutions were built. Those who have a romantic view of revolution may claim that because Islamic Iran is less free and more regressive than Pahlavi Iran, no revolution has taken place there. This tautological reasoning is a reflection of what they think revolution "ought to be" rather than what it "is" or "has been."

The Shah and the Experts:
An Iran That Was Not

It was not for lack of information that the experts were bewildered by the Shah's fall and the ulama's victory, for information was abundantly available. Rather, the problem was what I call "theoretical glaucoma," the roots of which may be traced back to the prevalent assumptions in social sciences about the nature and consequences of modernization in the Third World. Many of these ethnocentric assumptions were designed to provide intellectual justification for U.S. interventionist foreign policy in the era after World War II.[14] They reflected the arrogance of power and the utter insensitivity of the United States to the cultural and religious orientations of Third World nations. This is why, as Sheldon Wolin eloquently pointed out, "the Third World understood itself in one way, while social science understood it in another."[15]

Perhaps the source of all misleading assumptions was and is that the Western model of development has universal applicability, one that no nation can escape and all nations should emulate wholeheartedly.[16] What is altogether ignored in this simplistic model is the undeniable fact that the domestic and international conditions under which Western Europe was modernized have been qualitatively different from those that the developing world has faced. What has effectively worked for Western Europe and for the United States may not prove fruitful for the Third World, and what has been good for the West may not be good for the Third World, whose religion, culture, and history are often different from those of the West.

Based on the universality of the Western model, a number of other erroneous conclusions were drawn. For example, it was assumed that economic growth is a catalyst for stability and a deterrent against communist temptation, an idea that originated from the success of the Marshall Plan in rebuilding the ruined Western Europe after World War II. It was in that spirit that the United States provided economic assistance to the Third World. It was only in the mid-1960s that some scholars began to challenge the direct correlation postulated between economic growth and stability, at least for the Third World.[17]

Another misleading assumption was the dismissal of religion as a relevant force in revolutionary movements. The unfolding of modernization in the Third World, as in the West, was thought to go hand in hand with secularization—the emancipation of politics from religion.[18] Ironically, both Marxist and non-Marxist paradigms generally viewed religion as a dying and anachronistic force, as the "opiate of the masses." Thus, secular ideologies such as nationalism and socialism, not religion, and the peasantry and the middle class, not the religious groups, were identified as the potential agents for radical change in the Third World.

Many of these myopic assumptions had also permeated the discipline of Iranology. James Bill, for example, argued in 1972 that the middle class posed the greatest menace to the Pahlavi regime, a view shared by many other experts.[19] It was fashionable to consider the leftist and the nationalist groups as the most radical agents of revolutionary change in Iran.

Islam as a political force was hardly discussed. I know of no expert or policy-maker who predicted the ascendance of Islam in Iran. It is true that Bijan Jazani, a young Marxist activist, declared in 1964 that Khomeini would most likely play a major role in any future revolutionary movement, and Professor Hamid Algar wrote in 1969 that "protests in religious terms will continue to be voiced and the appeals of men such as Ayatollah Khomeini to be widely heeded."[20] But neither declaration should be confused with predicting a religious uprising in Iran.

The dominant view was that Islam had become a peripheral force. Professor Leonard Binder echoed this view:

> The Shah has striven to weaken the religious institution as an autonomous force without alienating his traditional religious support. ... By successfully putting down religious opposition in 1963 and by preventing anyone from being acknowledged as "Ayatollah al-Uzmah" or chief mulla [mullah] the Shah strengthened the relative position of his supporters among the clergy, even though it is now more than ever known that the Shah is not a friend of orthodox Shi'ite Islam.[21]

Professor Bill, too, fell into this trap. In 1979, he wrote that the "middle class was the main force behind the revolution" and "the ulama would never participate directly in the formal governmental structures."[22] In October 1979, when the new constitution had legitimized the Velayat-e Faqih provision, or the rule of the ulama, Bill stated: "However, in the long run the ayatollahs do not have the ability to erect a new political structure. Historically, the Shi'i clergy have always been outside the government and have acted as a negative force. They are mentally and emotionally unprepared for the challenge of rebuilding Iran."[23] To his credit, Bill was among the first in the United States to predict the inevitability of the Shah's collapse.[24]

The U.S. Embassy in Teheran, too, failed to foresee the threat the ulama could pose to the Shah. The confidential embassy report in 1972 was typical of the way the ulama's role was analyzed:

> Should a marked faltering of the economy or an apparent weakening of the government's firm hand, lead other segments of the population to challenge the government, the embittered Mullahs within the Muslim hierarchy could draw up considerable following, especially among the bazaaries and lower classes. Even in those circumstances, it is unlikely that they will ever return to a historic role such as that of 1892, when they led the attacks against the Belgian [actually British] Tobacco Concession, or of 1907, when they played a big role in the Constitutional revolution, or of 1952, when they rallied behind the government in the break with the British.[25]

Thus, in January 1978, a year before the Shah's regime crumbled, the U.S. ambassador to Iran, William Sullivan, reported to Washington that although the ulama possessed an impressive organizational network, "they would probably find it difficult to generate additional demonstrations immediately for purely political purposes."[26] Until November 1978, just three short months before the Shah's forced exile from Iran, the ambassador advocated supporting the Shah as the best alternative for the United States.

Nor was the record of the U.S. intelligence agencies any more impressive than Sullivan's. The Central Intelligence Agency (CIA) seemed more interested in gathering information about the Soviet Union by operating its two monitoring stations at Behshahr and Kapkan than in scrutinizing events in Iran. So it should come as little surprise that U.S. intelligence agencies had concluded in 1978 that the "Shah will be an active participant in Iranian life well into the 1980s."[27]

Nor were the Marxists immune to this blindness about religion. In February 1979, the editors of *Monthly Review,* an independent socialist publication, wrote that once the Shah was forced out of Iran the "question of class will come to the fore and religion will cease to play the leadership role it enjoyed during the revolutionary period."[28] In June 1979, Professor Ervand Abrahamian predicted that the "religious reactionaries will soon begin to lose their hold over the labor movement and the left will then have an easy entry into an arena that includes more than two and half million wage earners."[29] (The French ambassador to Iran, Raoul Delaye, was quoted by L. Bruce Laingen, U.S. chargé d'affairs in Teheran, as saying, "Khomeini will inevitably fail and the immediate gain will be by the left."[30])

Why were so many policymakers, academics, and intelligence agencies unable to predict the coming of the Islamic Revolution? In a way, the question itself is misleading because revolutions are intrinsically unpredictable. We should give up the idea of predicting revolutions because they are the outcome of interactions among various complicated factors some of which, like Machiavelli's idea of *fortuna* and the leadership quality of leaders during crises, can never be accurately assessed in advance.[31]

The experts should not be blamed for failing to predict the Islamic Revolution, but they do deserve to be rebuked for not even placing the Iran of the late 1970s in a prerevolutionary stage.[32]

There were specific flaws in the way prerevolutionary Iran was analyzed. The first one stemmed from U.S. ignorance about Iranian culture. Examples were abundant. In his *Counter-coup,* published shortly after the Shah's fall, Kim Roosevelt, one of the organizers of the 1953 CIA coup against Dr. Mossadeq, describes a camel-driven oil mill in the Isfahan bazaar, which was well known to tourists visiting the bazaar, as a secret opium processing plant.[33] The mistake about the oil mill, trivial as it appears on the surface, was symptomatic of a much deeper problem. In fairness to Roosevelt, he was not unique in having only a minimum acquaintance with the intricacies of Iran's complicated culture and customs. Americans living in Iran, and they were many, had created a colony for themselves. "This transplantation of America into Iran," Bill argued perceptively, "established an atmosphere of isolation that severely crippled the capacity of official Americans to understand Iran."[34] U.S. officials had little or no contact with ordinary Iranians. Fewer than 10 percent of U.S. diplomatic personnel, compared with 40 and 70 percent of their British and Russian counterparts, respectively, spoke Farsi, the Persian language. Not one U.S. ambassador to Iran ever spoke Farsi.[35] To think that it is possible to understand Iran without speaking that country's language, the gateway to its soul, is simply preposterous.[36]

The second flaw in the analysis of prerevolutionary Iran was political in nature. To protect its interests, the United States had made a decision not to see what was wrong with Iran. Hoping not to antagonize the Shah, who had become one of the closest Middle East allies of the United States and one of the pillars of the strategy to contain communism, Washington discouraged or ignored any negative reports about Iran. It could be argued that because the United States relied on SAVAK, Iran's secret service, for information, and because SAVAK, under the Shah's personal command, was not a reliable source, Washington was kept in the dark. But this argument is superficial. As a U.S. Embassy officer in Teheran cogently argued in 1978, there were signs that Iran was not actually what the United States wanted it to be, "but we [Americans], with increasing stubbornness, insisted on ignoring them."[37]

The Pahlavi regime and its many powerful supporters in the United States portrayed Iran as a stable, modernizing nation. The Pahlavis had established critical contacts with some influential members of the U.S. Congress, the military, the mass media, the intelligence agencies, the business community, and academia. The Iranian Embassy in Washington frequently showered the Shah's supporters in the mass media with gifts such as champagne, Persian caviar, diamond watches, and silk scarves.[38] Generous grants were given to major U.S. universities: More than fifty U.S. universities, including Harvard, Massachusetts Institute of Technology, University of Southern California, and Georgetown University, maintained official contact with the Shah's regime. The Pahlavis also had powerful friends, like the Rockefellers, in the business community. And the Shah's multibillion-dollar military purchases certainly made him popular among the executives of the military-industrial complex, whose clout in Washington is well known to all.

Gradually, the Shah came to be perceived by many Americans and Iranians as invincible; hence the prevalence of what I call the Supershah Syndrome. President Carter's praise of the Shah for creating an island of stability a year before the monarch was overthrown was but one example of how deeply the Supershah Syndrome had penetrated the U.S. foreign policy establishment. Academics were not immune to the contagious syndrome either: A U.S. economist wrote a book in the late 1970s about the direction of the Iranian economy under the Shah in the 1980s.[39] Soon after its publication, Iran celebrated the end of the monarchy.

An astute and objective observer of Pahlavi Iran could see three contradictory Irans, as if they represented three different nations. The first Iran was that of the rich, of the Western educated, of the high-rise buildings and discos, and of modern factories and armed forces. It was the Iran that the Pahlavis wanted the world to see and accept. And that was basically the Iran that most Americans knew. In their propaganda to depict Iran as what it really was not, the Pahlavis and their U.S. allies became victims of their own self-deceptions and therefore became even more divorced from the realities of the Iranian society.[40]

The second Iran was that of the middle-class, anti-Shah dissidents. Small in number, the components of this Iran were the focus of attention of U.S. experts, not only because they were seen as a serious threat to the Shah's rule but also because it was relatively easy to communicate with this Western-oriented segment of the population.

But the third Iran was unknown and mysterious except to those who composed it. It was not the Iran that made multibillion-dollar deals with the West. Nor was it the Iran that bought staggering amounts of sophisticated weapons from the West. It was not the Iran that generated easy research money. It was the powerless Iran that supposedly posed no threat to anyone and which those in power ignored. It was the Iran of the mosques, the flagellation processions, the shanties, the bazaars, the peasants, the workers, and the poor. Only intermingling with these people, not reliance or raw statistics, could have provided a clue to their modes of thinking. If this Iran was studied at all, it was done as an exciting intellectual exercise to uncover its mysterious and idiosyncratic dimension.[41] Consequently, this Iran remained unknown, and when the ulama, as the representatives of this Iran, rose to power, the experts were bewildered.

In response to my question about why the experts failed to predict the ulama's victory, President Ali Akbar Hashemi Rafsanjani said: "They were unaware of our contact with, and influence over, the masses. According to their logic, we did not have a political party or an official organization. It is extremely difficult for those who do not hold religious views to comprehend how influential religion could become and what a momentous force it really is."[42] Only by intermingling with the masses and understanding the nuances of Iran's culture could the experts have appreciated the mobilizing power of Shi'ism.

A Holistic Approach to the Study of the Islamic Revolution

There is a plethora of theories about the preconditions of revolution.[43] Although some of these theories can explain specific aspects of the Islamic Revolution, none of them single-handedly and convincingly can explain the totality of that revolution.[44] But this should not be surprising. As bafflingly complex phenomena, revolutions defy the application of any universal theory of revolution for several reasons: the ever-changing conditions of history; the idiosyncrasies of rulers and cultures (the threshold for enduring suffering, for example, varies from one culture to another); and the interaction of *fortuna* with the objective preconditions of revolutions (what would have happened to the Russian Revolution if Lenin had died before entering Russia from Germany in 1917?). Paul Feyerabend was on the mark when he wrote: "Are we really to believe that the naive and simple-minded rules which methodologists take as their guide are capable of accounting for such a maze of interactions? ... A complex medium containing surprising and unforeseen developments demands complex procedures and defies analysis on the basis of rules which have been set up in advance."[45] The contention here, the basis of my conceptual framework, is that an eclectic approach based on a synthesis of, and an addition to, various theories of revolution is preferable to an application of a grand theory of revolution. As such, I will apply different theories of revolution to different phases of the Islamic Revolution.

Societies in which socioeconomic development outpaces the institution building of an incumbent regime, Samuel Huntington argued, are most prone to experience political instability.[46] This explanation, known as the gap theory, seems logical: Socioeconomic development accelerates the rate of social mobilization, which increases the rate of literacy, exposure to new ideas, and so forth, which in turn increases the demand for political participation by various groups. To deny participation to those who desire to become involved in politics is to create the fertile ground from which a revolution grows.

Useful as it is, the gap theory suffers from two flaws.[47] First, it offers a shallow treatment of institution building and is oblivious to the critical issue of regime legitimacy. To survive, every regime has to rely either on diffuse or specific support. The former exists independent of the "reward the members may feel should be obtained from belonging to the system," and the latter is proportional to the benefits the state provides the citizens.[48] Institutions based on diffuse support are invariably more durable than those founded on specific support.

The second problem with the gap theory is its limited applicability. The presence of a gap may be a necessary precondition of revolutions, but it is not enough in itself. There are large gaps between economic development and institution building in most Third World countries, yet revolutions are still rare.

Two conditions must be present if the otherwise acquiescent population is to engage in the audacious act of making a revolution. James Davies has identified one such condition. According to his J-curve hypothesis, revolutions are likely to occur when a period of economic development, which increases expectation, is followed by a period of sharp reversal, which widens the gap between expectation and gratification.[49] This hypothesis is based on the supposition that economic development increases people's expectation and its reversal generates deprivation and unfulfilled expectations, which can lead to collective violence. Davies's hypothesis alone cannot explain why revolutions occur: The United States experienced the Great Depression after a period of economic growth, yet did not experience a revolution. The utility of the J-curve is enhanced if we combine it with another hypothesis: The potential for revolution is high when the perception of what I call the "support linkage" between a dependent Third World state and its foreign supporters is, or is perceived to be, weakened. The weakening of the "support linkage" is vital because a large number of the Third World states owe their survival to the multifaceted aid they receive from the Western governments.

But the presence of all these conditions does not necessarily set off a revolution. Revolutions do not "come," as the structuralists would have us believe; they are made by the heroic actions of committed revolutionaries. This is why the making of revolution is the ultimate act of political creativity.

Because "the human capacity to withstand suffering and abuse is impressive, tragically so," regardless of its form and intensity, neither discontent nor suffering alone can produce revolution.[50] Were this not the case, the rigid caste system in India or the apartheid regime in South Africa could not have so pertinaciously survived for so long. Nor do repression, economic depression, poverty, relative deprivation, or failure to build institutions automatically lead to revolution.

What is also needed is the recognition by the masses that fundamental change in the constitution of power is desirable and possible. For the masses to accept this new inevitability, revolutionaries must articulate a revolutionary ideology that is understandable to the masses and contains a utopian ingredient. As Barrington Moore, Jr., has observed, "since the time of the Apostles, and perhaps earlier, no social movement has been without its army of preachers and militants to spread the good tidings of escape from the pain and evils of this world."[51] In short, if there is no revolutionary ideology, there is no revolution.

Nor is it possible to overthrow the modern state, which has at its disposal many instruments of repression, without being organized.[52] Lenin, for example, effectively used the communist party to mobilize the workers and the peasants against the Romanovs. The internal structure of organizations, the nature of the relationship between leaders of organizations and the rank and file, and the financial resources at the disposal of organizations often determine how effectively they can challenge the incumbent regime. Successful revolutionary leaders have invariably been great organizers and mobilizers.[53]

And finally, revolutions cannot succeed unless a united, multiclass coalition is formed against the state. No one class or group is powerful enough to single-handedly stage a revolution against the modern state, which is often well fortified. Revolutions, Anthony Oberschall argued, require the participation of several groups, "including those that are not among the most downtrodden and underprivileged."[54]

This holistic approach is most useful for explaining the Islamic Revolution. Under the Pahlavis, the Iranian economy was somewhat modernized, whereas the state, despite a gargantuan expansion in its size and role, retained its autocratic and traditional essence. Simply put, the economic sphere developed while the political sphere did not. Mohammad Reza Shah's modus operandi was not much different from that of the Qajar despots who ruled Iran until 1926. He was an autocrat who believed that he alone had discovered the "secret path" to Iran's modernization and therefore denied political participation to all but his most trusted allies. As such, he inadvertently unified his opponents and sowed the seeds of the revolution that ended his dynasty.

In the late 1970s, the gap between socioeconomic development and institution building was ruptured because of the presence of two conditions: the coincidence of an economic contraction following a period of stupendous economic expansion with the liberalization of the polity after years of repression and the prevalent perception that U.S. support for the Shah had diminished. The vulnerability of the Shah's regime to such endogenous and exogenous pressures was a function of the nature of the state itself.

The prerevolutionary Iranian state was a rentier one, which "on a regular basis received substantial amounts of external rent," or oil revenues.[55] The state funneled the oil revenues into the economy, which, in turn, became vulnerable to price fluctuations in the international oil markets and experienced unpredictable cycles of expansion and contraction. Following a period of phenomenal expansion, Iran experienced a period of sharp decline starting in 1975. The economic reversal adversely affected those Iranians, and there were many of them, who were dependent for their prosperity on the state, which had monopolized the distribution of the oil wealth. At this juncture, the Shah lost his "specific support."

The prerevolutionary state was also dependent on the United States. The foundation of this dependent relationship was laid after the 1953 coup against Prime Minister Mohammad Mossadeq. Because of the coup, the Shah lost his "diffuse support." Then, the promulgation of the human rights policy in 1977 and the inconsistent policy of the Carter administration weakened the Shah's "support linkage" to Washington and made his opposition more belligerent. The Shah's own confusion and indecisiveness about quelling the burgeoning revolutionary movement of 1977–1979 certainly facilitated his overthrow.

Once the Shah's regime began to liberalize and loosened its repressive policy, the Shah's opponents mobilized the discontented masses against the monarchy. The masses were mobilized on massive and unprecedented scales by the leftists, the nationalists, and by the ulama. Of these, the ulama's organization proved most effective.

The ulama had access to a traditional, sophisticated, and nationwide network ideal for mobilizing the masses.[56] Unlike their Sunni counterparts, who have been an integral component of the state bureaucracy and who receive direct stipends from the state, the Shi'i ulama in Iran enjoyed considerable financial and political independence from the state. Their traditional system of mobilizing the faithful from the mosques, *takiyes*, Islamic associations, and the bazaar proved effective and unusually difficult for the Shah's regime to contain. In 1975, in Teheran alone, there were 983 mosques, each one administered by a *pish-namaz* (prayer leader), who had a following of his own, the size of which depended upon his popularity.[57] Altogether, there were more than 8,439 mosques throughout the country. In Teheran, there were also 164 permanent *takiyes*, each with a considerable membership. There were also hundreds of Islamic associations. Add to this massive network the *asnaf* (guilds), of which there were more than 135 in Teheran alone, each with a large membership. Together with the thousands of street vendors and shop assistants, they were a formidable force. The *asnaf* and the ulama's network were organically connected. No other group had access to so massive a network as did the ulama.

Finally, it was Shi'ism, as a revolutionary ideology, that justified the struggle against the Pahlavis and promised a bright future to the masses. The ulama were one of the main "traveling salesmen" of Iran's Revolution, and Shi'ism was the ideological umbrella under which the Shah's opponents forged a broad-based coalition that was able to cut across the fragmented groups and unify them.

Having elaborated the general conceptual framework for the first four sections of this study, let us begin our investigation by identifying the tensions and contradictions that eventually erupted into a popular revolution in 1979. Our journey begins in the middle of the nineteenth century, when the fabric of the Iranian society started to break down.

Notes

1. George Pettee, *The Process of Revolution* (New York, 1938), p. 96.

2. Arthur Hatto, "Revolution," *Mind*, 58 (January 1949), p. 498.

3. Ibid., p. 499.

4. Eugene Kamenka, "The Concept of Political Revolution," in G. Kelly and C. Brown, eds., *Struggles in the State* (New York, 1970), pp. 107–121.

5. Karl Griewank, "Emergence of the Concept of Revolution," in A. Kaledin, ed., *Revolution: A Reader* (New York, 1971), pp. 13–18.

6. Edmund Burke, *Reflections on the Revolution in France* (New York, 1979). Reprint.

7. According to Bernard Lewis, the word *enqelab* (revolution) was first used in the Moslem world by the Young Ottoman exiles who published a journal with that name ("Islamic Concept of Revolution," in P. J. Vatikiotis, ed., *Revolution in the Middle East* [Totowa, N.J., 1972], p. 40.)

8. Hannah Arendt, *On Revolution* (New Haven, Conn., 1979), pp. 59–114.

9. Raymond Tanter and Manus Midlarsky, "A Theory of Revolution," *Journal of Conflict Resolution*, 11, 3 (September 1967), pp. 264–280.

10. Charles Tilly, *From Mobilization to Revolution* (Reading, Mass., 1978), p. 191.

11. Arendt (1979), p. 4.

12. Samuel Huntington, *Political Order in Changing Societies* (New Haven, Conn., 1968), p. 264.

13. Theda Skocpol, *States and Social Revolutions: A Comparative Analysis of France, Russia and China* (New York, 1979), p. 4.

14. Robert Packman, *Liberal America and the Third World Political Development* (Princeton, N.J., 1973); and I. Wallerstein, "Modernization, Requiescat in Pace" in his *The Capitalist World Economy* (New York, 1979), pp. 132–137.

15. Sheldon Wolin, "The Politics of the Study of Revolution," *Comparative Politics*, 5:3 (April 1973), p. 345.

16. See G. Almond and J. Coleman, eds., *The Politics of Developing Areas* (Princeton, N.J., 1960), pp. 3–58.

17. S. Huntington, "The Change to Change: Modernization, Development, and Politics," *Comparative Politics*, 3, 3 (April 1971), pp. 283–322.

18. Leonard Binder, *Iran: Political Development in a Changing Society* (Berkeley, Calif., 1962), p. 46.

19. James Bill, *The Politics of Iran* (Columbus, Ohio, 1972).

20. Hamid Algar, "The Oppositional Role of the Ulama in Twentieth-Century Iran," in N. Keddie, ed., *Scholars, Saints and Sufis* (Berkeley, Calif., 1972), p. 255; and Bijan Jazani, *Tarhe Jame-e Shenacy Va Mabani-ye Strategy* (Sociological Design and Strategic Foundation) (Teheran, 1978), p. 144.

21. Leonard Binder, "Iran's Potential as a Regional Power," in P. Hammond and S. Alexander, eds., *Political Dynamics in the Middle East* (New York, 1972), p. 378.

22. James Bill, "Iran and the Crisis of '78," *Foreign Affairs*, 57, 2 (January 1979), p. 333.

23. *Asnad-e Lane-ye Jasusi* (Documents of the Spy Nest) (Teheran, n.d.), vol. 16, October 15, 1979, p. 135; "Memorandum of Conversation: The Current Situation in Iran" (speech given at 33d Annual Conference of the Middle East Institute).

24. James Bill, *Eagle and Lion: The Tragedy of American-Iranian Relations* (New Haven, Conn., 1988), p. 254.

25. *Asnad*, 8 (May 2, 1972), p. 31; "Religious Circles in Iran."

26. *Asnad*, 12 (January 24, 1978), pp. 28–29; from U.S. Embassy in Teheran to State Department, prepared by William Sullivan.

27. Gary Sick, *All Fall Down: America's Tragic Encounter with Iran* (New York, 1985), p. 92.

28. *Monthly Review*, 30 (February 1979), p. 2.

29. Ervand Abrahamian, "Political Forces in the Iranian Revolution," *Radical America*, 13, 3 (June 1979), p. 55.

30. *Asnad*, 16 (October 25, 1978), p. 158; "Memorandum: Comments by the French Ambassador A. Raoul Delaye," prepared by L. Bruce Laingen.

31. Afsaneh Najmabadi, "States, Politics, and the Radical Contingency of Revolutions," *Research in Political Sociology*, 6 (1993), pp. 197–215.

32. Thomas Ricks, "Iran and Imperialism: Academics in the Service of the People or the Shah," *Arab Studies Quarterly*, 2 (Summer 1980), pp. 265–277.

33. Richard W. Bulliet, "Middle East Policy and Middle East Studies," unpublished, p. 1.

34. Bill (1988), pp. 370–374.

35. Ibid., p. 389.

36. According to Eugene Tighe, head of the Defense Intelligence Agency who visited Teheran in December 1978, "the CIA Station Chief there was pleading for more Farsi speaking agents. We didn't get them, almost no one was able to find out what was going on." See Bob Woodward, *Veil: The Secret Wars of the CIA, 1981–1987* (New York, 1987), p. 101.

37. *Asnad*, 14, 5 (March 1979), p. 24.

38. Bill (1988), p. 392.

39. Robert Looney, *A Development Strategy for Iran Through the 1980s* (New York, 1977).

40. Marvin Zonis, *The Political Elite of Iran* (Princeton, N.J., 1971).

41. Peter Chelokowski, ed., *Taziyeh, Rituals and Drama in Iran* (New York, 1979).

42. Personal interview with President Hashemi Rafsanjani, Teheran, August 5, 1992.

43. On revolution, see A. Cohan, *Theories of Revolution* (New York, 1975); Issac Kramnick, "Reflections on Revolution: Definition and Explanation in Recent Scholarship," *History and Theory*, 11, 1 (1972), pp. 26–63; Hal Draper, *Karl Marx's Theory of Revolution: The Politics of Social Classes* (New York, 1978), 3 vols.

44. See Cheryl Benard and Zalmay Khalilzad, *The Government of God* (New York, 1984), pp. 1–24.

45. Paul Feyerabend, *Against Method* (London, 1975), pp. 17–18.

46. Samuel Huntington, "The Political Modernization of Traditional Monarchies," *Daedalus*, 59, 3 (Summer 1966), pp. 763–788.

47. See Mark Kasselman, "Order or Movement? The Literature of Political Development as Ideology," *World Politics*, 26, 1 (October 1973), pp. 139–154.

48. David Easton, *A Framework for Political Analysis* (Princeton, N.J., 1965), p. 125.

49. James Davies, "The J-Curve of Rising and Declining Expectation as a Case of Some Great Revolutions and a Contained Rebellion," in Hugh Davis Graham and Ted Robert Gurr, eds., *Violence in America* (New York, 1969), pp. 671–709.

50. Barrington Moore, Jr., *Injustice: The Social Basis of Obedience and Revolt* (New York, 1978), p. 13.

51. Ibid., pp. 472–473.

52. Tilly (1978).

53. Thomas Greene, *Comparative Revolutionary Movements* (Englewood Cliffs, N.J., 1990), chaps. 4–10.

54. Anthony Oberschall, *Social Conflict and Social Movements* (Englewood Cliffs, N.J., 1973), p. 82.

55. Hossein Mahdavi, "The Patterns and Problems of Economic Development in Rentier States: The Case of Iran," in M. A. Cook, ed., *Studies in the Economic History of the Middle East* (London, 1970), p. 428.

56. On the organization of the *marja'-e taqlid* see Leonard Binder, "The Proofs of Islam: Religion and Politics in Iran," in G. Makdisi, ed., *Arabic and Islamic Studies in Honor of Hamilton A. R. Gibb* (Cambridge, Mass., 1965), pp. 118–140.

57. *Gozaresh-e Farhangi-e Iran* (Iran's Educational Report) (Teheran, 1975), p. 107.

Part Two

Historical Background

2

The Constitutional Movement
and the Creation
of the Pahlavi Dynasty

To be ignorant of what occurred before you were born is to remain always a child. For what is the worth of human life, unless it is woven into the life of our ancestors by the records of history.

Cicero, 46 B.C.

Iran has one of the world's oldest civilizations. In its long history, it has witnessed the rise and fall of the great Persian empires and has frequently been invaded and occupied by powerful foreign adversaries. But each time it has been invaded and occupied, the country not only has managed to retain much of its cultural and linguistic integrity but also has started a process of political unification and intellectual renaissance. Remarkably, most invaders have had their culture absorbed into the Persian way of life.

After defeating the Medes (c. 546 B.C.), the Persians created the Achamanid Empire, which ruled over a good portion of the known world (c. 546–334 B.C.). Their empire, perhaps the first of its kind, was the largest the world had seen. Then, Alexander, from Macedonia, conquered Persia (c. 333 B.C.). After a long period of occupation by the invaders, a few Persian dynasties established their rule over parts of Persia, but it was the Sassanids (c. A.D. 226–642) who at last restored Persian sovereignty. Their empire also grew to become one of the main superpowers of the time. In many ways, the world was divided between Rome and Iran. Under the Sassanids, Iranian civilization flowered. Their religious, political, and military influence had an international impact. Then, about A.D. 642, the Arab invasion ended the Sassanid rule. Long after its conversion from Zoroastrianism to Islam, Persia experienced a remarkable intellectual, artistic, and literary renaissance that was among the most profound achievements of the Islamic civilization. That period of creativity was interrupted in the eleventh century, to be followed by five dark centuries of periodic invasions by the Seljuks (1037–1220), the Mongols (1220–1380), and the Timurids (1380–1500). From the darkness of this period the Safavid dynasty (1501) ascended to power. Under the Safavids, the country was unified, Shi'ism, a Persianized version of Islam, was established as the state religion, and Persian art and architecture flourished again and gained much fame.

Since the Safavids, Iran has not been completely occupied. However, over the past two centuries, since the advent of the Industrial Revolution in Europe around 1776, Iran has confronted another powerful force: the West. Unlike the invaders of the earlier three millennia, the West has no territorial ambitions over Iran. Still, the Western influence on Iranian politics, culture, and economy has been every bit as strong as when the country was conquered. Consequently, any analysis of modern Iran is incomplete unless it addresses the dynamics of Iran's cooperation or confrontation with the Western powers. This introductory chapter intends to do just that. It explains the evolution of such important institutions as the state, kingship, and Shi'ism and their interaction with one another and with the West.

The Iranian Encounter with the West

At the turn of the nineteenth century, Persia (named Iran in the early 1930s) was a predominantly agrarian and fragmented society. The most important groups within the urban class structure were the ulama, the merchants/shopkeepers, and the working masses.[1] Above the society stood the state, personified in the shah, whose power was absolute and arbitrary. There was little reciprocity and no contractual basis for the relationship between the state and the social groups that were not powerful enough to challenge the state. Whatever its shortcomings, Iranian society had its own unique form of government, its own code of laws, its own system of justice, and its own social equilibrium. But Western penetration of Persia became a catalyst for the breakdown of the country's social fabric.

With an efficient production system, powerful armies, and a monopoly over modern technology, the Western nations expanded their colonial empires in the nineteenth century. The Islamic world was not immune to this global expansion. India, with its large Moslem population, was colonized by England. By the nineteenth century, the mighty Ottoman Empire had become no more than a semi-colony of the West, as some of its strategic provinces had been lost to it.

The fate of Iran was not much happier than that of the Ottomans. Persia's subjugation to the West began after its humiliating defeat in the wars of 1803–1814 and 1828 against Russia, which, among other things, forced the ruling Qajar dynasty (1796–1926) to cede to Russia two fertile provinces and to levy low tariffs on Russian goods.[2] For the rest of the nineteenth century, Russian policy was to "make Persia obedient and useful" and to capture "the major share of the Persian market."[3] To realize these imperialistic goals, Russia had to compete with Britain, which valued Persia both as a buffer zone protecting its enormous investments in colonized India and as a lucrative market for its goods. The commercial treaty of 1841 between Persia and England granted British merchants the same privileges previously given only to their Russian counterparts, including exemption from the exorbitant road tolls (which the Persian merchants had to pay) and immunity from the local courts and laws. It was ironic that the competition between England and Russia and their determination to prevent one another from dominating the country saved Persia from becoming a colony.

For the rest of the century, England and Russia obtained a multitude of favorable concessions from the ineffectual Qajar rulers, such as telegraph concessions to Britain in 1862 and to Russia in 1881. The most notorious of these concessions, granted to Baron Julius de Reuter in 1872, included monopoly over the construction of railroads, roads, and tramways and the exploitation of forests and mines (except those closest to the Russian borders). The Reuter concession was, in the words of an apologist for British colonialism, "the most complete and extraordinary surrender of the entire industrial resources of a kingdom."[4] Faced with the vociferous opposition of the ulama, merchants, and Russia, Naser ad-Din Shah (1848–1896) annulled the concession in 1873. But Persia continued to be placed on auction: In 1889, Reuter opened Persia's first bank, the Imperial Bank of Persia, which enjoyed exclusive rights to issue bank notes, and later Russia opened its bank in Iran too.

Concessions to foreign nations and invasions of foreign goods gradually integrated Persia's local and regional markets into the world markets. This integration had far-reaching consequences. Although increasing the volume of foreign trade, it contributed to chronic problems: an unfavorable balance of payments, high inflation, increased bankruptcy among merchants and *asnaf*, and economic depression in certain areas of the country. Merchants with sufficient capital to compete with foreign capital and those who had become middlemen in the service of foreign companies made enormous fortunes, whereas the many merchants who were unable to compete with their foreign counterparts went bankrupt, especially those in the textile industry.[5]

In either case, the problems and concerns of the merchants and the *asnaf* (guilds) became national in scope. Thanks to the newly built telegraph lines, communication among them increased, and the presence of an identifiable foreign enemy (foreign capital) unified them. This is why the merchants and the *asnaf*, who controlled the jugular vein of the Iranian economy, became the first group to challenge the Qajars, demanding protection against foreign intrusion and imposition of laws to regulate commerce. The Qajars' failure to satisfy the merchants made them more belligerent.[6] Because by themselves they could not seriously challenge the Shah, they sought and received the critical support of the ulama, their traditional allies.

Ever since 1501, when Shah Isma'il imposed Twelve Shi'ism as the state religion, the ulama have been critical players in Iranian politics and part of the elite structure. (According to Twelver Shi'ism, after Prophet Mohammad, Ali, and his male descendants from the line of Fatemeh, the Prophet's daughter, were the legitimate imams of the Islamic community chosen by God. The twelfth and the last of these imams, the Mahdi, disappeared by God's fiat at the age of five. The Hidden Imam will appear at the end of time to impose godly justice.[7]) Under the Qajars, the ulama taught, interpreted, and administered Islamic law. They were judges, teachers, managers of the traditional educational institutions, prayer leaders of the mosques, guardians of famed shrines, prosperous landlords, and administers of *auqaf* (charitable-religious endowments).[8]

The ulama had connections with all segments of the population. The high ulama were a part of the elite structure: They were close to the court and held important posts, and many of them were integrated into the state bureaucracy. There were also "alliance marriages" between the Qajars and the high ulama.

The symbiotic relationship between the ulama and the monarchy was based, it must be stressed, on the subordination of the former to the latter. As a whole, the ulama gave their blessing to the Qajars, though at times rhetorically questioning their legitimacy. Mirza Mohaqiq-e Qommi, one of the leading ulama of the Qajar era, for example, argued that "kingship is God-given and its sanction moral."[9]

The high ulama were also linked with the merchants and the *asnaf*. The merchants and *asnaf* sent their children to schools administered by the ulama. They needed the ulama as legal advisers and as judges to settle their differences. At the same time, the ulama needed the merchants and the *asnaf* for their lavish financial contributions. Intermarriage among the three groups was quite common. The presence of a mosque in every major part of the bazaar was—and still is—symbolic of the mutually beneficial relations between the ulama and the merchants/*asnaf*.

The ulama's connection with the lower classes was equally strong. Because Shi'-ism was an inseparable part of the Persian psyche and popular culture, the ulama, as protector of the faith, enjoyed widespread support among the lower classes. This is why a few of them had organized their own private armies in some provinces and in some cities had created a state within a state and had become both "governor and executor of the law."[10] Moreover, the gradual separation of the Shi'i institutions from the state and the disassociation of some of the ulama from the state officials turned them into the "people's protector against the rulers."[11]

Although Western penetration in many ways adversely affected the fortunes of the ulama, it increased their political clout. Some of the ulama became opponents of Western imperialism and a component of the rising Persian nationalism. Alone they did not have the resources to oppose the Great Powers and the Qajar kings, but together with the merchants they became a force to be reckoned with. Consider the Tobacco Regie episode.

In 1890, Naser ad-Din Shah granted to a British company for a meager sum complete monopoly of the production, distribution, sale, and export of tobacco. At the time, well over 200,000 people were involved in the tobacco industry and approximately a quarter of the country's approximate population of 10 million consumed tobacco.[12] Those in the industry (which included the ulama), from the retailers to the cultivators, opposed the concession, at first peacefully but later violently. The decisive moment came when at the urging of Seyyed Jamal ad-Din Asadabadi (also known as al-Afghani), a radical Shi'i *mujtahed* and activist, and under pressure from the merchants, the *marja'-e taqlid,* Haj Hassan Shirazi, issued a *fatva* that made the use of tobacco "tantamount to war against the Imam of the Age."[13] As the Shah failed to placate the protesters, he abrogated the treaty in 1892, even though he had to pay a heavy penalty to the British for annulling the treaty.

The uprising demonstrated that the Shah's decision could be reversed. But it was only a victory over one concession. It neither slowed the growing influence of Russia and England nor shook the foundation of the Shah's autocracy. Comprehensive reforms were essential for guaranteeing Persia's independence and curbing the Shah's unlimited power. Neither the ulama nor the merchants had such a plan. The secular reformers shouldered the burden of designing those reforms.

Reforming the Political System: The Constitutional Movement

The secular reformers were few in number. They were the product of Iran's slow modernization that had started in the 1820s after the war with Russia when Abbas Mirza, the heir-apparent, created a small but modern army and sent a few students to study in Europe. The bulk of the reformers consisted of some high government bureaucrats, diplomats stationed in Persian embassies abroad, the few Western-educated Persians, and some graduates of the Darolfonun, Iran's first modern school built around the middle of the century. Despite a diversity of opinion, two concerns unified them: the creation of a code of written law and modernization from above, which most of them, regrettably, equated with the blind emulation of aspects of the European political system. By writing their travel memoirs, translating European books, publishing newspapers, and creating secret *anjomans* (associations), they disseminated ideas such as the Rousseauean concept of popular sovereignty, rule of law, protection of private property and life, and parliamentarianism.[14]

How could they disseminate such modern ideas in a country where the large majority of the people, as Malekolsho'ara Bahar wrote, "favored despotism" and were "reactionary"?[15] Mirza Malcolm Khan, a pioneer reformer, found a solution, which many others seem to have followed: "I knew that it was useless to attempt a remodeling of Persia in European forms, and I was determined to clothe my material reformation in a garb by which my people would understand, the garb of religion."[16] Mirza Aqa Khan Kermani took Malcolm's proposition to its logical conclusion and favored an alliance between the secular reformers and the ulama.

In the last decade of Naser ad-Din Shah's rule (1886–1896) the necessity of comprehensive reforms became even more evident. It was at this time that the Shah, who at times was enthusiastic about reforms, turned reactionary, increased repression, and became excessively hedonistic. In 1896, a bankrupt merchant and an avid supporter of Asadabadi assassinated the Shah. Mozaffar ad-Din Shah was quickly crowned. It was under the rule of that timid shah (1896–1907) that the Constitutional Movement flourished.

The virtual domination of the country by England and Russia, societal dislocations, economic stagnation, and lawlessness in the second half of the nineteenth century had generated strong resentment among many Iranians. The Constitutional Movement was the political manifestation of this discontent. It was a popular urban reform movement generated by the merchants, the secular reformers, and the prominent Shi'i ulama. Its objectives were to loosen the shackles of foreign domination, to save the country from bankruptcy, to put an end to lawlessness, and to limit the arbitrary power of the king by framing a written constitution and creating a consultative assembly, the Majles. The merchants and shopkeepers gave the movement financial support and manpower, the ulama religious legitimacy, and the secular reformers ideological direction. Japan's victory over Russia in 1904–1905 and the aborted revolution of 1905 in Russia gave psychological encouragement to Persian reformers, and the existing economic depression helped the reformers to mobilize the discontented groups.

Persia entered the twentieth century with its economy in a shambles and its state virtually bankrupt. Deficit spending and foreign borrowing were common: Between 1901 and 1903, Persia borrowed from England and Russia the equivalent of its entire budget in 1900.[17] To increase its revenues, the state reorganized the Customs Administration, among other things. Joseph Naus, a Belgian who was appointed minister of Customs Administration by Mozaffar ad-Din Shah in 1898, increased import and export duties and taxes on land and reduced pensions to the nobility.[18] The merchants, enthusiastically supported by the ulama, who were unhappy with the proposed taxes on land and with a Christian managing Persia's customs, called for his dismissal. As their demands landed on deaf ears, a rift was created between the state and the merchants and the ulama. This rift was widened by the impetuous action of Teheran's governor, who bastinadoed two sugar merchants accused of speculation in price. This angered a large number of ulama and merchants, who took sanctuary in a holy shrine and demanded the creation of a house of justice and the dismissal of the governor. Mozaffar ad-Din Shah dismissed the governor and promised to create a house of justice. He failed to keep his promise, thus precipitating bloody confrontations between the police and the protesters.

Finally, on August 5, 1906, Mozaffar ad-Din Shah signed the royal proclamation ordering the creation of a Majles and the drafting of a constitution by the

Majles deputies.[19] Five days before his natural death on December 30, 1906, he signed Persia's first written constitution.

The Dual Personality of the Persian Constitution of 1906

The Persian Constitution of 1906, which included the Supplementary Law to the Constitution, was the product of a fragile compromise between the secular reformers and the ulama.[20] The secular reformers, aspiring to create a European-style constitutional monarchy, manipulated the ulama to gain objectives they could not have achieved alone. "Because the Iranian people need fanaticism," Mirza Aqa Khan Kermani admitted, "if we receive assistance from the half-alive group of the ulama, we probably will achieve our goals sooner."[21] The ulama participated in the movement because of their myopic vision of constitutionalism and their desire to be recognized as promoters of progressive ideas. The eminent Ayatollah Mohammad Tabataba'i frankly acknowledged that he scarcely understood constitutionalism; he could only say "he had heard" it would bring security and prosperity.[22]

The Persian Constitution sought to reconcile the irreconcilable demands of these two groups. Consequently, it contained glaring contradictions. Thus, although the constitution talked about popular sovereignty, Article 2 limited the people's power by creating an "ecclesiastical committee" consisting of five ulama with veto power over all Majles legislation deemed contrary to Islamic law. Moreover, the constitution guaranteed equality before the law and freedoms of assembly and press provided that they were not inimical to Islam.

Not surprisingly, the Persian Constitution created a major rift within the camp of the ulama and accentuated the differences between the secular reformers and the constitutionalist ulama. Despite many concessions to the ulama, including the declaration of Shi'ism as the official state religion (Article 1), a small faction of the ulama opposed the constitution. Most notable among them was Ayatollah Sheikh Fazlollah Nuri, who called the Supplementary Law a "book of error" and labeled the constitutionalists atheists. For Nuri, sovereignty belonged exclusively to God. The Quran, he argued, contains all the regulations for administration of the state; therefore any legislative assembly was superfluous. He favored an Islamic government based on the fusion of Shi'ism with monarchy in which the Majles was an extension of the ulama's power. In many ways, he pioneered the fundamentalism of today and has therefore been praised by the Islamic Republic as a hero.[23]

It was against Nuri that the ulama's most comprehensive defense of constitutionalism was formulated by the sagacious Mirza Mohammad Hossein Gharavi Na'ini (1860–1936). Regarding all temporal authorities as illegitimate in the absence of the Hidden Imam, he argued that a constitutional form of government that limits the ruler's arbitrary power and grants people limited sovereignty was less abhorrent than other forms. Sovereignty of the people and equality before the law, Na'ini concluded, were the foundation of the government set up by the Prophet in Mecca.[24]

The division of the ulama into two hostile factions of constitutionalist and anticonstitutionalist, on the one hand, and the rancorous relationship between the secular reformers and the constitutional ulama, on the other hand, had weakened the Constitutional Movement. Mohammad Ali Shah, the successor to Mozaffar ad-din Shah, took advantage of this weakness and betrayed the constitution he was sworn to protect. He was simply unprepared to accept any limitations on his powers. He played his last card by appointing Colonel Vladimir Liakhoff, a Russian officer in command of the Cossack Brigade (a small but disciplined army created during the last decade of Naser ad-Din Shah's reign), to administer martial law in Teheran. Some prominent constitutionalists were jailed, chained, and killed, while many fled Teheran. Free assembly was forbidden, the press was muzzled, and the Majles building was bombarded.

The Constitutional Movement seemed defeated, but not quite. The constitutionalists unified their forces from various parts of Iran and surrounded Teheran. On July 16, 1909, Mohammad Ali Shah took refuge in the Russian Legation and ipso facto abdicated his throne. Ahmad, his eleven-year-old son, was declared the shah with Naserolmolk as regent.

With Mohammad Ali Shah out of the picture, the second Majles became the dominant force in Iranian politics, but only for a short time. When the Majles invited an American, Morgan Shuster, to come to Iran to reform the country's chaotic finances, both Russia and England opposed the appointment of this concerned adviser, fearing that his reforms would be detrimental to their interests. The Russians, probably with British consent, gave the Majles an ultimatum to dismiss Shuster, which it ignored. As Russian troops marched toward Teheran, Shuster was dismissed and the twenty-month-old Majles itself was dissolved, not to be convened again until three years later in 1914.[25] Thus, once again, the foreign powers imposed their will on Persia by forcing the dissolution of the Majles, marking the end of the Constitutional Movement.

The breakdown of the alliance between the ulama and the secular reformers and the defeat of the Constitutional Movement can be attributed to two factors, among others. First was the ideological incompatibility of the members of the alliance itself. The alliance was founded on political convenience rather than any compatibility of vision and program. Second was the secular reformers' flawed strategy to modernize Iran: They looked at Europe as a model. Constitution and parliament were the symbols of Europe's modern political system. They sincerely believed that Persia, too, must have a constitution and a parliament. But these impatient reformers did not look deep into Western Europe's democratization, a long and slow process that began from below. In Persia, they wanted to democratize from above. Thus, rather than focusing on grass-roots institution building and on party building, they first built a Majles, then wrote a constitution, and finally formed short-lived parties. Their ideas were thus devoid of solid mass support. This is why once the ulama, who enjoyed popular support, withdrew from the Constitutional Movement, the secular reformers failed to usher Iran into a new age.

Despite these and other shortcomings, the Constitutional Movement legitimized elections, popularized the notion that the king's power cannot be unlimited and arbitrary, and granted people rights and powers they hitherto had not enjoyed, such as equity before the law. In many ways, it was an auspicious victory for the Persian democrats.

Reza Shah Pahlavi and His Reforms

In the decade following the dissolution of the Majles in 1911, Persia was in turmoil. The central government was weak and increasingly manipulated by England and Russia, and despite its declaration of neutrality in World War I, parts of the country were occupied by the antagonists of that bloody war. The most consequential development, however, was the victory of the Bolsheviks in Russia in October 1917. The momentous event changed the balance of power in Persia in favor of England. The new Soviet regime, preoccupied with its own internal problems, annulled most of Russia's previous treaties with Persia and recalled its troops from that country. Hoping to take advantage of this new situation, England attempted to impose the Anglo-Persian Treaty of 1919, which would have virtually turned Persia into a British protectorate. Having failed in its plan, Britain, determined to stop the spread of Bolshevism and to assure the orderly flow of oil from Persia, sought to strengthen Persia's central government. The agents for this task were Seyyed Zia and Reza Khan.

In the early 1920s, Major General William Edmund Ironside, a local commander of British forces in Persia, was especially impressed with the leadership ability of Reza Khan Mir Panj, a self-made man of humble origins and one of the commanders of the 8,000-man British-controlled Cossack Brigade. In February 1925, Seyyed Zia Tabataba'i, an Anglophile journalist/politician, and Reza Khan staged a bloodless coup. If not actively involved in the planning and logistical operation of the coup, Britain had certainly given its blessing in advance.[26]

Zia and Reza Khan immediately imposed martial law in Teheran and other cities. Ahmad Shah appointed Zia prime minister and Reza Khan commander of the Cossack Brigade. The Zia cabinet quickly ordered the arrest of those who might have opposed his government. To conceal its dependence on England, the cabinet annulled the Anglo-Persian Treaty of 1919, which was never ratified by the Majles, and announced the withdrawal of the British troops from Persia.[27]

Zia's unremitting attacks on politicians with close contact with the Shah's court and his unvarnished ambitions had frightened Ahmad Shah. To neutralize Zia, Ahmad Shah gave greater power to Reza Khan and eventually dismissed Zia, forcing him into exile. Poor Ahmad Shah was unaware that in less than five years Reza Khan would dethrone his dynasty.

Reza Khan's fascinating accession to the throne involved two stages. In the first stage (1921–1923), he portrayed himself as lacking any political ambition and as the champion of law and order. Three veteran politicians formed five short-lived cabinets in this period, and Reza Khan remained the minister of war in all five, testimony to the consolidation of his power in the army. With the assistance of his army, Reza Khan violently suppressed the centrifugal movements in the provinces and emerged as the man with an iron will. In a period when chaos and rule by fragmentation had become the order of the day, restoration of order and imposition of central authority were precious achievements for which Reza Khan received much credit.

The second stage began when Ahmad Shah appointed Reza Khan prime minister in late 1923 and left for Europe, ostensibly for medical treatment, but never returned. (When Ahmad Shah left Persia, the caliphate institution had been dissolved in Turkey and Mostafa Kamal Pasha had become the first president of modern Turkey.) As prime minister, Reza Khan retained his post as minister of war and successfully brought gendarmerie forces under his personal command. Now he controlled the executive branch and the two disciplined armed forces in the country, the gendarmerie and the Cossacks.

At the time, there was also some talk of republicanism in Persia. Although the idea of establishing a republic in Persia can be traced to 1911, the creation of a republic in neighboring Turkey in October 1923 made republicanism somewhat popular in Persia, but only briefly. The ulama were unequivocally opposed to republicanism, which they identified with Ataturk's secularization. The leading ulama, like Ayatollah Abdol Karim Ha'eri Yazdi, declared republicanism contrary to Islam. Aware of their apprehension, Reza Khan manipulated the ulama: At first, he skillfully flirted with the idea, most probably to promote his own ambitions, but eventually he abandoned his opportunistic advocacy of republicanism in exchange for the ulama's endorsement of his accession to power.[28]

With the support of the ulama, the army, and the British, Reza Khan then convinced the Majles to dethrone the Qajars. In November 1925, the Majles chose Reza Khan as the caretaker of a provisional government. It also called for an elective constituent assembly to decide the future government of Iran. Of the eighty-five deputies, only five voted against the resolution, among them Dr. Mohammad Mossadeq, who would become Persia's prime minister in 1951, and Seyyed Hassan Modares, the deputy speaker of the Majles.[29] And then the Constituent Assembly voted to support the creation of the new Pahlavi dynasty, the first dynasty ascending to power without the assistance of any tribe.

Once enthroned, Reza Shah and a group of capable men he had gathered around him began a comprehensive modernization program that affected every facet of the society. Its ideological basis was Iranian nationalism based on glorification of pre-Islamic Persia.[30] Reza Shah's brand of jingoism was symbolized by the selection of the name Pahlavi, the language of pre-Islamic Persia, the changing of the country's name from Persia to Iran in the early 1930s, and the emphasis on Iran's Ari'yan heritage. A passionate but ruthless nationalist with little formal education, Reza Khan had a clear vision for Iran's transition to modernity, often using Ataturk's Turkey as a model.

Reza Shah moved decisively to strengthen and centralize the state. He used the meager oil revenues to modernize the armed forces (conscription laws were introduced in 1925). Relying on his disciplined army, he curtailed the centrifugal power of the landlords and the tribal khans. The state's financial institutions were reformed. A relatively large state bureaucracy was created. Hundreds of modern schools were built, and for the first time, some of them became coeducational. The University of Teheran was founded in 1934, and the government sent hundreds of students to Europe for higher education.[31]

Reza Shah sought to secularize Iranian politics. Toward this goal, he drastically reduced the ulama's power and suppressed those who dared to challenge him. The power of the religious courts, administered by the ulama, was greatly diminished. Because all judges were required to have a formal degree, many of the ulama, who had traditional education, were forced out of the judicial branch. European civil and penal laws gradually replaced Islamic laws. Newly created state agencies deprived the ulama of their control over the administration of civil services. Hundreds of modern schools were built to the detriment of the traditional *maktabs* administered by the ulama. Moreover, the state began to directly manage some religious schools, and a theology department was created at the new University of Teheran, breaking the ulama's monopoly on teaching religion. New regulations limited the ulama's control over the charitable lands. Passion plays and self-flagellations in public were forbidden.[32] Equally significant was Reza Shah's forced unveiling of women in 1936, making Iran the first Islamic country to declare veiling illegal. Veiled women were harassed by the police, forcing many of them into virtual exile, as they refused to appear unveiled in public.[33]

But perhaps the greatest achievement of Reza Shah was to lay the foundation of a modern economy and a relatively large infrastructure. In 1927, the Customs Administration was removed from Belgian control and returned to Iran. In 1930, the right to issue money notes was taken from the British and granted to the newly created Bank-e Meli-ye Iran. Uniform tax laws were drafted. New roads and ports were built and transportation became safe from bandits. The 850-mile Trans-Iranian Railroad was constructed. Electricity was introduced into most cities. Telephone and radio use increased. By 1940, more than 200 industrial plants with employment exceeding 60,000 had been built.[34] In Julian Bharier's assessment, by the middle of the 1940s, "Iran appeared to be well on the road to establishing a sizeable industrial sector."[35]

Despite Reza Shah's sincere desire to reduce foreign power in Iran (in 1928, the capitulation laws were abolished), the West continued to influence the Iranian economy. His modernization relied mostly on Western technology, and Britain continued to control the Anglo-Persian Oil Company, which provided a portion of state revenues for development projects.

But Reza Shah's impressive achievements suffered from a number of weaknesses. Most historians would agree with Arthur Millspaugh's assessment that the heaviest burden of the expensive development projects was borne by the poor classes. The construction of the Trans-Iranian Railroad, for example, was financed entirely from the imposition of rapacious tax rates on such items as tea and sugar. The poor financed these projects, but the merchants, monopolists, contractors, and some politicians with connection to the court, as Millspaugh pointed out, were its main beneficiaries.

Another problem was, as Ann Lambton argued, that "the old structure of society was destroyed, but no new mechanism through which [Reza Shah] could undertake effective social action replaced it."[36] Force was often used for political and economic ends. Millspaugh wrote: "Fear settled upon the people. No one knew whom to trust; and no one dared to protest or criticize."[37]

The ascendancy of Reza Shah was both a victory and a defeat for the architects of the Persian Constitution: It was a victory because many of his programs were precisely the ones they demanded but could never implement, and a defeat because under Reza Shah, the constitution was blatantly violated and the ugly face of autocracy resurfaced. The Majles was turned into a submissive body, the "ecclesiastical committee" was never convened, and the principle that the people can participate in politics was mocked. Reza Shah failed to institutionalize his support, a mistake his son was to repeat. He did not create any political party and excluded most groups from participating in the political process. Despite all these weaknesses, Iran under Reza Shah experienced remarkable economic and social development, perhaps unprecedented in the country's modern history.

When the Allied forces entered Iran in August 1941, Reza Shah ordered a general mobilization of his armed forces, presumably to challenge them. Accused by the Allies of being pro-German, he was forced to abdicate in September 1941. Thus, one more time, external forces blatantly interfered with Iran's internal affairs. Reza Shah was placed aboard a British ship and exiled to the island of Mauritius, then a British colony, and later to Johannesburg, South Africa. Then in 1944, he died in grief.

When external pressure finally loosened Reza Shah's iron grip, a centralized and powerful state had been built, a burgeoning professional middle class was in place, the size of the working class had increased substantially, and politics had been somewhat secularized. The age of mass politics had begun. So had the reign of his twenty-two-year-old son, Mohammad Reza Shah Pahlavi.

Notes

1. See Ann Lambton, "Persian Society Under the Qajars," *Royal Central Asian Studies*, 48 (April 1961), pp. 123–139.

2. Firuz Kazemzadeh, *Russia and Britain in Persia, 1864–1914: A Study in Imperialism* (New Haven, Conn., 1968).

3. As quoted in L. S. Stavrianos, *Global Rift: The Third World Comes of Age* (New York, 1981), p. 227.

4. George Curzon, *Persia and the Persian Question,* vol. 1 (London, 1892), p. 480.

5. Abbas Amanat, ed., *Cities and Trade: Consul Abbott on the Economy and Society of Iran, 1847–1866* (London, 1983), p. xvi.

6. Ahmad Ashraf, *Mavane'e Tarikhi-ye Roshd-e Sarmayedari dar Iran* (Historical Obstacles to the Development of Capitalism in Iran) (Teheran, 1980).

7. On Shi'ism, see 'Alama Tabataba'i, *Shi'i dar Islam* (Shi'ism in Islam) (Teheran, 1974).

8. Hamid Algar, *Religion and State in Iran, 1785–1906: The Role of the Ulama in the Qajar Period* (Berkeley, Calif., 1969).

9. Ann Lambton, "Some New Trends in Islamic Political Thought in Late 18th and Early 19th Century Persia," *Studia Islamica,* 39 (1974), pp. 95–128.

10. Morteza Ravandi, *Tarikh-e Ejtema'i-ye Iran* (The Social History of Iran), vol. 3 (Teheran, 1976), pp. 495–496.

11. Sir John Malcolm, *The History of Persia* (London, 1829), vol. 2, p. 316.

12. Faridoun Adamiyat, *Shuresh Bar Emtiyazname-ye Regie* (Rebellion Against the Regie Concession) (Teheran, 1981), p. 11.

13. Ann Lambton, "The Tobacco Regie: Prelude to Revolution," *Studia Islamica,* 22 (1965), p. 145.

14. Shaul Bakhash, *Iran: Monarchy, Bureaucracy and Reform Under the Qajars* (London, 1978).

15. Mohammad Taqi Bahar, *Tarikh-e Ahzab-e Siyasi-ye Iran* (The History of Political Parties in Iran) (Teheran, 1978), p. 1.

16. Bakhash (1978), p. 18.

17. Sir Percy Sykes, *A History of Persia* (London, 1921), p. 373.

18. For details, see Gad Gilbar, "The Big Merchants (*tujjar*) and the Persian Constitutional Revolution of 1906," *Asian and African Studies,* 11, 3 (Winter 1977), pp. 275–304.

19. Nezamolislam Kermani, *Tarikh-e Bidari-ye Iraniyan* (History of the Awakening of the Iranians), vol. 2 (Teheran, 1968); and Edward Brown, *The Persian Revolution of 1905–1909* (London, 1966), p. 133.

20. Medhi Malekzadeh *Trarikh-e Enqelab-e Mashruteh* (History of the Constitutional Revolution), vol. 2 (Teheran, 1949), p. 170.

21. Faridoun Adamiyat, *Ideoloji-ye Enqelab-e Mashruteh* (The Ideology of the Constitutional Movement) (Teheran, 1976), p. 30.

22. Adamiyat (1976), p. 226.

23. Abdul-Hadi Hairi, "Shaykh Fazl Allah Nuri's Refutation of the Idea of Constitutionalism," *Middle East Studies,* 13, 3 (1977), pp. 333–334.

24. Abdul-Hadi Hairi, *Shi'ism and Constitutionalism in Iran* (Leiden, 1977), pp. 165–197; and Hamid Enayat, *Modern Islamic Political Thought* (Austin, Tex., 1982), pp. 160–174.

25. See Morgan Shuster, *The Strangling of Persia* (New York, 1912).

26. For different interpretations of the British role in the coup, see Sir Dennis Wright *The British Among the Persians* (London, 1977), pp. 180–184; and Richard Ullman, *Anglo Soviet Relations: 1917–21,* vol. 3 (Princeton, N.J., 1972), pp. 383–394.

27. Hossein Maki, *Tarikh-e Bist Sale-ye Iran* (The Twenty-Year History of Iran), vol. 1 (Teheran, 1945), pp. 125–129.

28. Maki (1945), p. 344.

29. Ibid., vol. 3, p. 447.

30. See Amin Banani, *The Modernization of Iran, 1921–41* (Stanford, Calif., 1961).

31. A. Arasteh, *Education and Social Awakening in Iran, 1850–1968* (Leiden, 1969).

32. Shahrough Akhavi, *Religion and Politics in Contemporary Iran* (Albany, N.Y., 1980), pp. 32–59.

33. Margaret Laing, *The Shah* (London, 1977), p. 52.

34. Quoted by Fred Halliday, *Iran: Dictatorship and Development* (New York, 1979), p. 45.

35. Julian Bharier, *Economic Development in Iran, 1900–1970* (London, 1971), pp. 69–72.

36. Ann Lambton, "The Impact of the West on Persia," *International Affairs,* 33, 1 (January 1957), p. 23.

37. Arthur C. Millspaugh, *Americans in Persia* (New York, 1976), p. 34.

3

Reform from Above and Resistance from Below: The June Uprising of 1963

At the inception of our land reforms that January, I had predicted that the forces of the clergy, the Black reaction, and of the communists, the Red destruction, would attempt to sabotage this program: the former, because they wished the nation to remain submerged in abject poverty and injustice; the latter, because their aim was the complete disintegration of the country.

Mohammad Reza Shah Pahlavi, 1979

We have come to the conclusion that this regime also has a more basic aim: they are fundamentally opposed to Islam itself and the existence of the religious class. They do not wish this institution to exist; they do not wish any of us to exist, the great and the small alike.

Ayatollah Ruhollah Khomeini, 1963

With the forced abdication of Reza Shah in 1941 and the occupation of war-riddled Iran by the Allied forces, Mohammad Reza Shah Pahlavi inherited the Peacock Throne. The era of monarchical despotism came to a temporary halt, and a period of parliamentary democracy began, lasting until 1953.

During the first decade of his rule, the inexperienced Shah, generally portrayed as a Swiss-educated king with a passionate love for fast cars and beautiful women, was hardly taken seriously either by veteran politicians or by the Allied forces that had occupied parts of Iran in 1941. Mohammad Reza Shah recalls that in November 1943 when Roosevelt, Churchill, and Stalin held a conference in Teheran, "neither Churchill nor Roosevelt bothered with international protocol that required they call on me, their host. Instead, I paid courtesy visits to both their embassy residences."[1]

Internal conditions were also not conducive to his ascension as an autocratic ruler. On one side, his father's court patronage had dissipated, and the armed forces, upon whose might his father's rule had depended, were in abysmal condition. On the other side, with the breakdown of Reza Shah's autocracy, political forces he had long suppressed surfaced and committed themselves to preventing the reemergence of an imperial despotism. As a result, the Majles became the real source of power, and the Shah was pushed aside by forces he could hardly contain or control. But the young Shah was determined to monopolize power, a process that took slightly more than two decades and involved a myriad of crises and in which, through a combination of luck, good policy, and foreign assistance, he succeeded. Challenges by Mohammad Mossadeq and Ayatollah Ruhollah Khomeini were the most significant of the crises he faced.

Iranian Nationalism in Action: Mossadeq and the 1953 Coup

In the 1940s, the Shah focused on reorganizing and revigorating the armed forces and on forming an alliance with a new foreign power in Iran, the United States, whose troops had entered Iran to help transport military supplies to the Soviet Union between 1942 and 1943. After the war, victory and competition with the Soviet Union awakened in the United States an increased interest in Iran because of its oil, lucrative markets, and strategic location: Arthur Millspaugh once again came to Iran to reorganize the state's finances. Norman Schwarzkopf, a U.S. colonel who later played a role in organizing the coup of 1953 and the father of the commander of U.S. forces in the Persian Gulf War against Iraq in 1991, headed the gendarmerie and reorganized internal security. In 1947 the U.S. firm of Morrison-Knudson proposed the first developmental plan for Iran.

Iranian-U.S. relations became more congenial during the Azerbaijan crisis. In 1945, after the war ended, the Soviet Union refused to withdraw its troops from Iran, as it had pledged to do earlier. This led the Shah's opponents to create two so-called autonomous republics in the Azerbaijan and Kurdestan provinces. The negotiations with Joseph Stalin for troop withdrawal were conducted by Ahmad Qavam, an independent-minded and seasoned prime minister. Qavam's legendary negotiation skills, timely maneuvering in the United Nations, and generous U.S. support bore fruit, and the Soviets withdrew in 1947.[2] What followed was the signing of the Mutual Defense Agreement between Iran and the United States in 1950 and U.S. recognition of Iran as a vitally strategic country for implementing its doctrine of containing Soviet expansionism.[3]

As the Shah was moving closer to Washington, new political parties, representing Marxist, Islamic, and nationalist ideologies, were being formed. With logistical support from the Soviet Union, the Tudeh Party became the most organized and disciplined party of the period.[4] Espousing a Persianized Marxism-Leninism, the Tudeh Party enjoyed considerable support among the working class, university students, and intellectuals. In the 1943 elections, its candidates won eight seats in the Majles.

There was also a revival of activity by some of the ulama.[5] Because of the towering influence of Ayatollah Hossein Borujerdi, who became the sole *marja'-e taqlid* in the second half of the 1940s, the majority of the ulama resorted to quietism. Only a few of them, under the leadership of Ayatollah Abul Qasem Kashani, became politically active. Kashani had a long and active anti-British career: In 1919, he had opposed the British mandate in Iraq; in 1942, he was arrested by the British and exiled because of his alleged support for Germany; in 1948, he went back to Iran and created the Mojahedin-e Islam, a group that won some seats in the Majles. He was also reputed to be one of the spiritual pedagogues of the Fada'iyun-e Islam, a fundamentalist party formed by Navab Safavi in 1946 that enjoyed support among the bazaaries and was responsible for the assassination of prominent figures, including the historian Ahmad Kasravi.

But it was neither the Tudeh Party nor the Islamic groups but rather a charismatic and nationalist prime minister, Dr. Mohammad Mossadeq, who challenged the young Shah and changed the destiny of his homeland. In October 1949, Mossadeq, a Western-educated Qajar aristocrat and in 1925 one of the few opponents of the creation of the Pahlavi dynasty, formed the National Front.[6] From the inception, the National Front was a reformist organization that represented the aspirations of the middle class, with the objectives of safeguarding the 1906 Constitution. It was a coalition of some loosely organized and sometimes antagonistic groups whose ideological orientations spanned the gamut, including Marxists, pan-Iranists, and pan-Islamists. Had it not been for the charismatic personality of Mossadeq himself, this conglomeration of hostile forces could never have come together under the same banner.

Mossadeq's National Front quickly gained popularity by calling for the nationalization of the oil industry. This gradually evolved into a nationalist movement that represented the aspirations of a whole nation and transcended the parochial interests of any one group. Even though Mossadeq and his allies represented only a small percentage of the Majles deputies, the nationalist sentiment was so powerful that many deputies, the majority of whom were conservative landowners, supported the audacious call for nationalization of the oil industry.[7] After the assassination of Prime Minister Hajali Razmara by Khalil Tahmasebi of the Fada'iyun-e Islam in March 1951, and after the fleeting tenure of Prime Minister Hossein 'Ala, the Shah, under mounting pressure from the Majles, named Mossadeq prime minister in April 1951.

During Mossadeq's twenty-eight-month tenure (April 1951 to August 1953), the oil industry was nationalized and the National Iranian Oil Company was subsequently formed, the Shah was forced to reign and not to rule as the 1906 Constitution had stipulated, and democracy flourished. Mossadeq was the first Middle Eastern leader to defiantly nationalize a major Western-controlled industry. This is why he was never supported by the major Western powers. In the beginning of his rule, he counted on support from the United States: The Truman administration, probably influenced by the U.S. oil companies that were anxious to find their way into Iran, lent moral support to the nationalists. Consequently, Averill Harriman went to Iran in July 1951 to work out a compromise between England and Iran.[8] U.S. intervention bore no fruit, as Mossadeq demanded nothing short of complete control over the oil industry, and the British refused to accept this plan.

Meanwhile, Britain resorted to every conceivable method to undermine and denigrate Mossadeq. The British press, and to a lesser extent the U.S. press, portrayed Mossadeq, Iran's national hero, as an old, stubborn, deceptive, and demagogic prime minister who would eventually hand Iran over to the communists. After Iran took over the oil installations, Britain threatened to use military force to recapture them. Britain boycotted Iranian oil, imposed economic sanctions, and took Iran to the International Court in the Hague and to the United Nations, all to no avail.[9]

Meanwhile, Mossadeq sought to increase his personal power. On July 17, 1952, he asked the Shah to grant him control of the Ministry of War. The Shah, who knew better than anyone else how his father had exploited his role as minister of war to dethrone the Qajars, rejected Mossadeq's bid. Mossadeq resigned and Ahmad Qavam replaced him. During Qavam's five-day tenure, the pro-Mossadeq/Kashani forces brought Iran to a standstill. They were encouraged by the *fatva* from Ayatollah Kashani that made it a religious duty for the faithful to confront the army. To avoid bloodshed, the Shah dismissed Qavam and asked Mossadeq to form a new cabinet.[10]

This victory turned the National Front into an apparently impregnable force. When diplomatic relations between Iran and Britain were severed in August 1952, Mossadeq was revered for having defeated a mighty foreign power. But deliberate provocations by the Tudeh Party, internal splits within the National Front, and some imprudent decisions by Mossadeq weakened his power.

The Tudeh Party played a treasonous role. Although it was formally illegal, the Tudeh, thanks to Mossadeq's liberalism, was conducting its activity in the open and expanding its constituency. As the mouthpiece of the Soviet Union's foreign policy, the Tudeh opposed Mossadeq, labeling him the representative of the "regressive national bourgeoisie" and an anti-British aristocrat who was serving the interests of "American imperialism." The Tudeh tried, with some success, to drive a wedge into the National Front and used its propaganda machinery to prevent any resolution of the oil crisis. The problem with the Tudeh leadership was that it analyzed Mossadeq's popular movement from the perspective of the Cold War and not from that of Iranian national interests.[11] Despite the Tudeh's provocation, Mossadeq refused to crush it. As the Tudeh became more powerful and visible, some of the ulama and the elites became frightened at the prospect of a communist takeover and withdrew their support for Mossadeq.

Mossadeq also faced immense economic difficulties. Because of the Western boycott of Iranian oil and the economic sanctions imposed on the country, the government cut its budget, the volume of foreign trade was reduced, and inflation became rampant. The deteriorating economic conditions undermined Mossadeq's popular base of support.

Within the National Front, too, Mossadeq faced difficulties. The first two splits within the National Front by Hossein Maki and Mozaffar Baqa'i were inconsequential. Neither man showed much perspicacity in estimating Mossadeq's popularity, as they were swept away to oblivion. But the defection by Ayatollah Kashani, the powerful speaker of the Majles, was indeed serious. Concerned about the growing power of the communists and critical of Mossadeq's "un-Islamic" policies and his intention to monopolize power, in August 1952 Kashani split from the National Front.[12] Thus, a valuable link between the religious community and the National Front was severed. Moreover, Kashani, and to a lesser extent Baqa'i, had access to an ideal network for the massive mobilization of the bazaaries and the lower classes. In an age when the course of politics was increasingly being determined by the size of the crowds in the streets of Teheran, the breakdown of this mobilizing network was debilitating to the National Front. Moreover, Mossadeq's unconstitutional dissolution of the Majles, based on a national referendum in early July 1953, had convinced many Iranians that he might have other ambitions besides nationalizing the oil industry.

But the fatal threat to Mossadeq came from his foreign enemies. Under President Eisenhower, the United States began its covert activities against the Mossadeq movement. Influenced by Britain, the United States came to believe that Mossadeq's bold nationalization policy would adversely affect Western interests in the oil-rich Persian Gulf and even beyond. This is why Washington denied Mossadeq's repeated requests for aid and illegally interfered in Iranian domestic affairs. Paid British and U.S. saboteurs did everything possible to divide and weaken the nationalists. Finally, in a MI-6/CIA operation named AJAX, Mossadeq was toppled on August 19, 1953.[13] Four days earlier, General Fazlollah Zahedi, the chief of the Imperial Guard, delivered a royal decree to Mossadeq that named Zahedi the prime minister. Mossadeq arrested the general and declared that a coup against his government had been crushed. Upon hearing the news of the arrest, the timid Shah fled Iran, first to Iraq and then to Rome, and both pro- and anti-Shah forces poured into the streets. The Tudeh Party and some of Mossadeq's close advisers, including Hossein Fatemi, his foreign minister, began to speak of creating a republic. Teheran was tense. Mossadeq ordered the army to impose order, but this intervention only enabled the agents of the coup to complete their operation. On August 19, with the collaboration of the army, civilians like the Rashediyan brothers, thugs like Sha'ban "the Brainless," "and a conglomeration of south Teheran illiterates collected by Behbahani's [one of the ulama] organization with the assistance of Kashani, and other lesser mullas, and a wide assortment of *chaqu keshan* leaders [knife-wielders]," the nationalist movement was crushed.[14] Mossadeq was arrested and the Shah returned home. Although orchestrated by foreign powers, the coup had the support, albeit implicitly, of the landlords, the wealthy merchants, a significant portion of the ulama, and the majority of the top echelon of the armed forces.

That the coup was a rather simple and inexpensive intelligence operation is a sad commentary on the nature of Mossadeq's government and his movement.

The coup of 1953 had drastic consequences for Iran and for U.S.-Iranian relations. Because it was generally believed that the United States had saved his throne, the Shah lost much of his political legitimacy. His relationship with the nationalists was irrevocably damaged. From then on, he was tainted as the U.S. shah, a label that stuck to him throughout his life. The coup also created for the Shah a psychological dependence on Washington, thus depriving him of the ability to act independently during a crisis, which proved fatal during the last year of his reign.

Shaken by Mossadeq's meteoric rise to power, the Shah became determined never to allow anyone to become too powerful. In an ironic way, Mossadeq's legacy provided the Shah with the personal justification to become an autocrat. The United States, too, paid for its support of the Shah. Because the United States had not been a colonizing Western power, Iranians had deep admiration for the United States prior to the coup. After the coup, however, the United States lost much of its credibility and respect among many Iranians. The United States could have supported a popular, liberal, anticommunist and pro-Western nationalist leader, but it sided with the Shah. On the positive side, the coup guaranteed access to cheap Iranian oil for the United States and the Western governments for the next two decades.

The coup also marked the start of Iran's ever-increasing dependence upon the United States and became a catalyst for the emergence of the United States as the hegemonic foreign power in Iran.

The logic of Washington's support for the Shah was succinctly summarized in a report submitted to President Eisenhower's National Security Council in 1953:

"Over the long run, the most effective instrument for maintaining Iran's orientation towards the West is the monarch, which in turn has the army as its only real source of power. U.S. military aid serves to improve army morale, cement army loyalty to the Shah, and thus consolidate the present regime and provide some assurance that Iran's current orientation towards the West will be perpetual."[15] The United States, therefore, was laying the foundation of its policy in Iran based on a relationship with one man, whose only source of support was the army. Its primary objectives were to keep Iran immune from communism, to have easy access to its oil, and to perpetuate Western domination over the strategically vital Persian Gulf region. For these reasons, the United States became the staunchest ally of the Zahedi government.

The immediate objectives of the Zahedi government were to restore order and settle the oil dispute. Mossadeq was tried in a military court, found guilty of high treason, and sentenced to jail. (He was jailed for three years and then put under house arrest until his death in 1967.) Hossein Fatemi, Mossadeq's foreign minister, was placed before a firing squad. Mossadeq's prominent associates were either given jail sentences of different durations or forced into exile.

But the bloodiest edge of this terror was directed at the Tudeh Party. In 1954, a network of Tudeh members that had been created by Khosrow Roozbeh and that included some 600 officers of middle and low rank was accidentally discovered inside the armed forces.[16] About 450 officers were tried, and many were sentenced to death or long-term imprisonment. A large number of the Tudeh Party's high officials, however, fled Iran and found sanctuary in Eastern Europe.

Zahedi quickly settled the oil dispute. The United States granted $45 million in emergency financial assistance to Zahedi. In return, according to a twenty-five-year oil agreement negotiated by Ali Amini, Zahedi's finance minister, an oil consortium consisting of the major Western oil companies was created in which the British oil companies lost their dominant position and a group of U.S. companies became one of the major shareholders.[17]

By the end of 1954, Zahedi had exhausted his usefullness: Order had been restored and the oil industry was denationalized. Now the Shah was determined to destroy all sources of independent power in his drive toward absolute rule. The first victim of this drive was Zahedi, who, in early 1955, was replaced by Hossein 'Ala, a Shah confidant. The next victim was the Majles, which contained some independent-minded deputies. The Shah saw to it that his obedient servants packed the new Majles.

But perhaps the most critical move was to consolidate the Shah's power over intelligence-gathering agencies. In 1957, with generous support from the CIA of the United States and MOSSAD of Israel, SAVAK, the Sazeman-e Ettela'at Va Amniyat-e Keshvar (Information and Security Organization of the Nation), was established. General Teymur Bakhtiyar, one of the key figures in the 1953 coup, headed the organization. At the same time, the Shah created the Second Bureau within the ranks of the armed forces to prevent any coup against the Pahlavis. He also organized the Royal Inspection Organization to supervise all state activities. All three agencies were directly accountable to the Shah. Thus, Mohammad Reza Shah had moved a long way, from a powerless monarch in 1941 to a powerful autocrat in 1960. But the early 1960s were more turbulent than he had ever anticipated. The Shah was soon faced with the second crisis of his rule.

The Shah and His White Revolution

Secure on this throne, the Shah promised free elections for the upcoming twentieth Majles in 1960. In the course of the election, Prime Minister Manuchehr Eqbal was accused, and justifiably so, by his archrival Asadollah Alam of rigging the elections. Quickly, the opposition called for Eqbal's resignation, and gradually this intraelite dispute developed into a political quagmire for the regime. In the rigged elections, Eqbal's supporters scored a landslide victory.[18] After a news conference in which the Shah expressed displeasure with the elections, Eqbal resigned, and Ja'far Sharif Imami replaced him. Meanwhile, public pressure to nullify the elections intensified. Finally, in September 1960, the Shah bowed to the pressure: Before the Majles convened, he asked the deputies to resign. They all did. Nor did Imami's government stay in power for long. What led to Imami's fall was the killing of a teacher by the police during one of the strikes for higher wages by the Society of Iranian Teachers. It was during these critical moments that the Shah opened the twentieth Majles. The bazaar closed down again and this time Imami was forced to resign.[19]

More significant than the issue of election fraud was the inauguration of President John F. Kennedy in January 1961. Most Iranians believed that the liberal Kennedy was critical of the Shah's autocracy and was an advocate of genuine reform. At one time, the Kennedy administration did evaluate its options in Iran but after careful assessment decided to support the Shah. The incisive intelligence report prepared by John W. Bowling for Kennedy in March 1961 elaborates why that decision was made:[20]

> Traditional leaders—clergy, landlords, and really big merchants—offer little hope for providing competent leadership, and are blind to the threat which the urban middle class represents. It might conceivably still be possible to "bypass" the urban middle class by providing a dynamic to the inert traditional-minded peasantry and proletariat, perhaps based on a regeneration of Shi'i Islam with new values adjustable to semi-Western values and to modern techniques of production and organization. But there is no sign of the gigantic creativity which would be necessary for such a reversal of the current historical trend.[21]

Included in the fourteen recommendations Bowling made to the Shah were reduce military expenditures, withdraw from an openly pro-Western posture, make public scapegoats of scores of "corrupt" high officials, relax political repression, and, finally, proceed ostentatiously against the big landlords with at least a token land distribution program.

The Shah was nervous, and for good reason. In less than one year, two prime ministers, his close confidants, had been forced to resign and the United States was pressing for reform. In his search for a reformer, he turned to Ali Amini, a Qajar aristocrat and a minister in both the Mossadeq and Zahedi cabinets. The Shah recalled: "The U.S. would have oil and its own man in as prime minister. This man was Ali Amini, and in time the pressure became too strong for me to resist, especially after John F. Kennedy was elected president."[22] Amini's precondition for accepting the post was that the Shah dissolve the Majles and grant him temporary power to rule by decree without legislative obstruction. The Shah agreed, and on May 5, 1961, Amini became prime minister.

Amini's administration was a whirlwind of reforms, the linchpin of which was land reform. He acted decisively: Censorship was relaxed, the National Front leadership was offered cabinet posts, a controversial anticorruption campaign was started in which many prominent members of the ruling elites were arrested and tried, the teachers' strike was settled, and a land distribution program was enacted.

The Kennedy administration considered land reform an effective deterrent against communist expansion or an agrarian revolution of the Chinese type and a prerequisite for the success of any industrialization program. Julius Holmes, the U.S. ambassador in Iran, emphasized that the success of such a reform "is fundamental to our interests and that we need to exploit every occasion which presents itself for our assistance, both in following up land distribution and in stimulating recovery in the economy."[23]

Amini was not the first to advocate such reforms. In 1959, Prime Minister Eqbal introduced a bill to the Majles with a clause restricting the amount of land one could own, but Ayatollah Borujerdi publicly declared the incompatibility of such legislation with Islamic principles. To show obeisance to him, the Majles fundamentally modified it and turned it into a harmless bill. Finally, the Land Reform Act of 1962 was introduced.

The principal architect of land reform was Hassan Arsanjani, Amini's minister of agriculture.[24] On January 9, 1962, when the Majles had been dissolved, his land reform proposal was approved by Amini's cabinet. The program had a threefold objective: to curtail the power of the large landowners, to turn the *nassaq* holders (those who enjoyed the right of cultivation under the traditional sharecropping system) into a large landowning stratum, and to demolish the archaic structures of rural areas by the imposition of capitalism. The landowners were allowed to keep one village, or a total of six *dung*s (each *dung* is one-sixth of a property) from different holdings. The tea plantations, orchards, and mechanized fields were to be exempted from this provision. Landowners were required to sell the excess land to the government, which would resell it to the peasants at the purchase price plus a 10 percent surcharge for administrative costs.

The growing popularity of Arsanjani and Amini and the intensity of opposition to land reform by the landlords and some of the ulama alarmed the Shah. He was placed in a precarious position, caught as he was in the cross fire between the forces advocating reform and those opposing it. He had two realistic options: undo the damage by removing Amini or form a new alliance and proceed with reform. At his visit with President Kennedy in Washington in early 1962, the Shah seemed to have struck a deal to support land reform in return for full U.S. assistance. Two months later, in April 1962, Amini resigned, ostensibly because of insufficient U.S. aid to his administration and because the Shah had refused to accept his proposal for a reduction of military expenditures.

Part of the problem was that Amini's popular base of support was quite narrow. The success of his reform required the support, or at least the impartiality, of the Second National Front formed by, among others, Karim Sanjabi, Shahpur Bakhtiyar, and Mehdi Bazargan. But the Second National Front was looking for an excuse not to cooperate with Amini. Having no reform program of its own, it requested the dissolution of SAVAK, a demand that the Shah and Amini would never have accepted. There were good reasons to mistrust Amini: He had quit Mossadeq's cabinet, he had negotiated the notorious 1954 oil treaty with the Western oil companies, and he was a potential rival to the National Front's leadership. But the new conditions demanded much cerebration. Amini's government represented a progressive faction of the ruling class and advocated a comprehensive reform program. The issue was not whether Amini's government was the best alternative but what could have replaced it. The leadership of the Second National Front, living vicariously through Mossadeq's image, followed the suicidal line of undermining Amini's government by asking for his resignation and calling for free elections. Nothing could have been more pleasing to the Shah, for what he feared most was the formation of any kind of alliance between Amini and the Second National Front. The Second National Front's hostility toward Amini was based on the tenuous theory that should Amini collapse, the Shah and the United States would definitely turn to them to form a new government. Amini did fall, but it marked the beginning of an era of imperial despotism, one in which the forces of the Second National Front came to play the role of frustrated bystanders.[25]

Fearful that Amini could challenge him, the Shah replaced Amini with Alam. Arsanjani, however, remained in the new cabinet, symbolizing the Shah's commitment to land reform. In late 1962, when Arsanjani organized the Congress of Rural and Cooperative Societies in Teheran, in which thousands of peasants and agricultural workers gathered to express their support for him, the Shah reacted in alarm. He wasted no time asking for Arsanjani's resignation. If Amini had spoken of reform, the Shah was now talking of revolution—the "White Revolution." By championing the land reform program, he was hoping to win the hearts and minds of the lower classes and thereby achieve the dual objectives of enlarging his popular base of support and preventing the opposition from mobilizing them against his regime.

The White Revolution originally included six provisions: land reform, nationalization of forests, sale of state-owned enterprises to the public, a workers' profit-sharing plan, women's suffrage, and creation of the Literacy Corps. To legitimize the White Revolution, the Shah called for a national referendum in early 1963 in which 5,598,711 voted for the reforms and 4,115 voted against. The fraudulent referendum was boycotted by the opposition to the Shah. However, President Kennedy immediately sent a telegram congratulating the Shah on his "victory in the historic referendum."[26]

With Arsanjani out of the picture, land reform took a more conservative turn in its second and third stages. In the second stage landowners were allowed to keep as much as 150 hectares of their land and were offered a variety of options for the excess land, ranging from renting or selling it to the farmers to buying the peasant's right of cultivation. In the third phase, started in 1969, the goal was to increase productivity through mechanization and to terminate tenancies by providing for the sale of all lands leased by the landowners on a thirty-year basis. This was to be accomplished by creating farm cooperatives.

The land reform program had far-reaching consequences. First, it drastically curtailed the political power of the landed upper class and for all practical purposes eradicated absentee ownership. Second, it created a large petty-landowning stratum from the ranks of the *nassaq* sharecroppers. In 1961, there were more than 2.1 million *nassaq* sharecroppers. By 1971, 1,766,625, or 92 percent of them, had received legal title to the land they worked.[27] If the average household consisted of five members, more than 9.6 million people benefited from the reform. Third, the absolute authority of the landlords was replaced with that of the state as manifested in the creation of dozens of new institutions in the rural areas such as Anjoman-e Deh (Village Organization), Khane-ye Ensaf (House of Justice), the Literacy Corps, the Health Corps, and the Religious Corps. Most important, state-controlled banks penetrated the rural areas and made new landowners and the entire rural community dependent upon the state.

Fourth, because land reform did not provide necessary capital for the peasants who had acquired lands and did not create a sufficient infrastructure in the rural regions to assist the new landowners in managing their lands, agricultural output drastically declined during the 1960s and 1970s. This increased the need for exports and Iran's dependence on Western nations. Fifth, even though land reform contributed to the political stability of rural communities, it indirectly caused tension in urban areas as millions of landless peasants migrated to the major cities to become the foot soldiers of the Islamic Revolution. Sixth, the land reform generated acrimony between the ulama and the Shah's regime. There were more than 40,000 *vaqf* holdings (lands endowed for charitable purposes) in 1960. Under the provisions of the second phase of land reform, *vaqf* holders were required to negotiate a ninety-nine-year tenancy agreement with the *nassaq* sharecroppers. In most cases, the annual rents paid by the *nassaq* sharecroppers came to less than they had paid under the old system. This curtailed the ulama's revenues from the *vaqf* holdings.[28] It was not surprising that the ulama posed the greatest threat to the Shah's rule in 1963.

Ayatollah Khomeini and the Shah's Reforms

From 1953 to early 1960, the relationship between the Shah and the ulama was peaceful if not amicable. After all, the leading ulama, including Ayatollahs Borujerdi, Behbahani, and Kashani, had tacitly supported the military coup of 1953. In fact, Ayatollah Borujerdi was one of the first to send a welcome telegram to the Shah after his return to Iran from Rome in the aftermath of that coup. His reward was easy access to the throne.

The Shah saw in the ulama a powerful force against the radicalism of the left and the liberalism of the middle class. Anxious to demonstrate his commitment to Shi'ism, he made frequent trips to the sacrosanct shrines in Mashhad and Qom and contributed handsomely to their refurbishment as well as to major Shi'i theological centers. As a gesture of goodwill toward the ulama, in 1955 his government did not stop an angry mob from attacking the Baha'is' main temple in Teheran. This action met with the ulama's approbation. Both Ayatollahs Borujerdi and Behbahani sent a widely publicized telegram congratulating the Shah and assuring him of the vigorous support of the faithful.[29]

The introduction of a land reform bill in 1959, however, put an end to this brief honeymoon. On February 23, 1960, Ayatollah Borujerdi wrote a letter to Seyyed Ja'far Behbahani, one of the Majles deputies, stating explicitly that the imposition of any limitation on landownership was ignominious to the Islamic laws and that the two houses of Parliament should "refrain from approving the bill."[30] In no position to antagonize the popular ayatollah, the government reached a rapprochement with Borujerdi and withdrew the bill. But with Borujerdi's death in March 1961, the Shah implemented the land reform.

Borujerdi's death created a leadership vacuum within the Shi'i hierarchy. A number of prominent ayatollahs, all with impressive credentials, were in competition to replace Borujerdi: Mohammad Hadi Milani in Mashhad, Kazem Shariatmadari in Tabriz, Mohsen Hakim in Najaf, Iraq, and Mohammad Reza Golpayegani and Ruhollah Khomeini in Qom. The Shah attempted in vain to influence the selection process. On the occasion of Borujerdi's death he sent a telegram of commiseration to Ayatollah Mohsen Hakim, recognizing him as the leading *marja'-e taqlid*. The monarch was thus hoping to move the center of Shi'ism from Qom to Najaf and to elevate a non-Iranian ayatollah unfamiliar with and perhaps unconcerned about Iranian politics to the highest position of Shi'i leadership. But none of the candidates ascended to the position of the sole *marja'-e taqlid* and Shi'ism once again became polycephalic.

The period immediately following Borujerdi's death also coincided with the revival of the ulama's fervent opposition to the government. Several factors contributed to this activism. First, those ulama who had not approved of Borujerdi's conciliatory and cooperative policy with the Shah were now in a position to publicly express their grievances against the government. Second, Iran, having experienced a sustained rate of expansion from the coup of 1953 through the late 1950s, was now plunged into a depression.

By the early 1960s, the government deficit grew to immense proportions, the balance-of-payments situation deteriorated, and inflation became rampant. Because of pressure from the International Monetary Fund (IMF), Iran was forced to implement its Economic Stabilization Program in the late 1960s.[31] As a result of the imposition of this program, the government lowered its budget and its investments, froze hiring, cut employee salaries by about 3 percent, lowered drastically the amount of loans and credit to the private sector, and reduced imports. These policies increased bankruptcy among merchants and created much discontent among the bazaaries who sought and received support from their historic allies, the ulama. Third, issues such as land reform, women's suffrage, and the de facto recognition of the state of Israel united the ulama against the state. In July 1962, 150 religious figures meeting at Al-Azhar in Cairo issued a *fatva* calling on Moslems of the world to begin their *jahad* (holy war) against the Shah for his pro-Israeli policies.[32]

The ulama's opposition to the government intensified when Amini announced his land reform program in 1961. To appease the clergy, Amini made some cosmetic public relations moves, such as appointing a deputy minister for religious affairs and making frequent visits to the residence of the leading ulama, including the ailing Ayatollah Kashani. But the ulama's opposition was more deep-rooted than Amini had imagined.

It was during the tenure of Asadollah Alam as prime minister that the ulama's opposition against the Shah's policies reached its zenith. They vehemently opposed the proposed Local Council Elections Bill of November 1962. And it was in connection with this bill that Ayatollah Khomeini first came to national attention as a political figure.

Khomeini's opposition to the Shah revolved around three issues: the Local Council Elections Bill, the National Referendum of 1963, and the granting of capitulatory rights to U.S. advisers and military personnel and their dependents in Iran in 1964.

The Local Council Elections decree that was approved by Alam's cabinet (in the absence of the Majles that had been dissolved by the Shah) granted suffrage to women and replaced the term "holy Quran" in the mandatory oath of office with "holy book." The ulama argued that the substitution of "holy book" for "holy Quran" would increase the infiltration of religious minorities, especially the heretical Baha'is, in the government and the armed forces. In a country where men do not enjoy the freedom to elect their representatives, they insisted, the granting of suffrage to women was no more than a recipe for increasing corruption and decadence. The three grand ayatollahs of Qom—Golpayegani, Shariatmadari, and Khomeini—sent telegrams to the Shah, declaring the decree unconstitutional and inimical to Islam. After a week, the Shah responded to the telegram, derogatorily referring to the signatories as *hojatolislams*, a rank below that of ayatollah.[33] In a separate telegram to the Shah, Khomeini sounded the tocsin: "You are surrounded by the sycophants and slaves who would attribute all antireligion and unlawful acts to the person of His Majesty; and the approval of their treasonous and mistaken bill [decree] would undermine the Constitution which is the protector of sovereignty and kingship."[34] At this stage, Khomeini was cautious not to antagonize the Shah by dissociating him from the policies of Alam. The Shah did not even bother to respond to the telegram.

Throughout the country, the ulama used the pulpits in the mosques to incite the population against the government. Under pressure, Alam withdrew only the provision of the decree dealing with the oath of office. This concession did not appease the ulama. On the night when the ulama had planned a gathering at a Teheran mosque, Alam withdrew the entire bill. The ulama had scored a temporary victory, leading to a lull in their activism.

Khomeini's opposition to the government intensified in January 1963 when the Shah, hoping to legitimize his White Revolution, called for a national referendum. Included in the White Revolution was a provision granting suffrage to women. Khomeini argued that the constitution was ambiguous about which authority may call for a national referendum, implying that the Shah enjoyed no such privilege. Moreover, he maintained, "essentially referendum or national approval has no validity in Islam ... and the voters should have sufficient knowledge to understand what they are voting for. Consequently, a large majority [of Iranians] do not have the right to vote [for the referendum]."[35] (Ironically, sixteen years later, he relied on a national referendum to legitimize the creation of the Islamic Republic.) He asked the people to boycott the referendum and suggested the innovative idea that the ulama stage a strike during the holy month of Ramadan, the month of fasting, by not attending the mosques. Although Golpayegani and Shariatmadari issued a joint declaration with Khomeini condemning the referendum, they were unprepared to support Khomeini's call for a strike by the ulama.

The regime reacted violently against the ulama who opposed the referendum. The Shah's paratroopers attacked the theological Feyziyeh school in Qom, the stronghold of Khomeini. Young *tollab* (theology students) were beaten and several were killed. The government began drafting theology students for mandatory military service. The mass media portrayed the opponents of the referendum as "black reactionaries" supported by feudal lords who wished to return Iran to the dark ages. The attacks only intensified the spirit of contumacy in Khomeini. On June 3, 1963, Khomeini declared war on the Shah but not on the institution of monarchy: "Let me give you some advice, Mr. Shah! Dear Mr. Shah. ... Maybe those people [advisers and the government in power] want to present you as a Jew so that I will denounce you as an unbeliever and they can expel you from Iran and put an end to you! Don't you know that if one day some uproar occurs and that tables are turned, none of these people around you will be your friends. They are friends of the dollars; they have no religion, no loyalty."[36] So open an attack on the person of the Shah, combined with Khomeini's call to the Iranian army to join him for the "salvation of Islam and Iran," was intolerable. It was the first time since 1953 that an opposition leader had the courage to openly attack the person of the Shah. This is why on June 4, 1963, Khomeini was arrested by the government.

The arrest precipitated boisterous antigovernment disturbances in some major cities for a week. The climax of these activities was the June Uprising in Teheran. Khomeini's supporters made an aborted attempt to take over Teheran's main radio station but succeeded only in inflicting heavy damage on some government buildings, some liquor stores, and a Pepsi Cola bottling facility reportedly owned by a Baha'i. The rioters were small in number but strong and devoted in their commitment to Khomeini.

The government acted decisively. General Ne'mattollah Nassiri was appointed the military governor of Teheran as martial law was imposed in Teheran and some other cities. The government ordered the police to kill, and kill they did. One reporter observed that on June 5, "machine-gun fire still echoed through the rubble-strewn streets of the bazaar area. ... The bazaar area looked as if a tornado had hit it."[37] The official government estimate was that 20 were killed and 1,000 injured. The opposition claimed that thousands were massacred.

Not all the data about those who were arrested, injured, or killed are available. What is accessible is the information about 580 individuals who were injured or arrested by the government. Of those arrested and injured in the June Uprising, 27.6 percent were the skilled workers, followed by the ulama (15 percent), retailers and shopkeepers (13.4 percent), and the students (11.9 percent) (Table 3.1). The average age was about twenty-three years (Table 3.2).

The official explanation for this rebellion was that Khomeini and his supporters were against land reform and the progressive ideals of the White Revolution. To exculpate itself from any wrongdoing, the regime declared, without evidence, that Khomeini had a direct connection with President Abdul Naser of Egypt, one of the Shah's enemies, and that Egypt had financed the rebellion.[38] Unable to back up its claim, the government's accusation against Khomeini served only to make him more popular.

As calm was restored, Ayatollahs Shariatmadari, Najafi Mar'ashi, Hojatolislam Hossein Ali Montazeri, and others orchestrated a campaign for the immediate and unconditional release of Khomeini. They demanded television and radio time to clarify their views about government reforms. Moreover, Shariatmadari warned the authorities that according to Article 2 of the Supplementary Laws, high-ranking Shi'i ulama enjoy immunity and may not be jailed, tortured, or exiled—a reference to Khomeini's arrest.[39] After spending six weeks in jail, Khomeini was released but was denied permission to return to Qom and was kept under house arrest in Teheran. In a communiqué, the government announced that Khomeini had promised not to intervene in the affairs of the state, a claim that he subsequently denied having made.[40]

Khomeini was in no mood to compromise with the Pahlavi regime. As the Majles election approached, Khomeini's supporters asked the people to boycott the elections. The elections, open only to the Shah's loyalists, resulted in the victory of the Progressive Center group, led by Hassan Ali Mansur, who was named prime minister by the Shah. To improve relations with the ulama, Mansur allowed Khomeini to return to Qom.

By the time he returned to Qom in January 1964, Khomeini had emerged as a popular religious leader. He was given a hero's welcome. Immediately, his students at the Feyziyeh school submitted a ten-point proposal to the government. Among other things, it included a demand for the implementation of the 1906 Constitution, especially Article 2 of the Supplementary Laws, which gave the ulama veto power over Majles legislation. It called for annulling all un-Islamic de-

TABLE 3.1 Occupational Backgrounds of the Arrested and Injured in the June Uprising, June 2 to June 10, 1963

Job Background	Number	Percentage of Total
Skilled workers	163	27.6
Ulama	88	15.0
Retailers, shopkeepers	79	13.4
Students	70	11.9
Apprentices, assistant shopkeepers	47	8.0
Merchants and middlemen	36	6.1
Unskilled workers	32	5.4
Unemployed	16	2.7
Unspecified and others	16	2.7
Private and public employees	15	2.5
Farmers	14	2.4
Professional groups	12	2.3
Total*	588	100.0

*Data do not include the dead because the information on their backgrounds is not yet available.
Source: Data from Dahnavi, *Qiyame-e Khunin-e Panzdah-e Khordad-e Chehel-o Dau* (The Bloody Uprising of June 5, 1963) (Teheran, 1984), various pages. Calculations by author, figures rounded.

crees, ending the influence of colonialism and Zionism in Iran, cleansing television and radio programs of corrupt content, and preventing production and consumption of alcoholic beverages.[41] (Most of those demands are now being implemented under the Islamic Republic.)

In Qom, the cantankerous Khomeini continued to oppose the Shah's regime, this time over Mansur's proposal to the Majles granting capitulatory rights to U.S. advisers and requesting approval for a $200 million loan from the United States for the purchase of military equipment. (The capitulations were legal and taxation exemptions obtained by the Europeans in the Middle East. The first capitulations were granted by the Ottoman sultan, Suleiman the Magnificent, to the French in 1535. In the eyes of the Middle Easterners, the capitulations are the very symbol of European colonialism.) The bill was passed with only a few deputies opposing it. This infuriated Khomeini. In a sermon in Qom, he portrayed the Shah as sanctimonious, called the White Revolution a U.S. conspiracy against Islam, and asked all Iranians to rebel against the proposed bill, "which would turn Iran into a U.S. colony": "Even if the Shah himself were to run over a dog belonging to an American, he would be prosecuted. But if an American cook runs over the Shah, the head of state, no one will have the right to interfere with him. ... If some American's servant, some cook, assassinates your *marja'* in the middle of the bazaar, or runs over him, the Iranian people do not have the right to apprehend him![42]" Convinced that Khomeini could not be peacefully silenced, the Iranian regime exiled him. Pakistan and India rejected Iran's request to provide a sanctuary for Khomeini, but Turkey agreed and on November 4, 1965, he was forced to leave Iran for that country. From Turkey he went to Najaf, Iraq, where he resided until 1978.

TABLE 3.2   Average Age of the Arrested and Injured in the June Uprising, June 2 to June 10, 1963

Age	Number	Percentage of Total
10–14	12	5.2
15–17	41	17.9
18–20	61	26.7
21–25	49	21.4
26–30	32	14.0
31–35	19	8.3
36–54	15	6.5
Total	229	100.0
ulama[a]		
26–40	6	40.0
41–62	9	60.0
Total	15	100.0

[a] Includes *tollab*, or the theology students. Actual number of the arrested ulama is larger than this figure; data on all those arrested are not available.

Source: Data from Dahnavi, *Qiyame-e Khunin-e Panzdah-e Khordad-e Chehel-o Dau* (The Bloody Uprising of June 5, 1963) (Teheran, 1981). Calculations by author, figures rounded.

The Historical Significance of the June Uprising

By crushing the June Uprising and exiling Khomeini to Iraq, the Shah won the battle but not the war. In many ways, it was in the June Uprising that the seeds of the Islamic Revolution of 1979 were sown. The Shah's opponents learned valuable lessons from their defeat that later helped them demolish the Pahlavi regime. After the June Uprising, a growing portion of the opposition rejected the possibility of peaceful coexistence with the Shah and resorted to the armed struggle against the Pahlavis.

The secular and religious oppositions to the Shah had a golden opportunity to manipulate the favorable economic and political conditions of 1963 to enhance their interests. But they were divided and confused. The conservative and languid leadership of the Second National Front had lost all political creativity. By the early 1960s, it had become obvious that the Second National Front, like the Shah's regime, was a one-man show. Without Mossadeq, who was still under house arrest, the Second National Front could not manage its own internal disputes, to say nothing of the destiny of a nation. It had no comprehensive program, as was reflected in its absurd slogan "Reform Yes, Dictatorship No." It did not want to oppose the Shah's reforms, nor could it surrender to him or support him.

With the exception of its symbolic and belated support for the June Uprising, the Second National Front did not cooperate with the pro-Khomeini forces. Two months before the June Uprising, Nadar Saleh, a member of the Second National Front, informed the U.S. Embassy in Teheran that "on the possibility of religious agitation during Moharram [June] ... the National Front would under no circumstances cooperate with the clergy should there be disturbances." He quoted

Alahyar Saleh, one of the leaders of the Second National Front, as saying that "since the ultimate aims of the Front were diametrically opposed to those of the *mullas,* the Front would never combine their forces with them against the government."[43]

But if the Second National Front separated its destiny from the religious forces, Bazargan's Liberation Movement, a small group of Islamic intellectuals, chose a different path and collaborated with the clergy. Nadar Saleh seemed to have offered an accurate analysis of the Liberation Movement as "the only people ... who could and did work actively with the *mullahs,* and if it came to a test, the Liberation Movement would at present undoubtedly have greater support among the common people than the National Front."[44]

With alacrity, some of the ulama stood firm against the Shah. With the collaboration of some shopkeepers, merchants, and intellectuals, they challenged the Shah and lost. The defeat made it abundantly clear that more than a faction of this and a faction of that class was needed to seriously challenge the Shah. This is perhaps why, in 1978, Khomeini formed the broadest possible anti-Shah coalition, one that cut across class distinctions.

If a major segment of the opposition was confused, the Shah's regime appeared confident and decisive. It had a stratagem of dealing with the opposition that worked well. Its brutality against the demonstrators cannot be attributed to the Shah, who apparently opposed violence. The decision to attack Khomeini's supporters on June 5 was made by Alam, not the Shah.[45] The regime's quick response and its lack of compunction to apply brute force was also attributable to the full support of the United States for the Shah's policy toward the belligerent opposition.

The impact of the June Uprising on the ulama community was dramatic, too. Khomeini's courage to confront the Shah politicized a whole generation of the ulama and left a legacy in Qom. His arrest and exile increased cooperation among the ulama in general and among his own students in particular. After Khomeini's exile, seventy of his supporters were defrocked by the government and denied the right to use the pulpit. This small core kept Khomeini's legacy alive. They were often jailed or sentenced to internal exile.

The events leading up to the uprising also paved the way for the formation of a new Islamic organization. Following Khomeini's orders, three small Islamic groups formed the United Islamic Societies. Less than two months after Khomeini's exile, Mansur was assassinated by Mohammad Bokharai. The government identified the twenty-year-old assassin as a member of the Fada'iyun-e Islam. Years later, the United Islamic Societies claimed responsibility for the assassination. Much mystery surrounds the assassination, but it is known that many of Khomeini's supporters were arrested and jailed.

But the most significant consequence of the June Uprising was the emergence of Khomeini as religio-political leader. Khomeini's themes of anti-Americanism, his fervent opposition to Zionism, his opposition to the Shah's autocracy, and his emphasis on Islam attracted a large audience. Hossein Mahdavi, a member of the Central Committee of the National Front, was on the mark when he said: "He

[Khomeini] is regarded by Iranian intellectuals, even those who have little regard for Islam, as learned, extremely intelligent and courageous ... not since Mossadeq has one man brought so many diverse elements together."[46] As Khomeini went into exile, his boldness to confront the Shah, his spiritual leadership, his ability to speak a language understood by the ordinary people, and his magnetism to unify divergent groups were qualities that combined in the national memory to become a national myth. That he emerged in 1979 as the symbol of the revolutionary movement was no historical accident.

Notes

1. Mohammad Reza Pahlavi, *Answer to History* (New York, 1980), p. 72.

2. Faramarz Fatemi, *The U.S.S.R. in Iran* (New York, 1980), chaps. 4 and 5; and Richard Cottam, *Iran and the United States* (Pittsburgh, Penn., 1988).

3. Yonah Alexander and Allan Nanes, eds., *The United States and Iran: A Documentary History* (Frederick, Md., 1980), pp. 290–311.

4. Sepehr Zabih, *The Communist Movement in Iran* (Berkeley, Calif., 1966).

5. L. P. Elwell-Sutton, "Political Parties in Iran: 1941–1948," *Middle East Journal*, 3, 1 (1949), pp. 45–62.

6. Khalil Maleki, *Tarikhche-ye Jebhe-ye Melli* (The History of the National Front) (Teheran, 1954).

7. Fereidun Fesharaki, *Development of the Iranian Oil Industry* (New York, 1976).

8. Rubin, Barry. *Paved with Good Intentions: The American Experience in Iran* (New York, 1980), pp. 54–73; and Nikki Keddie, *Roots of Revolution: An Interpretive History of Modern Iran* (New Haven, Conn., 1981), pp. 132–137.

9. Homa Katouzian, *The Political Economy of Modern Iran: Despotism and Pseudo Modernism, 1926–1979* (New York, 1981).

10. The details of the event are described by S. Zabih, *The Mossadeq Era* (Chicago, 1982), pp. 40 and 56–66.

11. Faridoun Keshavarz, *Man Motaham Mikonam Komite-ye Markazi-ye Hezb-e Tudeh Ra* (I Condemn the Central Committee of the Tudeh Party) (n.p., 1981).

12. Richard Cottam, *Nationalism in Iran* (Pittsburgh, Penn., 1964), pp. 152–156.

13. Kermit Roosevelt, *Counter Coup: The Struggle for the Control of Iran* (New York, 1979); David Wise and Thomas B. Ross, *The Invisible Government* (London, 1965); and A. Tully, *The Inside Story* (London, 1962).

14. Cottam (1964), p. 155.

15. Alexander and Nanes (1980), p. 268.

16. Farhad Kazemi, "The Military and Politics in Iran: The Uneasy Symbiosis," in Elie Kedouri and Sylvia Haim, eds., *Towards a Modern Iran* (London, 1980), pp. 217–240.

17. For the composition of the consortium, see Ronald Ferrier, "The Development of the Iranian Oil Industry," in H. Amirsadeghi, ed., *Twentieth Century Iran* (London, 1977), pp. 108–109.

18. *New York Times,* August 18, 1960, p. 9.

19. Andrew Westwood, "Elections and Politics in Iran," *Middle East Journal,* 15, 2 (Spring 1961), pp. 153–164.

20. Alexander and Nanes (1980), p. 313.

21. Ibid., p. 327.

22. Mohammad Reza Pahlavi (1980), pp. 22–23.

23. Alexander and Nanes (1980), p. 349.

24. A.K.S. Lambton, *The Persian Land Reform, 1962–1968* (Oxford, 1969); Eric Hooglund, *Land and Revolution in Iran, 1960–1980* (Austin, Texas, 1982); Afsaneh Najmabadi, *Land Reform and Social Change in Rural Iran* (Salt Lake City, Utah, 1988).

25. Susan Siavoshi, *Liberal Nationalism in Iran* (Boulder, Colo., 1990).

26. President John F. Kennedy, *Public Papers of the President* (Washington, D.C., February 12, 1963), p. 160.

27. Hooglund (1982), pp. 72–73.

28. Ibid., pp. 80–81.

29. Shahrough Akhavi, *Religion and Politics in Contemporary Iran: Clergy-State Relations in the Pahlavi Period* (Albany, N.Y., 1980), p. 79.

30. Willem M. Floor, "The Revolutionary Character of the Iranian Ulama: Wishful Thinking or Reality," *International Journal of Middle East Studies*, 12, 4 (December 1980), p. 504.

31. On the IMF's austerity program, see Cheryl Payer, *The Debt Trap: The International Monetary Fund and the Third World* (New York, 1974), chaps. 1 and 2.

32. Quoted by Hamid Enayat, *Modern Islamic Political Thought* (Austin, Texas, 1982), p. 50.

33. Seyyed Hamid Rauhani, *Barresi Va Tahlili Az Nehzat-e Imam Khomeini* (Review and Analysis of Imam Khomeini's Movement) (Teheran, 1979), p. 151.

34. Ibid., p. 156.

35. Ibid., p. 230.

36. Ruhollah Khomeini, *Islam and Revolution: Writings and Declarations of Imam Khomeini*. Trans. and annotated by Hamid Algar (Berkeley, Calif., 1981), pp. 178–179.

37. *New York Times*, June 6, 1963, p. 8.

38. *Ettela'at* (Teheran), Khordad 16, 1341/June 6, 1963, pp. 1 and 3.

39. Rauhani (1979), p. 570.

40. According to Rauhani, while Khomeini was in jail, Hassan Pakravan, SAVAK's chief, told him that politics is "all lies and deception and, therefore, the ulama should not participate in such endeavors." Khomeini agreed and added that "from the start we [the ulama] were not engaged in this kind of politics." SAVAK read this as the Ayatollah's agreement that he would no longer be involved in politics. That SAVAK had reached this conclusion, Rauhani wrote, was also attributable to the fact that Ayatollah Khomeini was actually committing *taqiye*—a Shi'i concept that allows a prudent concealment of one's opinion in a hostile environment (Rauhani, 1979), pp. 656–659.

41. Algar (1981), p. 650.

42. Ibid., pp. 181–182.

43. *Asnad-e Lane-ye Jasusi* (The Documents of the Spy Nest) (Teheran, 1980), 21, 2 (April 15, 1964), p. 101.

44. Ibid., p. 100.

45. As quoted by Marvin Zonis, "Iran: A Theory of Revolution from the Accounts of the Revolution" (unpublished paper, 1984).

46. *Asnad-e Lane-ye Jasusi*, 22, 3 (June 5, 1963), p. 50; Memorandum of Conversation Between Hossein Mahdavi and William G. Miller, U.S. Embassy, Teheran.

Part Three

Preconditions of the Islamic Revolution

4

Economic Development and Political Decay

So long as men worship the Caesars and Napoleons, Caesars and Napoleons will duly risk and make them miserable.

Aldous Huxley, Ends and Means, *1937*

In the 1960s and 1970s, the Shah's regime embarked on a massive development project that led to uneven development of the economic and political spheres, modernizing the former without changing the nature of the latter. Thus, a gap was created between Iran's rapidly growing productive forces and the regime's institution-building initiatives. The Shah hoped to fill this gap by a combination of limited elite circulation, forced institution building, the infusion of more petrodollars into the economy, and unfettered economic growth. The more doses of these policies he injected into the body politic, the more explosive the political atmosphere became, paving the way for the Islamic Revolution.

Economic Development and the Class Structure of Prerevolutionary Iran

The Shah's first major program of modernization was the first Seven-Year Development Plan (1949–1955),[1] which focused mostly on improving agriculture, transportation, and communications. Most of the objectives, however, were unfulfilled because Iran was plunged into economic difficulties during the struggle to nationalize the oil industry in the early 1950s. The second Seven-Year Development Plan (1955–1962) concentrated on modernizing some old factories, constructing new factories and dams, and improving the transportation and communication systems. In the third, fourth, and fifth development plans, covering the 1960s and 1970s, the government financed an import-substitution industrialization program that relied heavily on Western technology and managerial skills. This strategy led to economic expansion, unequal distribution of wealth, height-

TABLE 4.1 Sectorial Contribution to Gross Domestic Product (as Percentage of GDP and at Current Prices) for Selected Years, 1963–1978

	1963–1964	1969–1970	1972–1973	1975–1976	1976–1977	1977–1978
Agriculture	27.9	22.5	16.9	9.8	9.4	9.3
Oil	18.6	17.4	22.2	45.0	36.8	31.8
Industry/mining	15.8	22.5	20.8	15.4	19.3	22.5
Services	37.7	37.6	40.1	29.8	34.5	36.4

Source: *Bank-e Markazi-ye Iran: Annual Reports,* Tehran, 1973, 1975–1976, and 1977–1978 issues.

ened social mobility, profound changes in the class structure, and a decline in the agriculture sector. In other words, Iranian society and economy underwent major transformations.

The Triangle of Fortune

The coalition that overthrew Mossadeq in 1953, consisting of the Shah's court, the landlords, some top clergy, rich merchants, the armed forces, and the United States, began to crumble as the Shah launched land reform in 1963. The dissolution of that coalition marked the formation of a "triple alliance" whose nucleus consisted of the Iranian state, the indigenous industrial bourgeoisie, and foreign capitalists, especially from the United States.[2] The decision to form the triple alliance was essential for the continuation of Pahlavi rule and for Iran's industrialization. What united the three partners in the triple alliance was their unremitting insistence on rapid economic growth and an "open-door policy" toward the West. These dual goals were pursued with little consideration of their pernicious consequences. Evaluated by economic standards, the record of the Shah's regime was impressive: The gross domestic product (GDP), at constant 1974 prices, rose from $10.4 billion in 1960 to $51 billion in 1977, an increase of over 389 percent in less than two decades.[3]

This expansion of the economy changed the orientation from agriculture/services to industry/services and increased the size of the labor force. Before the land reform in 1963, Iran was a predominantly agrarian society. The agricultural sector accounted for about 24.5 percent of GDP and over 56 percent of the total labor force. By 1976, the sectorial contribution of agriculture to GDP had dwindled to a negligible 9.4 percent, attracting only 34 percent of the labor force (Tables 4.1 and 4.2). A conspicuous shift from landownership for agricultural production to investment in commercial and industrial projects also occurred. Symbolic of this transition was that Mohammad Reza Shah had become the country's largest industrialist, in contrast with Reza Shah, who was its largest landowner. The Shah, his Pahlavi Foundation, and the Pahlavi family controlled a giant financial empire whose influence reached far beyond Iran.[4]

As the significance of agriculture diminished, that of industry increased. Not only was a significant portion of the state's revenues allocated to the development

TABLE 4.2   Iran's Employed Population Aged Ten Years and Older by Major Occupational
Backgrounds and as Percentage of Total Labor Force, 1956, 1966, 1976

	1956	1966	1976
Total labor force	5,907,666	7,115,787	8,698,947
	(100)	(100)	(100)
Agriculture	3,325,721	3,380,023	2,991,869
	(56.3)	(47.5)	(34.0)
Industries	1,187,843	1,886,988	3,112,773
	(20.1)	(26.5)	(35.4)
Services	1,394,102	1,848,766	2,694,778
	(23.6)	(26.0)	(30.6)

Source: National Census of Population and Housing, total country (Teheran, 1956); *National Census of Population and Housing,* total country, no. 186 (Teheran, 1981).

of industries but also the state enthusiastically promoted the participation of the private sector by providing lavish financial incentives such as low-interest loans and easy credit. In 1980, of 5,288 industrial units, 409 (about 7 percent) were state controlled and more than 89 percent were owned by the private sector.[5]

As the role of the state and indigenous industrialists increased, so did that of foreign capital. In 1971, $304 million of capital and loans entered Iran through the Center for the Attraction and Protection of Foreign Investments. This was increased to $804 million in 1977.[6] (Most foreign investments were in the rubber, pharmaceutical, chemical, petrochemical, metallurgical, and electronic sectors.) The foreign role in the banking industry also increased. Even more significant was the signing of numerous economic treaties. In 1974, a ten-year, $5 billion developmental agreement, including provisions for the sale to Iran of five 1,000-megawatt nuclear reactors, was signed between France and Iran. In 1975, a major $15 billion economic agreement was signed between the United States and Iran.[7]

Concomitant with increased foreign involvement was the deepening of Iran's dependence on the West. The imports of capital and intermediate goods rose from $89 million in 1963 to $886 million in 1977.[8] The dependent industrialists of Iran had become the junior partners of elites in the metropolis countries.[9] They identified with and emulated the West to such an extent that they became alienated from their own culture. This created a ubiquitous cultural gap between this small portion of the population and the bulk of Iranians.

There is a paucity of reliable data on the size of the "comprador industrial bourgeoisie" in Iran, with estimates ranging from one thousand to a few thousand persons. In any case, it is clear that a minuscule percentage of the population controlled a vast industrial fortune. In this triangle of fortune, the court stood at its peak and the native and Western industrialists occupied its corners. There was no alternative route to prosperity but through this triangle. Without access to it, or short of a venal agreement with one of its members, no one could engage in a large-scale economic project in Iran. The Islamic Revolution, in some ways, was directed against the abuses of this group.

The Modern Middle Class

The middle class in general and the modern middle class in particular was considered by the Shah's regime as the greatest menace to stability. The modern middle class refers to that segment of the population that came into existence as a result of modernization. The intelligentsia is at its core. The term refers to those "social groups whose special task it is to provide an interpretation of the world" for the society they live in.[10] In this Mannheimian definition are included both the intellectuals (students, professors, teachers, writers, and poets) and the professional-bureaucratic intelligentsia (doctors, lawyers, technocrats, and bureaucrats). Between 1966 and 1976, the number of teachers and authors slightly more than doubled whereas that of college professors and secondary school students more than tripled. The number of college students also increased substantially.

As Huntington wrote, "the students are the most coherent and effective revolutionaries within the intelligentsia."[11] Iranian students have played an important role in every major social movement of the post–World War II era. The higher institutions were hotbeds of opposition to the regime.[12]

In 1966, there were 52,294 students in higher educational institutions. One decade later, there were 437,089 students, an eightfold increase.[13] Despite impressive achievements in education, higher educational institutions could not produce sufficient numbers of professional and skilled personnel. Iran had to turn to the Western nations for help. In 1978, 67,000 Iranian students pursued their studies in the Western nations. Of those, 54,340 were in the United States, 4,445 in the Federal Republic of Germany, and 4,336 in England.[14]

Many of the Iranian students studying in foreign countries were highly political. In the 1960s, some of them formed the Confederation of Iranian Students (National Union) and the Moslem Students Association. These student organizations were the main anti-Shah propaganda machine outside Iran and were a large pool from which various communist, Maoist, Islamic, and nationalist groups recruited members.

The confederation organized periodic anti-Shah demonstrations and was involved in violent takeovers of Iranian embassies in Europe and the United States. The success of Iran's modernization depended on the active participation of professionals, administrators, and bureaucrats. Résumés of the members of the 24th Majles, for example, reveal that 110 of the deputies held either a bachelor's or master's degree, 21 had Ph.D.s, and 29 were doctors of medicine.[15] An overwhelming majority of those who opposed the Shah also came from these groups.

Because of the dualistic character of these groups, the Iranian regime pursued a policy combining repression and concession. It was prepared to lavishly reward those who refrained from agitational activities and to violently suppress individuals who dared challenge the Shah. Professional associations, like the labor unions, were under SAVAK's surveillance and could not engage in any anti-Shah activity. Newspapers critical of the regime had difficulty obtaining a license to publish. And student associations could be formed only if they were explicitly apolitical.

The Traditional Middle Class

Modernization adversely affected the fortunes of the bazaar merchants and shop-keepers and the ulama. The bazaar, a cluster of thousands of small shops located in a well-demarcated section of urban areas throughout the country, was for centuries the jugular of Iran's economic system. Its internal structure in the 1970s, as at the turn of the century, consisted of three groups. The merchants and the money lenders were the smallest and most prosperous and powerful group. The shopkeepers were highly organized, as each trade was represented by its own *senf* (singular for *asnaf*, or guild). Together, these two groups numbered 376,687. The third group was made up of salesmen, shop assistants, street vendors, canvassers, and so on. There were 158,149 of them in 1976. Altogether, the size of the retail and wholesale sectors, which included all the bazaars, grew from 481,026 persons in 1966 to 561,583 in 1976. Of these, more than 67 percent were self-employed in 1976, reflecting their relative financial independence from the state.[16]

The Shah's regime gave lip service to a hands-off policy toward this bastion of conservatism. But in reality, its developmental policies ran counter to the interests of the bazaar. The Shah candidly admitted this: "The bazaaries are a fanatic lot, highly resistant to change because their locations afford a lucrative monopoly. I could not stop building supermarkets. I wanted a modern country. Moving against the bazaars was typical of the political and social risks I had to take in my drive for modernization."[17] In this "drive for modernization," the economic and social status of the bazaar, in comparison with that of the industrialists, was adversely affected.[18] The proliferation of modern financial institutions outside of the bazaar eroded the bazaar's independent power. These enterprises were operated by a new breed of businessmen who were worlds apart from the bazaaries in their ideological outlook and life-styles.

The bazaar, however, remained financially powerful with access to a remarkable network of quick mobilization. This network was to be found in the *asnaf* organization. In the 1960s, there were 135 *senfs* represented in the High Council of the Asnaf, which was infiltrated by the regime. In 1970, the Majles granted the government the prerogative to appoint the director of the *asnaf*.[19] This intrusion was considered to be an unjustifiable move by the government to bring the bazaar under its thumb.

The ulama's fate was not much happier than that of the bazaaries. According to the 1976 census, the number of ulama was only 23,476, about twice as many as a decade earlier, but the actual number was probably higher. Despite disagreements among the ulama, the Shah's frontal attacks on the institution of Shi'ism eventually united them. The Shah did not try to destroy the institution of Shi'ism. Rather, he attempted, but failed, to bring this institution under his control—what I call the Pahlavization of Shi'ism.

After 1963, the regime moved to bring religious schools under its tight control by reducing their number, thus depriving the ulama of their last stronghold. From 1960 to 1975, for example, Teheran lost nine of a total of thirty-two *madreses.*[20] The authorities also contemplated creating an Islamic university in the 1960s in the city of Mashhad. Many ulama considered this an invidious scheme to undermine their influence. From exile, Ayatollah Khomeini vociferously opposed the plan.[21]

The state also attempted to deprive the ulama of their role as the propagators of Shi'ism. The Shah ordered the creation of the Religious Corps in August 1971. The corpsmen were to be chosen from the graduates in Islamic Studies from different universities and were to be sent to various parts of the country. In addition, the Shah ordered the creation of Religious Propagandists. The Religious Corps and the Religious Propagandists had a three-pronged objective: to spread a conservative, apolitical version of Shi'ism, one that emphasized the compatibility of Shi'ism and monarchical government; to gradually strengthen the intermingling of Shi'ism with the state bureaucracy; and to demonstrate the commitment of the state to Shi'ism.

But more important than these issues was the ulama's opposition to the expansion of a Western-oriented culture and the Shah's glorification of pre-Islamic Persia. The presence of thousands of Westerners, plus the proliferation of hundreds of cinemas showing "decadent" Western films, as well as discos and bars, symbolized the rise of a perfidious culture, considered by the ulama pernicious to Shi'ism. It was no accident that attacking cinemas was a favorite exercise of the Islamic revolutionaries during the riots of the 1977–1979 period. The grandiloquent celebration of the 2,500th anniversary of the Persian Empire staged by the regime and the panache of royal ceremonies designed to glorify pre-Islamic Persia were also strongly condemned by some of the ulama, including Khomeini. Many of the ulama were jailed or internally exiled for their opposition to the celebration.

The Working Class

The industrial working class was the largest urban class in the 1970s; it included those in manufacturing, mining and electricity, gas, water, and health services. Its number increased from 1,377,210 persons, or 19.3 percent of the labor force in 1966, to 1,924,053 persons, or 22.0 percent of the labor force in 1976. Manufacturing was by far the largest segment of the industrial working class, constituting 20.2 percent of the total labor force.[22]

Despite its large size, the working class as a whole posed no serious threat to the Shah's regime. It often resorted to political apathy. A number of factors accounted for this rather low level of revolutionary activism. First, because the working class was a heterogeneous class, no collective consciousness developed. There was a division between skilled and unskilled workers, between literate and illiterate, and finally between those working in the traditional industries with low wages and those in the modern industries with high wages. Second, a large number of the workers were concentrated in a few big cities such as Teheran and Esfahan, rendering the control of that class by the vigilant SAVAK more manageable.

Third, the government followed a policy that in many respects benefited the workers, even to the dismay of the capitalists. Attempts to appease the workers included insurance for workers, numerous housing projects, a private and public ownership extension scheme implemented in 1975 that required the sale of 49 percent of the shares of all private manufacturing units to the workers, and the minimum wage standard set by the Shah's regime in the 1970s. Fourth, although free labor unions were suppressed, the regime allowed the formation of many small syndicates and unions, all under the surveillance of SAVAK.[23] Consequently, by the eve of the Islamic Revolution, a small but influential labor aristocracy had been created, one that was under the regime's control.

Despite these policies, there were many workers' strikes, especially during the 1970s. The strikers, however, were more concerned with bread-and-butter issues than with politics. So the regime's policy paid off, as the workers were among the last groups to join the opposition to the Shah in 1978. The situation was somewhat different for the unskilled workers.

The lumpenproletariat refers to the lowest stratum of wage earners in the urban areas, which includes construction workers, domestic servants, and so on. Unskilled and often uneducated, the main bulk of this group was once the agricultural proletariat. Farhad Kazemi estimates that from 1966 to 1976 more than 2.1 million people migrated to the major urban centers.[24] The lumpenproletariat made up 18.2 percent of the total labor force (1,598,108 persons). It was the fastest-growing portion of the labor force.

Generally this group was politically passive but had strong religious commitments. Their passivity could be attributed to a host of factors. First, there was usually a marked improvement in their living conditions and a "feeling of relative reward."[25] Kazemi's data testify to this: Eighty percent of the migrant poor considered themselves better off in the city than in their villages.[26] Second, they could not join any unions or organizations. Their only channel of communication with the rest of society was through attendance at the local mosque, or *takiye*, which often unified them with the people from their own towns or villages. Here they reinforced their religious values and also became part of a religious community. This partially explains why they become the foot soldiers of the Islamic Revolution of 1979.

The regime considered this group to be politically innocuous. However, in the late 1970s there was a direct confrontation between those living in shantytowns and the police. The regime acted impetuously and from that moment on, the lumpenproletariat became ever more active in riots and demonstrations against the regime.

The Dynamics of Social Mobilization

One inevitable consequence of economic growth is social mobilization, defined by Karl Deutsch as "the process in which major clusters of old social, economic and psychological commitments are eroded or broken and people become available for new patterns of socialization and behavior."[27] The faster the rate of social mobilization, the greater the chances of political tension.

In the 1960s and 1970s, Iran experienced rapid social mobilization as established norms and standards were constantly challenged by the exposure of a large portion of the population to new ideas and modes of living. More than two decades of state-sponsored modernization from 1953 to 1976 radically altered the structure of the Iranian population. In the early 1950s, the population was small, predominantly agrarian, and highly illiterate. By 1979, it had grown much larger, more urbanized, and more literate.

With an annual growth rate of about 2.3 percent in the 1970s, Iran had a population slightly larger than 33.7 million in 1976.[28] The median age was 16.9, as over 18.6 million (55.3 percent of the population) were under twenty years of age in 1976.[29]

This population increase was concomitant with a rapid pace of urbanization and the growth of large cities. In the 1950s, 68.6 percent and 31.4 percent of the population lived in the rural and urban areas, respectively (Table 4.3). By 1976, slightly more than 47 percent of the population lived in urban areas, an increase of 50 percent in two decades. The number of large cities also increased: In 1966, Teheran was the only city with a population over 500,000. By 1976, four cities had populations over 500,000. Major cities were ill-equipped to deal with this population explosion, and polarization was the most visible consequence. Teheran is a case in point: The rich and the middle class lived in the northern section and the lower classes in the south. Not only was the southern section of the city packed with mendicants, but its population had a perception of life that differed from that of northern Teheran.

Benjamin Disraeli's description of the gap between the upper and lower classes in England in his 1845 novel *Sybil* was still valid for the Iranian society of the late 1970s: "two nations between whom there is no intercourse and no sympathy, who are ignorant of each other's habits, thoughts and feelings, as if they were dwellers in different zones, or inhabitants of different planets."[30]

Rapid urbanization also coincided with a substantial increase in literacy. In 1956, only 14.9 percent of the total population over ten years of age was literate (Table 4.3). By 1976, this increased to more than 47 percent. The number of students rose significantly, from 1,054,181 in 1971 to 7,572,822 in 1976. These improvements were possible because government expenditure per capita for education increased from $11 in 1970 to $103 in 1978.[31]

Not only had the population become more literate, but it had also been exposed to new ideas. In the 1960s, ownership of both television and radio sets was so limited that the 1966 census did not even include statistics about them. In the 1970s, more than 65 percent of private households owned radios. In urban areas, the figure was more than 75 percent. In the same decade, more than 24 percent of the country's households and more than 55 percent of urban dwellings had television sets.[32] Although both radio and television stations were under the state's

TABLE 4.3   Iran's Total Population by Urban and Rural Division and by Literacy Rates, 1956–1976 (percentage of total)

	1956	*1966*	*1976*
Total population	18,954,704	25,788,722	30,708,722
Total literates	14.9	28.9	47.1
Urban population	31.4	37.9	47.1
Urban literates	33.3	50.4	65.2
Rural population	68.6	62.1	52.9
Rural literates	6.0	14.6	29.6

Source: *National Census of Population and Housing* (Teheran, 1956); *National Census of Population and Housing*, no. 186 (Teheran, 1981). Calculations by author.

tight control, the broadcasting of Western films reached every corner of the country and exposed the population to new ideas. At the same time, the number of Iranians visiting foreign countries, especially those in the West, increased from 311,492 in 1971 to 1,377,325 in 1977.[33]

Political Participation and Repression

The most significant consequence of social mobilization was the intensified demand by various groups to participate in the political process. How did the Shah's regime respond to this demand?

Aware that political participation was necessary for the success of his modernizing efforts, the Shah, from 1958 to 1975, pursued a strategy that was founded on a combination of controlled elite circulation and outright suppression of all manifestations of dissent. After the coup of 1953, the Shah opted for what Huntington called an "autocratic model of development" in which political participation, especially by the middle class, is suppressed.[34] The Shah considered the middle class, especially those with nationalistic and communistic tendencies, to be the greatest menace to political tranquility. To neutralize them, the regime sought in vain to secure the support of the lower classes by promoting economic growth, a more egalitarian distribution of wealth, higher wages, and the granting of economic concessions to the workers. This strategy was based on the Pollyanna belief that the lower classes and the conservative ulama were an effective deterrent against the threat of the middle class. Ironically, as the Shah's intelligence network allocated much of its resources to combating communism and nationalism, the Islamic forces had some opportunity to expand.

In 1958, a two-party system was created by royal decree. Of the Melliyun and the Mardom parties, both headed by the Shah's close confidants, neither had the integrity of an opposition party. Nor did they differ ideologically one from the other. Their constituencies were limited to court favorites and the upper classes. But the Shah could not even tolerate the side effects of the competition between these loyal parties, as the rivalry among their leadership in the early 1960s resulted in embarrassing charges of election fraud. Determined to destroy the genesis of all independent sources of power and to end intraelite competition for power, the Shah demolished the token two-party system in 1964 and, with the assistance of Hassan Ali Mansur and Amir Abbas Hoveyda, created the Iran Novin Party.[35] These changes led to the rise to positions of power of a younger breed of Western-educated technocrats, mostly U.S.-educated, which generated strong resentment in the old courtiers, many of whom were now pushed into oblivion. As it was subservient to the court, the Iran Novin Party, too, failed to enlarge the Shah's political bases of support.

The tide turned with the oil boom of the early 1970s, which made the state rich enough to begin bribing dissidents and apathetic groups. The campaign was relatively successful, as many Iranians chose to become partners in the exploitation of the oil riches. But a mass mobilization of the middle class was required for the management of the phenomenal oil wealth. Thus, in spring 1975 the Shah, now terminally ill with cancer, again used Iranians as guinea pigs in his experiments with political participation. By royal fiat, the Rastakhiz Party was created overnight. Perhaps the dying monarch was hoping to rely on the Rastakhiz for a smooth transition of power to his heir apparent, Reza Pahlavi.[36]

The official justification for its creation was based on two dubious assumptions. First, it was emphasized that for Iran's industrialization to succeed, the luxury of diversity of opinion could not be tolerated; unity of purpose was imperative for entering the gates of the "Great Civilization." The Rastakhiz Party was to develop just such a national consensus. Second, as a consciousness-raising instrument, the party was to allow the participants to air their grievances against unpopular state policies in a legal fashion.

To give the party the facade of democracy, it was divided into two competitive wings: the progressive liberal and the constructive liberal. The former was under the leadership of Jamshid Amuzegar, the latter under Hooshang Ansari, both ministers in Hoveyda's administration. Occasionally, the progressive wing expressed reservation about the consequences of rapid growth, but differences between the two wings were minor.

To mobilize the masses, the party opened branches all over Iran, organized pro-Shah rallies and political seminars, and established a political science college to indoctrinate its members. It attempted to penetrate the bazaar and mobilize the merchants and the shopkeepers. It claimed a membership exceeding 6 million.

The cultural insensitivity and arrogance of the Rastakhiz's leadership reached cataclysmic proportions when, in 1975, they impetuously recommended that the Shah change the Islamic calendar to the Imperial calendar, which began over two and a half millennia ago with the creation of the Achaemenid Empire by Cyrus the Great. If the French revolutionaries began their revolution with the year 0, the Rastakhiz Party began its journey to the "Great Civilization" with the year 2535. With unlimited oil wealth at its disposal, the regime used the Rastakhiz Party as a channel for financial remuneration of loyal supporters. The Shah's motto was simple—"Those who are not with us are against us." He arrogantly declared:

> The place of those who oppose the Constitution, the monarchical system and the People-Shah Revolution is either in jail or outside of Iran. Those who do not wish to enter into this political organization (the Rastakhiz) have two alternatives: They either belong to an illegal political party, like the Tudeh, in which case they should be jailed. Or, with gratitude and without asking them to pay for a foreign exit visa, they may have their passport and go anywhere they would like.[37]

This was autocracy Iranian fashion, par excellence. It was an attempt to demolish the genesis of any opposition to the monarchy and create an image of a people united under the leadership of the Shah. It was a travesty of democracy, as the Rastakhiz was obsequious to the king.

The Rastakhiz Party inadvertently intensified the spirit of contumacy against the incumbent regime. It was an admission of failure of the entire political strategy of the regime in the previous decades. Convinced that the old policy of controlled elite participation would not enlarge the narrow basis of the monarchy's popular support, and in desperate need of trained cadres to assist in managing the oil wealth, the regime turned to forced institution building.

But the opposition to the Shah refused to join the party. From his exile, Ayatollah Khomeini expressed the opposition's stance on the party: "Because this party is against Islam ... participation in it is religiously forbidden ... and is against the Constitution."[38] While in exile in 1979, the Shah finally admitted his egregious error in creating this party.

For the alert reader, the question is: Why did Iran remain a stable country despite the Shah's failure to create durable institutions and despite his execrable policy of excluding all but his subservients from the decisionmaking process? Iran's stability was the product of three factors: international support for the Shah, the economic expansion of the last two decades of the Shah's rule, and repression.

The Western countries, especially the United States, provided political, economic, and intelligence support to the Shah. During the Cold War, Iran, with its oil riches and its more than 1,500 miles of common borders with the Soviet Union, was among Washington's most valuable strategic allies. Further, the Shah's congenial relationship with the Soviet Union and with East European nations buttressed the Shah's facade of invincibility. From 1953 to 1979, Moscow seemed content with the Shah's government, and its agents refrained from directing any major agitation against the Shah.

That a large portion of the population benefited from Iran's economic growth also contributed to stability, because that portion often resorted to political passivism. The regime's monopoly over distribution of the oil wealth permitted it to reward loyal supporters and punish the opposition. Therefore, many people refrained from provocative political activity.

But perhaps the single most significant reason for stability was the Shah's effective use of repression against his perceived opponents. He relied on the might of the armed forces, SAVAK, and his court, providing huge financial rewards to these pillars of power. The pervasive perception of SAVAK's omnipotence and wanton ferocity gave the Shah's regime an aura of invincibility. Eugene Walter persuasively argued that during much of the rule of the Zulu's chief Shaka (1818–1828), who ran one of the bloodiest and most repressive regimes in Africa, seldom were gas chambers, guillotines, or guns used. What forced the population into quietism was the fear that Shaka had generated early in his reign.[39] In Iran, SAVAK did rely on atrocious methods of torture such as "whipping and beating, electric shock, and extraction of nails and teeth, boiling water pumped into the rectum, heavy weights hung on the testicles, etc."[40] Ignominious as such methods are, most if not all developing nations rely on them to protect the status quo. Moreover, only a small segment of the Iranian population became victims of torture. The stability of the Shah's regime, like that of Shaka's rule, was based less on torturing dissidents and more on the general perception of the Shah's invincibility and the fear he had generated and perpetuated.

Moreover, in many countries, including some European nations and the Soviet Union, there seems to have been a direct correlation between the rapidity of the rate of industrialization and the level of repression. In Iran, as in many other countries, rapid industrialization and repression went hand in hand. It is hard to assess how much of this repression was attributable to the needs of a changing society, how much of it was a function of a political culture accustomed to dictatorship, and how much of it originated in the Shah's deliberate policy.

The Flaws in the Shah's Modernization Strategy

The Shah's modernization strategy, which created a multitude of tensions, suffered from three shortcomings. First, unable to completely break the back of Iran's traditional society, it created pervasive dualisms in the economy, in cultural arenas, and in modes of thinking. It increased the power of the modern sectors of the economy without destroying the power of the bazaar, and it somewhat secularized the society but fell short of substantially diminishing the ulama's power. Second, it led to an uneven development of the economic and political systems by modernizing the former without changing the nature of the latter. Third, the Shah's modernization drive had a narrow base of support and lacked a solid, supporting ideology. Little was built over the ruins of the much that was destroyed, creating in the process, among other things, an ideological vacuum and a sense of bewilderment for the masses.

Nations have taken different routes to modernize their societies. In England, where some democratic institutions and traditions were entrenched before the advent of industrialization, the process proceeded somewhat peacefully and gradually as the old and new classes shared political power. In France, it proceeded peacefully through the principle of power sharing but only after the creation of democratic institutions subsequent to the bloody French Revolution. In both countries, modernization enjoyed the support of a growing entrepreneurial class and was buttressed by a legitimizing, democratic ideology that had an anesthetic impact, especially for those adversely affected by such a transformation. Where democratic institutions and traditions have been absent or not fully developed, as in Russia and China, modernization was launched with relative success through a socialist revolution. In both countries, the communist party incorporated a relatively large portion of the population into the political process. The party relied on the repressive capability of the state, imposed a national discipline on the population, and formulated, through coercion and persuasion, a national consensus of sorts—a communist ideology to legitimize and facilitate modernization.

In Iran, like China and Russia but unlike France and England, the state—not the bourgeoisie class—has been the main modernizing agent. In contrast to prerevolutionary China and Russia, the Pahlavi state was not creative enough to impose a national discipline on the population, to create a party with mass support, to develop an ideology legitimizing its modernizing initiatives, and to create a powerful state to withstand the transformations it championed. The few democratic institutions, like the Majles and the labor unions, which were created before the birth of the Pahlavi dynasty, were ignored or brought under the control of the Shah's regime.

The Shah's reforms alienated the bazaaries, the ulama, and the landed upper class—the three traditional bastions of support for the monarchy. The Shah pursued an egregious strategy of containing the modern middle class, whose advocacy of nationalism and socialism was considered the greatest threat to stability, by seeking the support of the lower classes and the conservative Shi'i ulama. But the Shah's system was unable to sanction any drastic distribution of wealth or restructuring of the power structure that could win the hearts and minds of the lower classes. Nor did the Shah receive the complete support of the conservative ulama because his reforms had generated acrimony between his regime and the clerical establishment. Most important, by suppressing the modern middle class, he deprived himself of a major source of support, one that was capable of developing a supporting ideology for his modernization and acting as a deterrent to the radicalism from the left and fanaticism from the right. Having devoted most of its intelligence resources to suppressing the modern middle class, the Shah's regime became vulnerable to agitation by the fundamentalist ulama.

As more and more groups were alienated from the regime, the state was plunged deeper into isolation. To survive it had to rely on repression and foreign support, mainly from the United States. Consequently, the state stood on one side and all other groups, except the ruling elite, on the other.

Mohammad Reza Shah's notorious SAVAK brought under its control professional and student associations and trade unions; imposed censorship of the press; and suppressed all political parties that were critical of the Shah's regime, even those loyal to the constitution. Despite these efforts, SAVAK was unable to eradicate the roots of discontent against a repressive regime. All that was required was a spark to ignite the revolutionary volcano. The loosening of repression in 1977 and President Carter's human rights policy combined to become that spark.

Notes

1. H. Razavi and F. Vakil, *The Political Environment of Economic Planning in Iran, 1971–1983* (Boulder, Colo., 1984), pp. 19–36.

2. On Triple Alliance, see Peter Evans, *Dependent Development* (Princeton, N.J., 1979), pp. 14–54.

3. Iran, Imperial Government, Plan and Budget Organization, *Economic Trends of Iran* (hereafter *Trends*) (Teheran, 1978), pp. 15–16.

4. On the Pahlavi Foundation, see Robert Graham, *The Illusion of Power* (New York, 1979), pp. 251–254. Also informative is Mark Hulbert, *Interlock* (New York, 1982), pp. 47–70.

5. Iran, Islamic Republic, Plan and Budget Organization, *Amar-e Kargahha-ye Bozorg-e San'ati* (Statistics on the Large Industrial Units) (Teheran, 1981), p. 14.

6. The first set of data for 1971 is from *Bank-e Markazi* (1973), p. 183; the second set is from *Bank-e Markazi* (1978), p. 114.

7. *New York Times*, June 27, 1974, and March 4, 1975.

8. *Trends* (1979), p. 515.

9. For a general discussion, see Richard Barnet and Ronald Buller, *Global Reach* (New York, 1974).

10. James Bill, *The Politics of Iran* (Columbus, Ohio, 1977), pp. 53–72.

11. Samuel Huntington, *Political Order in Changing Societies* (New Haven, Conn., 1968), p. 290.

12. See James Bill, "The Politics of Student Alienation: The Case of Iran," *Iranian Studies*, 2, 1 (Winter 1969), pp. 8–26.

13. *National Census of Population* (Teheran, 1976).

14. UNESCO, *Statistical Yearbook* (New York, 1981), p. 480.

15. Hassan Mohammadi, "The Iranian Parliamentary Elections of 1975," *Indian Political Science Review*, 10 (July 1976), p. 215.

16. All the statistics in this section are from *Census* (1966), pp. 74–94, and *Census* (1981), pp. 94–110. For the internal organization of the bazaar, see Howard Rotblat, "Social Organization and Development in the Iranian Provincial Bazaar," *Economic Development and Cultural Change*, 23, 2 (January 1988), pp. 292–305.

17. Mohammad Reza Pahlavi, *Answer to History* (New York, 1981), p. 156.

18. *Salnameye Arzi* (Teheran, 1979), p. 205.

19. Personal interview, Naser Ouliya'i, a leader of the *asnaf* (Los Angeles, September 1984).

20. Shahrough Akhavi, *Religion and Politics in Contemporary Iran* (Albany, N.Y., 1980), p.

139.

21. *Dar Bare-ye Qiam-e Hemaseh Afarin-e Qom Va Tabiz* (On the Heroic Uprisings of Qom and Tabriz), vol. 3 (Teheran, 1979), p. 9.

22. *Census,* total country (1981), p. 82, and *Census* (1966), p. G.

23. Habib Ladjevardi, *Labor Unions and Autocracy in Iran* (Syracuse, N.Y., 1985).

24. Farhad Kazemi, *Poverty and Revolution in Iran* (New York, 1980), p. 262.

25. The idea of relative reward is borrowed from Soares, as quoted by Huntington (1968), p. 279.

26. Kazemi (1980), p. 84.

27. Karl Deutsch, "Social Mobilization and Political Development," *American Political Science Review,* 55, 3 (September 1961), p. 493.

28. United Nations, *United Nations Demographic Yearbook* (New York, 1980), p. 139.

29. My calculation based on *Census* (1976), p. xvii.

30. Quoted by Robert Goldstein, *Political Repression in 19th Century Europe* (London, 1983), p. 97.

31. International Monetary Fund, *Government Finance Statistical Yearbook,* vol. 6 (1982), p. 429.

32. *Census* (1981), p. LIV.

33. *Salnameye Amari Keshvar* (Teheran, 1979), p. 965.

34. S. Huntington and J. Nelson, *No Easy Choice* (Cambridge, Mass., 1976), p. 177.

35. Marvin Weinbaum, "Iran Finds a Party System: The Institutionalization of Iran Novin," *Middle East Journal,* 27, 4 (Autumn 1973), pp. 228–239.

36. On the Rastakhiz Party, see Mehdi Mozaffari, *Nezamha-ye Tak Hezby Va Rastakhiz-e Mellat-e Iran* (The One-Party Systems and the Resurrection of the Iranian Nation) (Teheran, 1976).

37. *Kayhan* (Teheran, Esfand 1352 [1975]), p. 2.

38. *Kalam-e Imam: Goruhha-ye Siyasi* (Imam's Sayings: Political Groups) (Teheran, 1983), p. 13.

39. Eugene Victor Walter, *Terror and Resistance: A Study of Political Violence* (New York, 1969), pp. 133–177.

40. Amnesty International, *Annual Report, 1974–1975,* p. 8. Not enough is known about the SAVAK: The Shah admitted to 3,500 full-time members, the opposition estimated 100,000. For the creation of SAVAK, see James D. Rudolph, "Public Order and International Security," in R. F. Nyrop, *Iran: A Country Study* (Washington, D.C., 1978), pp. 372–374.

5

Opposition to the Pahlavi Regime: Its Ideological and Organizational Bases

> I, at this part of the world and at this moment of history, am expecting, in a future that might be tomorrow or any other time, a sudden world Revolution in favor of Truth and Justice and of oppressed masses; a Revolution in which I must play a part; a Revolution which does not come about with prayers ... but with a banner and a sword, with a holy war involving all responsible believers. I believe that this movement shall naturally triumph.
>
> *Ali Shari'ati,* "Entezar: Mazhab-e E'teraz," *1982*[1]

The Shah's repressive policy could not obliterate the roots of discontent against his regime. In fact, it radicalized the opposition to the throne and gave it a special mystique—a sense of righteousness and legitimacy—and created an environment where the intensity, not the essence, of condemnation of the Shah's policies was the barometer for measuring the revolutionary credentials of the opposition.

The response to repression in the 1960s and 1970s varied from passivity to violent confrontation with the authorities. A large silent majority was mesmerized by the Shah's power and the unconditional support he was receiving from the United States. Preferring the existing order with all its evils to the chaos and unpredictable consequences of rapid change, and benefiting from the country's economic development, this majority sank into quiet apathy.

However, a small minority, the activists, carried the torch of struggle against the regime. They were organized into a variety of organizations, ranging from nationalist to Marxist to Islamic. Their activities politicized a whole generation of Iranians both at home and abroad and shocked the foundation of the Pahlavi rule.

Marxist Organizations:
The Tudeh and the Fada'iyun-e Khalq

Although the Persian Social Democratic Party, formed in 1904, espoused socialist ideas, it was only with the victory of the Bolsheviks in Russia in 1917 that Marxist ideas began to penetrate Iran. Marxism gradually attracted a growing portion of Iran's intellectuals.

The Tudeh Party of Iran was chiefly responsible for popularizing Marxism in Iran.[2] Soon after its creation in the 1930s, most of its founding members were either jailed or killed by the government and the party itself was declared illegal by Reza Shah. With Reza Shah's forced abdication in 1941, the party resurfaced and with support from Moscow expanded its network and constituency. Some of its members even became ministers in Qavam's cabinet.

The Tudeh's fortune began to reverse when Mossadeq nationalized the oil industry. The Tudeh leadership's treacherous policy toward Mossadeq (see Chapter 3) and its unconditional support of the Soviet Union irrevocably tarnished its image. Many Iranians began to perceive the Tudeh as no more than Moscow's Fifth Column. After the coup d'état, many Tudeh members were either killed or jailed by the Shah's regime and the party's secret network within the armed forces was discovered and dismantled. Some top leaders, however, escaped and moved the party's headquarters to Eastern Europe. In exile, the party operated an anti-Shah radio station, published subversive literature, and infiltrated the Iranian student movement. The Tudeh's popularity in the 1960s and 1970s diminished further as it occasionally flirted with the Shah's regime. Equally damaging were the revelations in 1962 and 1972 that two high-ranking cadres, Hossein Yazdi and Abbas Shahriyari, "the man with a thousand faces," were SAVAK infiltrators. By 1975, lamented Nurredin Keyanuri, the Tudeh's first secretary (1979–1983), "we did not have even one connection or unit inside Iran."[3]

Despite these problems, the Tudeh remained a powerful force within Iran's fragmented leftist movement. It was a pioneer of Marxism and was the left's main agenda setter.

Inside Iran, the leftist movement in the 1960s and 1970s was dominated by those who were critical of the Tudeh Party. After the coup of 1953 and again after the crushing of the June Uprising of 1963, activists began questioning the wisdom of peaceful coexistence with the Shah. The spread of the guerrilla movement in Latin America inspired them to experiment with guerrilla warfare.

In the mid-1960s, two independent groups of Marxists began building and expanding underground organizations. The Jazani group was created in 1963 by Bijan Jazani, a former member of a Tudeh Party youth organization, and a few others.[4] While they were still in the preparatory stage of building a secret network, SAVAK infiltrated the group and arrested most of its members, including

Jazani. The few who escaped arrest later formed the Jangal group. The second group, the Ahmadzadeh, was created in 1967 by Mas'ud Ahmadzadeh, a former member of the National Front, and a few university students. This group believed from the start that armed struggle was the road to political salvation. Amir Parviz Poyan, one of its founders, contended that the only way to shatter the existing "myth of the regime's invincibility" and the only way to overthrow the incumbent regime was to violently inflict heavy casualties upon it.[5]

To put their idealism into practice, some members of the Jangal group went to the forests of Mazandaran province to establish a training camp. A member of the group was accidentally arrested by the local police in early 1971. Fearful that the arrested comrade might break down under torture and reveal the group's secret network, the Jangal group attacked the gendarmerie post in Siyahkal, precipitating a violent reaction by the government during which the police killed most members of the group. The Siyahkal episode marked the beginning of the urban guerrilla war against the Pahlavis. With the unification of the remainder of the Jangal and Ahmadzadeh groups a month after this incident, the Fada'iyun-e Khalq organization was born. In the 1970s, it was the most popular Marxist organization.

The assassination of the chief of the military tribunal in charge of trials of political dissidents was the Fada'iyun's first military operation. From 1971 to 1978, many prominent officials of the regime and a few Americans fell victim to the Fada'iyun's terror. The organization's other activities included bombings of government buildings, kidnappings, robbings of banks (which they called liberation of the people's wealth), and distribution of revolutionary literature.

The authorities took the Fada'iyun's challenge seriously. The state-controlled mass media began a blaring campaign of attacking the guerrillas as terrorists and as agents of foreign nations. The Shah's SAVAK intensified its interrogations and torture of suspected sympathizers and members of underground organizations. It infiltrated these organizations, obtained sensitive information, and organized relatively successful raids on their hiding places. The campaign resulted in the killing of 106 Fada'iyun by the police. According to Ervand Abrahamian, of the total of 341 guerrillas killed by the Pahlavi regime in the 1970s, 91 percent belonged to the ranks of the intelligentsia, 41 percent of whom were college students.[6]

Gradually, the Fada'iyun's credulous leadership came to the unavoidable conclusion that their violent activities had not demonstrated the vulnerability of the regime as Poyan had so amateurishly theorized earlier. This recognition caused a split within the organization. By late 1975, one faction stressed education of the masses and secret party building whereas the other faction continued with guerrilla warfare. Although some degree of collaboration continued to exist between the two factions for the remainder of the decade, the Fada'iyun organization as a whole became less effective in challenging the regime.

By 1977, the Fada'iyun was in crisis. Its leadership was divided; most, if not all, of its founding members had been killed or jailed; and its constituency was limited to only a small percentage of the young. Despite these setbacks, the Fada'iyun enjoyed a great deal of popularity.

The National Front

The National Front was the major secular nationalist organization. After the coup in 1953, it was substantially weakened when Mossadeq was placed under house arrest and some of its leaders were either jailed or killed. With the limited liberalization of the early 1960s, the National Front resurfaced. With Mossadeq still under house arrest, the National Front leadership was divided, confused, indecisive, and devoid of political creativity. Consequently, its temporary activities were mostly inconsequential. But what proved to be most damaging in the long run was the 1961 split from the National Front by Mehdi Bazargan and his associates, who subsequently formed the Nehzat-e Azadi-ye Iran (the Liberation Movement of Iran), an Islamic-nationalist entity. The split deprived the National Front of much of its connection to the ulama community.

During most of the 1960s and 1970s, the National Front, whose constituency had been narrowed to a small portion of the middle class, remained an innocuous and reformist organization under surveillance by the SAVAK. Until the last phases of the revolutionary movement in 1978, it remained loyal to the 1906 Constitution.

In exile, however, the National Front took a somewhat different approach. Created by those who escaped Iran after the 1953 coup, the National Front in exile was also split into rival Islamic and secular organizations, each claiming to be the true representative of Mossadeq's line. Both were instrumental in creating the Confederation of Iranian Students in Western Europe and North America. Both groups were ideologically more radical than their counterparts in Iran. One group had connections with both Bazargan's Liberation Movement and with Ayatollah Khomeini in Iraq. The other group, headquartered in Lebanon and espousing to socialism/nationalism, was largely responsible for distributing in Europe and the United States the revolutionary literature written by the guerrilla organizations operating inside Iran. It also served as a link between the guerrillas and radical groups in the Middle East.

The National Front was a potentially powerful force because of its adherence to Iranian nationalism and its role as an inheritor of Mossadeq's legacy. This is perhaps why SAVAK considered it a threat to the Shah's regime.

Cultural Revivalism: Shadman, Bazargan, Al-e Ahmad, and Shari'ati

From the early 1960s onward, a number of prominent intellectuals profoundly influenced the evolution of Shi'i political thought. Mehdi Bazargan, Ali Shari'ati, and Jalal Al-e Ahmad (1923–1969) were at the top of this list. Despite their diversity of outlooks, they all shared the conviction that in Shi'ism one may find all the ingredients of a liberating, progressive ideology capable of neutralizing the cultural hegemony of the West in Iran, ending the endemic alienation of educated Iranians and protecting the country's identity and heritage. The messages of these thinkers—a well-crafted mixture of Iranian nationalism, Shi'ism, and some Western ideas—won the hearts and minds of a large segment of the educated population. They were the bridge builders and peacemakers between Shi'ism and the secular intelligentsia. Their pioneer work convinced many secular intellectuals that Shi'ism is a progressive religion.

One of the earliest pioneers of this powerful revivalist movement was Seyyed Fakhreddin Shadman Valavi (1902–1967). Born into a clerical family in Teheran, he completed his secondary education at the Darolfonun School and received his doctoral degree from the University of London. A prolific writer and a seasoned statesman, Shadman was well acquainted with Western history and literature and had taught at major European and U.S. universities. His understanding of Islamic and Iranian history was equally impressive: He was a professor of Islamic and Iranian history at the University of Teheran.

Shadman was among the first intellectuals to warn that the modernization of Iran was not tantamount to the complete rejection of all things Iranian and the acceptance of all things European. In 1948, in a beautifully written book, *Taskhir-e Tamaddon-e Farangi* (The Conquest of Western Civilization), Shadman, a passionate nationalist, lamented that in its 2,500- year history, Iran had witnessed vicissitudes in its fortunes, from glory to humiliation. But Iran had managed to survive as a nation. Recently, however, Iran was facing its most powerful enemy, Western civilization: "But Western civilization is a different kind of enemy and it has a different tactic, and in my opinion the victory of Western civilization in Iran will be Iran's last defeat, that is, after this defeat no longer will the Iranian nation survive."[7] Western civilization, Shadman wrote, was seeking to dehumanize Iranians, to deprive them of their identity and religion, and to enslave them. It sought to do so not by military force but by reliance upon its superior scientific knowledge. The only way to deal with this formidable enemy was to conquer the Western civilization before it could conquer Iran. This could be done first and foremost by learning about Western civilization and by incorporating into Iranian culture what was beneficial from it and disregarding what was harmful. Shadman insisted that it would also require protecting, purifying, and enriching the Persian language, the symbol of Iran's national identity, and safeguarding Iran's historical and cultural heritage, both in its pre-Islamic and Islamic forms.

Shadman was highly critical of what he called the *farangi-ma'ab* (pseudo-Westerner) or the *fokoli* (the bow-tie wearer). He relentlessly attacked them as deceptive, ignorant, and selfish: They knew little of Western civilization and even less of Iran's. The *fokoli* was interested only in bringing to Iran the West's most decadent social products and in denigrating the richness of Iran's culture, language, and historical heritage. The *fokoli*s attacked Islam as a cause of Iran's backwardness because they had never bothered to study the glorious history of Islam and its contribution to science and civilization. The *fokoli*s praised the peaceful facade of Western civilization because they had not studied the Crusades and the

Dark Ages. In short, the *fokoli* was an agent for Western civilization whose task was to defeat Iran. The *fokoli*, therefore, must be exposed and defeated.

Regrettably, Shadman's influence was confined to a small and highly educated constituency. Because his creative ideas were to be realized within the confines of the existing political structures, and because he had developed congenial relations with the Shah's court and had held numerous ministerial positions in Abdul Hossein Hazhir and Fazlollah Zahedi's cabinets, he was mistrusted by many radical intellectuals. Fortunately, some of his thought-provoking concepts, such as the *fokoli*, were picked up and politicized by Jalal Al-e Ahmad.

A popular novelist and former member of the Tudeh Party who split from the party in the late 1940s, Al-e Ahmad was the most outspoken critic of what he called *gharbzadegi*, or Westoxication—a concept that had striking similarities to Shadman's *fokoli*. *Gharbzadegi* is blind imitation of Western culture. Al-e Ahmad's hatred of *gharbzadegi* probably had much to do with his opposition to "Western imperialism" as the cause of Iran's problems. After the June Uprising of 1963 and after his pilgrimage to Mecca in 1964, he called for a return to Shi'ism and the rejection of all Western ideologies, including Marxism. He strongly attacked "co-opted" intellectuals of past generations for collaborating with Western-supported regimes.

If Al-e Ahmad the Marxist saw in the proletariat the social force destined to create a classless society, Al-e Ahmad the Shi'ite saw in the ulama a potential force capable of leading Iran to liberation. He looked to the ulama as the bastion that could protect Iran's identity and independence from the onslaught of Western imperialism. He pleaded for a close alliance between the ulama and the intellectuals in the fight against despotism and imperialism: "We have witnessed success, progress, and social development whenever the ulama and the intelligentsia were allies struggling for a common cause."[8]

Moving along the same lines, Bazargan and Shari'ati had a more profound impact on the Islamic Revolution than did Al-e Ahmad. They adroitly combined some aspects of Western social democracy, and in Shari'ati's case fragments of Marxism, with Shi'ism.

Mehdi Bazargan was born into a merchant family in Tabriz in 1905. He completed his high school education in Iran and his higher education in France. Unlike Al-e Ahmad, Bazargan attributed Iran's backwardness not to Western imperialism but to internal conditions such as despotism and ignorance.[9] One of the prerequisites to progress, he argued, is reliance on the true teachings of Shi'ism and on the creation of an Islamic government to be run not by the Shi'i ulama but by experts who are committed Shi'ites.

Bazargan, a committed but nonclerical Shi'ite, has been a champion of political and religious reforms in Iran. He was one of the pioneers of a reform movement in the early 1960s that sought to reorganize the *marja'-e taqlid* organization and to make it more compatible with the exigencies of a modern world.[10] Greater centralization for the *marja'-e taqlid* institution and the creation of a *shura-ye fatva* (council of *fatva*), where the leading ayatollahs could exchange their views, were advocated.

Bazargan was also one of the founding members of the Nehzat-e Azadi-ye Iran (the Liberation Movement of Iran), the nationalistic/Islamic organization that began its activities in June 1961.[11] Most of its founding members came from the high ranks of the National Front.[12] Its reformist political orientation was succinctly summarized by Bazargan: "We are Moslems, Iranians, the followers of the Constitution, and are Mossadeqites."[13] It rejected the notion of the separation of Islam and politics and regarded political activity by the ulama and the faithful as a religious responsibility. Bazargan and his associates were also instrumental in creating a number of Islamic organizations, like the Society of Moslem Engineers. During most of the 1960s and 1970s, the Liberation Movement continued its activities against the Shah surreptitiously.

In the United States, too, the Liberation Movement was active. Two of its members, Dr. Ebrahim Yazdi and Dr. Mostafa Chamran, helped create the Moslem Students Association, which had direct contact with Khomeini in Najaf, Iraq. Some of the students who occupied the U.S. Embassy in 1979 were members of this student organization.

The Liberation Movement, despite its small size, could have performed a stabilizing role in Iranian politics. Its loyalty to the institution of the monarchy and its liberal, reformist ideology could have been effectively used as a deterrent against radicalism of the left and fanaticism of the right. By suppressing the Liberation Movement, the Shah's regime severed the bridge between the Shah and the reform-oriented segment of the middle class.

Ali Shari'ati's influence was stronger and more pervasive than that of Bazargan. He was one of the most popular Shi'i thinkers of this century. Shari'ati's pictures were carried alongside Ayatollah Khomeini's during the revolutionary demonstrations of 1977–1979.

Ali Shari'ati was born in 1933 and received most of his secondary and undergraduate education in Mashhad, Iran.[14] In the mid-1950s, he was jailed briefly for his pro-Mossadeq activities. In 1960, he went to France to continue with his higher education. There his ideas were heavily shaped by the Algerian liberation movement and the works of Frantz Fanon and Jean-Paul Sartre. In 1964, shortly after he completed his doctoral degree in sociology at the Sorbonne, Shari'ati taught at the University of Mashhad for a brief period. Because of his political activism, he was dismissed from his post and went to Teheran. He lectured at the Hosseiniye-ye Ershad from 1969 until 1974, when the Hosseiniye, now turned into an intellectual center of agitation against the Shah, was shut down by SAVAK.[15] Banned from lecturing, he went into seclusion and was put under virtual house arrest by SAVAK. Thanks to the Shah's liberalization policy, Shari'ati was allowed to leave Iran in 1977. Shortly after his arrival in London, he died of a heart attack.[16]

Although Shari'ati's productive years in the Hosseiniye-ye Ershad were short, his contribution was immense. His emotionally charged lectures, which were then made available in tapes and transcripts, attracted a large audience composed mostly of the educated and young. In these lectures, he covered a variety of issues, ranging from the history of Islam to a harsh criticism of Marxism to the justification of the struggle against despotism.

Shari'ati, like Bazargan, was most concerned about the decline of Shi'ism in Iran. He attributed this decline to the infusion of Western ideas, such as Marxism and liberalism, and to the failure of the ulama to spread the true teachings of Shi'ism. For him, the struggle against the Shah was inseparable from the rejection of alien Western ideologies.

For Shari'ati, the true Shi'ism, which he labeled Alavi Shi'ism, was from its inception the liberating ideology of the oppressed, the meek, and the downtrodden. But when it was imposed as the state religion in 1501, Shi'ism was transformed into Safavid Shi'ism, a conservative ideology for legitimizing monarchical absolutism and acting as social anesthesia.[17]

The conspicuous characteristics of this ideology are engagement by the faithful in religious trivia and acceptance of suffering in the hope of the return of the Twelfth Imam, Shari'ati wrote. Sometimes implicitly and sometimes explicitly, Shari'ati attacked the ulama as defenders of Safavid Shi'ism. This is why he was not popular among the ulama, many of whom considered his interpretation of Islam to be misleading. Shari'ati was determined to reintroduce the true Shi'ism. In this difficult task, he made extensive use of allegories and analogies to avoid harassment by the agents of censorship.

For Shari'ati, Alavi Shi'ism is the faith of Hossein, the third imam of the Shi'ites who in A.D. 680 denounced the Ummayad's caliph as sacrilegious and proclaimed himself the legitimate imam. Despite incredible odds against his victory, Imam Hossein and seventy-one of his associates and relatives confronted the caliph's massive army in Karbela, in present-day Iraq. Hossein and most of his supporters were slaughtered. Since then, Imam Hossein has emerged as the paragon of the martyrs and martyrdom has become an integral part of the ethos of Shi'ism. Shari'ati hoped to rekindle the spirit of Imam Hossein among the young Iranians. Shi'ism, he insisted, is the religion of protest, of continuous struggle against tyranny, and of action. Its objective is to construct the city of God on this planet, a *tauhidi* (unitary) society free of oppression and exploitation. Unlike Marx, who assigned to the proletariat the task of building his utopia, Shari'ati looked to the Shi'i intellectuals to build the *tauhidi* society.

Shari'ati adroitly politicized many Shi'i concepts, including *entezar* (waiting for the return of the Hidden Imam). *Entezar,* for Shari'ati, had a new meaning: "belief in God's promise to the Muslims, in the final realization of the wretched masses' ideal and hope; in the final triumphant emergence of the classless society, a society freed from tyranny, injustice and deceit. Entezar means to say no to what is."[18] Aware that to say no to an armed regime could be fatal, he made a highly emotional argument that those who are actually killed in defense of Shi'ism will be eternally alive: "In our culture …martyrdom is death by choice, chosen by the strugglers with complete consciousness, logic, and awareness."[19]

Al-e Ahmad, Bazargan, and Shari'ati were men of the pen. Others were men of the sword. Consider the case of the Mojahedin.

The Organization of the Mojahedin-e Khalq-e Iran

The foundation for the Mojahedin-e Khalq-e Iran was laid by Mohammad Hanif Nejad and Sa'id Mohsen, both members of the Liberation Movement. Because of their anti-Shah activity, they were prisoners in the Shah's jails in the mid-1960s. In 1965, with the help of close associates like Ahmad Reza'i and Asghar Badizadegan, they informally created the Mojahedin organization.[20]

From the ideological debates among the founding members, it was concluded that only an indigenous ideology like Shi'ism could incite the population to rebel against the Pahlavis.[21] Influenced by the writings of Bazargan, Shari'ati, and Ayatollah Mohmood Taleqani, the Mojahedin offered a revolutionary interpretation of Shi'ism.

The Mojahedin, like the Fada'iyun, were inspired by Castro's victory in Cuba in 1959, and they, too, decided to resort to armed struggle. In preparation, some members were sent to the Palestine Liberation Organization's training camps in Lebanon. While the organization was still at a preparatory stage in Iran, many of its founding members, including Mohsen, were arrested by SAVAK. But the organization demonstrated a remarkable resilience and continued to expand its membership.

Soon after these arrests, and following the Siyahkal episode in 1971, the organization publicly declared its existence, pledging open war against the regime. The activities of the Mojahedin included the publication of radical literature, the bombing of government buildings, the robbing of banks, and the assassination of prominent members of the regime and a number of Americans.[22] Through the generous support of the National Front in exile, the Confederation of Iranian Students, and the Moslem Students Association, the Mojahedin and the Fada'iyun began to attract attention in the West.

In the early 1970s, the Mojahadin received some support from the pro-Khomeini clerics in Iran.[23] But Khomeini never explicitly supported the Mojahedin. He recalled that when he was in Najaf one of the Mojahedin approached him and asked him to declare his support for armed struggle against the Shah. This is how Khomeini recalled his encounter with that man: "For ten/twenty days, I listened to his talks, and did not give him any answer. … I listened and did not say a word, but when he said that we [the Mojahedin] wanted to start an armed struggle, I said no; it is not time for armed struggle, and you, too, will lose much of your resources and will not be able to accomplish much."[24]

At the zenith of its popularity, the Mojahedin suffered a split in its ranks in 1975 that marked the beginning of its decline.[25] A large faction within the organization had concluded that Marxism, not Islam, was the liberating ideology of the masses and that it should be adopted as the group's official ideology. The Marxist faction staged a coup and purged the non-Marxist elements. In 1978, the Marxist faction renamed itself Peykar and resumed its activities, and the Moslem members recaptured the leadership of the Mojahedin.

Moslem members of the Mojahedin insisted that the main ideologues of the Marxist faction were communists who had deliberately infiltrated the organization to denigrate Islam.[26] The validity of this assertion notwithstanding, after the creation of the organization it was obvious that the Mojahedin's ideological orientation was more than a revolutionary reinterpretation of Shi'ism. In the Mojahedin's published literature one could find Marxist ideas such as the workers' control of factories, centralized economic planning, and class struggle. Books like *Eqtesad Be Zaban-e Sadeh* (Economics in Simple Language) were but elementary regurgitations of Marxist economics.

The split lent credence to the regime's campaign of labeling the Mojahedin as Islamic-Marxist. Even though the Marxist elements have long since disappeared from the organization, the Mojahedin's ideological predilection today remains a strange blend of Marxist ideas and Shi'ism. This split, and the invidious scheme by which the Marxist elements took over an Islamic organization, not only enervated the Mojahedin but, more significant, reinforced the historic suspicion between the Islamic and Marxist forces.

Thus, from the middle of 1975 to 1979, there were two Mojahedin organizations. By 1978, the leading personalities of both factions had either been killed or jailed. Altogether from its creation up to 1978, 101 of the Mojahedin were killed, 71 from the Islamic faction and 30 from the Marxist group.[27] Neither of those two organizations posed a serious threat to the Shah's regime.

Ayatollah Khomeini and His Political Philosophy

In prerevolutionary Iran, the dominant Shi'i current was socially and politically conservative. This orthodox Shi'ism supported the monarchy and rejected political involvement by the ulama except in situations when the temporal authorities legislated un-Islamic laws or blatantly threatened the survival of the faith. The most notable advocates of this interpretation were Ayatollahs Hossein Borujerdi (d. 1961), Hadi Milani (d. 1975), and Kazem Shariatmadari (d. 1986).

From the June Uprising of 1963 to the middle of the 1970s, the Shah's regime sought this group's collaboration in neutralizing the threat of fundamentalist Shi'-ism and communism. Thus when Ayatollah Mohsen Hakim, a leading *marja'-e taqlid* in Iraq, died in 1975, the Shah sent his condolence telegram to Ayatollah Shariatmadari, thus recognizing him as the sole *marja'-e taqlid*.[28] In response to this intervention, eighty-six of the ulama in Iran sent their condolences to Ayatollah Khomeini in Najaf, thus elevating him to the position of sole *marja'-e taqlid.*

When censorship was prevalent, Ayatollah Shariatmadari's *Maktab-e Islam* was regularly published. A large number of books receiving permission for publication from SAVAK were religiously oriented texts that advocated an orthodox view of religion and politics.

The orthodox ulama, of course, had their moments of confrontation with the regime. During the early 1960s, many of them had opposed the Shah's initiatives, and they had done so again and again when family protection laws granted women the right to ask for divorce under certain conditions, when the Shah celebrated the 2,500th anniversary of the Persian Empire, and when he changed the Islamic calendar. These ulama were also angered by the spread of the West's "perfidious culture" in Iran. But those confrontations with the authorities were over specific policies, not against the institution of kingship. Thus, even if this group participated in the revolutionary movement of 1977–1979 and used its enormous organizational power to mobilize the masses, it was not until the very last stage of the movement that, under pressure form the fundamentalists, it reluctantly joined forces with them to demand the demolition of the monarchy.

If quietism and support for the monarchy were the characteristics of the orthodox Shi'ism, advocacy of the ulama's direct rule was the trademark of fundamentalist Shi'ism in prerevolutionary Iran. Ayatollah Khomeini was the most articulate proponent of Shi'i fundamentalism.

Ruhollah Mussavi Khomeini was born into a religious family in Khomain, Iran, in 1902. His father died when he was only five months old, his mother when he was sixteen.[29] Having learned Arabic and the basics of Shi'ism from his older half-brother, Morteza Pasandideh, Khomeini went to Arak, Iran, in 1920 to study to become a mullah. He learned theology, Islamic jurisprudence, and philosophy under Sheikh Abdul Karim Ha'eri Yazdi, a popular *mujtahed.* A year later when Ha'eri moved to Qom, Khomeini, his protégé, did the same. In 1926, when Reza Khan created the Pahlavi dynasty, the young Khomeini completed his studies.

When his mentor, Ayatollah Ha'eri, died in 1935, Khomeini actively campaigned on behalf of Hossein Borujerdi, who eventually emerged as the sole *marja'-e taqlid* and increased Khomeini's power as one of his close associates.

From the beginning, Khomeini was intensely interested in *erfan* (gnosticism), and when he was twenty-seven he wrote a book in Arabic about it. His interests in gnosticism and poetry, both quite unpopular among the ulama in Qom, set the young Khomeini apart from the vast majority of his cohorts. Fearful that some of the conservative ulama might defame him, Khomeini used the "Hendi" pseudonym, which means "from India," in his writings and poetry. This led to the rumor that he was of Indian, not Persian, descent. In reality, Khomeini chose the pseudonym because his Iranian grandfather had lived in India for some time and was known there as Mir Hossein Neyshaburi Hendi.

Khomeini's early political outlook was shaped by two significant events. As a student in his twenties, he somberly witnessed the disintegration of the Ottoman Empire, Islam's last empire, and the subsequent creation of a secular Turkey. As if this was not enough, he watched in pain as Reza Shah's reforms inflicted heavy damage on the power and fortunes of the ulama in Iran. The picture outside of Iran looked equally bleak: Nationalistic and socialistic ideologies were rapidly sweeping across the Islamic world, forcing Islam onto the backstage of politics. Because of such profound changes in his native land and in the Islamic world, Khomeini felt frustrated. But he was determined to make Islam politically relevant and powerful again.

Khomeini was a prolific writer and, as we learned after his death, a sensitive poet. By 1979, he was credited with some twenty-five books and monographs and hundreds of *fatva*s and short declarations, all written by Khomeini himself and not by his staff, as has been customary among the leading ayatollahs. His poetry, published posthumously, demonstrated his strong interest in *erfan.*

His writings are multifaceted, covering a wide array of religious, philosophical, social, and political issues. Some of them are based on simplistic arguments and written in easy-to-follow language, whereas others, aimed at a more erudite constituency, are serious scholarly treatises. Despite the richness of the topics covered in his voluminous works, three themes were central to Khomeini's scholarship: the urgency of reestablishing Islam as a way of life and a method of government, the legitimacy or illegitimacy of the monarchy, and the ulama's proper role in politics.

Khomeini's views regarding these three interconnected issues underwent major transformations. He began as a reformer, operating within the parameters of orthodox Shi'ism, and ended as a revolutionary interpreter of Islam and the founder of a new form of Islamic government.

Khomeini's first major overtly political treatise was *Kashfol Asrar* (Secrets Unraveled), which was published in 1941, shortly after Reza Shah's forced abdication. In *Kashfol Asrar* we meet Khomeini the reformer, the defender of the Persian Constitution and the monarchy, who was mainly concerned about Iranian politics. The book was a frontal attack on Reza Shah's policies and a response to *Secrets of a Thousand Years,* a book written by a member of Ahmad Kasravi's Pak Dini Movement, which denigrated the ulama as champions of superstition and the main cause of Iran's backwardness. Like Saint Augustine, who in *The City of God* defended Christianity against the pagans' charge that it had caused the decline of the Roman Empire, Khomeini lambasted the propagators of the Pak Dini Movement and praised the ulama as defenders of Iran's national identity, independence, and even its monarchy.

Khomeini condemned Reza Shah for the forced unveiling of women, which was "enforced at bayonet point," for curtailing the power of the ulama, for spreading coeducation, and for proliferating "centers of corruption" such as bars and liquor stores. Opposed to the prevalent quietist Shi'i view of the time, *Kashfol Asrar* was replete with passionate pleas to the ulama to engage in politics.

Khomeini even suggested that the ulama should govern, but the parameters of their "rule" were narrowly defined: "That it is said that *hokumat* [governance] must belong to the *faqih* [jurisconsult] does not mean that the *faqih* should become the Shah or a minister, the commander of the army ... but that the *faqih* should be able to *supervise* the legislative and executive branches of an Islamic nation."[30] This, of course, was no more than a broad interpretation of Article 2 of the Supplementary Laws of the 1906 Constitution, which stipulated that the Majles legislation should be reviewed by an "ecclesiastical committee" consisting of five ulama with veto power over the Majles.

Not much is known about Khomeini's activities from the publication of the *Kashfol Asrar* until the early 1960s. Although he supported Ayatollah Kashani during the struggle to nationalize the oil industry, Khomeini did not play any consequential role in the politics of the time or produce any major political work. It was only with his vociferous opposition to the Shah's reforms in the early 1960s that he gained national fame. At that point he also emerged as a leading candidate to succeed Ayatollah Borujerdi, the sole *marja'-e taqlid* of the time.

In that critical period, Khomeini remained a reformist. Despite his opposition to such specific issues as the granting of suffrage to women, Iran's de facto recognition of Israel, the Shah's White Revolution, and the reenactment of the Capitulation Laws in Iran, Khomeini offered friendly advice to the monarch to reverse his policies. He did not denounce the monarchy, although he attacked the person of the Shah. Nor did he speak of creating an Islamic government.

Only after his forced exile to Iraq did Khomeini gradually abandon his reformism and preoccupation with Iranian politics and articulate his revolutionary concept of an Islamic government based on some pan-Islamic principles. Like many other Islamic thinkers, Khomeini was deeply distressed by Western domination of the Islamic world, by the repeated Israeli victories over the Arabs, and the progressive decline of the once vibrant Islamic civilization. For him, the abominable governments of the Moslem world, the majority of whom he viewed to be puppets of the imperialists and Zionists, were willing accomplices in the grand conspiracy to destroy Islam. In a time when it was fashionable for Middle Eastern intellectuals to advocate nationalism and socialism, and when others regarded Islam as a dying faith, Khomeini raised the banner of Islam as the one force that could solve the problems facing the Islamic world.

In a series of lectures in 1969, he declared Islam to be diametrically opposed to the monarchy, the existing form of government in many Islamic nations of the time, and argued that the ulama have a divine mission to rule over a government founded exclusively on Islamic laws. Islam and politics, he pointed out, are inseparable: The Prophet Mohammad was the head of the state, the commander of the army, and the spiritual leader of the community. Khomeini suggested that the ulama should perform all the responsibilities of the Prophet and the imams, even if they do not possess their miraculous qualities. In short, the ulama should become the expositors, enunciators, and executors of Islamic laws and traditions.

Once the satanic governments of the Moslem countries are demolished, the ulama should collectively collaborate to create, Khomeini wrote, "a large Islamic government which recognizes no limitation or boundary except the limitation of Islam."

Thus Khomeini was not simply a destroyer of the status quo; he was also a builder of a new order, which he labeled Islamic government. Khomeini's discussion of the nature and structure of his Islamic government, however, seemed rudimentary and blurred: "Islam consists of the laws which all of humanity should practice; and the Islamic Government is not constitutional, or tyrannical, or a republic: No one can interfere in it except God. ... In this kind of government, the head of the state should have two qualifications. One, he should have knowledge of the law, and two, he should spread justice during the implementation of the law."[31] Islamic government then, is a nomocracy, a government of laws—eternal and absolute laws. But Khomeini did not talk about the process by which the *fuqaha* could be elected or selected or about many other pressing issues.

Although condemnation of the monarchy was implicit in the Najaf lectures, it was not until 1971, on the occasion of the Shah's celebration of Iran's two-and-a-half millennia of monarchy, that Khomeini not only attacked the Shah for the ostentatious and expensive celebration but also made the unconventional declaration that Islam is fundamentally opposed to monarchy. He quoted the Prophet as having said that the title often used by Iranian kings *Shahanshah*, Shah of the shahs, "is for me the most hateful word."[32] Leaving no room for any compromise with the Shah, Khomeini became the first reputable religious leader to call for the overthrow of the monarchy in Iran. None of the leading Shi'i ulama endorsed Khomeini's unorthodox view.

Until 1978, Khomeini had only spoken of an Islamic government. In November of that year he was no longer rejecting, as he had in his 1969 Najaf lectures, the idea that an Islamic government could also be a republic. There were a variety of reasons for this critical change of opinion: First, November 1978 represented the first time Khomeini sensed victory. Second, under the banner of an Islamic Republic, he mobilized all the antimonarchist elements and established himself as the only leader who was offering an alternative to the monarchy. Finally, his advocacy of an Islamic Republic put unbearable pressure on the moderate faction of the opposition to reject the Shah's policy of national reconciliation and recognize Khomeini's leadership.

How can we explain the radical transformation in Khomeini's thought? Khomeini was about seventy years old when he radically changed his political outlook (assuming that the Najaf lectures were the turning point in the evolution of his thought). Although it is impossible to understand the exact process that facilitated this transformation at his mature age, we can identify some factors that probably influenced the Ayatollah's thinking. For one thing, he was fortuitously in exile in Iraq (1965–1978) and out of reach of SAVAK, which made it easier for him to denounce the monarchy in Iran. Three developments had convinced the Ayatollah that the Shah's regime was incorrigible: the Shah's decision to create the

Religious Corps, which somehow reduced the ulama's power in rural Iran; his plan to create a state-sponsored Islamic university in Mashhad; and the passage of the Family Protection Bill, which granted women the right to sue for divorce under certain conditions (see Chapter 4).

While in Najaf, Khomeini was in contact with some radical thinkers and organizations. Chief among those who had an impact on Khomeini's thought was Seyyed Mohammad Baqer Sadr, an Iraqi-born ayatollah who was noted as perhaps the most celebrated Shi'i economist. Sadr advocated direct rule by the ulama and argued that they should be acquainted with modern sciences and with the administration of the state. He was calling for the creation of an Islamic government, as was the Al-Da'wa Party, a radical Shi'i organization in Iraq. Sadr's ideas generated lively discussion in Najaf's seminaries, in one of which Khomeini was teaching, about the potential and prospects of the ulama's direct rule. Sadr was executed by President Saddam Hossein in 1980.

Ayatollah Khomeini was also in contact with Moussa Sadr, a highly educated and shrewd Iranian mullah. In the 1960s, Moussa Sadr had gone to Lebanon, where he had gathered around himself a considerable following. In 1969, he founded the Higher Shi'ite Council to represent Shi'ite interests in government and to help the poor. Moussa Sadr created a militia that trained many of Iran's Shi'ite revolutionaries in the 1970s. In 1975, he founded Amal, an organization designed to help the Shi'ites in Lebanon. Moussa Sadr's talent as an organizer and his emphasis on organization building probably influenced Khomeini's thought and political strategy.[33] Sadr vanished mysteriously during his visit to Libya in 1978; it is alleged that he was killed by Colonel Momarr Khadafi, who accused him of being a SAVAK agent.

But much more significant than speculation on the causes for the transformation of Khomeini's political philosophy were the consequences of his interpretation of the Velayat-e Faqih: It further politicized many of the young, pro-Khomeini ulama in Iran and Iraq. Relying on the massive and informal network of the ulama, Khomeini's followers began indefatigably to promulgate the new ideas on Islamic government and the illegitimacy of the monarchy. Khomeini's views began to be advertised daily during the pilgrimage to Mecca and through the smuggling of cassette tapes from Iraq to Iran.

But the most profound consequences of Khomeini's new interpretation were the explicit rejection of the compatibility of Shi'ism/Islam with monarchism, two institutions that share a long history of symbiotic coexistence in Iran, and the advocacy of the ulama's direct rule. In *Kashfol Asrar,* Khomeini's views were fundamentally different from those he expressed in the 1970s:

> So far no *faqih* has ever said or indicated in a book that we are kings or that kingship is our right. ... No one from this class [*fuqaha*] has ever opposed the principle of kingship. On the contrary many of the more prominent ulama like Tousi and Allameh Helli and Muhaqqiq-e Thani and Muhaqqiq-e Damad and Majlesi and others

have cooperated in the administration of the government with the kings; and in spite of the ill-treatment meted out to them by the king and in spite of the pressure brought upon them, they have however never opposed the foundation of the administration and the government.[34]

That he hoped to mix religion and politics was neither surprising nor new in Iran's long and turbulent history. Iranian kings have long manipulated religion to legitimize their rule and enhance their imperial ambitions: from Cyrus the Great, the founder of the Achaemenid dynasty who claimed to be the representative of the god Ahura Mazda; to Shah Esmail, the founder of the Safavid dynasty who insisted that he was the emanation of the Hidden Imam; to Mohammad Reza Shah Pahlavi, who was overthrown by the Islamic Revolution. In Iran's political culture, religion seems inseparable from politics.

The unique and surprising element about Khomeini's Velayat-e Faqih was that for the first time in Iranian history it legitimized the monopoly of power by one religious class, namely the ulama. Moreover, for the first time in the history of Shi'ism it sought to place one *faqih* above all other religious authorities, to transform Shi'ism from a polycephalic faith to a unicephalic or monolithic one. True, many leading ulama had spoken of the ulama as the *Nayeb-e Imam* (Imam's representative) and had emphasized the supremacy of their rule over the holders of temporal power. But Khomeini took a giant step beyond those thinkers: He believed that the "*faqih* should be not just one high official among the many who form the top echelon of the state administration but its supreme overseer, judge, and guardian."[35]

Whatever one thinks of Khomeini's new interpretation of the Velayat-e Faqih, it cannot be denied that he offered an alternative to the Shah's monarchy in Iran as early as 1969, something no other prominent leader had done. Even if the picture he drew of his Islamic government was blurred, the audacious declaration that Shi'ism/Islam and monarchy were incompatible earned Khomeini a special and highly respected place among the oppositional forces to the Shah. It reinforced his image as the most outspoken opponent of the Shah and as a religious innovator. And most important, Khomeini's ideas gave religious sanction to rebellion against the Pahlavis and challenged the religious legitimacy of the institution of monarchy. This was no minor accomplishment.

Notes

1. The quotation from Shari'ati can be found in "Entizar, the Religion of Protest," trans. Mangol Bayat, in John Donohue and John Esposito, eds., *Islam in Transition* (New York, 1982), p. 303.

2. See Sepehr Zabih, *The Communist Movement in Iran* (Berkeley, Calif., 1966).

3. *Mardom,* 23 Esfand 1357 (March 15, 1979).

4. *Hasht Sal Mobareze-ye Mossalahane* (Eight Years of Armed Struggle) (Teheran, 1979).

5. Amir Parviz Poyan, *Zarurat-e Mobareze-ye Mossalahane Va Rad-de Teoriye Baqa* (The Necessity of Armed Struggle and the Refutation of the Theory of Survival) (Teheran, 1972).

6. Ervand Abrahamian, *Iran Between Two Revolutions* (Princeton, N.J., 1982), p. 480.

7. Seyyed Fakhreddin Shadman Valavi, *Taskhir-e Tamaddon-e Farangi* (The Conquest of Western Civilization) (Teheran, 1948), pp. 25–26, and *Tragedy-ye Farang* (The Tragedy of the West) (Teheran, 1967).

8. Jalal Al-e Ahmad, *Dar Khedmat Va Khiyanat-e Raushanfekran* (On the Service and Treason of Intellectuals) (Teheran, 1978), p. 271.

9. Mehdi Bazargan, *Serr-e Aqaboftadegi-ye Melal-e Mosalman* (The Secret of the Backwardness of the Islamic Nations) (Boston, 1983).

10. *Bahsi Dar Bare-ye Marja'iyat Va Rauhaniyat* (A Discussion on Marja'iyat and Rauhaniyat) (Teheran, 1963).

11. For a brief history of the Liberation Movement, see *Tarikh-e Mo'aser-e Iran: Asnad-e Nehzat-e Azadi-ye Iran* (History of Contemporary Iran: Documents of the Liberation Movement of Iran) (hereafter *Asnad-e Azadi*), vol. 1 (Teheran, 1981).

12. For details, see H. E. Chehabi, *Iranian Politics and Religious Modernism* (Ithaca, N.Y., 1990).

13. *Asnad-e Azadi*, p. 17.

14. See Abdulaziz Sachedina, "Ali Shari'ati: Ideologue of the Iranian Revolution," in John K. Esposito, ed., *Voices of Resurgent Islam* (New York, 1983), pp. 191–214; and Shahrough Akhavi, "Shari'ati's Social Thought," in Nikkie Keddie, ed., *Religion and Politics in Iran* (New Haven, Conn., 1983), pp. 125–144.

15. In 1972, Shari'ati was jailed again. During the OPEC Conference, the president of Algeria, whom Shari'ati knew personally, asked the Shah to release him and he was released.

16. The opposition to the Shah blamed SAVAK for Shari'ati's death. The British coroner's report attributed his death to a heart attack.

17. Ali Shari'ati, *Khod Sazi-ye Enqelabi* (Revolutionary Self-Building) (Teheran, 1979), and *Che Bayad Kard* (What Is to Be Done?) (Teheran, n.d.).

18. Shari'ati (1979), p. 303.

19. *Shahadat* (Martyrdom) (Teheran, 1971), p. 64, my translation.

20. See *Sharh-e Ta'sis Va Tarikh Va Vaqaye-e Sazeman-e Mojahedin-e Khalq-e Iran* (Explanation of the Formation and Historical Account of the Events of the Organization of the Mojahedin of Iran) (Teheran, 1979).

21. See Ahmad Reza'i, *Nehzat-e Hosseini* (Hosseini's Movement) (Beirut, 1973).

22. On these acts, see *Shah: Doshman-e Khalq, Doshman-e Mojahedin* (Shah: The Enemy of the Masses, the Enemy of the Mojahedin) (Teheran, 1979).

23. Ali Akbar Hashemi Rafsanjani, *Enqelab Ya Be'sat-e Jadid* (Revolution or a New Mission) (Teheran, 1985), pp. 134–150.

24. R. Khomeini, *Kalam-e Imam: Goruhha-ye Siyasi* (The Imam's Words: Political Groups), vol. 13 (Teheran, 1984), pp. 247–248.

25. For the split, see *Bayaniye-ye E'lam-e Mavaze-e Ideologic* (Declaration on the Ideological Positions) (Teheran, 1975).

26. See *Asnad-e Azadi*, vol. 9, pp. 9–15.

27. Abrahamian (1982), p. 480.

28. As quoted by Michael Fisher, *Iran: From Religious Dispute to Revolution* (Cambridge, Mass., 1978), pp. 188–189.

29. For a general background on his life see *Khomeini Va Jonbesh* (Khomeini and the Movement) (Teheran, 1978); Ruhollah Khomeini, *Islam and Revolution: Writings and Declarations,* trans. and annotated by Hamid Algar (Berkeley, Calif., 1981), pp. 13–21; Michael Fischer, "Imam Khomeini: Four Levels of Understanding," in John Esposito, ed., *Voices of Resurgent Islam* (New York, 1983), pp. 150–174; and *Zendeginame: Biographi-ye Pishva* (Life Story: The Biography of the Leader) (n.p., 1974), a book that was published before the Islamic Revolution, most likely in Iraq, and which contains Khomeini's thoughts regarding a variety of issues.

30. Ruhollah Khomeini, *Kashfol Asrar* (Secrets Unraveled) (Teheran, n.d.), p. 185.

31. R. Khomeini, *Hokumat-e Islami Ya Velayet-e Faqih* (The Islamic Government or Velayat-e Faqih), lessons 3 and 4 (Najaf, 1969), p. 5.

32. *Khomeini Va Jonbesh* (Khomeini and the Movement) (Teheran, 1983), p. 50.

33. See Hanna Batatu, "Iraq's Underground Shi'i Movements: Characteristics, Causes, and Prospects," *Middle East Journal* (Autumn 1981), pp. 578–594.

34. Khomeini (n.d.), pp. 186–187.

35. Hamid Enayat, "Iran: Khumayni's Concept of the Guardianship of the Jurisconsult," in James P. Piscatori, ed., *Islam in the Political Process* (New York, 1983), p. 161.

6

The Crisis of Wealth

Nature has so constituted men that, though all things are objects of desire, not all things are attainable; so that desire always exceeds the power of attainment, with the result that men are ill content with what they possess and their present state brings them little satisfaction. Hence arise the vicissitudes of their fortune. For, since some desire to have more and others are afraid to lose what they have already acquired, enmities and wars are begotten, and this brings about the ruin of one province and the exaltation of its rival.

Niccolò Machiavelli, Discourses, *1517*

The astronomical increase in oil revenues in Iran led to phenomenal economic expansion during the 1970s. It created a national euphoria, what I call a crisis of wealth, which eventually changed Iran's destiny.

That the Islamic Revolution followed a decade of prosperity is not astonishing. Tocqueville astutely observed that "in those parts of France where there had been the most improvement ... popular discontent ran highest. For it is not always when things are going from bad to worse that revolution breaks out."[1] Eric Hoffer perceptively expanded Tocqueville's argument and wrote that "the revolutionary temper is generated in the irritation and difficulties inherent in the realization of dramatic change."[2] The drastic changes imposed on Iran in the 1970s were the immediate economic preconditions of the Islamic Revolution. In the mid-1970s Iran resembled a fast-accelerating ship whose captain and passengers had lost all sense of direction and purpose as they bitterly fought over the distribution of a newly found treasure. They all sank.

Oil and the Shah's Great Civilization

The history of the oil industry in Iran is a fascinating chronicle of foreign intrigues, conspiracies, assassinations, and even a coup.[3] Oil has indeed been both a blessing and a curse for Iran. It all began in 1901, when a lucrative sixty-year oil concession was granted to William Knox D'Arcy, a British subject. D'Arcy's prudent investment in Qajar ignorance and greed paid off lavishly when oil was discovered in 1908. By 1909, he had founded the Anglo-Persian Oil Company (APOC), the first of its kind in the Middle East. Since the discovery in 1908 of rich oil deposits in Kermanshah, the destiny of Iran and the policies of the powerful nations toward it have been increasingly molded by petropolitics.

For decades, the British dominated the Iranian oil industry. Often the British government earned more revenues from taxation of the British oil companies in Iran than did the Iranian government. By the late 1940s, when the Majles passed the first comprehensive Seven-Year Development Program, it became abundantly clear that financing the development projects would require sustained increases in oil revenues. This would be possible only by nationalizing the oil industry, and this is exactly what Mossadeq did. Infuriated by this bold initiative, the Western nations boycotted Iranian oil, and diplomatic relations were severed between England and Iran. Finally, Mossadeq was overthrown in a coup, and General Zahedi took over.

After the coup of 1953, Ali Amini, a minister in the Zahedi government, quickly signed an oil treaty with the newly created oil consortium, which consisted mostly of American and British oil companies. The treaty was to last until 1979. In a way, the Iranian oil industry was denationalized and brought back under foreign domination. The members of the consortium, for example, had reached a secret agreement in the late 1950s to unilaterally decide Iran's oil production level based on their own needs, thus determining Iran's oil revenues and, hence, the rate of the country's economic growth.[4]

Despite the consortium's control of the Iranian oil industry, the struggle for higher oil revenues was enthusiastically pursued by the Shah. From the late 1950s to the late 1960s, the price of a barrel of oil was increased from 75.6 cents to 85.8, a substantial reduction when adjusted to inflation. After the Teheran Agreement of 1971, the price of a barrel of oil was increased by 33 cents. By 1973, Iran had regained full control over its oil industry, including production level and pricing—a dream Mossadeq had audaciously fought for two decades earlier but had taken to the grave.

Subsequent to the Arab-Israeli War in 1973 and the oil embargo on the United States and European nations that had assisted Israel, imposed by the major Arab oil producers, including Saudi Arabia, the price of oil almost quadrupled, reaching $11.65 per barrel in 1974. Although the Shah refused to participate in the embargo on the grounds that oil should not be used as a political weapon, Iran, which was among the world's largest oil exporters, became the recipient of the largest transfer of wealth in its history.[5]

Intoxicated with the new oil wealth, the Shah's regime began a stentorian propaganda campaign both abroad and at home. Internationally, it portrayed its monarch as a world statesman. Iran's role as policeman of the strategically important Persian Gulf and its newly acquired role as a benefactor to thirty-four nations, including England and Italy, substantially increased the Shah's prestige in international affairs. Despite his vehement insistence that his oil policy served the long-term interests of the Western nations, the Shah's propaganda war backfired. He emerged as the villain responsible for the West's economic difficulties and became a target of mounting international criticism. Negative rumblings about the Shah were evidenced in U.S. secretary of the Treasury William E. Simon's famous statement that the Shah "is a nut" who wants Iran "to be a superpower," the intriguing observation by General George S. Brown, chairman of the U.S. Joint Chiefs of Staff, that the Shah had irredentist ambitions and was working to revive the mighty Persian Empire, and the publication of Paul Erdman's best-seller *The Crash of 79,* in which the Shah expands his power throughout the Middle East.[6] The Shah fueled the West's sense of suspicion. Thus, to President Gerald Ford's warning that the Organization of Petroleum Exporting Countries (OPEC) should not increase oil prices, the Shah responded, "We can hurt you as badly if not more so than you can hurt us."[7]

On the domestic front, the regime inundated the population with the claim that the Shah was independent of oil companies and Western nations and was diligently spending petrodollars to push Iran into the era of the Great Civilization.[8]

The cornerstone of the Great Civilization was a crash program of economic growth that exacerbated all the latent contradictions of a society already experiencing the tumultuous consequences of modernization from above. The Shah poured salt on the wound by raising people's expectations in vain. He promised to distribute the new oil wealth fairly, to increase the average per capita income of Iranians to $2,069 before the end of the decade, and to create a new Iran:[9] "In the next 25 years ... we shall rank among the five biggest powers."[10] The regime made the egregious error of promising too much and of failing to deliver what it had promised. This only created relative deprivation among the people.

Iran's Oil Boom and Bust

The unexpected increase in the price of oil provided the Shah's regime with a golden opportunity to transform Iran into a regional economic and military superpower. But the Pahlavi regime turned this opportunity into a revolution.

The abrupt rise in oil revenues left the government with little time to design a rational economic program compatible with the needs of the economy. Total revenues for the Five-Year Development Plan (1973–1978) were projected at about $49 billion.[11] After the unexpected jump in revenues, the Planning and Budget Organization revised its original estimates. Despite repeated warnings by some planners about the limitations of Iran's absorptive capacity and the pernicious consequences of a sudden economic expansion, the Shah persistently insisted that the original goals of the Five-Year Development Plan be followed at an accelerated rate on an even larger scale. Thus, the expenditures in the Five-Year Development Plan surpassed $145 billion, running $100 billion more than the original estimate, which translated into a per capita increase in government expenditures from $112 in 1970 to $853 in 1978.[12]

A major portion of the petrodollar was allocated to investments in infrastructure, such as road construction.[13] State expenditures for economic affairs jumped from $1.54 billion in 1972 to $7.38 billion in 1976.[14] A small but significant fraction of the petrodollar was channeled to the private sector through low-interest loans. These led to increased investment, which was accompanied by rises in aggregate demand and demand for labor. The high demand for labor made unemployment almost nonexistent and increased the general index of wages.[15] Internal sources could not meet the demand, and hundreds of thousands of workers rushed into Iran. Unskilled workers came from Afghanistan, Pakistan, and the Philippines; skilled labor came from the Western nations, especially the United States. That U.S. and European workers were better paid than their Iranian counterparts increased the cultural tensions between Westerners and Iranians.

Aggregate demand, however, was growing faster than the inefficient, highly protected industrial and manufacturing sectors could respond. The automobile industry is a case in point: Despite the increase in the number of cars manufactured in Iran from 352,000 in 1973 to 1,136,000 in 1979, the value of imported vehicles jumped from $234 million in 1972 to $1.3 billion in 1977.[16] Altogether, the total volume of imports increased from $2.57 billion in 1972 to $14.2 billion in 1977.[17] Increased imports strengthened Iran's dependence on Western nations, contributed to inflation, and further worsened the balance of payments, to name just a few consequences.

The limitation of Iran's absorptive capacity was also reflected in the expansion of the construction sector. Private investment in construction (in constant prices) rose from $1.4 billion in 1972 to $3.1 billion in 1977.[18] Perhaps the most significant consequence of this expansion was the increase in the power of the urban landed class, a class that was to come into direct conflict with the state in 1978.

Not all of the oil revenues were allocated to economic and social programs: The Shah also strengthened the armed forces. As the policeman of the Persian Gulf, the Shah spent much on advanced weaponry. In May 1973, after signing the SALT (Strategic Arms Limitation Talks) Treaty in Moscow, Nixon and Kissinger visited Teheran and assured the Shah that he could purchase the most sophisticated weaponry of the United States short of nuclear weapons. President Nixon ordered the State Department to fill the Shah's orders for the purchase of any weapons without the usual review of such deals by State Department authorities. Consequently, the Shah purchased sophisticated military weapons, most of which could not be operated without direct U.S. supervision. Thus, defense expenditures rose from $77 million in 1970 to more than $7.8 billion in 1978, increasing expenditures per capita from $27 to $220.[19] By 1975, Iran was the world's number one buyer of export military equipment and the world's seventh-largest military spender.[20] The militarization of Iran deepened the country's dependence on the

United States and became a rallying point for the Shah's opponents, who considered so expensive an initiative a plunder of a precious natural resource.[21]

In short, Iran experienced a stupendous economic expansion during the 1972–1976 period: Non-oil GDP, at constant prices, increased from $16.3 billion to $30.5 billion and per capita income rose from $550 to $1,600.[22] The previous state deficits gave way to an impressive $2 billion surplus in 1975 and the net foreign assets of the government exceeded $7.7 billion.[23] The Shah's regime was flying high, indeed.

But the Shah's conception of the petrodollar as an elixir capable of ameliorating all ills was tragically misleading. France's financial support for the American Revolution is rightly claimed to have contributed to the financial crisis of the state that precipitated the French Revolution. It can also be suggested that the economic crisis that befell Iran in the late 1970s paved the way for the Islamic Revolution.

As early as 1975, there were ominous signs of bleak days to come. The limitations of Iran's absorptive capacity had become visible in rapacious rates of inflation, uncontrollable expansion of unproductive activities such as land speculation, and infrastructural bottlenecks such as a dearth of skilled labor and lack of proper port facilities to quickly unload the imported goods. Moreover, because there were no institutional mechanisms for checking the abuse of the authorities in distributing the oil wealth, favoritism, nepotism and corruption had become ubiquitous. The lucky recipients of government loans and subsidies lost what little respect they had for the regime, as they knew that without connections or bribery their fates would have been very different. Those without access to the center of power could not benefit from the many amenities offered by the state and therefore became increasingly disenchanted with the regime.

Despite these warnings, the Shah refused to decelerate the rate of economic growth. In fact, the government increased the taxes and resorted to foreign borrowing because the Shah's ambitious projects had drained the treasury. As such, Iran's surplus of $2 billion in 1974 was turned into a whopping deficit of $7.3 billion in 1978, constituting 24 percent of total government expenditures.[24] Taxes levied on salaried groups increased from $4.02 billion in 1975 to $5.86 billion in 1978.[25]

The Shah's remedy for the imminent economic crisis was based more on political considerations than on sound economic calculation. Thus, the government now took a populist turn.[26] The objectives of this maneuver were threefold: to enlarge the regime's popular base of support by granting concessions to the lower classes and distributing the oil wealth more equitably; to lower rampant inflation; and to exculpate the regime of any wrongdoing by identifying the merchants, the shopkeepers, and the industrialists as the principal culprits of the economic chaos. In that spirit, in August 1975 the Shah added two new articles to the other twelve provisions of his White Revolution of 1963, namely a private and public ownership extension scheme and a price stabilization and antiprofiteering campaign. The private and public ownership extension scheme required the sale of 49 percent of shares of all private manufacturing units and 99 percent of shares of all state-owned factories (with the exception of oil and a number of other strategically vital industries) to the workers, farmers, and the general public. The government was to provide low-interest loans to the workers and farmers who wished to participate in the program. The Shah claimed that in three years more than 4.5 million Iranians would be shareholders in the country's major industrial units.[27] The government, to the dismay of the industrialists, set a minimum wage standard and on many occasions forced the industrialists to capitulate to the higher wage demands of the workers. These policies were adamantly opposed by the industrialists as an unjustifiable intervention of the state in the economic sphere.

To control inflation, the government put into practice its price stabilization and antiprofiteering program.[28] The fight to lower inflation began in 1975 when the government gave the private sector one month to voluntarily lower prices and rents. This method, as expected, proved ineffective. Then the government set restrictive price guidelines for hundreds of items. The government targeted the industrialists, the shopkeepers, and the merchants. The Shah declared that because he had destroyed the feudal lords in 1963, he was now determined to fight the "industrial feudalism" until victory. The government directed a demagogic mass-media blitz against the "irresponsible rich or the parasites of our nation," who, if not controlled, would "plunder the nation." At the same time, the Committee for Protection of the Consumers was established by the government. This committee and the young zealots of the Rastakhiz Party were empowered to identify the price gougers. Prison terms of up to five years, forced internal exile, and confiscation of property were the penalties for price violators. The Shah claimed that 8,000 price gougers were tried in the courts.[29] Others estimated that 17,000 persons were taken to the court and 11,500 of them were convicted.[30] These actions accentuated the antagonism between the state and the bazaar, which shouldered the heaviest burden of the antiprofiteering and price control campaign.

The surgical strikes to this or that sector of the economy were inadequate for realizing the objectives of the Shah's "populism." In mid-1977, because of an energy shortage, different sections of Teheran experienced daily electricity shutoffs, sometimes for as long as six or seven hours. On the eve of the Islamic Revolution, the economy was still overextended, government deficits were high, inflation was high, and the plan to redistribute oil wealth was rendered counterproductive. Most ominous was the sharp decline in the production of Iran's oil exports and oil revenues.[31] The Shah's dream of pushing Iran into the Great Civilization seemed shattered.

Amuzegar's Austerity Program

In the middle of 1977 and in the midst of this economic crisis, the Shah replaced Amir Abbas Hoveyda, the longest-serving prime minister in recent Iranian history. In June 1977, William H. Sullivan, former U.S. ambassador to the Philippines, became the new U.S. ambassador to Iran. In a meeting with the Shah, he expressed his reservations about Iran's economic program. Sullivan recalled that after the meeting, "there was a long gap in which the Shah did not initiate any contact with me." But soon after that meeting, the Shah appointed Jamshid Amuzegar prime minister. Amuzegar was a U.S.-trained technocrat and the leader of the Constructive wing of the Rastakhiz Party. He advocated a slower rate of economic growth and less government intervention in the economy. Sullivan's conclusion reveals the monarch's psychological dependence on U.S. support: "I did not know exactly what cause and effect there was between my conversation with the Shah and the actions that he subsequently took to revise economic programs. ... It suggested that ... a brief word of concern from a friendly outsider could alter significantly the course of his nation's economic future."[32]

In an address to the new cabinet, the Shah set the agenda for the government: to improve housing conditions, lower inflation, put an end to the electricity shortages, and slow down the pace of economic growth.[33] To achieve these objectives, Amuzegar imposed an austerity program, reminiscent of the one implemented by the government in the early 1960s, and moved to improve the state's unfriendly relations with the private sector. To demonstrate his good faith, he appointed four well-known entrepreneurs to ministerial positions in his cabinet. He also promised to stop the expansion of the public sector, lift price controls, and end the antiprofiteering campaign started earlier. Some of his objectives, however, were contradictory. For example, Amuzegar lifted price controls and simultaneously advocated a wage and salary freeze, thus reducing the buying power of the salaried classes. The free-price policy only increased inflation. By mid-1978, Amuzegar reversed his policy and consented to a large increase in wages. Oscillating between satisfying the grievances of the private sector and the demands of the workers and the salaried middle class, he not only failed to improve the deteriorating economic conditions but also intensified public discontent with the incumbent regime.

To compensate for declining oil revenues, Amuzegar increased taxes, began investigating previous tax records to penalize tax evaders, and proposed a new tax system that would have increased taxes. These policies infuriated the merchants and the *asnaf*, among whom the evasion of taxes had become a common practice. He also curtailed a wide range of governmental activities. For example, some monarchists have maintained that a major contributing factor to the ulama's opposition to the Shah's regime was Amuzegar's injudicious decision to substantially lower the allocation of a secret fund from which the ulama received lucrative stipends.[34]

Estimates of the total reduction in state expenditures in the two years preceding the Islamic Revolution range from $6.9 billion in 1977 to $10.2 billion in 1978.[35] Reductions of that magnitude had drastic consequences: Total fixed capital formation by the public sector (at current 1977 prices) decreased from $12.2 billion in 1977 to $7.6 billion in 1978.[36] The total amount of loans granted to the private sector was lowered. The allocation for government-sponsored housing projects for workers, which had risen substantially in the mid-1970s, was lowered.

By 1977, the rate of economic growth had declined considerably. Whereas the average annual rate of increase at constant prices was about 7 percent between 1972 and 1976, it decreased to only 1.7 percent in 1977.[37] The manufacturing sector's average annual rate of increase slowed from 15.8 percent between 1972 and 1976 to only 10.7 percent in 1977.[38] These reductions were ordered precisely when, according to the government, housing shortages and high rents had become a major national issue. The austerity program created a recession within the construction industry. The annual rate of increase in the construction industry was lowered from 14.4 percent in the 1972–1976 period to only 3.2 percent in 1977.[39] This led to the layoff of thousands of construction workers. Moreover, to control land speculation and lower the prices of land and rent, Amuzegar moved against large urban landowners by limiting real estate transactions to one per annum for each individual. In short, every major segment of the economy suffered from declining oil revenues and the austerity program of the Amuzegar administration.

Compounding these difficulties was the government's confrontation with the poor migrants who had erected a shantytown outside the city limits of Teheran. To stop the rapid expansion of this type of dwelling, the regime required the owners to obtain city permits for them. In late 1976, when the police demolished some dwellings for which city permits were not obtained, the residents organized themselves and confronted the police. It was probably the first open confrontation between the state and the people before the start of the revolutionary movement one year later.

As I pointed out in Chapter 1, the specific support given by the population to the state is proportional to the benefits and rewards the state provides the citizens. The Shah's regime used the huge oil wealth to increase this kind of support. As long as the economy was prospering, this policy remained beneficial. Once the oil boom became a bust, the regime quickly lost much of its specific support, which proved devastating.

But as bad as the economic conditions were, I do not suggest that the Islamic Revolution came about because of such conditions—far from it. All available data substantiate the claim that a majority of the population benefited from the oil boom, though not equally. The general standard of living of the large majority of Iranians was even higher during the economic contraction of the late 1970s than in the 1960s. My contention is that the economic expansion, which increased expectations, followed by a period of economic contraction, intensified discontent among many groups. The Shah's regime pursued policies that created a rift between the state and the industrialists and the bazaar merchants and shopkeepers. Despite this situation, had it not been for the coincidence of the economic crisis with the looming political crisis ahead, the Shah's regime would have been financially capable of weathering the storm.

Notes

1. Alexis de Tocqueville, *The Old Regime and the French Revolution* (New York, 1955), p. 176.

2. Eric Hoffer, *The Ordeal of Change* (New York, 1952), p. 4.

3. For the history of oil, see Fereidun Fesharaki, *Development of the Iranian Oil Industry* (New York, 1976).

4. Anthony Sampson, *Seven Sisters* (London, 1976), pp. 140–145, 184–187.

5. Immanuel Wallerstein, "Semi-Peripheral Countries and the Contemporary Crisis," *Theory and Society: Renewal and Critique in Social Theory*, 3 (Winter 1976), pp. 461–483.

6. On Simon's remark, see *New York Times,* July 15, 1974. On Brown's statement, see ibid., October 19, 1976. For an analysis of the coverage of Iran in the 1970s by the major newspapers, see Martin Walker, *Power of the Press* (New York, 1980), pp. 342–393.

7. *New York Times,* March 14, 1976.

8. See Mohammad Reza Pahlavi, *Be Su-ye Tamaddon-e Bozorg* (Toward the Great Civilization) (Teheran, 1977).

9. *Kayhan* (Teheran), September 8, 1975.

10. Quoted by R. K. Karanjia, *The Mind of a Monarch* (London, 1977), p. 243.

11. Iran, Imperial Government, Plan and Budget Organization, *Iran's 5th Development Plan: 1973–1978* (Teheran, 1973), p. 19.

12. Ibid.

13. See Robert Graham, *Iran: The Illusion of Power* (New York, 1979).

14. International Monetary Fund, *Government Finance Statistics Yearbook,* vol. 3 (New York, 1984), p. 98.

15. Ibid., vol. 35 (1982), p. 247.

16. United Nations, *United Nations Statistical Yearbook (1979–80)* (New York, 1981).

17. *Bank-e Markazi-ye Iran: Annual Report and Balance Sheet* (Teheran, 1978), p. 155.

18. Ibid., pp. 154–155.

19. International Monetary Fund, vol. 5 (1981), p. 300.

20. For details, see R. K. Ramazani, *The United States and Iran: The Patterns of Influence* (New York, 1982).

21. Government expenditures for army personnel, which included salaries, rose from $217 million in 1969 to $2,371 million in 1978 (Iran, Imperial Government, *The Budget,* various issues).

22. *Bank-e Markazi-ye Iran* (1979), p. 109; the data on per capita income is based on my calculation from the International Monetary Fund, vol. 35 (1982), p. 249.

23. Ibid., p. 247.

24. International Monetary Fund (1982); *Bank-e Markazi-ye Iran* (1979).

25. *Bank-e Markazi-ye Iran* (1981), p. 34.

26. *Kayhan* (Teheran), September 23, 1975.

27. Ibid., August 7, 1975.

28. Cyrus Sassanpur, "The Influence of Foreign Inflation on the Domestic Economy of Iran," *OPEC Review,* 3 (Winter/Spring 1980), pp. 116–127.

29. Mohammad Reza Pahlavi, *Answer to History* (New York, 1980), p. 156.

30. *Wall Street Journal,* October 16, 1976, p. 1; *Kayhan International,* October 2, 1978; *New York Times,* August 21, 1975.

31. *Bank-e Markazi-ye Iran* (1979), p. 109.

32. William Sullivan, *Mission to Iran* (New York, 1981), p. 71.

33. *Teheran Economist,* August 13, 1977, p. 5.

34. According to the Shah, many of the Shi'i ulama were on the state payroll and in 1977 "due to the exigencies of our economy, Prime Minister Amuzegar was forced to eliminate these payments." Pahlavi (1980), p. 155.

35. Based on my calculation from International Monetary Fund (1982), and *Bank-e Markazi-ye Iran* (1979).

36. *Bank-e Markazi-ye Iran* (1978), p. 78.

37. International Monetary Fund (1982), p. 344.

38. United Nations, *Yearbook of National Accounts Statistics,* vol. 2 (New York, 1980), p. 323.

39. *Bank-e Markazi-ye Iran* (1979), p. 94.

Part Four

The Mechanics of the Transfer of Power

7

The Anatomy of Iran's Revolutionary Movement: From Demanding Reforms to Dethroning a King

He whom many fear, has himself many to fear.

Publilius Syrus, ca. 1 B.C.

The most important thing which a king needs is sound faith, because kingship and religion are like two brothers; whenever disturbance breaks out in the country religion suffers too; heretics and evil doers appear; and whenever religious affairs are in disorder, there is confusion in the country.

Nezamolmolk, Siyasat-nameh (The Book of Government), *1063–1073*

Iran's fascinating revolutionary movement, which started in 1977 and culminated in the Shah's downfall on January 16, 1979, went through eight stages. Benefiting from hindsight, we can see that in the 1977–1979 period the Shah made faulty assumptions about the nature of the emerging movement; that he was reluctant to put to work all the repressive resources at his disposal; and that he acted belatedly to prevent the formation of the alliance of convenience between the secular and Islamic forces. We can see how the United States, the Shah's main bastion of support, was unable to define precisely the objectives for its human rights doctrine and oscillated in its policies toward the beleaguered monarchy, sometimes overestimating the Shah's ability to diffuse the crisis and sometimes underestimating the power of Ayatollah Khomeini's supporters to take over the government. We can see an opposition fragmented and moderate in 1977 but which under the umbrella of Shi'ism and the charismatic leadership of Khomeini gradually became more united and revolutionary in 1978, effectively manipulating all the resources available to it.

Carter's Human Rights Policy and the Shah's Opponents

The beginning of the popular movement that eventually overthrew the monarchy can be traced back to the liberalization of the polity in 1977. Before the liberalization, the organized opposition to the Shah was almost checkmated by SAVAK. The two main guerrilla organizations, the Fada'iyun and the Mojahedin, had suffered internal splits and their leaders had either been killed or jailed by SAVAK. Their constituencies were confined to a very small faction of the population. The Tudeh Party was devoid of any effective organization within Iran. The National Front was kept under the watchful eyes of SAVAK. The Liberation Movement, also under SAVAK's surveillance, was no more than a small group of unarmed Islamic intellectuals who, like the National Front, hoped to make the Shah's autocracy a bit more tolerable. The ulama's ranks were divided, and most of them were not against the institution of the monarchy.

It was SAVAK and the fear it had generated within Iranian society that had kept all these groups at bay. The Shah's regime appeared impregnable, as it enjoyed the support of the Iranian armed forces, the United States, and the major European powers. Because of the combination of these factors, analysts considered Iran an archetypical modernizing, stable society.

But they were wrong. Behind the facade of the Shah's omnipotence stood an insecure regime whose ideas and ideals were basically alien to the majority of the population. Beneath the apparent stability was a closed society on the verge of explosion, brimming with individual frustration, alienation, and hatred of the Shah's regime. True, the organized opposition to the Shah was fragmented, but it had the organizational and financial potential to challenge the government should an opportune moment present itself. The liberalization policy provided this opportunity. Because liberalization coincided with the economic reversal of the 1976–1979 period, which had created acrimony between the state and the merchants, shopkeepers, and industrialists, it allowed the organized opposition to channel the people's deep-seated grievances into collective action.

The Shah was exceptionally sensitive to his image in the international community as a benevolent ruler. A vulnerable aspect of his regime was its ignominious human rights record. The exiled opposition to the Shah in Western Europe and North America in the 1960s and 1970s adroitly manipulated this weakness by contacting human rights organizations and providing them with exaggerated and sometimes fallacious information about a so-called political holocaust in Iran, a country alleged to have had more than 100,000 political prisoners. In 1972, a United Nations panel found Iran guilty of consistent violations of human rights,

probably

3000

and in 1975, Amnesty International conferred on Iran the notoriety of having the world's most terrifying human rights record.[1]

The Shah also occasionally experimented with new ideas to color his regime with an appearance of liberalism. In 1975 the Rastakhiz Party, the symbol of the Shah's utter intolerance for criticism, encouraged the masses to engage in constructive criticism of the government. But this policy was regarded by the cynical population as a vacuous initiative to divert attention from the economic crisis Iran was experiencing.

A second attempt at reform in 1977, however, had drastic consequences and marked a clear discontinuity with the Shah's past policies. Not accidentally, the inauguration of such a reform program coincided with the presidency of Jimmy Carter. Undoubtedly, President Carter's human rights policy, formed amid the internal turmoil and malaise in the United States after its defeat in Vietnam and the Watergate fiasco, pressured the Shah to liberalize his autocratic rule. This development should not be surprising: A dependent country, imperial Iran was not immune to the reverberations of the political vicissitudes of a powerful nation like the United States.

The doctrine that U.S. foreign policy should reflect the most cherished values of the United States, such as respect for human rights, has been a recurring theme in U.S. diplomacy.[2] Thanks to the civil rights and anti–Vietnam War movements of the 1960s, this doctrine became popular in Congress in the 1970s. The passage of the Foreign Assistance Act of 1973, which denied U.S. assistance to any government that practiced "the internment or imprisonment of that country's citizens for political purposes," was a reflection of this trend.[3] This and other initiatives had symbolic significance because the executive branch, which conducted foreign policy, was controlled by those who stressed strategic imperatives, rather than moral considerations, as the cornerstone of foreign policy. "When policy becomes excessively moralistic," wrote former secretary of state Henry Kissinger, "it may turn quixotic or dangerous. A presumed monopoly on truth obstructs negotiation and accommodation."[4]

Campaigning for the presidency, Carter challenged this Kissingerian outlook by advocating the enhancement of human rights around the world. Carter declared that his policy would "remove the reasons for revolutions that often erupt among those who suffer from persecution."[5] Emphasis on human rights as an instrument of foreign policy was to serve as a double-edged sword. Domestically, it was designed to restore the eroded public confidence in the presidency and heal the wounds of the Vietnam nightmare. Internationally, it was to win the hearts and minds of millions suffering under the iron heels of despotic rulers and to expose, in East-West rivalry, the savagery of the East's totalitarian regimes. Carter's shrewd campaigning helped him win the election.

With the new administration came a breed of ideologues and bureaucrats who sincerely wished to weaken, and if possible to sever, U.S. ties with the despotic regimes of the Third World. Products of the antiwar and civil rights movements, they orchestrated a selective campaign against some countries that were in violation of human rights.[6] Iran and Nicaragua were the favorite targets. Zbigniew Brzezinski, Carter's national security adviser (1977–1979), recalled that "the lower echelons at State, notably the head of Iran desk, Henry Precht, were motivated by doctrinal dislike of the Shah and simply wanted him out of power altogether."[7]

Once Carter was inaugurated, his sincere moralistic concerns had to be balanced against the U.S. strategic and economic interests in Iran. Gradually, therefore, the humanitarian rhetoric of the administration and its actual foreign policy became worlds apart, almost hypocritical.

As the ruler of a geopolitically critical and oil-rich country, and an old ally of the United States, the Shah presented a delicate dilemma for the administration: Could human rights be enhanced without offending the Shah and without damaging the economic and military ties between the two countries?[8] The United States continued to sell limited quantities of armaments to Iran while pressuring the Shah to liberalize. William Sullivan, U.S. ambassador to Iran (1977–1979), suggested that through the intermediation of a third nongovernmental organization, reform proposals should be submitted to the Shah so that "the appearance of having been hectored into these improvements by a foreign, albeit friendly, government" would be eliminated.[9]

Thus the Carter administration pursued a self-defeating and inconsistent policy toward Iran.[10] This course of action was mainly the result of the deep division within the Carter administration.[11] One faction, represented by Brzezinski and the National Security Council (NSC), foresaw unpredictable and destabilizing consequences for sudden liberalization. Another faction, championed by the State Department, regarded liberalization as a prerequisite to Iran's long-term stability and ability to resist the communist temptation.[12] And Carter, preoccupied with the negotiations for SALT II and the Camp David Accord, paid little attention to Iran during the early phases of the revolutionary movement. When he did focus on Iran, his record was one of oscillation between the two factions.

Although no major shift in the overall pattern of relations between the two nations was discernible in the 1977–1978 period, political ties between Washington and Teheran were damaged by misunderstanding. This only increased the Shah's suspicion that Washington's real intentions for liberalization were to weaken or perhaps overthrow his regime. In a candid conversation with his friend Nelson Rockefeller, the Shah echoed this suspicion when he asked if "Americans and Russians have divided the world between them."[13] For a shah whose throne was saved by direct U.S. intervention two-and-a-half decades earlier, this perception had catastrophic decisionmaking implications. The human rights campaign worried the Shah, who had never trusted liberal elements of the Democratic Party as his true friends. He not only was politically dependent upon U.S. support but also desperately needed U.S. military equipment to continue modernizing the military. Although the Shah received most of the items he asked for, there were straws in the wind that disturbed him. The Presidential Decision Memorandum 13 in 1977, for example, imposed a dollar ceiling on arms sales to all countries except the members of the North Atlantic Treaty Organization (NATO), New Zealand, and Israel.[14] It infuriated the Shah that Iran was excluded. Moreover, in the congressional debates over the sale of airborne warning and control systems (AWACS), the magnitude of opposition to the Shah became abundantly clear. Also, the Shah's request for the sophisticated "wild weasel" aircraft and some other items were denied. David Aron, a member of the NSC, warned that "if the Shah thinks that he can get everything he wants in the arms field, he is in for a surprise."[15]

Having had carte blanche to buy whatever he wanted short of nuclear weapons during the Nixon and Ford presidencies, the Shah saw these restrictions as ominous. Therefore, early in 1977, most probably to develop a congenial relationship with the new Democratic president and to soften the growing international criticism of his regime, he initiated a liberalization program. Perhaps the terminally ill monarch was planning to abdicate in the early 1980s in favor of his heir apparent and therefore set in motion a series of reforms to facilitate a smooth transition to power for his son, Reza Pahlavi.

The Shah's liberalization program was far-reaching. On the political level, the Shah promised Iranians to "create a free political atmosphere." A braggart regime that only a year earlier was intolerant of diversity of opinion suddenly promised free elections and loosened press censorship.

In the judicial arena and in the treatment of political prisoners, the reforms were also substantial. The Majles passed legislation in November 1977 that required prosecutors to complete preliminary interrogations of the accused within twenty-four hours after arrest. It granted the accused the right to civilian counsel and trial in public rather than by military courts and assured the judges of judicial independence.[16] The Shah declared that political prisoners would not be tortured and ordered the security forces to be tolerant toward dissidents. Hundreds of prisoners were given amnesty. The Red Cross was permitted to inspect the jails. Western observers were allowed to attend the trials of dissidents. The Shah met with the representatives of Amnesty International and the International Commission of Jurists, who personally proposed to him a number of reform measures.

But the most profound impact of Carter's human rights policy and the Shah's liberalization initiatives was psychological: They changed the attitude of the opposition to the Shah and the Shah himself.[17] The U.S. human rights policy generated a perception in Iran that Washington's previous policy of unconditional support for the Shah had changed and that Carter was pressuring the Shah to reform his political system. Gradually, this perception gained more and more acceptance among Iranians. Whether or not this perception was accurate, it gave the opposition a new lease on life, strengthened the spirit of defiance among the population, and slowly shattered the myth of the Shah's invincibility, a myth SAVAK had so painstakingly created in Iran. After all, perceptions in politics are as important as reality.

It soon became obvious that the human rights campaign severely limited the Shah's ability to apply brute force. The opposition to the Shah understood the significance of this new development. In a letter to the ulama in September 1977, Khomeini wrote:

> Today in Iran, a break is in sight; take advantage of this opportunity. ... Today, the writers of political parties criticize; they voice their opposition; and they write letters to the Shah and to the ruling class and sign those letters. You, too, should write; and a few of the Maraja' should sign it. Write about the difficulties and declare to the world the crimes of the Shah. Write the criticism and submit it to them [the authorities], as a few other people who have done so and have said many other things and nobody has bothered them.[18]

Other groups shared the Ayatollah's optimism. One of the forty signatories of an open letter by the Writer's Guild of Iran to Prime Minister Amir Abbas Hoveyda, which was highly critical of the Shah's regime, frankly admitted: "All 40 signed because the government would not dare jail all of us in the present climate of human rights."[19]

The Eight Phases of
Iran's Revolutionary Movement

Phase One: Defensive Mobilization
by the Opposition

Sudden liberalization, albeit limited, in a nation long forced into submission and with no recent encounters with freedom, awakened the dormant opposition against the Shah and created political pandemonium that the regime failed to contain.

The Shah's approach toward liberalization was naive. He had no clear objectives for liberalization nor any well-defined policy on how to loosen the reins. He was prepared to grant the opposition a little room to breathe, but he was unprepared to share power with anyone. Consequently, his policies oscillated erratically between reconciliation with the opposition and repression. This policy was doubly detrimental to the Shah: It diminished his supporters' confidence in his leadership ability and further alienated and radicalized the moderate opposition, which in 1977 was anxious to cooperate with him.

The protest movement against the Shah began in early 1977 when the leaders of the National Front, plus Asghar Haj Seyyed Javadi, a famous writer, and some fifty prominent lawyers began circulating open letters to the Shah and the prime minister lamenting the prevalence of corruption and repression and of the Shah's autocracy.[20] That the signatories of these three letters were not harassed by SAVAK was perceived by the opposition as an auspicious end to the period of outright repression. This perception was reaffirmed by two other incidents. In August, a small group of pro-Khomeini followers demonstrated in front of the Teheran bazaar and demanded the return of the exiled Ayatollah. Surprisingly, the police did not apply force to disperse the crowd. Then on November 3, at the funeral of Khomeini's son, Haj Mostafa, audiocassettes of Khomeini's sermons, smuggled from Iraq, were distributed. To the bewilderment of the opposition, the police did not disturb this gathering.

Gradually, dozens of professional associations like the Association of Iranian Jurists and the Iranian Writers Association were reactivated, and some new ones, like the Iranian Society for the Defense of Human Rights, were created.[21] In October, the Writers Association organized ten nights of well-attended poetry reading in Teheran in which the lifting of government censorship, among a host of other issues, was demanded.[22] The students at the universities were allowed to have peaceful marches and gatherings. Most encouraging to the opposition to the Shah was the violent confrontation in Washington, D.C., between supporters and opponents of the Shah during his formal trip to the United States in November 1977, which was nationally televised in Iran. The opposition in Iran regarded it as another indication that Washington was abandoning its unconditional support for the Shah.

In short, the liberalization policy provided the opposition with its first opportunity since 1963 to begin mobilizing its resources and to plan its strategies against the regime.

In this phase, the protest movement was essentially reformist and nonviolent, with students and secular intellectuals its most vocal components. There is no evidence that the ulama were engaged in any agitational activities at this time, although they could have been involved in revitalizing their network. The fledgling movement represented the aspirations of the modern middle class, which desired to transform Iran into a genuine constitutional monarchy. The emerging movement posed no threat to the Shah because it lacked a charismatic leader to unify its different components and because its leaders, who did not call for the Shah's overthrow, were prepared to collaborate with the Shah.

The government strategy in this phase (March 1977 to December 1978) was to neutralize the emerging movement by organizing, through the Rastakhiz Party, its own pro-Shah rallies; to degrade the opposition leaders as the fossils of a bygone era; and to resist rescinding the liberalization program. More political prisoners were released and more promises for freedom were made.

Washington, meanwhile, continued to pressure the Shah for reforms. In July 1977, William Sullivan became the new U.S. ambassador to Iran, replacing Richard Helms, former CIA director and a schoolmate of the Shah in Switzerland. He welcomed the Shah's liberalization initiatives. Because of the fragmentary character of the reform movement, he reported to Washington that the Shah was in full command of the country and that the opposition was no match for the well-fortified regime. Such optimistic reports encouraged the human rights advocates in Washington to intensify their pressure on the Shah for further liberalization.

Phase Two: Offensive Mobilization and the Entry of the Islamic Forces

On the first day of 1978, President Carter visited Teheran and praised the Shah for creating an oasis of stability in a troubled area.[23] Ironically, soon after Carter's visit, Iran's upheaval entered a new phase. The poorly organized, reformist, non-violent, and decentralized movement that was contained within Teheran gradually transformed into a more coordinated, radical, violent, and centralized movement that was spreading to the major urban centers. Most important, the ulama captured the leadership of the movement, Khomeini in Iraq and Kazem Shariatmadari in Iran, never to relinquish it. Shi'ism became the umbrella under which divergent groups came together and destabilized the government.

The resurgence of Shi'ism should not have been surprising to an alert observer of Iranian politics. In the previous two decades, the revival of Shi'ism as an ideology of protest had become alarmingly visible (see Chapter 5). From 1965 to 1975, for example, some twenty-six exclusively religious publishing houses were established in Teheran alone, and religious books, considered innocuous by state censors, had the highest circulation of any category.[24] In the universities, there was a visible increase in the number of veiled women and Islamic student associations. The imposition by the government of a quota system, in which a predetermined number of students from different provinces were to be admitted to the universities, packed the universities with students from provincial towns and cities. Often from conservative backgrounds, these students were repelled by the decadence of city life and were attracted to the puritanical overtones of Shi'ism, as were the millions of agricultural workers who had migrated to the urban centers. That hundreds of students rioted against coeducation at Teheran University in 1976 was symbolic of the resurgence of Islam.

The spark that precipitated the transformation of the protest movement was the publication of a crass article in two of Teheran's newspapers in early January 1978. It attacked Khomeini as an agent of colonialism and a traitor of non-Persian descent.[25] Perhaps to quell the increasing popularity of Khomeini, the Shah, encouraged by Carter's public declaration of support in Teheran, approved the article.[26] Or perhaps, as was rumored, Hoveyda, the minister of court, not having forgiven Amuzegar for replacing him as prime minister, had the article published to foment internal turmoil, which could lead to the toppling of Amuzegar. Whatever its reasons, the entire opposition condemned the fatuous attacks on Khomeini. The three grand ayatollahs, Shariatmadari, Mohammad Reza Golpayegani, and Najafi Mar'ashi, demanded the article retracted and a public forum created to reply to its contents, but to no avail.[27]

The indignant ulama organized a peaceful rally in Qom on January 9. In support of the protest, the bazaaries closed their shops. When the police arrived, the rally turned violent. More than a dozen people were killed, hundreds were injured, and a few government buildings were set on fire. In condemning the killing, Shariatmadari expressed bewilderment as to why the police had not used tear gas and fire hoses to disperse the crowd.[28] (The armed forces were more trained to deal with external threats and therefore did not know how to apply crowd-control techniques. Iran's request for tear gas from Washington was at first blocked by the human rights activists in the State Department. After one year of waiting, Teheran received its order in November 1978. But it was too late.) Soon after the Qom episode, riots broke out in seven other cities. The bazaars in these cities closed in sympathy with the ulama, marking the entry of the shopkeepers and merchants into the revolutionary movement and their historic alliance with the ulama.

The tempestuous incidents, reactions to the scheme to vilify Khomeini, backfired and elevated Khomeini and Shariatmadari as symbols of the opposition to the Shah's regime. With the new leadership came new methods of mobilization. From now on, the slogans and objectives of the popular movement were carefully crafted in order not to antagonize any faction of the opposition to the Shah and to attract the largest possible audience at home and abroad.

Other characteristics of the second phase were the manipulation of Shi'i symbols and rituals and the bombing of government buildings, all manifested in February in an uprising in Tabriz.[29] The ulama had planned to commemorate the fortieth day of the death of the martyrs of Qom, an Islamic tradition, in the mosques of Tabriz, the home of Shariatmadari. The government, determined to prevent the spread of the movement to Tabriz, ordered the police to block people from entering the mosques. The angry mourners took to the streets and in a few hours burned the Bank-e Saderat, a number of theaters and liquor stores, and the headquarters of the Rastakhiz Party and of the Women's Association. The army intervened at once. It killed some protesters, arrested hundreds, restored calm, and left the city. Disappointed with the performance of the civilian governor of Azerbaijan, the Shah replaced him with a general and demoted some SAVAK officials. The government attributed the riot to a "foreign conspiracy."

Shariatmadari condemned the government for its brutality but did not condone violence by the opposition. From Iraq, Khomeini praised the heroic resistance of Tabriz, implicitly legitimizing revolutionary violence. It was now clear that the orthodox and the fundamentalist ulama had substantial differences in their tactics against the government.

With the Tabriz uprising as inspiration, protests quickly spread to other cities. As more protesters were killed in every uprising, the subsequent forty-day commemorations to honor the dead became larger and more potent. The pulpits were now used by the ulama to implicitly attack the Shah. The ulama relied on thousands of mosques, *hey'at*s, Islamic associations, and the bazaar to mobilize the masses against the government. This massive network of mobilization proved effective and extremely difficult for the authorities to contain. It was perhaps not accidental that the first major uprising occurred in Tabriz and that martial law was first imposed in Esfahan in 1978; Tabriz and Esfahan had more mosques and *takiyes* than any other city except Teheran.[30] And no other group exploited this network as effectively as Khomeini's supporters. They were convinced that direct confrontation with the government, even if it involved bloodshed, would but radicalize the movement and expose the regime's atrocities.[31]

The government was still in control, and SAVAK was monitoring the activities of the leaders of the protest movement. Nor was there any evidence that antigovernment activities were coordinated through a hierarchical command structure. More significant, moderates in the protest movement and some of the ulama were prepared to collaborate with the Shah. They were uncertain about the Shah's sincerity, though, and needed tangible assurance that the promise of free elections would not be used as a catalyst for restoration of order to be followed by suppressive measures, as the Shah had done so often before. Mehdi Bazargan, from the Liberation Movement, for example, informed the U.S. Embassy on May 30 that "if the Shah is ready to implement all provisions of the Constitution, then we are prepared to accept the monarchy and participate in the elections."[32] The National Front expressed similar views.

In retrospect, what proved most detrimental to the government was the Shah's indecision. On the one hand, he continued with his liberalization: The Free Election Bill, which promised free elections in June 1979, was submitted to the Majles; more prisoners were released; General Ne'matollah Nassiri, SAVAK's director for many years, was replaced with the "liberal" General Naser Moqaddam; the royal family was forbidden to engage in business deals with the government; the antiinflation/antiprofiteering campaign was stopped to appease the shopkeepers and the merchants; and the Shah made a visit to the holy shrine in Mashhad and promised to reopen the Feyziyeh theological school in Qom to please the ulama. On the other hand, he took strong actions to suppress the growing revolutionary movement. Constant surveillance of target areas, such as banks, by the police and harsh punishment of the arrested suspects led to a temporary lull in bombings in the major cities. To flaunt its popularity, the government organized large rallies in the major cities. It formed secret Action Committees and Resistance Corps, which physically attacked the regime's opponents, and arrested a number of opposition leaders.[33]

In short, the Shah hoped to be the impossible: a "democratic autocrat," to liberalize with one hand and to take away what he had given with the other. His "democratic" side created confusion for his security forces, which were sometimes asked to maintain order without relying on brute force. His autocratic side alienated his constitutionalist critics as concessions followed by harassment made them skeptical of the Shah's intentions.

Rather than redress the opposition's grievances, the government orchestrated a campaign to discredit its opponents as puppets of foreign powers. A bloody military coup in neighboring Afghanistan in April 1978, in which the civilian government of President Mahmmoud Dawud was overthrown by a pro-Moscow faction of the armed forces, gave the Shah a new propaganda theme to attack the opposition as communist inspired. By treating the entire opposition movement as a homogeneous entity, which it certainly was not, the regime was weakening the moderates and inadvertently strengthening the radicals. The Shah and many policymakers in Washington made the fallacious assumption that the moderate secular forces would not form an alliance with the ulama. Hence, no serious initiative was launched to prevent the eventual alliance between these forces. Nor did the regime attempt to manipulate the differences between the fundamentalist and orthodox ulama by driving a wedge between them.

Ambassador Sullivan was aware of both the growing power of the Islamic forces and the Shah's confusion. His evaluation of both issues, however, changed as the crisis unfolded. Only a week after the Qom riot of January 1978, he reported to Washington that although the ulama had an impressive organizational network, "they would probably find it difficult to generate additional demonstrations immediately for purely political purposes."[34] He also reported that the Shah was in full command of the situation. Four months later in May, he cabled Washington that "the normal conclusion that many draw is that he [the Shah] is losing his touch."[35] He also expressed his growing unease about the power of the ulama and indicated his desire to contact them. Although Secretary of State Cyrus Vance instructed Sullivan in June 1978 to "meet with low-level figures [ulama] to find out about the nature of the opposition,"[36] Sullivan claimed that during 1978 he met with Ayatollah Mahdavi Kani only late in the year. But as it turns out, the U.S. Embassy had some contact with the Islamic forces throughout the second half of the year.

Phase Three: The Shah in Retreat

In this phase, the Shah's indecision and confusion became even more visible. The opposition could easily observe the signs of lassitude in the Shah: He had no appetite to confront the movement with decisive and shrewd maneuvering. In a system long dominated by one man, nothing could have been more fatal than this perception by the opposition. At the same time, all the opposition forces moved one step closer to unification. The hit-and-run tactic of the opposition in the earlier phases gave way to direct confrontation with the security forces. And with Khomeini gaining free access to the Western media, a war of nerves had begun between him and the Shah—a war in which the Ayatollah proved to be the master tactician.

By the end of July 1978, the situation had reached so critical a level that the Shah postponed a scheduled Eastern European trip. In early August, a new spate of uprisings struck the major cities, especially Esfahan. There the arrest of an obscure clergyman precipitated a bloody riot that resulted in substantial loss to property and the imposition of martial law. A few days later, Shiraz, Ahvaz, and Tabriz also went under curfew, making the revolutionary movement truly national in scope.

Still reverberating from these uprisings, the regime was jolted by another bombshell. On August 19, more than 400 men, women, and children were burned to death when the Cinema Rex in Abadan was set ablaze by arsonists. The government blamed the Islamics/Marxists and the opposition castigated the regime for having committed the atrocity to discredit its opponents.[37] The tragic accident galvanized the revolutionary movement, led to the first massive and peaceful anti-Shah rally in Teheran, and forced the government into a defensive posture. Amid growing chaos, Premier Amuzegar, not known for his political savvy, was dismissed by the Shah.

Iran was now on the brink of revolution: Riots showed no signs of abating and the opposition was becoming more bellicose. The opposition was still divided into two camps. The moderates, which included the National Front, the Liberation Movement, and a considerable number of orthodox ulama under the leadership of Ayatollah Shariatmadari, favored peaceful reform and were not calling for the Shah's overthrow. The revolutionary camp, consisting of the pro-Khomeini forces and the guerrilla organizations, demanded radical change.

To weather the storm, the Shah had to act decisively. He either had to crush the growing movement or to relinquish some of his power and strike a deal with the moderate faction of the popular movement. He opted to do neither.

Contradictory counsel was offered to the Shah. On the one hand, William Sullivan and British ambassador Anthony Parsons admonished him that their respective governments would not tolerate an ironfisted approach and favored a peaceful resolution to the crisis. Sullivan, Brzezinski wrote, never explicitly urged the Shah to be tough.[38] Some of his advisers, especially those gathered around the Queen (Farah), also urged the Shah to grant more concessions to the opposition. On the extreme other hand, the hawks, including General Gholam Ali Oveyssi and Brzezinski, pressured the Shah to rescind the liberalization and to begin a mass arrest of the more powerful members of the opposition. Brzezinski argued that "the deliberate weakening of the beleaguered monarch by American pressure for further concessions would simply enhance instability and eventually produce complete chaos."[39]

The Shah finally succumbed to the forces that favored a peaceful resolution of the crisis. But he was unprepared to relinquish power and to become a figurehead monarch by appointing an independent-minded figure from the moderate faction of the protest movement to head the government. His refusal to relinquish power revealed his ignorance about the nature of the ongoing upheaval. The Shah appeared completely isolated from the realities of the revolutionary movement. He was truly a prisoner of the system he had created, a system that rewarded sycophancy and submission and punished constructive criticism and truthfulness.

In late August 1978, the Shah appointed Ja'far Sharif Imami to lift him out of the political quagmire. In retrospect, Imami was the Shah's last chance to diffuse the explosive turmoil. Imami, a prime minister in the early 1960s, was politically astute but devoid of popular support. He was a symbol of the decadent system that the opposition was struggling to demolish.

To save the beleaguered monarchy, Imami called for national reconciliation. His top priorities were to appease the ulama and, if possible, to drive a wedge into their front. He abolished the portfolio of the minister of state for women's affairs; created a new ministry for religious endowments; shut down the few operating casinos; closed many nightclubs; restored the Islamic calendar; granted freedom of activity to political parties; lifted censorship of the media; allowed parliamentary debates to be televised; began an anticorruption campaign; gave an across-the-board salary increase to government employees; ordered swift punishment for the officials responsible for killing the protesters in Tabriz and Esfahan; and, finally, dissolved the Rastakhiz Party, the Shah's last organized source of civilian support.[40] The bulk of these concessions had been demanded by the opposition just a few short months earlier but had been rejected by the Shah, who always seemed to be a few steps behind the popular demands. These concessions polarized the division between the hawks and the doves within the Shah's small circle of advisers, but they were welcomed by thousands of exiled Iranians, many of whom returned to Iran and joined the bandwagon of the revolutionary movement.

The response by the opposition leaders to Imami's reforms ranged from conditional approval to outright rejection. Ayatollah Shariatmadari declared that he would give the new government three months, until November 1978, to resolve the tension between the people and the government. The National Front, under the leadership of Karim Sanjabi, called Imami's reforms a sham and publicized its own twelve-point program, which, among other issues, demanded the dissolution of SAVAK and immediate release of all political prisoners. No mention was made of dismantling the monarchy.[41]

Unfortunately, the Black Friday tragedy on September 8, which took place only a few weeks after Imami's appointment, dashed the hopes for any rapprochement between the government and the moderate faction of the opposition. The exact course of events leading to the tragedy is not known. What is clear is that the opposition forces planned a demonstration into Jaleh Square. The army, alarmed by the size of the previous rallies, pressured Imami to impose martial law and curfew in Teheran and eleven other cities on the evening of September 7, 1978. Imami agreed and appointed General Gholam Ali Oveyssi military governor of Teheran. On September 8, there was a major demonstration in and around the Jaleh Square in Teheran. Because the demonstrators ignored the curfew restrictions,[42] the police opened fire on the crowd. According to government sources, 86 protesters were killed; according to the opposition, 3,000 protesters were killed.[43]

The bloody incident had a devastating impact on the ailing Shah.[44] British ambassador Anthony Parsons found the Shah on September 16 "exhausted and drained of spirit." To heal the wounds of Black Friday, the Shah granted amnesty to some 1,400 more political prisoners, including some of Khomeini's supporters; restricted SAVAK's power; and promised lavish financial support to families of the victims of the Cinema Rex fire and the Black Friday massacre.

In desperation, Imami turned to Ayatollah Khomeini. He declared that Khomeini was free to return to Iran and that government representatives would go to Najaf to negotiate with him. But the cantankerous Ayatollah intensified his virulent attacks on the Shah, calling Imami's concessions "cosmetic." In response, Imami requested that the Iraqi government either limit Khomeini's agitational activities or force him out of Iraq. Saddam Hossein's government, having cordial relations with the Shah, expelled Khomeini. He was permitted by France, with the Shah's prior approval, to go to Neauphle le-Château, in the vicinity of Paris.[45] Iranian officials supposed that Khomeini's hegira to a Western nation would substantially reduce his activities and would expose to the world the reactionary mentality of the Ayatollah. But the exact opposite happened. During his 114-day residence in France, Khomeini's enigmatic personality became the focus of the Western media, and Neauphle le-Château became the Mecca for the opposition against the Shah. With the assistance of his Western-educated advisers like Ebrahim Yazdi, Abolhassan Bani Sadr, and Sadeq Qotbzadeh, Khomeini skillfully exploited the modern communication system to spread his gospel.

With Khomeini in Paris, the situation in Iran was irrevocably changed. Shariatmadari was by now disgusted with the regime's irrational policy of repression following concession; he began for the first time to express doubts about the possibility of any compromise with the regime.[46] In its now regular meetings with the U.S. Embassy officers, Bazargan's Liberation Movement requested a high-level meeting with U.S. officials to pave the way for "transition from present authoritarian government to a more democratic system" within the confines of the 1906 Constitution.[47]

Available documents about U.S. policy in this phase are contradictory and reflect the self-delusion of the policymakers. The U.S. foreign policy establishment, having for so long supported the Shah, was sluggish in adjusting to Iran's revolutionary situation. In one corner, the CIA in late August 1978 concluded that "Iran is not in a revolutionary or even prerevolutionary situation" and across the way the Defense Intelligence Agency (DIA) predicted in September that "the Shah is expected to remain actively in power for the next ten years."[48]

Despite such faulty analysis, the U.S. government at least tried to learn more about the opposition. We know that the U.S. Embassy was in frequent contact with the Liberation Movement and other groups and that Professor Richard Cottam, a prominent Iran expert, visited Khomeini in Najaf in August 1978. He reported that the Ayatollah did not endorse the idea of direct rule by the ulama in the post-Shah period.[49]

Phase Four: National Strikes and Unification of the Opposition

In October and November workers and public employees entered into the revolutionary movement. Months of paralyzing nationwide strikes ensued.

As soon as schools opened, the teachers were the first to go on strike, thus making thousands of students available for street demonstrations. Soon, government employees joined the strikers. In the beginning, the strikers' demands were exclusively economic in nature. But gradually, as the leadership of the trade unions previously under SAVAK's control was replaced by a new generation of radical elements, the strikers' demands became overtly political. Critical factors that prolonged the strikes were the financial support given by the prosperous bazaar merchants and shopkeepers to the strikers and Khomeini's *fatva* making it permissible for the ulama to give half of the religious tithes to the families of the strikers.[50]

Of the many strikes, those by the electrical and especially the oil workers hammered the final nail into the coffin of the Pahlavis. The former created periodic blackouts in Teheran and forced many factories to shut down and lay off workers. The latter deprived the government of much-needed oil revenues and led to shortages of heating oil in the cold winter.

As Imami's stratagem failed to end the strikes and restore order, the desperate Shah finally approached a number of secular opposition leaders to save him from imminent collapse. The venerable Hossein Saddiqi, a member of the National Front and a minister in the Mossadeq cabinet, agreed to form a new government contingent on the Shah's staying in Iran, as there was a rumor that he was planning to leave the country. Sanjabi was also approached by the Shah. He gave an ambivalent answer to the Shah and asked to be allowed to consult with the Ayatollah in Paris. The Shah welcomed the suggestion, and Sanjabi left for Paris in early November. In Paris, he changed his position. In a written statement signed by Sanjabi and verbally blessed by Khomeini, it was declared that the existing monarchy had no constitutional or religious legitimacy; that as long as the illegal monarchical order survived, the "Nationalist-Islamic Movement of Iran will not approve of any form of government"; and that in accordance with the precepts of Islam, democracy, and independence, and through a national referendum, the future political system of Iran would be determined.[51] (The Paris declaration was never approved by the Central Committee of the National Front in Iran.[52]) With this historic declaration, the secular nationalists formed a de facto alliance with the fundamentalists, the same force they had refused to collaborate with in June 1963. Strange bedfellows indeed. For all practical purposes, the declaration marked the start of the progressive decline of the National Front as a viable force. Sanjabi probably signed the declaration of unity with Khomeini believing that once the Shah was deposed, his National Front and not the ulama would inherit the government.

With the largest faction of the National Front joining Khomeini's forces, the historic alliance among the ulama, the bazaar, and the intelligentsia was now complete. The latest additions to the alliance were the workers, making the revolutionary movement multiclass in essence. Short of a miracle, nothing could save the Shah. The prosperous industrialists and the rich, two of the pillars of the Shah's regime, recognized the symptoms and accelerated the export of their capital to Western nations. They soon followed the path of their capital, moving by the hundreds to the Western nations.

As Iran plunged deeper into turmoil, the disagreement within the Carter administration also deepened. The Shah continued to receive contradictory messages: from the State Department to grant concessions and from the NSC to get tough. By late October, the State Department had concluded that the "Shah's autocracy was over" but perhaps not his rule. The State Department saw two possible successors to the Shah: "the generals and the secular political opposition."[53] But Ambassador Sullivan had cabled Washington on October 28 that "our destiny is to work with the Shah."

Ayatollah Khomeini, who at this phase had emerged as a popular alternative to the Shah, adhered to an effective three-pronged strategy. First, he called on the people to continue with their nationwide strikes. Second, he sent conciliatory messages to the rank and file of the Iranian armed forces, inviting them to join the revolutionary movement. And finally, he emphasized only the common objectives of the oppositional forces, such as national independence, freedom, and democracy.

Although many Marxists participated in the revolutionary movement and accepted Khomeini's leadership, Khomeini never formed an alliance with them.[54] In November 1978, the Tudeh Party's chief, Iraj Eskandari, recognized Khomeini's leadership in Paris and called for a united front against the Shah. Khomeini did not even bother to respond. The Marxists, like the National Front, deceived themselves into believing that after the Shah's departure from the political scene, Khomeini's movement would quickly vanish and they could emerge as a powerful force. They were so obsessed with overthrowing the Shah and so mesmerized by the growing mass movement that they failed to pose serious questions about Khomeini's intentions. Later, when Khomeini created a theocracy in Iran, they complained that he had deceived the population about his real intentions. But they had no one to blame but themselves, for they had chosen not to pay attention to Khomeini's ideas in *Islamic Government,* where they could have discovered his political predilections. They gambled that the Ayatollah would lose, but they lost.

Phase Five: Desperation
and Military Government

By November 1978, Imami's failure to settle the strikes, restore order, and reach consensus with any faction of the opposition on the one hand and the growing belligerence of the protest movement on the other left Mohammad Reza Shah Pahlavi in the most critical period of his long reign. To save his endangered throne, the ailing Shah finally turned to his most trusted ally, the armed forces.

On November 5, 1978, a jubilant crowd, celebrating the release of the popular Ayatollah Mohmood Taleqani from jail, went on a rampage and burned government buildings, theaters, and other favorite targets. Teheran was on fire. Apparently, General Gholam Ali Oveyssi, the martial law commander of Teheran, had ordered the soldiers not to intervene in order to persuade the Shah to give the hawks in the military a chance to begin a crackdown on the opposition. The Shah, terminally ill with leukemia, despondent over the contradictory signals he was receiving from Washington, and with his hopes of reaching a compromise with the moderate opposition all but dashed, selected with little perspicacity General Gholam Reza Azhari, an ailing old man and the chief of staff of the Iranian armed forces, to head the military government. His appointment was another defeat for the hard-liners in the military. The installation of the military government was to admonish the opposition leaders that the regime had unlimited repressive capabilities and that it would make sense for them to compromise with the Shah.

Azhari pursued a strategy of reconciliation and repression in order to buy the Shah more time to find a civilian prime minister. Consequently, the military government, which consisted of only six military ministers, turned out to be a farce, as the Shah had ordered Azhari to "do the impossible, to avoid bloodshed."[55] The Shah's inconsistency reached tragic proportions when one day after the installation of the military government he recognized the legitimacy of the people's uprising in a nationally televised speech. Looking pale and apprehensive, he said: "The Revolution of the Iranian people cannot be disapproved by me. ... Once again before the Iranian people I swear that I will not repeat the past mistakes and I assure you that previous mistakes, lawlessness, oppression, and corruption will not happen again. ... I, too, have heard the voice of your Revolution."[56] This was the obituary of the Pahlavis read by the Shah. Had the Shah truly heard the voice of the unfolding revolution, reason would have dictated that he not impose a military government. Further, having installed a military government, it was not an opportune moment to apologize for past policies. It was now clear that the Shah was paralyzed by an absence of will.

Khomeini grasped the Shah's weakness and exploited it by warning Iranians not to be credulous and give another chance to the "satanic Shah who has already admitted to being a traitor." He encouraged the continuation of the strikes and called for desertion within the army.[57]

The Shah's confusion and Khomeini's refusal to collaborate with the government made Azhari's job difficult, if not impossible. At first, it appeared that he might restore order: Oil production temporarily increased and a few strikes were settled. He stopped foreign currency exchange to halt the export of capital from Iran; he began an anticorruption campaign that included investigation of the business dealings of the Pahlavi family; and he ordered the arrest of prominent members of the regime like former prime minister Amir Abbas Hoveyda and former SAVAK chief Ne'mattollah Nassiri. These actions sent shock waves through the ruling class, which saw them as an invidious scheme by the Shah to sacrifice them to save his dynasty. Consequently, thousands of people, mostly those who could have provided support to the monarch during his hour of need, fled Iran.

Any positive impact of the concessions by Azhari to the opposition was quickly forgotten when he reimposed censorship, restricted freedom of assembly, and arrested some opposition leaders, including Bazargan and Sanjabi.

As the popular movement grew stronger, the Carter administration became more confused and divided. Only a day before the selection of General Azhari, Brzezinski, with Carter's authorization, had called the Shah to express U.S. support for whatever decision the Shah had to make, including a show of force.[58]

But the State Department and Ambassador Sullivan had different plans for the Shah. By mid-November, the State Department was adjusting itself to the realities of an Iran without the Shah, Secretary Vance recalled.[59] Sullivan, who was vehemently against the imposition of the military government, and who on October 28 had cabled Washington insisting that "our destiny is to work with the Shah" and saying "I would strongly oppose any overture to Khomeini," changed his mind three days after the appointment of Azhari.[60] In a cable to Washington that he called "Thinking the Unthinkable," Sullivan posited a situation in which after the army's failure to restore order not only the Shah but "most of the senior Iranian military officers would leave the country. Understandings about the nature of a successor regime would be reached between the religious leadership and the new, younger military leadership. In such understandings, Ayatollah Khomeini would have to choose a government headed by moderate figures like Bazargan and Minatchi, and eschew the 'Naser-Qadhafi' types, which I assumed he would prefer."[61]

Further, Sullivan predicted that Khomeini would play a Gandhi-like role in the post-Shah period and that an Islamic government, run by leaders of the National Front type, would be the most likely outcome of the revolution—a government that would be friendly to the United States. At least from that moment, Sullivan used his clout to lead Iran in the direction of an Islamic government, sometimes to the dismay of President Carter.[62]

Upon receiving Sullivan's cable, Carter finally realized both the gravity of the Iranian crisis and the misleading essence of the intelligence reports he had been receiving from different U.S. agencies. He tried to put his administration in order, but with little success.

As the Shah was looking for someone to save his sinking ship, Khomeini for the first time began publicly to elaborate some general ideas about the future form of government in Iran, namely an Islamic Republic. In his declaration on November 5, 1978, he explicitly indicated that the "goal of our Islamic movement is to demolish the monarchical order" and to establish an "Islamic Republic which is the protector of Iran's independence and democracy."[63] Convinced that religion was a dying force and confident that they would rule in the post-Shah era, the National Front and the leftists did not pressure Khomeini to discuss the nature of his Islamic republic. In retrospect, both Khomeini and his secular supporters refrained from discussing the system they strived to create in order to ensure the unity of their fragile coalition against the Shah.

Phase Six: A Walking Referendum
on the Monarchy

By early December, which coincided with the holy month of Moharram, when the faithful commemorate the Karbela tragedy through weeping and self-flagellation, it became abundantly clear that Azhari's military government was unable to contain the revolutionary movement. The leaders of the popular movement exercised much more control over the masses and proved to be more creative and effective manipulators of their mobilizing resources than the military government. When the military government forbade assembly after dusk, the Islamic leaders urged the masses to go to the roofs of their homes exactly at the beginning of the curfew hours and loudly chant "Allah is great." This peaceful show of force and unity, in which millions participated, turned Teheran into the largest chorus in the world. It truly demoralized the government.

The military government at first threatened to use force against the violators of martial law. Carter's press conference on December 7 was discouraging to the military government. When asked about the Shah's chances for survival, the President answered: "I don't know. ... This is something in the hands of the Iranian people."[64] (The White House quickly reiterated U.S. support for the Shah, but the damage had already been inflicted on the monarch.) At any rate, through the mediation of Ali Amini, the former prime minister, the opposition and the military authorities reached an agreement that in exchange for the government's policy of confining the soldiers to barracks and permitting the processions, the opposition would assure peaceful rallies.[65]

For Tasu'a and 'Ashura (December 10 and 11), the climax of Moharram ceremonies, the opposition called for two rallies. They thus killed two birds with one stone: A government ban on the processions would have further revealed the sacrilegious policies of the Shah, and approving them would have provided a golden opportunity for the opposition to show off to the world the immensity of their popular base of support. It was a skillful manipulation of religion for political ends.

The two days of rallying were peaceful and orderly. Millions of people participated in the anti-Shah marches in Teheran and other cities. The marches were superbly organized and massive. The rallies produced a seventeen-point declaration, a compromise between the Islamic and nationalist forces. This declaration recognized Khomeini's leadership and called for an end to the Shah's rule and the creation of a government based on Islamic precepts—this vague point should not be confused with the idea of the Islamic Republic elucidated in Khomeini's November 6 declaration—and for the implementation of such egalitarian measures as emancipation of women, distribution of wealth, and so forth. The document did not mention dismantling the monarchical order.

The horrified Shah saw the rallies as a machination by his foreign enemies. The dauntless opposition interpreted them as a walking referendum for dismantling the Shah's rule.

In the crowd were men and women from all walks of life, young and old, rich and poor, educated and illiterate. Studies of the banners carried and slogans chanted in the rallies revealed that hatred of the Shah was the unifying theme. One study showed that 38 percent of the slogans and banners were against the person of the Shah, 31 percent for an Islamic Republic, and 16 percent in praise of Khomeini.[66] Another study concluded that 50 percent of the more than 800 slogans identified were anti-Shah, 20 percent pro-Khomeini, and 30 percent for the Islamic forces.[67]

The rallies shattered any illusions the Shah might have had about Azhari's ability to end the turmoil. He had two alternatives: to surrender to the opposition by leaving Iran or to pursue an ironfisted policy. While he was contemplating his options, the Ball Commission, created by presidential order to study the Iran crisis, reached the conclusion that if the Shah "did not act immediately to cede real authority to a civilian government," his chances for survival were minimal.[68] Among its other proposals was the formation of a Council of Nobles, comprised of prominent anti-Shah figures, to facilitate the transition to a civilian government. For different reasons, Brzezinski and Sullivan opposed the Ball Commission's proposal: the former because it would have undermined a close ally, and the latter because it contradicted his own plans and was considered, rightly so, too late to have any merit.

Brzezinski and, to a lesser degree, Secretary of Defense Harold Brown advocated a tough policy by the Shah, even if it involved bloodshed. Vance, Sullivan, and George Ball favored a political solution, even if it meant the downfall of the Shah, because reliance on force not only contradicted the human rights policy but also could have led to the disintegration of the armed forces, whose integrity they deemed essential to U.S. interests. (According to Vance, this view was supported by Carter and the British ambassador to Iran, Anthony Parsons.) The feeling of the State Department was succinctly summarized by Henry Precht from the Office of Iranian Affairs at the State Department: "We must move with definite steps towards a post-Shah future in Iran."[69]

Aware of the division within the Carter administration, the Shah on December 26 asked Sullivan about U.S. reaction to a possible ironfisted policy. Sullivan was instructed from Camp David to inform the Shah that a civilian government was preferable but that only if it failed to restore order, and only if the armed forces were in danger of disintegration, should the Shah "choose without delay a firm military government which would [end disorder]."[70] The message, a compromise between the two factions of the administration, epitomized the ignorance of the policymakers about the unfolding crisis and further confused the Shah. As Secretary Vance frankly admitted, the cable was primarily intended to assure that the Shah not weaken the armed forces in order to save his throne. At this stage, nothing short of a massacre of the pro-Khomeini masses by the police could have saved the Shah.

Knowing that the Western nations would not tolerate an ironfisted policy, and that his military government could not even implement its own martial laws, the Shah desperately looked for a civilian prime minister. Ali Amini was approached. He requested control of SAVAK and of the armed forces, which the Shah rejected.[71] Once again the Shah turned to the National Front. Saddiqi was still asking for more time, and Sanjabi had switched to the Ayatollah's camp. Short on credible candidates, he negotiated with Shahpur Bakhtiyar, a junior member of the Mossadeq administration. Bakhtiyar agreed to form a government contingent upon the Shah's departure from Iran. The Shah agreed, and on December 31, Bakhtiyar announced his goal of resuscitating the corpse of the Pahlavi dynasty.

As the Shah was preparing for his inevitable departure, Khomeini made his first major move to create an alternative polity: In late December 1978, he asked Mehdi Bazargan to form a committee consisting of Hojatolislam Hashemi Rafsanjani, Mostafa Katira'i, and two other members to be selected by Bazargan himself to go to the oil fields and convince the workers to produce enough oil for domestic consumption.[72] The immediacy with which this committee realized its goal was a clear indication that it was Khomeini who was now Iran's strongman. That the National Front was not asked to participate in the settlement of the oil strike was the beginning of a series of actions by Khomeini to exclude it from important political positions.

Phase Seven: Neutralization of the Army and the Shah's Exile

With the announcement of the Shah's imminent departure, the political crisis suddenly took a new turn. Because no one believed that the Shah would peacefully capitulate, the prevalent view among the opposition was that the armed forces would eventually stage a bloody coup against them. Vance quoted Sullivan as saying in late December that the armed forces "are now determined to move, that they will not let the Shah leave the country, and that they are prepared for a massive crackdown which will involve a lot of blood being spilled."[73] Professor Richard Cottam, who visited Teheran in early January 1979, confirmed to the State Department the accuracy of Sullivan's report.

The opposition was perturbed by the prospect of a coup in the making.[74] Ayatollah Shariatmadari, through an intermediary, asked the U.S. Embassy to prevent a military coup.[75] So did Abbas Amir Entezam on behalf of the Liberation Movement.[76] In his first known meeting with Warner Zimmerman of the U.S. Embassy in Paris in mid-January, Ebrahim Yazdi, speaking for Ayatollah Khomeini, indicated that the U.S. blocking of a coup by the Shah's generals would be a positive gesture for building friendly relations between Washington and the soon-to-be-installed Islamic government.

The fear of military intervention was justifiable: When armed forces put their full might against insurgents, revolutions rarely succeed.[77] This is why the opposition to the Shah at this phase began contacting high officials of the armed forces, hoping to win their allegiance. Equally concerned was President Carter, who sent General Robert E. "Dutch" Huyser, the deputy commander of U.S. forces in Europe, to Teheran.

Without the Shah's prior knowledge, Huyser arrived in Teheran on January 5, 1979, a day after the convening of the Guadeloupe Conference, at which the leaders of the major Western nations decided to ask the Shah to leave Iran.[78] There is a universal consensus that two of Huyser's priorities were to protect the sensitive listening posts in place in Iran near the Soviet borders and to prevent sophisticated U.S. equipment like the F-14 jets and Phoenix air-to-air missiles from falling into unfriendly hands.[79] He also was to provide the President with an independent assessment of the capability of the Iranian military because the President was skeptical of Sullivan's reports.

The principal task of the Huyser mission, however, remains elusive. Was it, as British ambassador Anthony Parsons and so many Iranian generals claim, to nip in the bud any attempt by the generals to stage a pro-Shah coup?[80] Or, was it, as Huyser insisted, to prevent the disintegration of the armed forces, to convince the generals to support Prime Minister Bakhtiyar, and to prepare the army to take over the government should public order collapse?[81] Whatever its real goals, the mission was bound to fail before it was launched because Huyser "was asked to satisfy both American factions [Vance and Brzezinski] … and at once organize and prevent a *coup d'état,* encourage and restrain the Iranian generals, support Bakhtiyar and a military organization that had pledged its loyalty to the Shah."[82]

According to Huyser, the top echelons of the Iranian armed forces were hysterical. They unanimously agreed that the Shah should not leave Iran and that if he did, they would leave with him. They viewed the revolutionary movement as a communist conspiracy and blamed Sullivan for pressuring the Shah to leave.[83] General Amir Hossein Rabi'i, the chief of the Air Force, told Huyser that "your Ambassador is forcing our Shah to leave the country."[84] "My government," responded Huyser, "have always told me that the Shah's departure was to be at his own will."[85] But, as it turned out, Washington did in fact directly pressure the Shah to leave Iran.

Huyser confirmed that five of the Shah's generals, or Group of Five, were planning to stage a coup to prevent the Shah's departure.[86] To Huyser's amusement, however, the Group of Five had not worked out the logistical aspects of such a coup. Huyser attributed the lack of planning and the failure of various units in the armed forces to coordinate their activities during the revolutionary movement to the internal organization of the armed forces and to the quality of the Shah's leadership. To prevent a coup against his dynasty, the Shah had never permitted the service chiefs to collectively meet with the chief of the supreme commanders' staff or with him. The service chiefs reported to him individually. To win his confidence, they spied on and were suspicious of one another. Moreover, over the years they had become dependent on the Shah, who "made all decisions … even those [which] in most military organizations would have been made by lieutenant colonels or colonels."[87] The generals, Huyser concluded, were not trained to be problem solvers; they were only the executors of the Shah's orders.[88]

Of the generals who regularly met with Huyser, only Abbas Qarabaghi, the Shah's last chief of staff, has written his version of the events, which in many cases contradicts Huyser's. In his first meeting, Qarabaghi recalled, Huyser reiterated his government's support for the Shah and the necessity of smashing the opposition. In the second meeting a few days after his arrival, Huyser changed his position and argued that the immediate departure of the Shah was essential for the restoration of order.[89] Huyser recommended that Qarabaghi meet with Khomeini's representatives in Iran, Mehdi Bazargan and Ayatollah Mohammad Hosseini Beheshti. Qarabaghi reported this to the Shah. The Shah asked, "Do you know what the Americans are up to?"

At any rate, while Huyser was preoccupied with the affairs of the armed forces, Sullivan was moving in a direction incompatible with Huyser's stated objectives. It was official U.S. policy to support Bakhtiyar. Sullivan had strongly opposed such a strategy because of his accurate assessment that of the opposition forces, Khomeini's supporters were most powerful. Consequently, Bakhtiyar, with no support in the streets and expelled from the National Front, was correctly perceived as a catalyst for the Shah's removal. Sullivan, therefore, told Huyser that "we should just skip the Bakhtiyar interlude and move on to a Bazargan government," which Huyser interpreted as Sullivan's preference for an Islamic Republic rather than a military takeover.[90] In that vein, Sullivan had prepared a list of 100 top military officers who would be asked, or perhaps forced, to leave Iran with the Shah to facilitate the formation of an alliance between the younger military officers and the ulama through the good offices of the Liberation Movement.[91] (Vance was advocating the idea of a coalition among the armed forces, Bakhtiyar, and Khomeini's forces.) Timing was of the essence for this scheme, as it called for the immediate departure of the Shah and direct negotiation with Khomeini in Paris. But Washington went along only to inform the Shah to leave expeditiously. After some debate, on January 10, Washington finally decided to contact Khomeini through the French government, but only to admonish him that unless he stated his support for Bakhtiyar, the armed forces would stage a bloody coup.[92]

Meanwhile, Bakhtiyar, unaware of Huyser's goals and Sullivan's negative assessment of his regime, was desperately seeking to reach a compromise with the opposition. The orthodox ulama were prepared to give him a chance by not directly attacking him. Many of them preferred Bakhtiyar to a coup or to a communist takeover as the best of the three alternatives they could envision for a shahless Iran. Shariatmadari, for example, expressed serious doubts about the ability and wisdom of Khomeini supporters to take over the state.[93]

But as long as the Shah was in Iran, Bakhtiyar could not play his trump card as the man forcing the Shah into exile. Thus, the preparations for the Shah's departure proceeded quickly. On January 13, the nine-man Regency Council was set up.

With the creation of the Regency Council, in which none of the prominent opposition leaders participated, and with the confirmation of Bakhtiyar by the Majles, the Shah left Iran on January 16 for an "extended vacation." Before leaving, he finally met Huyser, who had accompanied Sullivan to the gloomy palace. The Shah's recollection of the meeting is revealing: "My departure was no more a matter of days, Sullivan said, but of hours, and looked meaningfully at his watch. Both talked of a 'leave' of two months, but neither seemed very convinced that I might return."[94] He never returned.[95] General Amir Hossein Rabi'i, the commander of the air force and one of the first to be executed by the Islamic authorities upon Khomeini's return, regretted serving a Shah who was "thrown out of Iran by Huyser like a dead mouse." The Shah's departure began a new chapter in the denouement of the Iranian drama.

The Price of Indecision

As the Shah showed indecisiveness in dealing with the burgeoning movement throughout 1977 and 1978, the entire system collapsed. Only fifty-three weeks elapsed between the first riots in Qom and the Shah's departure.

"The Shah's failure to act has to this day," Huyser wrote, "remained a mystery to me." The following factors may shed some light on the situation. First, the Shah did resort to the repression and killing of his unarmed opponents. The problem was that the Shah did not use violence at the right time or direct it at the right groups. It also appears that the Shah was not convinced that by force alone he could have saved his throne. Sullivan recalled the Shah telling him that by force he could "suppress the spreading of revolution only as long as he himself lived" but that eventually during the reign of his son the suppressed forces would blast away his dynasty.[96]

Second, the Shah was not noted for his decisionmaking ability during crises. He was a rather indecisive ruler with strong fatalistic views. The coup of 1953 was essentially organized for him by his U.S. and British allies, and the decision to crush his opponents in the June Uprising of 1963 was made by his prime minister, Alam. The side effects of treatment for his cancer understandably contributed to this innate indecisiveness during the revolutionary movement.[97]

Third, that the Shah left Iran so peacefully could have been partly the result of his Pollyanna belief that the United States might implement another miraculous scheme to save his throne, like the coup of 1953, or at least assure a smooth transition of power for his heir-apparent, Reza Pahlavi. Dependent on U.S. advice, he was waiting for the U.S. government to explicitly urge him to crack down. Instead, he received contradictory signals from Washington. Therefore he did not act when he had to.

To have been able to deal with the revolutionary movement the Shah would have had to be creative, consistent, and forceful. Tocqueville was on the mark when he wrote, "The most perilous moment for a bad government is when it seeks to mend its ways. Only consummate statecraft can enable a king to save his throne when after a long spell of oppressive rule he sets to improving the lot of his subjects."[98] The Shah could not blame the United States, as he did, for not giving him the green light to use brute force to stay in power. As a king, it was his responsibility alone to decide what course of action to take. The United States did what it considered to be in the best interest of that country. The Shah also should have done what he considered to be in the best interest of his country. The Shah, waiting for the United States to once again save him from collapse, acting indecisively, and consistently misreading the nature of the revolutionary movement, watched the demise of what he and his father had so painstakingly built over five decades. Ultimately, he had no one to blame but himself, for he lacked that precious "consummate statecraft" that Tocqueville so eloquently defined. It cost him the Peacock Throne. Like his father thirty-eight years earlier, he died in exile with a broken heart.

The Shah's closest ally, the United States, also came to pay a heavy price for its inconsistent policy. Debating policy alternatives in the marketplace of ideas is beneficial if it can generate a consistent policy. But oscillation and inconsistency are devastating to cunning diplomacy. There seemed to have been at least four different U.S. centers of decisionmaking during Iran's revolutionary movement: the White House, the State Department, the National Security Council, and the U.S. Embassy in Teheran. Their analyses of the turmoil and their proposed strategies of action often differed one from another. All four centers made flawed judgments about the Shah's regime and its opponents. None seemed to have understood the dynamics of Iran's revolutionary movement or its cultural and religious heritage—prerequisites to formulating sound policy. In short, the United States did not speak with one voice when, more than at any other time, unanimity of action was essential. If the contradictory policies of the U.S. administration were not a calculated move to undermine the Shah, as has been suggested by some Iranian monarchists, then one can only conclude that U.S. foreign policy establishment has no appropriate mechanism to deal with revolutionary crises.

The United States lost much credibility among the conservative forces in the Middle East for not having generously supported an old ally in his hour of need. Even a Soviet Embassy officer was reported to have told his U.S. counterpart that the United States did not fully support the Shah during the revolutionary movement.[99]

The Shah's exile marked the end of the short period when the United States was the dominant foreign power in Iran (1953–1979). Considering the abundance of resources available to the United States in Iran, its "loss of Iran" should be viewed as a masterpiece of flawed diplomacy.

Phase Eight: Dual Sovereignty

As soon as the Shah established the Regency Council on January 13, 1979, Khomeini publicly declared the creation of a secret Council of the Islamic Revolution to coordinate the activities of the opposition to the Shah. Bazargan recalled that at that time Khomeini told him from Paris that since he did not know too many people in Iran, Bazargan should recommend a few qualified candidates for that small council, and he did so—an indication of the absence of any large Khomeini network in Iran.[100]

Having been denied entry to the secret body, the National Front and other moderate groups vehemently opposed the formation of the Council of the Islamic Revolution. This dispute was the first major clash between the moderate and revolutionary elements of the anti-Shah coalition. The former desired a complete break with the past; the latter sought change in a context of continuity. Sanjabi, for example, who believed on January 18, 1979, that Khomeini would eventually accept a constitutional monarchy, was prepared to accept the rule of Reza Pahlavi, the heir-apparent to Mohammad Reza Shah.[101] He was also under the delusion that the National Front would eventually take over the government.[102] Ayatollah 'Alameh Tabataba'i, one of the main organizers of Black Friday, also favored some type of constitutional monarchy, a view shared by many other ulama who dared to express it publicly.[103]

With the Shah's departure and the formation of the Council of the Islamic Revolution, both Bakhtiyar and the revolutionaries under Khomeini's leadership began a fierce competition to win the allegiance of the masses and, more important, of the armed forces. To win public support and to create a wedge in the anti-Shah coalition, Bakhtiyar dissolved SAVAK, released political prisoners, lifted censorship of the media, severed diplomatic relations with Israel, promised lucrative compensation to political prisoners and to those killed during the demonstrations of the previous year, and sought to improve relations with the ulama by recognizing them as the legitimate leaders of the revolution.[104] These concessions were too little, too late. The continuation of nationwide strikes and resignations by Jalal Tehrani, the head of the Regency Council, by a number of Bakhtiyar's cabinet ministers and by seventeen Majles deputies revealed the vulnerability of the new government. Bakhtiyar's appointed ministers were often denied entry to their ministries by the revolutionaries.

Bakhtiyar's calculation that the armed forces would render their support to him in the event of a confrontation with the opposition was also erroneous. The first blow came when the Shah denied him the prerogative to appoint the chief of staff. Instead, the Shah appointed General Abbas Qarabaghi. And Bakhtiyar could not see, or chose to ignore, the diligent moves by the Council of the Islamic Revolution, backed by the U.S. Embassy, to form an "alliance of convenience" with the armed forces.

Information about the status of the Iranian armed forces is both inconclusive and contradictory.[105] A day after the Shah's departure, Huyser cabled Washington to indicate that the armed forces were prepared to stage a coup. Two days later Sullivan informed Washington that the armed forces were rapidly disintegrating.[106] Although the army's morale was low, and although there were about 100 desertions per day by the conscripts, not by the professionals, the fact is that the

450,000 members of the military still represented the most organized force in the country and simply could not be ignored.

This is why the Council of the Islamic Revolution did so much to neutralize the armed forces. What we know is that the hawks in the armed forces opposed any overtures to the anti-Shah coalition. But gradually the hawks' power diminished. First, in January, General Gholam Ali Oveyssi, known as the "butcher of Teheran" and the champion of the hawks, left Iran because of his opposition to the appointment of Bakhtiyar. (He was later assassinated in the streets of Paris.) The next victim was Major General Khosraudad, who was anxious to replace Oveyssi as the new leader of the hard-liners. A week before the Shah's departure, Khosraudad announced that the armed forces would not allow the Shah to leave. Bakhtiyar, with the Shah's blessing, quickly dismissed Khosraudad.[107] Thus, as Bakhtiyar was hoping to control the armed forces, he helped to reduce the power of the hawks who did not trust him and in the process facilitated the compromise between the doves in the armed forces and the anti-Shah coalition.

We also know that only a few days after Bakhtiyar's accession to power, Sullivan met with Bazargan and a representative of the ulama. After that meeting, Sullivan encouraged Bazargan to get in touch with Chief of Staff Qarabaghi, presumedly to facilitate a smooth transition of power to the revolutionaries.[108] Qarabaghi also claims that he was asked by Huyser to get in touch with Ayatollah Beheshti and Bazargan while the Shah was still in Iran. It is also clear that the mediator between the army and the Council of the Islamic Revolution was SAVAK's chief, General Moqaddam, and that a meeting was scheduled for January between Ayatollah Beheshti, Hojatolislam Rafsanjani, Bazargan, Y. Sahabi (from the Liberation Movement), and Qarabaghi.[109] It appears that Qarabaghi had reached some kind of understanding with the Council of the Islamic Revolution: When Bakhtiyar declared on January 20 that should his administration fail, the armed forces would take over, Qarabaghi quickly announced his resignation on the grounds that the armed forces should not intervene in political disputes. Because of pressure from Huyser and Sullivan, Qarabaghi stayed in his job. His announced resignation, however, was a defeat for Bakhtiyar.

There is ample evidence to suggest that while the U.S. Embassy, and perhaps General Huyser, was pressuring the armed forces not to stage a pro-Shah coup, there were policymakers in Washington who tried in vain to manipulate the possibility of a coup by the army in order to enhance U.S. interests. Consider the following contradictory evidence. On January 22, "Huyser asked that he be authorized to inform the armed forces that the United States would not support a coup," which, according to Secretary Vance, was denied, a proposition that also contradicts Huyser's account of events.[110] In a conversation with an officer of the U.S. Embassy in Teheran, a member of the Liberation Movement thanked the U.S. government for its successful attempts to prevent a coup.[111]

It was probably because of the understanding between the Council of the Islamic Revolution and the armed forces that Ayatollahs Shariatmadari and Najafi

Mar'ashi denied their support to Bakhtiyar. Naser Minatchi, Shariatmadari's representative and a member of the Council of the Islamic Revolution who was in close contact with the U.S. Embassy, probably informed the two Grand Ayatollahs that the armed forces would not support Bakhtiyar in any confrontation between the revolutionaries and the civilian government.

Unaware that the constitutionalist ulama had abandoned him and that serious negotiations were going on between the Council of the Islamic Revolution and the military, Bakhtiyar was in contact with the Council of the Islamic Revolution regarding the return of Khomeini from Paris. With Bazargan as mediator, the most significant of these discussions was a scheme, planned by the Council of the Islamic Revolution and approved by Bakhtiyar, in which Bakhtiyar, as an Iranian and not as a prime minister, would pay homage to Ayatollah Khomeini in Paris, recognizing Khomeini's leadership. He then would offer his resignation, and Khomeini would appoint him as his own prime minister.[112] (Bakhtiyar rejects this interpretation.) At first, Khomeini agreed to meet with Bakhtiyar. Influenced by his advisers, including Ebrahim Yazdi and Abolhassan Bani Sadr, the Ayatollah changed his mind and insisted that he would grant an audience to Bakhtiyar only if he resigned his post. Bakhtiyar refused to give in, and that ended the possibility of any rapprochement between Bakhtiyar and Khomeini.

Nor could Bakhtiyar prevent Khomeini's triumphant return to Iran. Under irresistible pressure from millions of Khomeini supporters, Bakhtiyar and the army had no alternative but to "approve" Khomeini's return. After some fifteen years of exile, Ayatollah Khomeini returned to Teheran amid national fanfare on February 1, 1979. From the airport, he went to the Behesht-e Zahra, the main cemetery of the martyrs of the Islamic Revolution. There, he made it abundantly clear that he was Iran's strongman. Saying that he "will give this government a punch in the mouth," he encouraged desertion within the armed forces and promised to quickly announce the formation of a provisional revolutionary government to prepare the ground for the establishment of an Islamic Republic.[113] Six days later, he asked Mehdi Bazargan to head the provisional government.

With the formation of the provisional revolutionary government, a period of dual sovereignty began. On one side stood Bakhtiyar's government and on the other side stood Bazargan's shadow government. With Khomeini supporting Bazargan, Bakhtiyar was quickly pushed to oblivion.

A week after his return, a group of *homa faran* (air force technicians) went to Khomeini's headquarters and hailed him as the new leader of Iran. (Even before Khomeini's return to Iran, Qarabaghi admitted that serious desertions had occurred within the ranks of the *homa faran*.[114]) This event precipitated violent confrontations between the air force technicians and the Imperial Guard, the Shah's most trusted soldiers. Finally, on February 10, some members of the 30,000-man Imperial Guard (the Immortals) attacked the mutinous air force technicians at the Dushan Tapeh base in Teheran. The revolutionaries, including the guerrilla organizations, most likely without Khomeini's approval, joined the technicians and a mini–civil war broke out. Soon the revolutionaries took over the garrison, seized thousands of weapons, and defeated the Immortals. The next day, the armed forces declared their neutrality to prevent further bloodshed. Bakhtiyar went into hiding. Quickly, the revolutionaries attacked the Shah's main prison at Evin (Iran's Bastille), freed the remaining political prisoners, and ransacked SAVAK's main headquarters in Teheran. General Abdul Ali Badre'i, the chief of the army, was assassinated outside his headquarters in Teheran. Manuchehr Khosraudad and other high-ranking officials were arrested. Soon they were sent to the firing squads.

That the Mojahedin and Fada'iyun played a role in defeating the Imperial Guard can hardly be disputed. But the significance of their role and of the entire confrontation between the Imperial Guard and the *homa faran* should not be exaggerated, as it often is by the leftists and the Mojahedin. First, the declaration of neutrality of the armed forces was the product of weeks of behind-the-scenes negotiations between the Council of the Islamic Revolution and the armed forces. But had that neutrality been declared from a position of strength and through the continuation of negotiations by Bazargan and his associates, the cohesion of the armed forces would have remained relatively high. As such, they most likely would have played an important moderating role in the postrevolutionary power struggle. The declaration of neutrality from weakness, therefore, was the first defeat for the forces of moderation in the anti-Shah coalition. Second, there is no evidence that the Shah, who was in Egypt at the time, had blessed the action by his guards. It appears that the Imperial Guard acted autonomously and did not enjoy the support of the armed forces as a whole. Thus, by causing the forced declaration of neutrality, the Immortals, like the leftists, weakened the possibility of the armed forces intervening in the post-Shah power struggle and, therefore, inadvertently helped radicalize the revolutionary movement.

While the masses were celebrating the victory of the revolution and destroying every visible symbol of the Pahlavi dynasty, including the Shah's statues in the cities, Washington was still pondering its predicament in Iran. On February 12, a day after the neutralization of the Imperial armed forces, the White House called Sullivan to instruct him to give the green light to the armed forces to stage a coup. Sullivan "gave a colorful, but unprintable, reply."[115]

With the Shah in exile in Egypt, Khomeini in Iran, Bakhtiyar in hiding, Bazargan in charge of the Provisional Revolutionary Government, and the armed forces demoralized and neutralized, a new chapter in Iran's history opened, one in which an Islamic order was built on the ashes of imperial Iran.

Notes

1. Amnesty International, *Annual Report 1974–75* (Geneva, 1975). Also see International Commission of Jurists, *Human Rights and the Legal System in Iran* (Geneva, 1976), pp. 1–72.

2. Sandy Vogelgesang, *American Dream, Global Nightmare* (New York, 1980); and A. H. Robertson, *Human Rights in the World* (New York, 1982).

3. Vogelgesang (1980), p. 128.

4. Ibid., p. 125.

5. Jimmy Carter, *Keeping Faith* (New York, 1983), p. 143.

6. The situation in Iran and Nicaragua in the late 1970s had striking similarities. See William M. Leogrande, "The United States and the Nicaraguan Revolution," in Thomas Walker, ed., *Nicaragua in Revolution* (New York, 1982), p. 65.

7. Zbigniew Brzezinski, *Power and Principle* (New York, 1983), p. 355.

8. Even before Carter's presidency, some doubts were expressed by some Americans about the benefits of U.S. relations with Iran (Robert L. Paarlberg, "The Advantageous Alliance: U.S. Relations with Iran, 1920–1975," in R. L. Paarlberg et al., eds., *Diplomatic Dispute: U.S. Conflict With Iran, Japan and Mexico* (Boston, 1978).

9. *Asnad-e Lane-ye Jasusi* (Documents of the Spy Nest), vol. 12 (Teheran, 1981), p. 20; January 11, 1978, "Ambassador's Goals and Objectives in Iran," from the American Embassy in Teheran (hereafter AET) to the State Department in Washington (hereafter SDW), prepared by William Sullivan. The *Asnad* were released by the Students Following the Imam's Line subsequent to the takeover of the U.S. Embassy in Teheran in November 1979. It is clear that not all captured documents were released. They are selective but do not appear inaccurate.

10. Richard W. Cottam, "Arms Sales and Human Rights: The Case of Iran," in P. Brown and D. Maclean, eds., *Human Rights and U.S. Foreign Policy* (Lexington, Mass., 1979), pp. 281–301.

11. For a critical analysis of Carter's human rights, see J. Kirkpatrick, "Dictatorships and Double Standards," *Commentary,* 68, 79 (November 1979), pp. 34–45; and Richard Sale, "Carter and Iran: From Idealism to Disaster," *Washington Quarterly,* 3 (Summer 1980), pp. 75–87.

12. For the list of officials in both camps, see Michael Ledeen and William Lewis, *Debacle: The American Failure in Iran* (New York, 1982), pp. 68–70.

13. Ibid., p. 155.

14. Cyrus Vance, *Hard Choices: Critical Years in America's Foreign Policy* (New York, 1983), p. 319.

15. Ledeen and Lewis (1982), p. 75.

16. U.S. Congress, House of Representatives, *Human Rights in Iran: Hearing Before the Sub-Committee on International Organizations of the Committee on International Relations,* House of Representatives, 95th Congress, Washington, D.C., October 26, 1977.

17. See, for example, Barry Rubin, "Carter, Human Rights, and U.S. Allies," in B. Rubin and Elizabeth Spiro, eds., *Human Rights and U.S. Foreign Policy* (Boulder, Colo., 1979), pp. 109–132.

18. Quoted by Mehdi Bazargan, *Enqelab-e Iran Dau Du Harekat* (The Iranian Revolution in Two Strokes) (Teheran, 1984), p. 26.

19. *Asnad,* vol. 8, July 25, 1977, p. 178; "Straws in the Wind: Intellectuals and Religious Opposition in Iran," from AET to SDW, prepared by William Sullivan.

20. For the text of the letter see Bakhtiyar *Sio Haft Ruz Pas Az Sio Haft Sal* (Thirty-Seven Days after Thirty-Seven Years) (Paris, 1981), pp. 140–142.

21. The Association of American Publishers urged Prime Minister Hoveyda to reactivate the banned Writer's Association (*New York Times,* August 5, 1977).

22. Naser Moazen, ed., *Dah Shab* (Ten Nights) (Teheran, 1978).

23. *Public Papers of the Presidents: Administration of Jimmy Carter* (Washington, D.C., 1978), p. 2221.

24. Said Amir Arjomand, "Shi'ite Islam and the Revolution in Iran," *Government and Opposition*, 6 (Summer 1981), pp. 311–312.

25. *Ettela'at*, January 7, 1978.

26. Dariyush Homayoun, the nominal writer of the article, insisted that the article was prepared by the court and approved by the Shah and that he simply published it (*Diruz Va Farda* [Yesterday and Tomorrow] [n.p., 1981], pp. 92–93).

27. *Asnad*, vol. 12, June 1, 1978, p. 119; "Iran in 1977–78: The Internal Scene," from AET to SDW, prepared by William Sullivan.

28. Ibid., January 24, 1978, pp. 26–27; from AET to Secretary of State, Washington, D.C. (hereafter SSW).

29. For details, see *Dar Bare-ye Hemase-ye Qom Va Tabriz* (On the Heroic Uprising of Qom and Tabriz) (Teheran, 1982).

30. In 1975, there were 1,125 mosques and 140 registered *takiye* in East Azerbaijan. In Esfahan, there were 719 mosques and 89 *takiye* (*Gozareshe Farhangi-e Iran*, [Teheran, 1975], p. 103). The first uprising was in Azerbaijan and Esfahan was the first city in which martial law was imposed.

31. For an excellent analysis of different phases of the Islamic Revolution, see Ahmad Ashraf and Ali Banuazizi, "The State, Classes and Modes of Mobilization in the Iranian Revolution," *State, Culture and Society*, 1, 3 (Spring 1985), pp. 3–40.

32. *Asnad*, vol. 24, July 18, 1978, p. 16; "Memorandum of conversation between J. Stempel and members of the Liberation Movement, M. Bazargan, Y. Sahabi, and M. Tavakoli."

33. *Kayhan International*, April 4, 1978.

34. *Asnad*, vol. 12, January 24, 1978, pp. 28–29; "Religion and Politics: Qom and Its Aftermath," from AET to SSW, prepared by William Sullivan.

35. Ibid., May 21, 1978, p. 108; "Public Reaction to Shah's Interview," from AET to SSW, prepared by William Sullivan.

36. Vance (1983), p. 325.

37. According to Ali Asghar Haj Seyyed Javadi, a prominent writer, General Razmi, Abadan's police chief, was partly responsible for the fire. He also makes the implicit assumption that SAVAK was behind the incident (*Jonbesh*, 8, 31 [Mordad 1557]).

38. Brzezinski (1983), p. 356.

39. Ibid., p. 355.

40. *Ettela'at*, 7 Mehr, 1357/August 29, 1978.

41. *Ettela'at*, 10 Shahrivar, 1357/September 1, 1978. Also *Asnad*, vol. 26, December 8, 1978, pp. 43–45; prepared by office of Central Reference, Central Intelligence Agency.

42. For details, see Abbas Qarabaghi, *Haqayeq Dar Bare-ye Bohran-e Iran* (Truth About the Crisis in Iran) (Paris, 1982), pp. 83–94.

43. Sullivan estimated that 200 persons died in that incident and that from then to January 8, 1978, some 1,000 people were killed by the police (*Asnad*, vol. 13, January 23, 1979; from AET to SDW, prepared by William Sullivan).

44. The Shah also points out that after Black Friday, he planned to organize a pro-Shah rally. He discussed the matter with the British and U.S. ambassadors. "The envoys shrugged and said, 'What is the point in that? ... It is a race you cannot win'" (Mohammad Reza Pahlavi, *Answer to History* [New York, 1980], pp. 163–164).

45. Sullivan points out that Imami was convinced that once Khomeini was forced out of Iraq, "he would fade from public view and probably never be heard from again" (W. Sullivan, *Mission to Iran* [New York, 1981], p. 166).

46. *Asnad*, vol. 24, September 28, 1978, p. 31; "Memorandum of conversation between John Stempel, political officer, U.S. Embassy, with Liberation Movement, Baharam Bahramian and Mohammod Tavakoli."

47. Ibid., September 25, 1978, p. 29.

48. As quoted by Gary Sick, *All Fall Down: America's Tragic Encounters with Iran* (New York, 1985), p. 92.

49. *Asnad*, vol. 24, p. 67.

50. Ruhollah Khomeini, *Neda-ye Haq: A Collection of Imam Khomeini's Declarations, Interviews and Speeches*, vol. 1 (Teheran, 1979), p. 16.

51. For the text, see Bakhtiyar (1981), p. 143. Abolhassan Bani Sadr claimed that he wrote the declaration (*Khiyanat Be Omid* [Betrayal of Hope] [Paris, 1983], p. 345).

52. Shahpur Bakhtiyar, *Yek Rangi* (Paris, 1982), pp. 148–149.

53. Vance (1983), p. 327.

54. In November 1979, Khomeini was asked why he was not cooperating with the communists. He answered: "We will not accept the communists, for their danger to the country is no less than that of the Shah. We cannot accept them." *Neda-ye Haq*, vol. 1 (1979), p. 93.

55. Mohammad Reza Pahlavi, *Answer to History* (New York, 1980), pp. 167–168.

56. Bazargan (1984), pp. 207–208.

57. Khomeini (1979), vol. 1, pp. 20–23.

58. Zbigniew Brzezinski, *Power and Principle* (New York, 1983), p. 365. Brzezinski confirms the Shah's statement that Sullivan did not inform the Shah that the U.S. government supports an ironfisted policy. Brzezinski recalled that when he told the Shah that more concessions to the opposition were most likely to produce a more "explosive situation," the Shah responded: "Is your Ambassador briefed?" (p. 365).

59. Vance (1983), p. 329.

60. Carter (1983), p. 439.

61. Sullivan (1981), p. 202.

62. Jimmy Carter complained that he was not getting accurate information from Sullivan and that he told Vance to get him out of Iran but "Cy insisted that it would be a mistake to put a new man in the country in the midst of the succession of crises" (Carter [1983], pp. 444–446).

63. *Neda-ye Haq*, pp. 16–17.

64. Quoted by Sick (1985), p. 110.

65. *Asnad*, vol. 26, December 8, 1978, p. 58; from the U.S. Embassy in Teheran (AET) to the State Department in Washington (SDW).

66. Bazargan (1983), pp. 37–40.

67. Mohammad Moqtar, "Barresi-ye Sho'arha-ye Doran-e Enqelab" (Review of the Slogans of the Revolutionary Period), *Ketab-e Jam-eh*, vols. 13, 20, and 21 (Teheran, 1979).

68. Vance (1983), p. 330; and Brzezinski (1983), pp. 372–373.

69. Sick (1985), p. 121. Henry Precht was, according to Sick, one of the first officials at the State Department to foresee the Shah's collapse.

70. Vance (1983), pp. 332–333; and Brzezinski (1983), pp. 375–378.

71. *Asnad,* vol. 26, December 8, 1979, p. 40; from the CIA to the AET. Amini, like Sanjabi and many other moderates, believed that once in Iran, Khomeini would drastically soften his views (*Asnad,* vol. 27, January 20, 1979, p. 88; from the SDW to all diplomatic missions in Europe, the Near East, and South Asia).

72. On the oil strike and other strikes, see *Asnad-e Nehzat-e Azadi-ye Iran: Rahandazi-ye Naft va Tanzim-e E'tesabat* (Documents of the Liberation Movement of Iran: Resumption of Oil and Coordination of Strikes), 9, 3 (Teheran, 1985).

73. Brzezinski (1983), pp. 379–380.

74. *Asnad,* vol. 10, January 8, 1979, p. 5; from the SDW to the AET, prepared by Vance. Cottam visited Khomeini in 1978. For his assessment of Khomeini, see *Asnad,* vol. 24, 1979, pp. 44–45.

75. *Asnad,* vol. 27, no. 3, January 10, 1979, pp. 36–38; from the AET to SDW, prepared by Sullivan. Ayatollah Shariatmadari desired a friendly relationship with the United States and expressed neutrality about Bakhtiyar's government.

76. *Asnad,* vol. 27, January 18, 1979, p. 79, from the AET to the SDW.

77. On the role of the armed forces in revolutions, see D. Russell, *Rebellion, Revolution and Armed Forces* (New York, 1974); Katherine Chorley, *Armies and the Art of Revolution* (London, 1973); and Alvin J. Cottrell, "Iran's Armed Forces Under the Pahlavi Dynasty," in G. Lenczowski, ed., *Iran Under the Pahlavis* (Stanford, Calif., 1978), pp. 389–431.

78. Carter (1983), p. 444.

79. See Ebrahim Yazdi, *Barresi-ye Safar-e Huyser Be Iran* (Investigation of Huyser's Trip to Iran) (Teheran, 1984); and Alvin Cottrell, "American Policy During the Iranian Revolution: The Huyser Mission," *International Security Review,* 4, 4 (Winter 1979–1980), pp. 433–444. See also Robert Huyser, *Mission to Teheran* (New York, 1986), p. 50.

80. Anthony Parsons, *The Pride and the Fall: Iran, 1974–1979* (London, 1984), p. 121.

81. Huyser (1986), pp. 17–18.

82. Ledeen and Lewis (1982), p. 180.

83. Huyser (1986), p. 50.

84. Ibid., p. 68.

85. Ibid.

86. Ibid., pp. 34–37.

87. Ibid., p. 27.

88. Huyser wrote that the Shah ordered the generals to "trust and obey Huyser." Ibid., p. 85.

89. Qarabaghi (1982), p. 170. For details of the discussions among the top generals before the Shah's departure, see *Mesl-e Barf Ab Khahim Shod: Mozakerat-e Shura-ye Farmandehan-e Artesh* (Like Snow We Will Melt: Negotiations of the Council of the Commanders of the Army) (Teheran, 1983).

90. Huyser (1986), p. 24.

91. Sick (1985), p. 136.

92. Vance (1983), p. 337.

93. *Asnad,* vol. 26, no. 3, January 17, 1979, p. 43; "Shariatmadari Reportedly Seeks U.S. Support," from the AET to the SDW.

94. Pahlavi (1980), p. 172.

95. The Shah did not want to set a date for his departure, but Sullivan pressured him to leave quickly (Vance [1983], pp. 334–335).

96. William Sullivan, "Dateline Iran: The Road Not Taken," *Foreign Policy* (Fall 1980), p. 178.

97. See Asadollah Alam, *The Shah and I* (New York, 1992), translated by Alinaghi Alik-hani. In his confidential diary, Alam provides us with a picture of the secrets of the Shah's court.

98. Alexis de Tocqueville, *The Old Regime and the French Revolution* (New York, 1955), pp. 176–177.

99. *Asnad*, vol. 48, November 15, 1978, p. 80. It appears that from November 1978 to January 1979, the Russians believed that the United States was contemplating the idea of a military coup in favor of the Shah (*Asnad*, vol. 48, September 10, 1978, p. 48).

100. Mehdi Bazargan, *Shura-ye Enqelab Va Daulat-e Movaqat* (The Islamic Revolutionary Council and the Provisional Government) (Teheran, 1983), p. 22. Bazargan wrote that in his first meeting with Khomeini in Paris he was shocked by Khomeini's indifference to political and management issues.

101. *Asnad*, vol. 27, no. 3, January 23, 1979, pp. 116–118; from the AET to the SDW, "Sanjabi's Views on Khomeini and the Government," prepared by Sullivan. Sanjabi complained about the negative impact of Sadeq Qotbzadeh and Ebrahim Yazdi on Khomeini. Sanjabi was also against the Council of the Islamic Revolution (CIR).

102. Ibid., January 18, 1979, p. 86; from the AET to the SDW, prepared by Sullivan.

103. *Asnad*, vol. 16, no. 2, December 8, 1978, pp. 65–66; from the AET to the SDW. Nuri was the leader of the Black Friday demonstration that led to the death of hundreds.

104. Bakhtiyar (1981), pp. 154–170; and *Ettela'at* (Teheran), Day 16, 1357/January 6, 1979.

105. Robert Huyser estimated 100 desertions per day during the first days of January 1979 (1986, p. 109). Gary Sick claimed that Huyser reported between 500 to 1,000 desertions, a major discrepancy between these two reports.

106. Huyser (1986), pp. 142 and 161.

107. *Kayhan* (Teheran), Day 20, 1357/January 10, 1979.

108. Sullivan (1981), pp. 236–237. We also know that Ayatollah Beheshti was in contact with the Iranian generals. See Vance (1983), p. 338.

109. *Asnad*, vol. 26, January 8, 1979, p. 139; "Clergy Organizing to Help Stabilize Public Order," from the AET to the SDW, prepared by Sullivan.

110. Vance (1983), p. 339. This also contradicts Huyser's statement that he favored a coup.

111. *Asnad*, vol. 10, November 1978, p. 19. For U.S. opposition to the coup, see *Asnad*, vol. 10, December 1987, p. 8.

112. Ebrahim Yazdi, *Akharin Talashha Dar Akharin Ruzha* (The Last Efforts in the Last Days) (Teheran, 1984), pp. 92–94; and *Ettela'at* (Teheran), Bahman 7, 1357/January 28, 1979.

113. Ruhollah Khomeini, *Islam and Revolution: Writings and Declarations of Imam Khomeini*, trans. and annotated by Hamid Algar (Berkeley, Calif., 1981), p. 259.

114. *Ettela'at*, Bahman 19, 1357/February 8, 1979.

115. Sullivan (1981), p. 342.

Part Five

The Postrevolutionary Power Struggle

8

The Rise and Fall of the Provisional Revolutionary Government: A Good Government for a Wrong Time

> So if the question were discussed whether Rome was more indebted to Romulus or Numa, I believe that the highest merit would be conceded to Numa; for where religion exists it is easy to introduce armies and discipline, but where there are armies and no religion it is difficult to introduce the latter.
>
> *Niccolò Machiavelli*, Discourses, 1517

> This rebellion ... is not a nationalist rebellion; this rebellion is a Quranic rebellion; this rebellion is an Islamic rebellion.·... It was the invisible hand of God which united the entire nation from school children to hospitalized old men.
>
> *Ayatollah Ruhollah Khomeini, 1980*

No single group had the power to dethrone the Pahlavis; hence the urgency for a multiclass coalition against the Shah. The nucleus of that coalition consisted of the ulama, the intelligentsia, and the merchants/shopkeepers who collectively provided it with legitimacy, organization, manpower, and financial resources. Fanatical hatred of the Shah and Khomeini's charisma kept the coalition united. Unity, however, was meteoric, lasting as long as the soul-soothing feeling of collective jubilation and release from years of oppression kept the coalition intoxicated with optimism for a roseate future.

As President John F. Kennedy remarked in the aftermath of the Bay of Pigs invasion, "Victory has many fathers while defeat is an orphan." The Islamic Revolution, too, had many "fathers," all claiming to be legitimate leaders. This is why immediately after the collapse of the ancien régime, solidarity among the participants in the anti-Shah coalition gave way to antagonism, which opened historical wounds. Old allies became new enemies, and a fierce struggle for the control of the state began. The Shi'i fundamentalists, under Khomeini's leadership, were the victorious force in that intense power struggle.

In the following two chapters, I will explain the anatomy of the fundamentalists' victory over their rivals and the creation of an Islamic theocracy based on the Velayat-e Faqih. The fundamentalists first controlled the revolutionary institutions and then created a state within the state to weaken and defeat their rivals. Gradually they expanded their domination of the various organs of government. By the third anniversary of the Islamic Revolution, in 1982, they were firmly in control of Iran.

The victory of the fundamentalists shocked many Iran experts who, having conveniently dismissed Islam as a "dying force," had predicted that the fundamentalist ulama were ill-equipped to manage the ruins of the Pahlavi state and would return to their mosques and seminaries as soon as the revolutionary hysteria subsided. Not only did they not return to their mosques in Iran, but they have also inspired others outside of Iran to make Islam the most potent political force in the Islamic world.

The Art of Winning a Revolution

Many groups must join together to make a revolution, but only one emerges victorious. The following factors may determine who wins: First, the emergence of an undisputed leadership in the process of overthrowing the ancien régime greatly facilitates victory for that leadership. Second, a favorable public perception about one's capability to eradicate exploitation and poverty—what Hannah Arendt called the social question—increases the chances of victory. This is logical, because revolutions, born out of compassion, popularize egalitarian and utopian ideas that mesmerize the masses. Third, challengers must be skilled mass psychologists, aware of, and prepared to exploit, the people's emotional idiosyncrasies, cultural symbols, and sometimes irrational demands for quick fixes. They must be apt in communicating with the masses, in using propaganda, in forming and breaking coalitions, and in applying force when necessary. Fourth, institutions must be built to absorb into the political process the previously disenfranchised forces. Theorizing about revolution sounds romantic, but winning it is no romantic enterprise. The verdict on those who refuse to treat revolution as a furious war has been unequivocally clear: oblivion or death.

The fundamentalists won the Islamic Revolution by surpassing their rivals in all these areas. But this victory was not inevitable; neither does it appear entirely preplanned by the fundamentalists.[1] It was a gradual process of trial and error. It involved shifting alliances with uneasy bedfellows, decisive and cunning leadership, institution building, positive response to the needs of the masses, wisdom to create an independent militia, and effective use of terror. It was also attributable to the nationalists' self-deceptions and abysmal failure to unify and exploit their abundant resources and to the left's suicidal animosity toward and weakening of the nationalists.

Revolutions are like wars: Those who play the game better will win and those who lose will become bitter, indicting everyone for their defeat except themselves. Therefore, when their opponents grumble that the fundamentalists "hijacked" the revolution, they reflect their self-deception about their own popularity and they misread the nature of Iran's revolutionary movement. The shallowness of this claim is exposed further when, with the wisdom of hindsight, we observe that not only were many features of the anti-Shah movement distinctly Shi'i, but also that the Shi'i ulama were the leaders of the revolutionary movement. This explains why the struggle among the Shi'i groups, and not between them and others, has shaped the politics of revolutionary Iran. Thus, the revolution would have been truly hijacked if the secular nationalists or the leftists had won.

The Provisional Revolutionary Government: Its Own Worst Enemy

When the Shah left, Iran was in chaos. Governmental authority was practically nonexistent and what little was left was being challenged by the autonomy-seeking ethnic minorities, the leftists, and the fundamentalists. The security forces were demoralized. The economy was in a shambles: Thousands of managers and bureaucrats had fled the country, oil production was low, strikers were reluctant to resume work, major industries were idle, unemployment was high, and inflation was rampant.

The appointment of Bazargan as prime minister of the Provisional Revolutionary Government by Ayatollah Khomeini was a shrewd maneuver. Khomeini did not trust the National Front. Nor could he rely on the ulama: They were devoid of the managerial skills to run the state and there was also strong opposition by the nationalists and by the orthodox ayatollahs to their engaging in politics. With impeccable religious credentials, Bazargan was respected and accepted by both the nationalists and the ulama and was feared by neither as power hungry. Thus, Khomeini declared that "opposition against his government is blasphemy and punishable."[2] He later admitted that he had turned to Bazargan out of desperation and lack of a better alternative.[3]

History will remember Mehdi Bazargan as Iran's Kerensky, for during his ten-month tenure Ayatollah Khomeini, who instinctively understood the nature of the revolution better than Bazargan, laid the foundation of a theocratic order. During those fateful months, the provisional government was hamstrung not only by its own flawed approach toward the revolution, but also by Khomeini's interventions in state affairs, by the various revolutionary institutions created after the Shah's fall, and by the hostile leftist parties.

The provisional government was an alliance of the secular and Islamic nationalists, the former represented by the National Front, whose members constituted some 33 percent of the cabinet, and the latter by the Liberation Movement and its affiliates, which controlled about 50 percent of the cabinet positions. In the early phases of the revolution, the provisional government enjoyed advantages no other groups had.[4] It symbolized both Iranian nationalism and modernist Shi'ism. Bazargan and many of his ministers were nationally and internationally known. The provisional government controlled the bureaucracy, had considerable influence within the remnants of the armed forces, and had the managerial skills to administer the state. Moreover, it received strong backing from significant portions of the middle class, the bazaar, and the orthodox ulama.[5]

Despite such advantages, the provisional government proved unable to facilitate the rise of Iranian nationalism as a major political factor in post-Shah Iran or to stop the ascendance of fundamentalism. As Bazargan stated, his government was "a knife without a blade." Although there were forces working against the government that Bazargan could not contain, the fact remains that he offered no revolutionary agenda to a country in the throes of a revolution.

To effectively govern, the provisional government needed to expand its popular base of support. The migration of thousands of middle-class Iranians to the West during the early days of the revolution had substantially diminished the size of the constituency from which the nationalist government could mobilize support. This situation made it more urgent to attract the lower classes, which by 1979 were the largest block of the urban population. Winning their allegiance was indispensable to winning the revolution. But the nationalists could not communicate with the lower classes or identify with their plight.

Of course, the real difficulty facing the nationalists was much deeper than communication with the lower classes. Their main shortcoming was their myopic vision of the revolution as a movement to expand democratic rights, civil liberties, and freedom. They were oblivious to the social question. Revolutions, and Iran's was no exception, usually begin with a moderate temperament, then shift toward radicalism or a reign of terror, and finally surrender to a Thermidorian reaction.[6] The impetus behind the initial radicalization is the entry into the revolutionary process of what Arendt called the social question. Proponents of the social question popularize egalitarian ideas such as eradication of poverty and equitable distribution of wealth. Those who embrace the social question are often the victors and those who swim against its tidal wave are the losers of revolutions. The more the social question is emphasized, the less relevant the stress on such issues as freedom and civil liberties becomes.[7]

From the start, the provisional government was justifiably perceived by the masses as insensitive to and even hostile toward the social question. In a time when one's popularity was proportional to how revolutionary, not necessarily how logical, one's proposals were for the future, Bazargan's government was portrayed as the champion of the rich, a "closet defender" of the monarchy minus the Shah. Bazargan explicitly stated that he had no intention of distributing wealth. He championed piecemeal reform.[8] This approach was a perfect recipe for disaster; his support quickly dwindled among the lower classes and the revolutionaries who controlled the streets, where the fate of the revolution was being determined.

Compounding these difficulties that the provisional government had created for itself was the irreconcilability of Bazargan's vision with Khomeini's. Influenced by Western ideas intertwined with Iranian nationalism, and moderate in temperament, the modernist Shi'ism that Bazargan represented reserved only an advisory role for the ulama. Untainted by Western thought and at times hostile toward it, Khomeini's fundamentalism sought to create a theocracy. Iran was simply too small for both visions.

Khomeini's Leadership and the Social Question

In the previous chapters I took some pains to establish Khomeini's undisputed leadership of the revolutionary movement because it was, for two reasons, critical to the rise of fundamentalism in the post-Shah era. First, the establishment of Khomeini's leadership during the course of the revolutionary movement prevented any radical shift of power from one group to another in the post-Shah era. During the French Revolution, for example, no one could quickly fill the vacuum created by the fall of the monarchy, so power oscillated from one group to another until Napoleon Bonaparte filled it and imposed order.[9] In Iran, there existed no such leadership vacuum: Khomeini was the revolution and the revolution was he. His old age and spartan lifestyle, which contrasted sharply with the Shah's ostentatious life, combined with his confrontationalist politics, decisive leadership, approval of revolutionary violence, and genius in communicating with the lower classes helped him personify the revolution.

The second factor that made Khomeini's leadership so critical to the fundamentalists' victory was the nature of the system that Khomeini inherited from the Pahlavis. It was a patrimonial and highly centralized system administered by a king and his personally chosen servants. In such a system, as Machiavelli argued, the most arduous task is the removal of the king. Once that is done, the victor can appoint his subservients to strategic posts and impose a new order.[10]

Khomeini did precisely that. As a U.S. diplomat stationed in Teheran observed, Khomeini "was alert not to repeat Kerensky's mistake of not using the weapons of revolution against sometime allies of convenience who would seize the moment for their own deed."[11] Khomeini alone called the important shots and determined the direction and tempo of change. When unopposed, he expeditiously consolidated his rule; when strongly opposed, he retreated, regrouped, and struck back. Most important, he had a clear vision of what he hoped to accomplish and suffered from no inferiority complex toward either his opponents or his Western enemies.

As soon as he came back to Iran, Khomeini shrewdly empowered his network within the clerical establishment and created a new network within both the state bureaucracy and the newly created revolutionary institutions. He appointed his supporters, many of them his former students, as the Friday prayer leaders in thousands of mosques throughout the country. He appointed the director of national television and radio and thus controlled the mass media. He alone appointed the members of the secret Council of the Islamic Revolution, whose power matched the government's. He sent his trusted allies as the Imam representatives to every important decisionmaking organ. Accountable to him, these "eyes and ears of the Imam" were more powerful than government authorities.

But two other factors ultimately made Khomeini Iran's most powerful man: (1) the undivided commitment of a large group of zealots prepared to defend Khomeini with their blood and (2) his prowess to lead a powerful Shi'i populist movement that swept across the country. Shi'i populism was a movement aimed at gaining power by those who had been kept powerless under the Shah, a movement that used chiliastic and apocalyptic overtones of Shi'ism to mobilize the poor masses. Like the French revolutionaries who introduced such new ideas as liberty and equality, Khomeini popularized the concept of the *mostaz'efin* (disinherited) and made it the essence of the populist movement. The creation of the Mostaz'efin Foundation was, therefore, not accidental. It was symbolic of Khomeini's determination to lead and direct the populist movement. The foundation became the inheritor of the massive fortunes of the Pahlavi Foundation, which consisted of a conglomeration of hundreds of companies, factories, buildings, and substantial holdings in the West. The fundamentalists, who controlled the foundation, exploited its wealth to mobilize the lower classes and to place their own supporters in its large financial network.

Thus, Khomeini became the defender of the poor, declaring that the revolution was made to serve their interests. He convinced many of them that fundamental change was essential if they were to have their fair share of power. He advocated such popular but unrealistic measures as free housing and free electricity for "the barefooted." This was soul-soothing to the lower classes, many of whom were recent migrants to the cities and who were often uneducated and religious. They became the foot soldiers of Khomeini's revolution and constituted the backbone of the Hezbollah.

The quality of Khomeini's leadership was also important in the victory of the fundamentalists. Unlike the Shah, Khomeini was decisive. He supported swift retribution against the perceived enemies of the revolution. Also unlike the Shah, he kept himself divorced from the administration of the state, which placed him in a favorable position to disassociate himself from bad government policy while taking all the credit for its more popular programs.

Ayatollah Khomeini and his supporters were also masterful institution builders in the postrevolutionary Iran. By controlling the revolutionary institutions, they gradually strangled the provisional government and won the Islamic Revolution.

Creating a State Within the State and Strangling Bazargan

Similar to Mao's strategy of first controlling the rural areas and then overcoming the cities, the fundamentalists first controlled the revolutionary institutions created after the collapse of the monarchy and then overtook the government. In fact, they formed a powerful and armed mini-state that stood parallel to, but outside the jurisdiction of, the provisional government. A channel for mobilizing and remunerating the lower classes, the mini-state was adroitly used by the fundamentalists to weaken the provisional government and consolidate their own rule. The Islamic Republican Party was one of the main components of that mini-state.

Less than a month after his arrival, Ayatollah Khomeini sanctioned the formation of the Islamic Republican Party. The party was founded by Ayatollahs Mohammad Hosseini Beheshti, Hojatolislam Seyyed Ali Khamenei, and Hojatolislam Rafsanjani, among others. Representing Khomeini's vision, the party sought to create an Islamic society in Iran by placing the ulama at the helm of the state. A coalition of diverse Islamic groups, it received much support from the traditional middle class, the bazaar, and the lower classes. The Islamic Republican Party championed many radical programs such as the nationalization of major industries. Its ideologues clothed many leftist ideas in a Shi'i garb and made them comprehensible to the masses.

The Islamic Republican Party quickly became Iran's largest and most powerful party.[12] It opened branches in major cities, published a daily newspaper, and had its own militia that included the Hezbollah, created by Hadi Ghaffari, and the Mojahedin-e Enqelab-e Islami, formed by Behzad Nabavi. Called "club wielders" by the party's opponents, these armed groups physically attacked dissidents.

In short, the Islamic Republican Party presented a revolutionary agenda and coordinated the activities of the fundamentalists. It was mostly through its leadership that the fundamentalists controlled the revolutionary institutions, one of which was the Council of the Islamic Revolution.

After the collapse of the Shah, the secret Council of the Islamic Revolution (henceforth referred to as the council) acted as an interim parliament, passing legislation that covered many areas. Whereas the provisional government was dominated by the nationalists, the council was controlled by the ulama, most of them members of the Islamic Republican Party. Originally, eight out of the seventeen members of the council came from the clerical establishment, and two other members often supported them. Although Bazargan and some of his associates were members of the council, the secular nationalists were excluded from the beginning by Khomeini. The assassination of Ayatollah Morteza Mottahari and the death of Ayatollah Mohmood Taleqani, both close associates of Bazargan and powerful members of the council, in May 1979 further diminished the power of the provisional government in the council.

Although the provisional government and the council collaborated on certain issues, such as the suppression of centrifugal activities by the rebellious ethnic minorities, mutual suspicion was the basis of their relationship. The fundamentalist ulama wanted to see a government strong enough to protect the Islamic Revolution and prevent the economy from disintegration but not powerful enough to allow the nationalists to disarm and outmaneuver them. With no administrative responsibility, the Council of the Islamic Revolution criticized many of Bazargan's programs while remaining immune to public criticism. In many cases, the council interfered in the affairs of the provisional government. For example, in April 1979 Karim Sanjabi, the leader of the National Front and foreign minister, submitted his resignation because he found himself unable to appoint ambassadors to foreign countries: His ministry was controlled by a small committee accountable to the ulama in the council.

Bazargan attempted in vain to reduce the ulama's growing power in the council by including four of them in his cabinet and by complaining to Khomeini. Although Khomeini publicly advised the government and the council to end their quibbles and to cooperate, in reality the council was implementing Khomeini's wishes. This is why he saw to it that the fundamentalists always controlled the council.

Ayatollah Khomeini also supported, to Bazargan's utter dismay, the fundamentalists' drive to control the Komites (committees). Their genesis can be traced back to the last months of the Shah's rule when, as ad hoc committees, they surreptitiously coordinated strikes and street demonstrations. In the chaotic days following the collapse of the Shah's regime, they sprang up everywhere—in the factories, in the government, in the universities. Having armed themselves after an army barracks was attacked in February 1979, the Komites became a powerful force. These "vigilante" entities hoped to protect the revolution by harassing, imprisoning, and executing—on the spot—officials of the ancien régime.

In the absence of a powerful central government, the Komites often reflected the ambitions of a local clergy or a small party, including the Mojahedin and the Fadae'iyun (Fada'iyun-e Khalq). The leftists were generally supportive of the Komites because they mistakenly believed that they would eventually evolve into a grass-roots workers' council. When they were purged from the Komites, the leftists' earlier approval quickly changed to disapproval.

From the beginning, the provisional government opposed the Komites, which often defied Bazargan's rulings and rejected his appointments. For Bazargan, the Komites symbolized anarchy; they were to be contained and preferably destroyed.[13] He attempted to dissolve the Komites by incorporating them into the national police. He was even supported by Ayatollah Shariatmadari, who insisted that the Komites should operate only in the areas where the government was weak or absent.[14]

Rather than opposing the Komites, the fundamentalists brought them under their own control by centralizing and purging them. By March 1979, Ayatollah Mahdavi Kani regulated the Komites' activities and in the following month the revolutionary prosecutor-general made unwarranted arrests and confiscation of property by the Komites unlawful and punishable.[15] Soon, Komite members were required to carry identity cards issued by the prosecutor-general that provided the fundamentalists with the opportunity to purge unfriendly elements. By November, Ayatollah Khomeini ordered Kani to dissolve some Komites and bring all of them under the supervision of fourteen regional districts, all to be headed by his trusted allies.[16]

Even more annoying to the provisional government than the Komites was the operation of the Revolutionary Courts. Their formation was the first move by the fundamentalists to monopolize the judiciary and to reintroduce the Shari'a. From their inception, the Revolutionary Courts were staffed by Khomeini's trusted lieutenants. As the paragon of Islamic justice, they decided the severity of punishment meted out against the convicted and determined the fate of the massive amounts of confiscated wealth. A few days after Khomeini's return to Iran, Sadeq Khalkhali, known in the West as "the hanging judge," executed four officials of the Shah's regime. In the ensuing nine months, some 600 people were executed by order of the Revolutionary Courts.[17] Ironically, many leftists praised the Revolutionary Courts for their swift retribution. Eventually the same courts sent many of them to the firing squads.

Bazargan, like most of the orthodox ulama and the secular nationalists, was infuriated by the Revolutionary Courts' closed trials, neglect of due process of law, the specious charges, such as "corruption on earth," that they leveled against the convicted, as well as the summary executions that were often carried out without his approval.[18] His plan to create special courts under the government's jurisdiction to deal with the counterrevolutionaries was neutralized by the fundamentalists who controlled the Revolutionary Courts.

Ayatollah Shariatmadari came to Bazargan's rescue. He maintained that courts in Islam must be open and the accused must have the right to a defense attorney.[19] Khalkhali responded that "there is no room in the Revolutionary Courts for defense lawyers because they keep quoting laws to play for time, and this tries the patience of the people."[20] But as domestic and international criticism intensified, Khomeini ordered summary executions temporarily halted in March 1979 and a new committee formed to establish rules of conduct for the Revolutionary Courts. After the new regulations were announced, the courts resumed their activities without losing their power.

The most powerful organ in control of the fundamentalists, however, was the Pasdaran, or Revolutionary Guards. Unlike Bazargan, who refused to create a national guard at the disposal of the prime minister and instead relied on the demoralized remnants of the imperial armed forces, Khomeini had the perspicacity to form an independent army. He recognized that the armed forces, despite their declared neutrality, posed a threat to the Islamic Revolution. Moreover, he knew that without the support of an armed group, the fundamentalists would be unable to defeat their rivals. Therefore, he pursued a two-pronged policy. First, he brought the armed forces under his control. During the first six months of the revolution, the Revolutionary Courts executed 248 officers of the former regime.[21] In addition, thousands were imprisoned or forced into exile. Moreover, Khomeini created in the barracks the Politico-Ideological Department of the Armed Forces and sent his representatives to all branches of the armed forces. The Politico-Ideological Department and the Imam representatives were in charge of indoctrination, dismissal of unfriendly elements, promotion of loyal supporters, and neutralizing the menace of a coup. (Thus they were much like the Bolshevik political commissars Lenin sent to the Russian army in order to keep it at bay.)

The second component of Khomeini's strategy was to create the Pasdaran. Fanatically loyal to him and to the ideals of the Islamic Revolution, the Pasdaran, which was recruited primarily from the lower classes, became an awesome force at the disposal of the fundamentalists. The fundamentalists employed the Pasdaran to suppress their opponents and to consolidate their rule. By September 1979, the Pasdaran numbered between 11,000 and 12,000, undoubtedly the largest militia of its kind in Iran.[22]

The provisional government was of course well aware of Khomeini's direct intervention into state affairs and of the growing power of the mini-state. Abbas Amir Entezam, Bazargan's deputy prime minister, informed the U.S. Embassy in Teheran that "Ayatollah Khomeini, the Komites, and the Pasdaran are campaigning against the government."[23] The U.S. Embassy went further than Entezam and reported that "Bazargan is overshadowed by the ulama establishment which is extending its authority into new areas [and] which is giving direct orders to government ministers nominally under the PRGI [Provisional Revolutionary Government of Iran] control."[24]

Bazargan, too, was aware of the proliferation of the centers of power that undermined his government. This is why he referred to Iran as a country with "thousands of sheriffs." He tried to convince the fundamentalists that progress was contingent upon the existence of one source of power: One bad commander, he quoted Napoleon, is better than two good commanders. The fundamentalists made sure that Bazargan's wishes were realized by making Khomeini the only source of power. Bazargan's numerous threats to resign and his schemes to dissolve or weaken the power of the mini-state proved fruitless. When he finally resigned in the wake of the Teheran hostage crisis, he blamed his "friends rather than the leftists" for his troubles, an unambiguous reference to the fundamentalists.

In short, from February to November 1979 the fundamentalists created a state within the state that remained outside the jurisdiction of the provisional government. Khomeini was its undisputed leader and its source of inspiration; the Islamic Republican Party was its parliament and brain; the Komites its local police; the Pasdaran its national army; the Revolutionary Courts its judiciary; and the Mostaz'efin Foundation its auxiliary source of revenue. This mini-state was a channel for the indoctrination and mobilization of the masses. It was skillfully used by the fundamentalists in the Islamic Republican Party to destroy their opponents and to pave the way for their own ascendancy.

In many ways, the events in the first three years of the Islamic Revolution were shaped by those who sought to dissolve this mini-state and those who wished to augment its power. If revolutions are the explosion of political participation, the existence of this mini-state was the symbol of that explosion.

Bazargan and the Left

In the first year after the revolution, the most influential parties of Iran's heterogeneous left movement were the Mojahedin, representing its Islamic component, and the Marxist Fada'iyun and Tudeh. Despite profound ideological differences among them, the leftists were all united in opposing "U.S. imperialism" and in advocating such measures as an equitable distribution of wealth, nationalization of the major industries and banks, and workers' and farmers' control of factories and farms.

Of course, none of Iran's leftist groups were strong enough to emerge as the victor of the revolution. As the U.S. Embassy in Teheran correctly reported in 1979, a leftist takeover was "an extremely unlikely possibility."[25] The simple fact was that the leftists lacked the resources to compete with the popular fundamentalists. There were other factors, mostly intrinsic to the left movement itself, that pushed the leftists to the political sidelines in the post-Shah era. First, they were too divided and could agree only to disagree with or denigrate one another: The Maoists denounced the Tudeh as revisionist, the Tudeh regarded the Maoists as traitorous to Marxism, the Marxists viewed the Mojahedin as religious zealots devoid of a "scientific" ideology, and the Mojahedin regarded the Marxists as atheists with no understanding of Islam. Second, the left's constituency was confined to the young, the intellectuals, and a small portion of the working class. Third, most of the leftist leaders were obscure figures. Fourth, most of the leftist organizations were more fitted to engage in guerrilla activity than to administer the state or mobilize the people. Finally, the leftists, especially the Marxists, often raised issues that appeared irrelevant to the masses. They were unable to communicate with those lower classes for whose interests they were supposedly fighting.

Despite these weaknesses, the left played an important, albeit indirect, role in the outcome of the ferocious competition between the provisional government and the fundamentalists. Their importance derived from their unrivaled ability to popularize the social question and to radicalize the revolution. The leftists were the most educated political group: Many prominent writers, poets, professors, artists, and a large proportion of the university students had strong leftist leanings. The leftist organizations also published dozens of newspapers and magazines. For these reasons the leftists, despite their exclusion from decisionmaking roles, were able to place many of their favorite programs at the top of the revolution's agenda. In the lexicon of prerevolutionary politics, for example, liberalism was a virtuous ideological posture. In the first year of the revolution, the leftists turned liberalism, which the provisional government supposedly represented, into a derogatory label.

For the left, the downfall of the Shah was an auspicious milestone, presenting them with alluring opportunities.[26] Viewing the power of the fundamentalists as ephemeral, many of them believed they would eventually rule Iran. The first obstacle in the way of that utopia was the provisional government. As the first step in their ambitious strategy to acquire power, the left developed an antagonistic policy toward the provisional government.

The left as a whole was a volunteer partner in the fundamentalists' crusade to defeat Bazargan—a partner that earned no dividend for its services. The intensity and effectiveness of their animosity toward Bazargan varied from case to case.

The Mojahedin leadership was hostile toward the provisional government, even if some of the founding members of the organization had once been closely associated with Bazargan's Liberation Movement and were influenced by his writings. On all major issues, from the proliferation of the Komites to the summary executions of the "counterrevolutionaries," the Mojahedin opposed Bazargan, deeming his policies too conservative.[27] But the Mojahedin were, not by their own choosing, more preoccupied with rebuilding their organization and neutralizing the fundamentalists' offensive against them than with attacking Bazargan. Recognizing that their ideology was more compatible with Bazargan's than with the fundamentalists', and seriously concerned about the ramifications of the fundamentalists' victory, the Mojahedin were a bit more cautious about their opposition to Bazargan than were most Marxist groups (see Chapter 10).

Compared to the Mojahedin, the Tudeh and the Fada'iyun mounted more powerful and systematic opposition to Bazargan's government. The Fada'iyun was the largest and the most popular of the leftist groups. But its neophyte leadership was manipulated by the more seasoned Tudeh leadership, which eventually caused a split in the organization.[28] Much smaller than the Fada'iyun, the Tudeh Party, whose leadership was undoubtedly the most experienced among all the leftist groups, formulated a strategy that many of the Fada'iyun followed. The Tudeh received generous support from Moscow. Its leaders were well known, its cadres disciplined, and its propaganda machinery effective. Therefore, the fundamentalists and Bazargan saw the Tudeh as far more threatening than any other leftist group. The Tudeh strategy toward Bazargan reveals much about Iran's left movement in the first year of the revolution.

The Tudeh strategy was based on identifying "the very center of the gravity, that center which moves the society. Then finding access to, or controlling, that center."[29] The Tudeh had correctly identified Khomeini as that center but it conveniently ignored the fact that Khomeini refused to recognize any Marxist group. In fact, he did not even meet with a Fada'iyun delegation that wished to present its proposal to him in February 1979.

To the Tudeh, Bazargan's government represented the liberal bourgeoisie that "will attempt to confine the Revolution within the content of its own narrow class interests."[30] Bazargan's government was portrayed as pro-Western and pro-capitalist, sworn to derail the revolution, whereas the fundamentalists were viewed as petit bourgois in class orientation, anti-imperialistic in outlook, and unpredictable and uncompromising in temperament, with some proclivity toward democratic values.

Attracted to the irresistible lure of power, the Tudeh and others under its influence were to manipulate Islam before reading its obituary. By supporting the fundamentalists and by defeating the provisional government, they hoped to push Iran toward socialism. They credulously assumed that with the nationalists eliminated, the fundamentalists would either have to invite them into a unity government or face worsening economic conditions, in which case the situation would be ripe for a socialist revolution.

The Tudeh Party proposed the formation of a broad anti-Bazargan coalition. It exaggerated the possibility of an imminent counterrevolutionary conspiracy, intensified the atmosphere of fear, and demanded fundamental change, all to the detriment of the provisional government and all with the hope of radicalizing the revolution. To widen the wedge between the provisional government and the fundamentalists, it relentlessly ostracized Bazargan's government as the U.S. link, calling it reformist and ill-suited to rule.[31]

In the bitter dispute between the provisional government and the revolutionary institutions, the Tudeh, like most leftists, ardently supported the latter because "they are trying much harder than the provisional government to eradicate the roots of the former regime."[32] These infant institutions provided enticing opportunities for infiltration by the Tudeh and the other leftist groups. The Tudeh deemed these institutions indispensable for neutralizing the menace of counterrevolution. For example, the Tudeh and its followers became, to Bazargan's dismay, staunch supporters of the Revolutionary Courts and their summary executions of the real or perceived enemies of the revolution. The Tudeh Party, which unequivocally supported Khalkhali, declared that "those who oppose the Revolutionary Courts are bedfellows with imperialism, Zionism, the monarchists, and SAVAK."[33] The Tudeh Party, like Khalkhali, denounced Amnesty International's call to halt the summary executions, calling it blatant interference in Iranian affairs. When Bazargan insisted that forgiveness, not revenge, is Islam's true legacy, the Tudeh responded that "real Islam" is based on *qesas* (retribution), as if it were an expert on Islam.[34]

Thus, the Tudeh Party facilitated the fundamentalists' ascendance to power. Had the Tudeh followed a different policy, the fundamentalists would have still emerged victorious, albeit after greater hardship and more compromises with the moderate elements, which would have decelerated the revolution's drive toward radicalism.

The policy of the Tudeh Party, indeed of the entire left movement, toward Bazargan became crystal clear during the drafting of a new constitution.

The Islamic Constitution

The struggle over the constitution began with the altercations over naming the new order. Whereas the Fada'iyun favored the "People's Democratic Republic" and the Liberation Movement talked of the "Democratic Islamic Republic,"[35] Ayatollah Khomeini insisted on an "Islamic Republic," arguing that the addition of adjectives such as democratic or progressive to Islamic Republic implied that Islam was neither.[36] Hojatolislam Rafsanjani quoted Khomeini as saying: "These people ... want Islam. From these people of Iran, 98 per cent cannot even pronounce the word 'democratic.' Say something that the people understand and have made a revolution for."[37]

Once it was decided to call the new order the "Islamic Republic," there were disputes over the wording of the referendum ballot, which generated the first open conflict between Ayatollahs Shariatmadari and Khomeini. The prepared ballot was to ask the voters, "Do you favor an Islamic Republic or a monarchy?" Complaining that the ballot gave the voters a Hobson's choice because the Islamic Revolution was the rejection of the monarchy, Shariatmadari, like many others, demanded that the voters should have more than one system to choose from. Although some leftist organizations and ethnic groups boycotted the referendum, the government claimed that 98.2 percent of more than 15.7 million votes were cast for an Islamic Republic. On May 1, 1979, Khomeini declared the first day of the Government of Allah on the earth: The Islamic Republic of Iran was born.

But the republic people had voted for remained obscure. True, in his writings Khomeini had urged the creation of an Islamic government, but he had not discussed its nature or structural configuration. This is perhaps why the draft constitution, prepared by six members of Bazargan's government, bore little resemblance to what Khomeini had written about. The 151-article constitution, which outlined a strong presidential system, had profound similarities with the 1906 constitution minus the monarchy. It made voting the basis of governance and left no privileged leadership status for the ulama. The document, however, proposed the creation of a twelve-member Guardian Council consisting of five members of the clerical community and seven laymen who were to assure the compatibility of all legislation with Islam.[38]

Strong opposition to the drafted constitution was voiced mostly by the left. The Fada'iyun criticized it for not addressing "dependent capitalism and imperialism," as if a constitution were a party resolution.[39] The Mojahedin slandered it for failing to propose the dissolution of the armed forces, the annulment of all "imperialistic treaties," and the establishment of a system based on workers' and peasants' councils.[40]

The Council of the Islamic Revolution, Ayatollah Shariatmadari, the National Front, and the Liberation Movement supported the draft.[41] Ayatollah Khomeini allegedly gave his approbation, only demanding retraction of the provisions granting women the right to judgeship and the presidency.[42] He suggested that it be submitted for referendum without being reviewed by a yet-to-be-formed constituent assembly, perhaps out of fear that the Islamic forces might not strike a decisive victory against the leftists and nationalists. But the provisional government insisted on a large constituent assembly, believing that the larger the size of the assembly, the less the chances of its domination by the fundamentalists. Hojatolislam Hashemi Rafsanjani perceptively warned these wishful thinkers that the ulama would win the majority and would doctor the drafted constitution so fundamentally that "you will regret your own decision."[43] Finally, in late June, after a unity meeting between Ayatollahs Shariatmadari and Khomeini, it was announced that a seventy-three-member Assembly of Experts would be established.[44]

It was during the campaign for the Assembly of Experts that the Velayat-e Faqih issue, which hitherto had not been stressed by the fundamentalists, became a national issue. Bani Sadr suggested that the fundamentalists introduced the concept as a defensive reaction because the leftists had opposed the draft constitution. Whatever the reasons for introducing the idea at the time, the fundamentalists' hard campaign paid off: Of the seventy-three seats, the ulama and their allies, most of them from the Islamic Republican Party, won the overwhelming majority. Only one woman and a handful of laymen were elected. Of course, the National Front and some leftist groups refused to participate in the elections on the pretext that they were denied equal time to campaign in the clergy-controlled media and that their headquarters and candidates were physically attacked by the Hezbollah. But in a spirit of unity, no one sabotaged the elections, in which hundreds of candidates competed.

Before the Assembly of Experts convened, the provisional government passed new laws that prescribed harsh penalties for insulting the ulama or denigrating Islam; these laws made others suspicious that it intended to suppress the opposition during the drafting of the constitution. More than forty newspapers, including *Ayandegan,* were shut down. By suppressing the leading newspapers, the government contributed to the suffocating atmosphere of censorship that was once again showing its ugly face.[45]

Mandated to review Bazargan's proposed constitution, the Assembly of Experts took some 560 hours of deliberation to write a constitution fundamentally different from the draft. (A somewhat similar situation had occurred in the United States: The Philadelphia Convention of 1776 was asked by the Constitutional Congress to revise the Articles of Confederation. But in a move some scholars call a coup, it wrote a new constitution that was ratified by each of the states and has survived until today.)

Ayatollah Khomeini's opening message to the Assembly of Experts unambiguously outlined the task ahead. Without mentioning the Velayat-e Faqih, he stated that the constitution must be inspired neither by the West nor the East but must be "one hundred percent Islamic."[46] In writing such a constitution, the fundamentalists first captured the leadership position. Although Ayatollah Montazeri was elected chair, Ayatollah Mohammad Hosseini Beheshti, the vice-chair, managed the Assembly of Experts. They then determined the composition of the seven closed-door committees that studied the draft and disregarded provisions deemed incompatible with Islam and wrote new ones.

In designing a political system that was simultaneously Islamic and republican, the fundamentalists faced major difficulties. First, they had to design a mechanism that would place the ulama in privileged governmental positions while eliminating the possibility that a strong president could emerge to challenge them in the future. Second, from a theological perspective, it was hard to legitimize their version of the Velayat-e Faqih because for centuries the dominant Shi'i thought had declared all temporal authorities illegitimate. Third, the Shi'i theory of government was primitive and the overwhelming majority of the framers had no previous experience in managing the state. As Rafsanjani once admitted: "Where in Islamic history do you find parliaments, presidents, prime ministers? In fact, 80% of what we now have has no precedent in Islamic history."[47] Finally, the fundamentalists were pressured by the masses to create a system in which the people could decide their own destiny.

The Islamic Constitution, like many other constitutions, contains a number of popular provisions. Consisting of twelve chapters, presumably symbolic of the Twelve Imams, and 175 articles, it calls for the creation of a single world community in the interests of the disinherited; it prohibits the interrogation of citizens; it requires the state to provide free education for all citizens up to the level of middle school, to eradicate poverty, to create full employment, to provide interest-free loans, and to prevent "foreign economic domination over the country's economy"; and it makes "nonalignment with respect to the hegemonic superpowers" Iran's official foreign policy posture. Although it grants various freedoms, the constitution limits them, too: Freedoms of press and assembly are tolerated unless deemed inimical to Islam and to the republic.

The Islamic Constitution, however, created a truly unique political system based on rule by a powerful *faqih*. Article 5, written by Ayatollah Beheshti, stipulated that during the occultation, "the governance and leadership of the nation devolve upon the just and pious *faqih* who is acquainted with the circumstances of his age; courageous, resourceful, and possessed of administrative ability; and recognized and accepted as leader by the majority of the people."[48] The constitution made it explicit that the *faqih* must be a *marja,* a highly respected authority with a considerable following who can make independent judgments about religious issues.

To justify the article, Beheshti conceded that Islam is incompatible with popular sovereignty but that the people had not voted to create a democratic order either. The selection of the *maktab* (ideology) was unequivocally made by the majority of the people when they overthrew the monarchy and subsequently voted for an Islamic Republic, he declared. And "with their first selection, they [people] will limit their future selections within the boundaries of the *maktab* [Islam]."[49] In other words, once people freely embrace Islam, they must obey its laws and limitations. Hassan Ayat used a Rousseauian analogy to justify such limitations: To leave the unhappy state of nature and enter into the tranquil and happy civil society, people forfeit certain freedoms.[50]

Once Khomeini was recognized as the center and soul of the new order, his powers and responsibilities, which certainly exceeded those granted to the king in the 1906 Constitution, were delineated. The reaches of the *faqih*'s power extended to every branch of the government. He was to serve, among other roles, as the commander of the armed forces; to declare war and peace; to appoint half of the members of the Guardian Council, which reviews the constitutionality of all legislation and regulations in the country; and to appoint the prosecutor-general and the chief of the Supreme Court. In a way, the constitution created, without admitting it, a fourth branch of the government, headed by a *faqih*, with no fixed term in office, and which is stronger than the other three and could intervene in their affairs. This did not disturb the fundamentalist framers: One of them declared that the separation of powers was a fatuous Western concept and that in Islam "all three branches emanate from one source [the *faqih*], which should supervise all activities of an Islamic government."[51]

Nor did the framers deem it essential to design an institutional mechanism, similar to the checks and balances in the U.S. Constitution, to prevent any possible abuse of power by the *faqih*. They were confident that by the time a person became a *faqih*, he would be immune to evil temptations and manipulation of power. Hojatolislam Seyyed Ali Khamenei offered the bottom-line argument: "The interpretation that the *Faqih* acts according to his own interests and is a dictator is misleading. One who acts on God's behalf is not a dictator."[52]

The framers were not even prepared to make the *faqih* accountable to any temporal powers. The Islamic Constitution makes the Majles deputies accountable to the entire nation and the prime minister to the Majles. Under the 1906 Constitution, the king, in a symbolic gesture of respect to the will of the people, must appear before the Majles to take the oath of office, declaring his unconditional support for the constitution. Although the king was also declared nonaccountable, there was a reciprocity of sorts between the king and the people, as loyalty was a gift given by the people to the king. Abuse of this divine gift, which the Majles was to determine, could justify the king's removal. But there is no reciprocity between the *faqih* and the people since he is primarily accountable to God. He does not take an oath of office before the Majles or any other authority, nor must he respond to, or appear in, the Majles. Moreover, only under extraordinary circumstances can the *faqih* be dismissed, a right reserved for the Guardian Council, half of whose members the *faqih* himself appoints.

There were practical reasons for placing the *faqih* at the apex of power: A powerful *faqih* was the best insurance for keeping Islam the basis of the new republic. His status as commander of the armed forces, for example, allowed Khomeini to place his supporters in the most strategic posts and to reduce the possibility of a coup d'état against the Islamic Revolution.

The framers also guaranteed that the ulama would retain a privileged position in the new order. The ulama's powers are most pervasive in the Guardian Council and in the judiciary. To complete the fusion of the state with Shi'ism, the Guardian Council was created. It consists of six ulama, appointed by the *faqih*, and six jurists, to be selected by the Majles from a list of candidates prepared by the Supreme Judicial Council, most of whose members are also appointed by the *faqih*. The ulama in that body exercise more power than the other members: Whereas the constitutionality of Majles legislation is to be determined by all the members, the ulama alone may express opinions on the congruity of legislation with Islam.

In the judicial branch, the ulama's power is visible and pervasive. The ministry is structured to eradicate the vestiges of all Western-inspired laws promulgated under the Pahlavis and to reimpose the Shari'a. All judges must find the basis of their judgment in the codified laws of Shi'ism and Islam or in the *fatva*s of reputable *marja'-e taqlid*. The Supreme Judicial Council, all of whose members must come from the clerical establishment, prepares bills on all judicial matters and appoints, dismisses, promotes, and demotes all judges.

In short, the framers diligently designed various constitutional mechanisms to preclude the emergence of a powerful figure who could challenge the *faqih* or the ulama's preferential status. The structural configuration of the executive branch illustrates this point.

The majority of the framers opposed a strong presidency because they regarded it as a prelude to a presidential dictatorship and a potential threat to the authority of the *faqih*. To create a weak presidency, the fundamentalists devised constitutional mechanisms of control both inside and outside of the executive branch and in the nominating process, which, in turn, diminished the effectiveness of the executive branch in formulating and implementing policy. Within the executive branch, power was decentralized and divided between the president, who held a ceremonial position, and the prime minister, who held real executive power. The activity of the executive branch was to be monitored by the *faqih*, the Majles, and the Guardian Council. The Majles, which the ulama believed they would control, was empowered to confirm the prime minister and the cabinet ministers. Thus in Iran, as in France's Fifth Republic, the divided executive branch was designed to live with "cohabitation," which denotes the coexistence of a president and a prime minister who may have different party affiliations.

Moreover, both the *faqih* and the Guardian Council were allowed to intervene in the nominating process by reviewing the credentials of all presidential candidates. (Khomeini exercised this right in the first presidential election when he banned Mas'ud Rajavi, the Mojahedin leader, from running.) This intervention was justified because of the perceived gullibility of the masses: Mohammad Keyavosh, a deputy in the Assembly of Experts, frankly admitted that "because there are those who can easily deceive the people and can dominate their lives and properties the *Faqih* must intervene to save the masses."[53]

The framers created a unique presidential system. Only in Iran's presidential system does an unelected religious figure, the *faqih,* have to approve, albeit symbolically, the election of the president and have the ability to dismiss the president if the Supreme Court or the Majles find him "incompetent," a prerogative Khomeini exercised when he dismissed Iran's first elected president, Abolhassan Bani Sadr. And only in Iran's presidential system was and still is the executive branch deprived of control over the armed forces.

The delegation of privileged roles to the ulama and the acceptance of limited popular sovereignty are harmonious with the Shi'i hermeneutics, temperament, and history. Shi'ism was born a minoritarian and esoteric movement with, as Hamid Enayat perceptively observed, "an attitude of mind which refuses to admit that majority opinion is necessarily right." The history of Shi'ism is replete with episodes in which a minuscule minority opposed a large majority. Thus, despite the consensus among the majority of the Prophet's companions to select Abu Bakr the caliph, a handful favored the succession of Ali. And Hossain defied all odds and confronted Yazid's intimidating army in Karbala with only seventy-two confidants. In these cases, the Shi'ites insist, Imams Ali and Hossein were right because their message was divine.

In Shi'ism, the truth is independent of the perception or belief of the masses. Moreover, the affairs of the state and religion are too exquisite to be delegated to those incapable of comprehending the real meaning of the Quran or the *hadith,* even if they enjoy majority support. This elitism in hermeneutics is manifest in the prevalent view that only the best of the best of the ulama can surmise the *baten* (secret meaning) of the Quran and the *hadith,* whereas the masses can only digest their *zaher* (apparent meaning). In the religious realm, this elitism has long been established since all the faithful must emulate a living ayatollah.

The Velayat-e Faqih has only extended this deep-rooted tendency into the political domain. This mistrust of the wisdom of the masses and their perceived tendency to, in Imam Ali's words, "follow every crowing," justifies the existence of a powerful authority—a shepherd, a religious superman of sorts—to protect and spread Shi'ism. The same mistrust is the underlying reason why the Guardian Council has the responsibility to examine the suitability of all candidates running for the Majles or the presidency so that, in the words of one of the framers of the constitution, the chances for the emergence of demagogic leaders are eliminated. The implicit assumption is that the people are often incapable of distinguishing good from evil and truth from falsehood, a view that a host of Western thinkers, ranging from Plato to Machiavelli, shared with the framers of the Islamic Constitution.

The other side of this coin of cynicism about the wisdom of the masses is the total trust placed in a gifted leader, an imam or a *faqih*. After decades of autocracy by the two Pahlavi shahs, the framers of the constitution designed no institutional mechanism, similar to the checks and balances in the democratic constitutions, to prevent the potential abuse of power by the *faqih*.

Challenging the Islamic Constitution

By approving of the Velayat-e Faqih, the Assembly of Experts created an irreparable crack within the anti-Shah coalition and formalized the inevitable split between the orthodox and fundamentalist ulama.

Within the Assembly of Experts itself there was some opposition to the Velayat-e Faqih. Bani Sadr, who later as president was sworn to defend the *faqih*, questioned the feasibility of ever finding a *faqih* with all the qualifications specified in Article 5.[54] He warned that granting of unlimited power to the *faqih* is a preliminary step for the reemergence of dictatorship. Ezatollah Sahabi argued that a "nefarious but secular government can be dismantled by the people, but a critical blunder by the faqih, even if inadvertent, would anathematize the ulama and calumniate Shi'ism."[55] Rahmatollah Moqaddam Maraqe'i reasoned that as long as Ayatollah Khomeini was alive, the new theocracy would endure, but because after Khomeini's death no one would likely enjoy his immense popularity, the system could collapse.[56] But these criticisms were inconsequential: Only eight votes were cast against the provision and four deputies abstained.

The second source of opposition was the nationalists and the leftists. The nationalists, with Bazargan's assistance, attempted in vain to convince Khomeini to terminate the Assembly of Experts on the procedural excuse of having failed to complete its mission according to the original schedule and for having doctored the draft constitution beyond recognition. The National Front declared that the Assembly of Experts was dominated by the "religious clique, monopolists and turban-wearers" and that it "had betrayed the ideals of the Revolution and is determined to create a theocratic order in which the ulama enjoy a privileged status."[57] The Fadae'iyun condemned the Velayat-e Faqih as a camouflaged effort to replace the Pahlavi with a Khomeini-style caliphate system.[58] The Mojahedin argued that since no group may claim a privileged status in Islam, the Velayat-e Faqih provision was a heresy.[59] The religious minorities were the third force of opposition to the constitution. The Kurdish Democratic Front and many other Sunni minorities rejected it because of its strong sectarian bias in favor of Shi'ism.

The last and most potent opposition was crystallized by the orthodox ulama who challenged the Velayat-e Faqih from the perspective of Shi'i jurisprudence. The assassination in 1979 of Ayatollah Morteza Mottahari, the chairman of the

Council of the Islamic Revolution, and the sudden death of the popular Ayatollah Mohmood Taleqani in September of the same year were disorienting blows to the forces of moderation among the ulama. It is hard to predict how either of those men would have reacted to the approval of the Velayat-e Faqih. Although it was only rumored that Taleqani stated his opposition to the Velayat-e Faqih before his death, Mottahari, before his assassination, explicitly stated that "the *Velayat-e Faqih* does not mean that the *Faqih* himself heads the government. The *Faqih's* role in an Islamic country is one of being an ideologue, not a ruler."[60]

It was Ayatollah Kazem Shariatmadari who had articulated the most rigorous opposition to the proposed constitution. Offering a strict interpretation of the Velayat-e Faqih, he argued that the primary roles of the *faqih* should include teaching; guiding the faithful; providing guardianship over the orphans, widows, and so forth; and acting as the state's ideological supervisor. Only under emergency conditions, he stated, could the *faqih* directly intervene in politics, as Ayatollah Khomeini did when he appointed Bazargan to head the provisional government.

Shariatmadari demanded the deletion of the Velayat-e Faqih provision altogether: "Because the foundation for the dissolution of the former regime was a popular referendum, the will of the people should also be the foundation for the new government."[61] He saw an irreconcilable contradiction in the constitution: It adheres to a vague notion of popular sovereignty (Article 56), but it also contains the Velayat-e Faqih, which denies the supremacy of the will of the people (Article 5).

Ayatollah Khomeini stood firm against the opponents of the Velayat-e Faqih. To the charge that it would restore dictatorship, he responded: "Was Prophet Mohammad who occupied the position of the *Velayat-e Faqih* a dictator?"[62] He equated opposition to it with a declaration of war on Islam and with wasting the "blood of the martyrs of the Revolution." He admonished the critics of the Velayat-e Faqih that they would not be able to run for the presidency.

The opponents of the Velayat-e Faqih, and they were many, failed to unify their forces. When the Velayat-e Faqih provision was approved by the Assembly of Experts in September 1979, the fundamentalists were not securely in power and could have been challenged. The orthodox ulama under Shariatmadari's leadership, the secular and Islamic nationalists, the Mojahedin, and the left were all unprepared to accept the emerging theocracy. But neither the leftists nor the nationalists gave their support to Shariatmadari, who was the only leader with the necessary religious credentials to force the fundamentalists to modify the proposed constitution. At the time, apparently, they could not see how Iran was gradually but unequivocally moving toward an Islamic theocracy. While the leftists and the nationalists were formulating their strategy toward the proposed constitution, the Teheran hostage crisis began. It radically altered the political mood of the country, prevented any meaningful debate about the proposed constitution, forced the nationalists and the leftists into a defensive posture, and irrevocably changed the balance of forces in the fundamentalists' favor. Once again the

United States, this time inadvertently, was instrumental in changing the direction of Iran's politics.

The United States, the Hostage Crisis, and Bazargan's Resignation

Having placed itself on the losing side of the revolution, the United States found itself confused and relatively powerless in revolutionary Iran. With the monarchy dismantled and the armed forces and SAVAK disintegrated, the United States lost the three channels through which it had traditionally influenced Iranian politics. Washington knew little about the new personalities who dominated Iranian politics and even less about the nature and dynamics of the ongoing power struggle. To gather intelligence, for example, the U.S. Embassy in desperation resorted to the visa weapon: To obtain visas, some Iranians had to provide the Embassy with information about the Islamic Republic. According to a memorandum from the U.S. defense attaché in Teheran, "visa referrals will only repeat *only* be handled to gain intelligence information useful to the United States government."[63]

Washington had much at stake in revolutionary Iran. It recognized that the Islamic Revolution had not diminished the importance of Iran's profitable markets, its role as major oil producer, its strategic and long borders with the Soviet Union, and its excellent position to control the flow of oil in the Persian Gulf. Despite this recognition, the United States, still bitter about the "loss of Iran," did not pursue a coherent policy toward Iran. It simply reacted, and not always wisely, to a series of events it neither understood nor controlled and made some serious blunders that radicalized the Islamic revolution and made the United States even more isolated in revolutionary Iran.

Was the real objective of U.S. policy to support Bazargan's provisional government, which it identified as moderate? Was the objective to open a dialogue with the fundamentalists? Was it to undermine the Islamic Revolution? Was it to avoid intervening in Iran's internal affairs by supporting neither the provisional government nor the fundamentalists in order to leave open the option of developing relations with whomever emerged victorious? Whatever the real objectives, the U.S. policy alienated both the fundamentalists and the provisional government and contributed to the consolidation of power by the fundamentalists.

Until November 1979, U.S. policy toward Iran was not a divisive national issue, despite consistent agitation and propaganda by the left under the ideological supervision of the Tudeh Party and despite Washington's unfriendly posture toward the Islamic Revolution and its self-evident ties with the exiled Shah. In fact, Bazargan's government worked arduously to lay the foundation for strong bilateral relations between Iran and the United States based on reciprocity and mutual respect. Among other things, Bazargan believed that all U.S.-Iranian treaties should be evaluated one by one, with only those deemed detrimental to Iranian independence being annulled. Regarding military treaties, he declared: "Those aspects of our military treaties that were not negotiated based on the Shah's ambitions and on his quest to become the policeman of the region, should not and will not be abrogated. After all, not all treaties reflected the Shah's ambitions."[64] In supporting this policy, Dr. Ebrahim Yazdi, the foreign minister, announced that whereas some U.S.-built weapons must be removed from the Iranian arsenal, others must be maintained. This required the delivery of spare parts from the United States or "our sophisticated weapons systems would turn into useless and worthless metal."[65] Abbas Amir Entezam reinforced the policy of not dismissing U.S. advisers: He warned that their expertise was essential if "Iran was to make maximum benefit from its military investments."[66] The significance of such conciliatory moves is better appreciated when we recognize that the leftists were calling for suspension of all military transactions, abrogation of all bilateral treaties, and dismissal of all U.S. advisers. In the most provocative language, the Tudeh Party, for example, lambasted the government for backing U.S. advisers who are "spies" and who have "supported and financed various assassination plots against the revolutionaries."[67]

Such a conciliatory posture toward the United States by the provisional government was never publicly condemned by Ayatollah Khomeini nor by the fundamentalists who wished not to antagonize a superpower. This is why the first attack on the U.S. Embassy in Teheran, orchestrated by a small group of armed Marxists a few days after the collapse of Bakhtiyar's government in February 1979, proved to be a minor diplomatic episode. For a short time, the armed group took captive the U.S. ambassador, William Sullivan, and a few members of his staff. However, Ayatollah Khomeini's refusal to approve the ordeal allowed Dr. Yazdi, representing the provisional government, to resolve the conflict peacefully and without much fanfare.

Although the provisional government sought to improve bilateral relations, Washington did not reciprocate; at least this is what the Iranian authorities believed.[68] Washington refused to deliver military spare parts for which Iran had already paid. From the viewpoint of those in Iran, Washington's total support for the Shah in the previous decades turned the United States into a suspected enemy of the revolution. Washington did little to change this perception, thus placing the provisional government in a difficult position. To show its goodwill and to make it easy for the provisional government to justify its good relations with the United States, Washington could have explicitly recognized the Islamic Revolution and Khomeini's leadership, admitting to its illegal campaign to overthrow Mossadeq's government in 1953 and its consistent intervention in Iranian affairs during the Shah's rule. But it refused to so do. Even Abbas Amir Entezam, who had frequent meetings with the U.S. Embassy and with U.S. intelligence officers in Teheran, accused Washington of "playing a wait-and-see" game "with the objective of interfering in Iranian affairs again in the future."[69]

Nor did Washington succeed in establishing contact with the fundamentalists, who, according to the U.S. experts in Teheran, were the dominant force in revolutionary Iran. Reason dictated the imperative of direct talks with Khomeini, without whose blessing bilateral relations could not have been normalized. Bazargan's government was well aware of this need. Through his mediation, there was to be a meeting between Khomeini and U.S. representatives in Teheran. There was even talk of inviting some prominent ulama to a religious conference in the United States.[70] Bazargan was also prepared to accept the new U.S. ambassador-designate, Robert Cutler. In May 1979, however, the U.S. Senate passed a resolution, drafted by two of the Shah's staunchest supporters, Senators Henry "Scoop" Jackson and Jacob Javits, condemning Iran for summary executions. Considering the resolution to be an interference in its affairs, the provisional government, under pressure from the fundamentalists and the leftists, announced that Cutler was no longer welcome, and Ayatollah Khomeini's office canceled the arranged meeting with the U.S. representatives. The leftists welcomed these developments but asked for more. The Tudeh Party said, "You must attack the Yankee imperialists because this is the only language they understand."[71]

But perhaps the most sensitive issue for Iran was the fate of the exiled Shah. The Shah's influential U.S. advocates were determined to prevent the resumption of friendly relations with Iran, believing that positive contacts would help institutionalize the Islamic Revolution. One of their most successful maneuvers was to pressure the Carter administration to admit the Shah to the United States for medical treatment.

As it had been during Iran's revolutionary movement, the Carter administration was again divided over the explosive issue of the Shah's admission.[72] Secretary of State Cyrus Vance reminded the president that "whatever chance existed [of] establishing relations with the new government would be surely destroyed if the Shah came to the States."[73] Zbigniew Brzezinski, the national security adviser, told Carter that "we must show our strength and loyalty to an old friend, even if it means personal danger to a group of very vulnerable Americans."[74] Former secretary of state Henry Kissinger, David Rockefeller, and a vocal group of the Shah's avid supporters also pressured Carter to admit the Shah to the United States.

The reference in Brzezinski's statement to the "vulnerable Americans" is significant because L. Bruce Laingen, the U.S. chargé d'affaires in Teheran, had advised Washington to delay the Shah's admission, predicting that such a move could lead to the seizure of the U.S. Embassy and to hostage taking. In discussing the issue with his advisers, President Carter is even quoted as saying, "What are you guys going to advise me to do if they overrun our embassy and take our people hostage?"[75]

It appears, therefore, that the Carter administration was aware of the potential consequences of admitting the Shah. When it informed the Iranian foreign ministry of the decision to admit the Shah, Yazdi, who had been assured by Secretary Vance a week earlier that Washington would not admit the Shah, protested and said "you are playing with fire."[76] He was not exaggerating.

Why did the Carter administration admit the Shah? Some say it was for humanitarian reasons. Some believe that Carter did not want to be accused in the upcoming presidential election of abandoning an old and dying ally. Still others advocate the "Kissinger-Rockefeller/Chase Manhattan" theory, according to which "Chase Manhattan engineered a freeze by convincing the government to permit the Shah to come to the United States, knowing that act would precipitate violence in Iran and make a freeze inevitable."[77] Indeed, one of Carter's first moves was to freeze billions of dollars of the Iranian assets in the United States, some of which had been placed with the Chase Manhattan Bank.

Whatever the reasons for the decision to admit the ailing Shah to the Cornell Medical Center on October 22, 1979, it changed the political landscape of Iran, renewed the bitter memories of the CIA-led 1953 coup, and generated much hatred toward the United States. It was yet another illustration of the insensitivity or perhaps ignorance of U.S. policymakers about the dynamics of Iran's internal politics. What the leftists had failed to accomplish in the previous nine months, Washington did for them: to create a hysterical anti-U.S. climate in Iran.

Taking maximum advantage of the existing freedom, the leftist parties, united as they were against "U.S. imperialism," orchestrated a disparaging campaign against Washington. To reactivate subliminally a sensitive nerve in the collective consciousness of Iranians, they identified Washington as the instigator of counterrevolution and Bazargan as its supporter. They stressed the incompatibility of Iranian independence with normal relations with Washington and the urgent need to eradicate U.S. influence as the prerequisite to the revolution's success. The Tudeh Party called, as it had for some time, for the extradition of the "criminal shah." It condemned the Shah's admission as a calculated move and "a conspiracy against the Islamic Republic."[78] The leftists accused the provisional government of not exerting enough pressure to return the Shah and of lacking the perspicacity to recognize Washington's conspiracy to restore the monarchy. The neighborhood around the U.S. Embassy in Teheran became a Mecca for the leftists who organized demonstration after demonstration against the United States. In short, to their utter pleasure and disbelief, the leftists' favorite theme, anti-imperialism, became the hottest issue of the Islamic Revolution.

But the militant Islamic groups were not about to be outmaneuvered by the leftists. One such group was the Students Following the Imam's Line, which consisted mostly of university students, many of them U.S. educated. In his interview with me, Sheikholislam Mohammad Mussavi Khoeiniha, the spiritual leader of this group, said the militant students believed that the provisional government was getting too dangerously close to the United States and that they viewed the Shah's admission to the United States as "an organized movement to destroy the Islamic Revolution. ... They were, therefore, looking for ways to inflict damage on the increasing U.S. intervention in Iran. Naturally, they concluded that the most effective action would be the temporary occupation of the American Embassy. Such an action, they thought, would have world-wide repercussions and would allow them to express their outrage against the Shah's admission to the

United States."[79] The militant students requested that Khoeiniha inform Khomeini of their plan to seize the U.S. Embassy. But Khoeiniha

> opposed contacting the Imam. I argued that the Imam is the leader of the Revolution and we should not expect his consent if we were to inform him of our plan to occupy the Embassy, an action which is in violation of international rules. ... I argued that political consideration would preclude the possibility of his consent for our action. We finally decided to execute the plan and then to inform the Imam. If he opposed the occupation, we were to quickly leave the compound, and if he approved, we were to continue with our operation.[80]

These militant students were simply waiting for an opportune moment to strike. That moment came when Bazargan and Foreign Minister Yazdi met with Zbigniew Brzezinski in Algeria in late October 1979. Both parties had acted impetuously to meet at that sensitive time. The meeting became the casus belli for the seizure of the U.S. Embassy. Three days after the meeting, and exactly fifteen years after Khomeini's forced exile from Iran to Turkey by the Shah, the U.S. Embassy in Teheran was attacked and seized by the Students Following the Imam's Line. Less than 500 in number, the students took Embassy personnel hostage, confiscated hundreds of documents not destroyed by the Embassy personnel, and created a major crisis that changed the destiny of Iran for years to come.

Immediately after entering the compound, Khoeiniha, ignoring the provisional government, "called the Imam's office and through Haj Ahmad [Khomeini's son] informed the Imam. My second call was to Ayatollah Montazeri. At first, he was surprised that we had undertaken such an action, but he did not oppose our move. I made these two calls to assure the Imam and Ayatollah Montazeri that the students were well-trusted and well-respected and would obey their orders."[81] At first, Ayatollah Khomeini did not enthusiastically support the takeover, but soon, recognizing its potential benefits, he called it "Iran's second revolution, more important than the first one."[82]

The first victim of the takeover was Mehdi Bazargan. He condemned the takeover as a violation of international law and civilized norms of diplomacy and demanded the immediate and unconditional release of the hostages. He lashed out against his critics and insisted that Ayatollah Khomeini knew in advance of his meeting with Brzezinski, even though he, Bazargan, was not obliged to obtain permission from anyone before going to meetings. Sarcastically, he said, "I am not Hoveyda; nor is the Imam [Khomeini] Mohammad Reza Shah."[83]

The fact that a small group of students refused to comply with Bazargan's demand exposed the powerlessness of his government. Therefore, two days after the takeover, Bazargan resigned. He attributed his resignation, which he happily referred to as his "second wedding," to the "interventions, disturbances, and oppositions" by the revolutionary institutions.[84] His forced resignation was a major victory for the militant students and the fundamentalists and was a defeat for the forces of moderation and the nationalists. The leftists welcomed Bazargan's defeat, but they soon paid a heavy price for their premature celebration as Iran moved closer to becoming an Islamic theocracy.

Notes

1. See, for example, Amir Taheri, *The Spirit of Allah and the Islamic Revolution* (Bethesda, Md., 1986). He argues that as early as 1976, the fundamentalists had planned the revolution but stood behind the scenes and directed the movement. A more realistic analysis is offered by Shaul Bakhash, *The Reign of the Ayatollahs: Iran and the Islamic Revolution* (New York, 1984).

2. Ruhollah Khomeini, *Kalam-e Imam: Nahadha-ye Enqelabi* (The Imam's Word: The Revolutionary Institutions) (Teheran, 1982), p. 21.

3. Ibid., pp. 31–32.

4. Mehdi Bazargan, *Shura-ye Enqelab Va Daulat-e Movaqat* (The Islamic Revolutionary Council and the Provisional Government) (Teheran, 1983), pp. 39–40.

5. See Mehdi Bazargan, *Be'sat Va Daulat* (Mission and State) (Teheran, 1981), pp. 9–48.

6. Scholars have described the Islamic Revolution according to Crane Brinton's classical model of the stages of revolution. According to this model, in all revolutions the moderates rule first and are then overthrown by the radicals. Finally, revolutions cool off and enter into the "thermidorean reaction." (The Anatomy of Revolution [London, 1953]).

7. Hannah Arendt, *On Revolution* (New York, 1965), pp. 59–114.

8. Mehdi Bazargan, *Avalin Sal-e Enqelab* (The First Year of the Revolution) (Teheran, 1981), pp. 33, 229–234.

9. For details, see Lynn Hunt, *Politics, Culture and Class in the French Revolution* (Berkeley, 1984), pp. 25–29.

10. Niccolò Machiavelli, *The Prince and the Discourses* (New York, 1950), pp. 15–16.

11. *Asnad-e Lane-ye Jasusi* (Documents of the Spy Nest), vol. 16, September 4, 1979, p. 67 (hereafter referred to as *Asnad*).

12. *Az Hezb Che Midanim?* (What Do We Know from the Party?) (Teheran, n.d.); and *Hezb-e Jomhuri-ye Islami: Mavaze'-e Ma* (The Islamic Republican Party: Our Positions) (Teheran, n.d.).

13. Bazargan (1981), p. 91.

14. *Foreign Broadcasting Information Service* (hereafter *FBIS*), August 14, 1979, p. R2.

15. Amnesty International, *Law and Human Rights in Islamic Republic of Iran* (February 1980), p. 24. The book contains an excellent account of the activities of the paralegal institutions. See also *Echo of Islam* (Teheran, 1981), pp. 1, 3, 4.

16. *Asnad*, vol. 16, October 4, 1979, pp. 136–141; "Weekly Political Report," from the American Embassy in Teheran (hereafter AET) to the State Department in Washington (hereafter SDW), prepared by Leigon. Abolhassan Bani Sadr quoted Mahdavi Kani as saying that he had purged 40,000 of the estimated 45,000 members of the Komites (Khiyanat Be Omid [Betrayal of Hope] [Paris, 1982], p. 96).

17. *Asnad*, vol. 16, October 10, 1979, p. 148.

18. *New York Times Magazine,* October 28, 1979 (Bazargan's interview with Orianna Fallaci).

19. *Asnad*, vol. 28, August 23, 1979, p. 40; "Divisions Within the Religious Community," from the AMT to the SDW, prepared by Charles Naas. Also Amnesty International (1980), pp. 40 and 52.

20. Amnesty International (1980), p. 52.

21. Gregory Rose, "The Post-Revolutionary Purge of Iran's Armed Forces," *Iranian Studies*, 17, 2 and 3 (Spring–Summer 1984), p. 160. See also William Hickman, "Ravaged and Reborn: The Iranian Army, 1982," Staff Paper, Brookings Institution, Washington, D.C., pp. 1–33.

22. *Asnad*, vol. 16, September 2, 1979, p. 61; "Threat Assessment," from the AET to the SDW.

23. Ibid., vol. 10, July 8, 1979, p. 78; from the AET to Secretary Vance.

24. Ibid., vol. 16, August 30, 1979, p. 55; from the AMT to the SDW.

25. Ibid., vol. 14, April 11, 1979, p. 78; "The Bazargan Government and the Future," from the AET to the SDW, prepared by Naas.

26. Sepehr Zabih, *The Left in Contemporary Iran* (Kent, 1986).

27. See *Majmu'e-ye E'lamiyeha Va Mauze'giriha-ye Siyasi-ye Mojahedin-e Khalq-e Iran* (Collection of the Declarations and Positions of the Organization of Iran's Mojahedin) (London, 1980).

28. *Kar*, Khordad 13, 1359/June 4, 1980.

29. *Mardom*, Esfand 23, 1357/March 15, 1979, p. 6.

30. N. Keyanuri, *Hezb-e Tudeh-ye Iran Dar Arse-ye Seyasat* (Teheran, 1980), p. 19.

31. For details, see Mohsen Milani, "Harvest of Shame: Tudeh and the Bazargan Government," *Middle Eastern Studies*, 29, 2 (April 1993), pp. 307–320.

32. *Mardom*, Khordad 21, 1358/June 13, 1979.

33. Ibid., Ordibehesht 17, 1358/May 9, 1979, and Khordad 13, 1358/June 5, 1979.

34. Ibid., Ordibehesht 14, 1358/May 6, 1979.

35. Bazargan (1981), pp. 73, 90.

36. Ruhollah Khomeini, *Kalam-e Imam: Enqelab-e Islami* (The Imam's Word: The Islamic Revolution) (Teheran, 1983), p. 175.

37. See Ali Akbar Hashemi Rafsanjani, *Enqelab Ya Be'sat-e Jadid* (Revolution or a New Mission) (Teheran, n.d.), p. 162.

38. *Asnad*, vol. 14, March 1, 1979, pp. 18–19; "The New Direction," from the AET to the SDW, prepared by William Sullivan.

39. *Kar*, no. 17, Tir 7, 1358/June 29, 1979.

40. *Mojahed*, no. 6, Mehr 23, 1358/October 15, 1979.

41. On Shariatmadari's view see *Khalq-e Mosalman-e Iran*, no. 9, Shahrivar 15, 1358/September 9, 1979. See also *Ayandegan*, Khordad 30, 1358/June 20, 1979.

42. As quoted in Bakhash (1984), p. 74.

43. Bani Sadr (1982), p. 61.

44. For Khomeini's original views on a constituent assembly, see his *Kalam-e Imam: Nahadha-ye Enqelabi* (1982), pp. 18, 21.

45. *FBIS*, August 6, 1979, p. R-11; *Kar*, nos. 26, 18, Mordad 18, 1979/August 9, 1979.

46. *Kayhan*, Mordad 10, 1358/August 3, 1979.

47. Cited by S. Bakhash. "Islam and Social Justice in Iran," in *Shi'ism, Resistance, and Revolution* (Boulder, 1987), p. 113.

48. *Constitution of the Islamic Republic of Iran*, trans. Hamid Algar (Berkeley, 1980), pp. 29–30.

49. *Surat-e Mashruh-e Mozakerat-e Majles-e Barresi-ye Nahai'e-ye Qanun-e Asasi-e Jomhuri-ye Islami-ye Iran* (The Detailed Deliberations of the Proceedings of the Council on the Final Review of the Constitution of the Islamic Republic of Iran; hereafter referred to as *Surat*) (Teheran, 1986), vol. 1, p. 380.

50. Ibid., vol. 2, pp. 1092–1093.

51. Ibid., vol. 1, p. 58.

52. Ibid., p. 54.

53. Ibid., p. 1195.

54. *Asnad,* vol. 16, September 1979, p. 105; "Work of Council of Experts Proceeds Slowly," from the AET to the SDW.

55. Ibid.

56. I am grateful to Rahmatollah Moqaddam Maraqe'i for providing me with a copy of his speech delivered to the AOE in opposition to the Velayat-e Faqih.

57. *FBIS,* September 25, 1979.

58. *Kar,* no. 33, Mehr 9, 1358/October 2, 1979.

59. *Mojahed,* no. 7, Mehr 30, 1358/October 22, 1979, pp. 1–2.

60. Morteza Mottahari, *Piramun-e Enqelab Islami* (On the Islamic Revolution) (Teheran, 1981), pp. 85–86.

61. *Ettela'at,* Mehr 19, 1358/October 11, 1979, p. 2.

62. Ibid., Aban 12, 1358/November 6, 1979, p. 10.

63. James Bill, *The Eagle and the Lion: America and Iran* (New Haven, 1988), p. 286.

64. *Mardom,* Khordad 15 and 19, 1358/June 7 and 11, 1979.

65. Ibid., Mordad 15, 1358/August 7, 1979.

66. Ibid., Ordibehesht 24, 1358/May 16, 1979, and Khordad 17 and 28, 1358/June 9 and 20, 1979.

67. Ibid., Mordad 6, 1358/July 29, 1979.

68. Bill (1988) p. 281.

69. *Asnad,* vol. 10, August 9, 1979, pp. 96–99, from the SDW to the AMT; "Meeting with Amir Entezam," prepared by Vance.

70. *Asnad,* vol. 16, 1979, p. 131; "Policy Initiatives: Talk with Perm Reps," prepared by Henry Precht; and *Asnad,* vol. 16, September 26, 1979, p. 110; "Public Diplomacy: Communication Between United States and Iran, October 1979–February 1980," from R. T. Curran to Harold Saunders in the SDW.

71. *Mardom* Khordad 2 and 3, 1358/May 25 and 26, 1979.

72. Most of the information in the next two paragraphs comes from Mansour Farhang, "U.S. Policy Toward the Islamic Republic of Iran," in Hooshang Amirahmadi, ed., *The United States and the Middle East* (Albany, 1993), pp. 151–157.

73. Ibid., p. 154.

74. Jimmy Carter, *Keeping Faith* (New York, 1983), pp. 452–453.

75. Quoted in Hamilton Jordan, *Crisis: The Last Year of the Carter Presidency* (New York, 1982), p. 5.

76. Farhang (1993), p. 155.

77. Bill (1988), pp. 295–298.

78. *Mardom,* Khordad 2, 1358/May 25, 1979.

79. Personal interview with Sheikholislam Khoeiniha, Teheran, August 1991.

80. Ibid.

81. Ibid.

82. Khomeini (1983), p. 301.

83. Bazargan (1981), p. 290.

84. Ibid., p. 67.

9

Iran's First Encounter with the Presidency and the Drive Toward Radicalism

The benefit of this Revolution is freedom from the domination of the East and the West, which is no small accomplishment.

Ayatollah Ruhollah Khomeini, Teheran, 1982

What is going on in Iran today is an antirevolutionary current for the purpose of destroying all our national accomplishments. In lieu of that Great Civilization that I had envisioned for my country, today Iran is heading toward a Great Fear.

Mohammad Reza Shah Pahlavi, in exile in Mexico, 1979

With the forced resignation of Mehdi Bazargan in November 1979 and the start of the Teheran hostage crisis, the fundamentalists took a giant step closer to consolidating their power and creating an Islamic theocracy. Quickly, a new Islamic Constitution was approved, Ayatollah Kazem Shariatmadari's vociferous opposition to the new constitution was silenced, and the fundamentalists emerged as champions of anti-imperialism in a country where such a reputation often guarantees success. The hostage ordeal brought to the core of Iranian politics some of the most radical elements of the fundamentalist camp and suffocated the moderate elements.

In 1980, a few months into the hostage crisis, Abolhassan Bani Sadr was elected Iran's first president. His presidency was defined and overshadowed by the hostage crisis, the Iraqi invasion of Iran, and his fierce competition with the fundamentalists. Thus, like Bazargan before him, President Bani Sadr found himself powerless and surrounded by antagonistic forces. Unlike Bazargan, who pursued a passive strategy toward the fundamentalists, Bani Sadr, emboldened by virtue of being the first and the only nationally elected official of the new republic, acted defiantly and aggressively to defeat them. Consequently, unlike Bazargan, who was politely forced to resign, Bani Sadr was forcefully but constitutionally kicked out of office by the fundamentalists. Reportedly, he left Iran incognito and now lives in Paris.

The Hostage Crisis, the Constitutional Referendum, and the Demise of the Orthodox Ulama

The hostage crisis led to the first major confrontation between Washington and the fundamentalists. From its beginning, it was closely connected to the ongoing power struggle among rival groups and ambitious personalities. The fundamentalists effectively exploited and prolonged it to traduce and weaken their nationalist opponents and the orthodox ulama, to pass a new Islamic Constitution, and to consolidate power. A Moslem statesman perceptively informed Secretary of State Cyrus Vance in January 1980 (a year before the Americans were finally released) that "you will not get your hostages until Khomeini has put all the institutions of the Islamic Revolution in practice."[1] His analysis was correct but not complete. Professor Richard Cottam has quoted Sadeq Qotbzadeh, one of Ayatollah Khomeini's early advisers, as saying that one of Khomeini's main objectives in prolonging the hostage crisis was to shake the United States into accepting Iran's sovereignty and independence and to awaken Iranians to the limited power of the United States.

The fundamentalists used anti-Americanism to solidify their position. They harshly condemned U.S. policy toward Iran in the previous decades and accused the U.S. Embassy of having acted as headquarters for Central Intelligence Agency operations in much of the Middle East; hence the later reference by the militant students to it as the "Spy Nest."

With Hojatolislam Khoeiniha as the Imam representative in the national radio and television network, the militant Moslem students had unlimited access to the mass media. With the blessing of the fundamentalists, they made opposition to the proposed constitution tantamount to collaboration with the United States and a treasonous betrayal of the Islamic Revolution.

The militant students' most effective strategy to push Iran toward an Islamic theocracy was their selective release of the documents they captured from the U.S. Embassy. The militant students painstakingly pieced together those documents, many of which had been shredded moments before the Embassy compound was attacked. Systematically organized, they eventually filled some sixty-five volumes. Called the "Documents of the Spy Nest," they cover a variety of issues ranging from U.S. interventions in Iran to Soviet policy in the Middle East to the operation of the Israeli MOSSAD.

The documents also contain psychological and political profiles of Iranian intellectuals and politicians and a detailed description of contacts between the U.S. Embassy and Iranians from all walks of life.[2] The Students Following the Imam's Line selectively and with much fanfare released the documents to defame the opponents of the Velayat-e Faqih. They accused hundreds of people, many of them nationalists, of being spies for the United States because they had visited with U.S. officials. Some people were imprisoned as a result, and many others were forced into exile. Abbas Amir Entezam, Bazargan's deputy who was assigned by the government to stay in contact with the Embassy, was the first victim of this well-orchestrated campaign: He was arrested and sentenced to life imprisonment. Bazargan's Liberation Movement attempted in vain to take the militant students to court, charging them with ruining the reputation of honorable men without granting them any chance to defend themselves.

Bazargan and policymakers in Washington failed to understand the organic connection between the hostage crisis and the ongoing power struggle in Iran. While the militant students were defaming hundreds of people and practically running Iranian foreign policy, none of the leading fundamentalists opposed them. Hojatolislam Khoeiniha, who held an office in the occupied Embassy, recalled that none of the ulama ever opposed the actions of the militant students:

> Among the ulama the only one who called me in the Embassy and declared his opposition was Mr. Mahdavi Kani. He requested that we leave the Embassy and release all the hostages. You mean to suggest, I responded, that the compound belongs to the Americans and our action is an illegal confiscation. He replied that it was. Are you declaring that performing prayers in the compound is not religiously sanctioned? I do, he responded.[3]

Nor did the leftists grasp the implications of the hostage ordeal. They were delighted to join the bandwagon of anti-Americanism. They praised the militant students' relentless attacks on the nationalists and often embellished them. The Fadae'iyun argued that liberalism (an unmistakable reference to the National Front, the Liberation Movement, and other nationalist groups) was as an *aba* (cover) for imperialism.[4] They claimed that Ayatollah Shariatmadari and the Moslem People's Republican Party that he supported, the two main bastions of opposition to the Velayat-e Faqih, had received substantial support from the SAVAK. The Mojahedin and the Tudeh Party were equally supportive of the militant students.[5] However, as some Mojahedin members, who were among the original 500 or so students who stormed the Embassy, were purged by the fundamentalists, Mojahedin's support for the takeover lost some of its steam.

The leftists were unaware that by recognizing the Students Following the Imam's Line as anti-imperialists they were hurting themselves: They were depriving themselves of the one last issue they could rely on to mobilize the masses, their so-called anti-imperialist posture. Many of the militant students and their supporters later became the backbone of the hard-line faction of the Iranian political elite.

While the whole country was frozen in the hysteria of the hostage crisis, the fundamentalists proposed a referendum for their draft constitution. The nationalists and the leftists continued to oppose the Velayat-e Faqih. What they did was too little, too late.

After Bazargan's fall, the National Front proposed to Khomeini that since the members of the Council of the Islamic Revolution remained secret and were not accountable to the public, he should create a Council for National Understanding to administer the state.[6] The National Front also demanded an indefinite postponement of the constitutional referendum. Ayatollah Khomeini did not even bother to respond to their two proposals.[7]

Bazargan, in his usual placating fashion, also asked Ayatollah Khomeini not to show favoritism to any one group, an unmistakable reference to the Velayat-e Faqih provision of the proposed constitution.[8] He, too, was ignored.

The greatest challenge to the proposed constitution was posed by Ayatollah Shariatmadari and the Moslem People's Republican Party, which he supported. Having failed to persuade the fundamentalists to amend the constitution, Shariatmadari issued a *fatva* against it, precipitating clashes in some major cities between his supporters and the fundamentalists.[9]

The divided opposition to the Velayat-e Faqih was no match for the fundamentalists. Thus the constitutional referendum was held on December 2 and 3, 1979, in the midst of the hostage crisis. The Council of the Islamic Revolution claimed that of the more than 15 million votes cast, only 30,866 were against the constitution. The National Front, the Moslem People's Republican Party, Ayatollah Shariatmadari, the Mojahedin, and many others boycotted the referendum. The new constitution, the most auspicious victory thus far for the fundamentalists, elevated the ulama as the plenipotentiaries of the Hidden Imam.

Despite the approval of the new constitution and despite the hostage crisis, Ayatollah Shariatmadari continued to vociferously oppose the new constitution. In a clash between his supporters and those of Ayatollah Khomeini, one of his bodyguards was shot to death. Khomeini hurriedly paid a visit to Shariatmadari's house and condemned the killing. But this did not prevent an uprising in Tabriz in which the protesters captured the radio and television stations.[10] The Islamic Republican Party demanded punishment for the killer of the bodyguard; lifting of censorship; annulment of the constitution, which it claimed had "legitimized dictatorship"; and the formation of a united front against the fundamentalists.[11] To prevent the spread of the Tabriz uprising to other regions, the fundamentalists promised Shariatmadari that "without his prior approval" no decision regarding the internal affairs of Azerbaijan would be made. This led to a short lull in the tension.[12]

Soon, however, Shariatmadari complained that the government had broken its promises, thus precipitating more bloody riots in Tabriz.[13] This time, the regrouped fundamentalists reacted violently: The Pasdaran attacked and occupied the Moslem People's Republican Party's headquarters in Tabriz. The Revolutionary Courts executed some of those who had participated in the earlier uprising. Shariatmadari and the Moslem People's Republican Party were accused by the Students Following the Imam's Line of collaboration with SAVAK and the United States.

The fundamentalists demanded that Shariatmadari be stripped of his ayatollah title, which they were unqualified to do. Ayatollah Shariatmadari was pressured to dissolve the Moslem People's Republican Party. He responded: "And the point that I should tell you, dear gentlemen, is that with the current policy of the regime there is no need on the part of the founders of the party to dissolve it because the regime, by labeling political parties as American, Zionist and un-Islamic, will gradually dissolve all of them."[14] He was soon silenced and put under a virtual house arrest and the Moslem People's Republican Party was dissolved before the Iranian presidential elections, scheduled for January 1980.

Thus, the opponents of the Velayat-e Faqih, forced into a defensive posture by the hostage crisis, failed to forge a coalition against the proposed constitution: The National Front, the Liberation Movement, and other moderates did not rally behind Shariatmadari. Shariatmadari knew that the nationalists and the leftists were vehemently against the Velayat-e Faqih, but he mistakenly assumed that they would support him should he confront Khomeini.

Although most leftists welcomed Shariatmadari's defeat and praised the hostage fiasco, they were unaware that soon they too would have to confront the fundamentalists face to face and become victims of their wrath.

Bani Sadr: A Man of Many Titles and Little Power

The constitutional design of a divided executive and a weak presidency reflected the fundamentalists' goals of precluding the possibility that a strong president might challenge them later. That structural configuration protected them, but it also created an ineffective government. Consider the brief tenure of Iran's first president, Abolhassan Bani Sadr.

Although Bani Sadr, running as an independent, won the first presidential race with 10.7 million of the 14 million votes cast, his victory can be attributed more to his identification as a creation of Khomeini and to the confusion within the Islamic Republican Party than to his own popularity, a fact that he refused to accept. Because of the strong opposition to the Velayat-e Faqih, Ayatollah Khomeini banned the ulama from running in the first presidential elections. The ban shattered Ayatollah Beheshti's bid for the presidency and created confusion in the Islamic Republican Party, which nominated the obscure Hassan Habibi. Khomeini, exercising his constitutional right, also banned the Mojahedin leader, Mas'ud Rajavi, because he had boycotted the constitutional referendum. These two developments, plus Khomeini's endorsement of his candidacy, greatly enhanced Bani Sadr's chances of victory.

Bani Sadr's brief presidency was marred and rendered ineffective by the growing power of the Islamic Republican Party and the revolutionary institutions, or the mini-state, it controlled. Bani Sadr enjoyed several advantages. In the early days of his presidency he was close to Ayatollah Khomeini. He was the only nationally elected official of the new republic and was appointed by Khomeini as the chair of the Council of the Islamic Revolution and the temporary commander of the armed forces. He also had some support among the nationalists and leftists. Despite these advantages, he lacked the wherewithal to compete with the fundamentalists in the Islamic Republican Party under the shrewd leadership of Ayatollah Beheshti.

Bani Sadr recognized that only by curtailing the centrifugal forces of the revolutionary institutions would he be able to govern. Toward this goal, he first attempted to control the Majles. Even though he campaigned tirelessly on behalf of his allies, only a handful were elected. In the double-ballot elections, a format that is universally advantageous to large parties, the Islamic Republican Party won more than 130 of the 234 seats in the Majles.[15] Having the majority, the fundamentalists further consolidated their power by rejecting the credentials of some elected National Front and pro–Bani Sadr Majles deputies, including Admiral Ahmad Madani, who was accused by the militant students of having connections with the United States. They also helped elect Hojatolislam Ali Akbar Hashemi Rafsanjani, a member of the Islamic Republican Party's central committee, as speaker of the Majles. Thus with the Islamic Republican Party dominating the Majles, Bani Sadr suffered his first major setback.

The dispute over selecting the prime minister created the first constitutional crisis for the new republic. The constitution stipulated that the president chooses and the Majles confirms the prime minister. Bani Sadr tried in vain to bypass the Majles and to pressure it to confirm his nominee, Mostafa Mir Salim. In the end, a committee, whose members were chosen by the Majles and the president, proposed a list of potential candidates to Bani Sadr. From that list, Bani Sadr chose Mohammad Ali Raja'i.[16] He later claimed that he was "pressured by that committee" to choose Raja'i.[17]

It was obvious from the start that the president and the prime minister could not "cohabit." Their different socioeconomic, educational, and ideological backgrounds turned them into bitter rivals, not partners.

They were both born in 1934, Bani Sadr into a prosperous clerical family in Hamedan and Raja'i into a family of humble origin in Qazvin. They both completed their high school education in Iran and then took two different paths. Bani Sadr continued his education at Teheran University, where he became active in the pro-Mossadeq politics in the early 1950s. Raja'i became a street vendor for a while, but eventually his mentor, Ayatollah Beheshti, helped him become a high school teacher. Raja'i collaborated with both the Liberation Movement and the

Fada'iyun-e Islam, an underground Islamic group responsible for assassinating a number of prominent Iranian statesmen. He was jailed and allegedly tortured by SAVAK. Unlike Raja'i, who stayed in Iran, Bani Sadr left for France in the early 1960s to begin his doctoral studies, which he reportedly never completed. There he continued with his anti-Shah activity, collaborating at different times with the National Front, the Liberation Movement, the Confederation of Iranian Students, and the Moslem Students Association. Bani Sadr was profoundly influenced by European social democracy, with its emphasis on individual freedom and pluralism, and by the dependency theory that focuses on the negative consequences of the Third World's dependent relations with the West. He mixed these two currents with Islamic philosophy and concentrated on economics, about which he wrote a few short pieces.

Both Bani Sadr and Raja'i were obscure figures until the former became a close adviser to Khomeini in Paris in 1979 and the latter was named prime minister in 1980. Raja'i became under secretary for education in Bazargan's provisional government and later won a seat in the first Majles. Bani Sadr returned home in the same Air France jet that brought Khomeini back to Iran. Calling him his "spiritual son," Khomeini appointed Bani Sadr to the Council of the Islamic Revolution, where he championed radical programs.

In many ways, these men represented two different breeds of activists. Raja'i had the perfect profile of a dedicated, homegrown Shi'i fundamentalist who bragged about his humble family background and his face-to-face confrontation with the Shah's regime inside Iran. He was unimpressed by Bani Sadr's Western education, nor did he appreciate Bani Sadr's "eclectic" interpretation of Islam. Bani Sadr, in contrast, exemplified those upper-class, Western-educated, Islamic intellectuals who, championing a version of the modernist Shi'ism that Ali Shari'ati had advocated, fought the Shah from their safe sanctuaries in the West. Bani Sadr could hardly hide his condescending attitude toward Raja'i for his lack of advanced formal education and his ignorance of the proper protocol of diplomacy.

Therefore, it was no surprise that the two men, representing two different constituencies and outlooks, could only agree to disagree with each other. Their first major dispute revolved around the selection of the cabinet members. Raja'i, like the Reds in the Chinese Cultural Revolution, focused on the ideological commitment of the ministers, whereas Bani Sadr, like the Experts in the Cultural Revolution, emphasized expertise. Unable to reach a consensus, they were forced to leave some of the cabinet posts vacant throughout Bani Sadr's term.[18]

Their dispute over the selection of ministers reflected their diametrically opposed views on the role and responsibilities of the president. Bani Sadr desperately sought to create an imperial presidency, with him formulating the policy and his prime minister implementing it. Raja'i, backed by the Islamic Republican Party and the Majles, was an advocate of a weak presidency, as the constitution stipulated. His goal was to keep the president a figurehead with merely ceremonial responsibilities.

To a large extent, Raja'i succeeded in his mission: During his tenure, Bani Sadr was outmuscled by the fundamentalists who controlled the revolutionary institutions, the Majles, the office of the prime minister, and the judicial branch. Recognizing early in his presidency that he had many impressive titles but little influence over domestic policies, Bani Sadr chose to focus on foreign policy. First he concentrated on the hostage ordeal and then on the Iraq-Iran war. Neither of these issues, however, could save his doomed presidency.

Bani Sadr, the Hostage Crisis, and the War with Iraq

President Carter's policy during the early phase of the crisis was inconsistent and indecisive. He granted sanctuary to the Shah, an old ally—a move that was surely justifiable on moral and humanitarian grounds. But his decision to force the dying Shah out of the United States was morally indefensible and politically imprudent. It exposed his inability to withstand pressure and made the Students Following the Imam's Line more belligerent. These two factors prolonged the crisis and contributed to Carter's defeat in the presidential election of 1980.

In response to Iran's intransigence in attempts to end the crisis quickly, the Carter administration began to implement its containment policy toward Iran. It was based on five pillars: (1) to freeze Iranian assets in the United States, estimated somewhere between $8 billion and $15 billion; (2) to impose economic and military sanctions on Iran; (3) to isolate Iran internationally; (4) to support the anti-Khomeini forces; and (5) to strengthen Saudi Arabia and befriend Iraq as counterweights against Iran in the Persian Gulf.

A few weeks into the crisis, Bani Sadr and Sadeq Qotbzadeh worked out a U.S.-supported plan whereby a United Nations Inquiry Commission would investigate Iran's grievances against the Shah in return for the release of all hostages.[19] Ayatollah Khomeini's declaration in February that only the new Majles would enjoy the prerogative of settling the crisis put an end to this plan. Despite this setback, a team of four—Bani Sadr, Qotbzadeh, Argentinian businessman Hector Villalon, and radical French lawyer Christian Bourguet—devised a plan to extradite the Shah to Iran from Panama—a plan that reportedly had the backing of Hamilton Jordan, Carter's chief of staff. The Shah was informed of the plan by his friends in Washington and in Panama and left Panama for Egypt before the extradition papers were submitted to the Panamanians. That the Shah escaped extradition was interpreted by Bani Sadr as a deliberate policy by the Carter administration to undermine him.[20] In protest, he detached himself from the hostage crisis.

As various diplomatic initiatives failed to bear fruit, President Carter, who broke diplomatic relations with Iran in early April 1980, was pressured to take punitive military action against Iran. Eventually, six months after the crisis began, Carter opted for a daring, but ill-advised, rescue operation called "Eagle Claw," which had been designed immediately after the taking of the hostages. If its main objective was to rescue the hostages, the operation had little chance of success: Groups of armed men, constantly in contact with each other and with a central command center, were guarding the hostages, who were spread out in different parts of the huge Embassy compound, which was located in a crowded section in the heart of Teheran.

According to the plan, eight Sea Stallion helicopters were to meet six C-135 transport planes, bringing men and equipment, in Tabas, about 260 miles from Teheran. From there, the rescuers were to be taken surreptitiously to Teheran, where they would storm the Embassy.[21] According to Colonel Charles A. Beckwith, leader of the operation, "it was our aim to kill all Iranian guards ... and we weren't going in there to arrest them; we were going there to shoot them right between the eyes, and to do it with vigor."[22] But in the first phase of the operation, three of the eight helicopters malfunctioned, forcing the commander of the operation to abort it. Returning to their bases at night in a sandstorm, one of the helicopters collided with a transport plane, killing eight servicemen. After the failure of the operation he had opposed from the start, Vance resigned.

The aborted mission further solidified the fundamentalists' position and weakened the nationalists. The astonishing ease with which U.S. helicopters and planes had penetrated Iranian airspace, and the strange decision by the commander of the Iranian air force to explode one of the helicopters abandoned in Iran that allegedly contained sensitive documents about the mission, increased the suspicion that the United States was instigating a coup.

According to the officials of the Islamic Republic, the United States planned a major coup to overthrow Khomeini in July 1980, three months after the abortive Tabas rescue mission. The coup, which was reportedly neutralized before it could be put into operation, was to begin from the Nuzheh air force base near Hamadan. Some twelve targets, including the residence of Ayatollah Khomeini in northern Teheran and the headquarters of the Pasdaran, were to be bombed by Iranian jets taking off from Nuzheh.[23] The discovery of this coup culminated in the arrest, imprisonment, and execution of hundreds of officers from the regular armed forces. The National Front and other nationalists were also implicated in the aborted coup. In retaliation, the Hezbollah seized the National Front's headquarters, arrested one of its leaders, and shut down its newspaper. In the ensuing months, some 4,000 bureaucrats and between 2,000 and 4,000 personnel of the armed forces were purged.[24]

In short, during the hostage crisis, the fundamentalists increased their anti-U.S. rhetoric, pushed the revolution toward radicalism, and solidified their control over the revolutionary institutions, the state bureaucracy, and the armed forces, all to the detriment of Bani Sadr, who was turned into a figurehead president. Once Iraq invaded Iran, however, Bani Sadr found a new opportunity to increase his power.

In September of 1980, Iraq invaded Iran.[25] Whatever Hossein's goals were for this naked aggression against Iran, the Iraqi invasion gave the Islamic Revolution a new lease on life as the whole country rallied behind Khomeini, and a combination of strong Shi'i fervor coupled with intense Iranian nationalism revitalized the armed forces and strengthened the Revolutionary Guards. Explicitly blaming the United States for "ordering" Iraq to invade Iran, the fundamentalists intensified their anti-U.S. rhetoric. As Saddam had calculated, the war intensified the rivalry between the fundamentalists and Bani Sadr, but this did not, as he had hoped, lead to the overthrow of the fundamentalists; in fact, it accelerated their consolidation.

In the first month of the war, the Iraqi forces scored a major victory as they occupied a considerable portion of Iranian soil. In the ensuing months, the Iraqis also captured the port city of Khoramshar and continued their successful offensive.

Bani Sadr attributed Iran's inability to win the war to the fundamentalists' flawed military strategies. This was an unmistakable reference to the role the Revolutionary Guards were playing in the war and their interventions in military decisions being made by the regular army. He saw in the war a golden opportunity to solidify his position within the regular army. He favored management of the war by military experts, whereas Raja'i and the Islamic Republican Party praised the actions of the Revolutionary Guards against the Iraqis.

Bani Sadr's strong support for the regular armed forces prompted suspicion among the fundamentalists that he might be cultivating the dangerous idea of eventually imposing himself as a new strongman, a Reza Khan in religious guise or, as the leftists preferred to say, as Iran's Napoleon. Bani Sadr, who had no prior military experience, fueled such speculations by often appearing in public in his military fatigues.

The devastation and hardship of the lingering war, along with the prevalent corruption and lack of security and freedom, gave the opponents of the fundamentalists an opportunity to resurface. It was in this context that Sadeq Qotbzadeh, the erstwhile foreign minister, publicly expressed his dissatisfaction with the state of affairs. He was quickly arrested by the Komites, which precipitated a strong protest by the nationalists and some bazaar merchants who were disenchanted with a pending bill to nationalize foreign trade. Qotbzadeh was released quickly. But a few months later, a leading bazaar merchant who had contributed lavishly to the Islamic Revolution and had supported Qotbzadeh was executed. The opposition to the fundamentalists was neutralized at every level: Their demonstrations were often interrupted violently by the Hezbollah; their open letters to state officials were ignored; and their criticism fell on deaf ears.

In the long run, the war proved a blessing for the fundamentalists in several ways. First, it solidified the organic link between them and the lower classes because they administered the Basij (Mobilization) organization, which was responsible for recruiting war volunteers. Second, it increased the Pasdaran's war experience and consolidated their position as dedicated defenders of Iran's territorial integrity. Third, because the armed forces were preoccupied with the war, the chances of a military coup against the Islamic Republic were substantially diminished. Fourth, on the pretext of a war emergency, the government increased repression of the dissidents. The Mojahedin's newspaper, for example, was shut down because of its critical stance on the government's war policy. Fifth, the war diverted public attention away from internal difficulties. And finally, the consequences of the war in addition to the U.S. economic sanctions over the hostage crisis led to a rationing of essential goods. The local mosques and the Komites became the distribution centers for the ration cards, hence putting the clergy at the helm of a massive distribution network. The rich obtained goods on the expensive black market, whereas the middle and lower classes relied on the mosques and the Komites for their supplies. The mosques thus became a powerful economic force at the community level.

Resolution of the Hostage Crisis and Bani Sadr's Removal

By the middle of 1980, the fundamentalists were in an excellent position: They controlled the Majles, the judicial branch, and the cabinet; they were unfolding a cultural revolution designed to eradicate all vestiges of Western culture from Iranian society; and they were in charge of the war with Iraq. The benefits of the hostage crisis, however, were gradually outweighing its costly consequences, which included Iran's diplomatic isolation, war with Iraq, and economic sanctions imposed on the country by the United States. Hence, Iran softened its demands for the resolution of the crisis. Ayatollah Khomeini announced four conditions for its resolution: a pledge by the United States not to intervene in Iran's internal affairs; the return to Iran of the assets frozen in the United States; the cancellation of all U.S. claims against Iran; and the extradition of the Shah's wealth to Iran. Subsequently, secret negotiations began between the two nations, with West Germany and Algeria as intermediaries.

In early October, a special Majles committee, headed by Hojatolislam Khoeiniha, was established to direct Iran's negotiating plans. Raja'i, without Bani Sadr's approval, dispatched Behzad Nabavi to represent Iran in the final negotiation with the U.S. government, represented by Warren Christopher, who later became President Clinton's secretary of state. Although the Iranians remained "deeply suspicious and often obstinate," Christopher recalled, "they made a number of far-reaching decisions rather quickly in the closing hours, permitting the release of the hostages."[26] Two days before Reagan's inauguration, the Majles approved the Algiers Agreement, and hours after Carter left office in January 21, 1981, the hostages were freed.[27] Later, the timing of this release fueled the suspicion that representatives of the Reagan/Bush campaign had covertly struck a deal with the Iranians: The Iranians allegedly promised not to release the hostages during the presidential campaign in return for a pledge by the Americans to provide Iran with weapons.

According to the Algiers Agreement, the United States pledged not to intervene in Iran's internal affairs and to prevent the hostages and their families from bringing lawsuits against their captors and against the Iranian government. It promised U.S. cooperation with the Islamic government in bringing lawsuits in U.S. courts to extradite the Pahlavi family's wealth. And it released some Iranian assets that were frozen in the United States. Only $7.98 billion was transferred to Iran's escrow account, "Dollar Account 1," at the Bank of England, of which about $3.67 billion was transferred to New York Federal Reserve to cover Iran's debts to U.S. banks.[28]

The accord provided the nationalists and the leftists with ammunition to attack the fundamentalists who had negotiated it single-handedly. Bani Sadr emerged as their spokesperson. He emphasized that the Americans made no apologies for their past activities in Iran, nor were the hostages tried in court, as the Students Following the Imam's Line had demanded. Not only was the Shah's wealth not extradited (and therefore unlikely to be returned), he maintained, but also during the 444 days the hostages were held Iran lost access to its massive assets in the West. The confrontation with the United States made Iran diplomatically isolated and vulnerable to the Iraqi invasion. Bani Sadr chastised Nabavi for failing to obtain a U.S. commitment to provide the much-needed military spare parts for Iran's war efforts against Iraq. Placing the blame for the humiliation of the accord on the Islamic Republican Party, he touched a historically sensitive Iranian nerve: He compared the accord with the disastrous Torkaman Chay and Golestan treaties imposed by Russia on Iran in the early nineteenth century.[29]

The fundamentalists were in no mood to listen to provocative criticism that threatened their collective interests. Emphasizing that the accord was blessed by Khomeini, they equated criticism of it with a personal insult toward him. Master propagandists, they represented the accord as the symbol of Iran's victory over the "Great Satan," as one of the "most important and constructive actions in the history of the world."[30] Speaker Rafsanjani argued that the entire ordeal proved that a Third World nation can challenge the world's mightiest military force: "We demonstrated that the decision is with us. When we desired, we talked. When we desired, we remained silent; we got everything we wanted."[31] Although he admitted that some minor economic damages were inflicted on Iran, he quickly added that such losses were expected because Iran was fighting a superpower. But, he pointed out, Iran can even turn the short-run economic loss into long-term gain: Economic sanctions by the United States have exposed Iran's dependency on the West and will force the country to move toward self-sufficiency. Finally, he concluded that "if hostages had not been taken, the person of the shah would perhaps still be alive and the focal point of the opposition [against the Islamic Revolution]. Either they [it is not clear who "they" refers to] killed him, or he died from sorrow; at least, his death came prematurely."[32]

Unable to unify the opponents of the fundamentalists over the Algiers Agreement, and outmaneuvered by the Islamic Republican Party on all major domestic and foreign policy issues, Bani Sadr felt frustrated and powerless. So when his speech to a large group commemorating the hundredth birthday of Mossadeq was interrupted by hecklers in March 1980, he ordered the police to arrest the hecklers, who were later identified as supporters of the Islamic Republican Party. The fundamentalists struck back: The general prosecutor began investigating an apparent violation of the law by the president for ordering the arrest, and some Majles deputies called for Bani Sadr's impeachment.

The different approaches of Bani Sadr and the Islamic Republican Party to domestic and foreign policies were pushing the Islamic Republic to the brink of collapse. At this time, Ayatollah Khomeini intervened. In mid-March, he called for a meeting of the Islamic Republican Party and Bani Sadr at his residence. He ordered the creation of a tripartite conciliatory committee to investigate the grievances of the feuding factions. He kept Bani Sadr as the commander of the armed forces but ordered him and the Islamic Republican Party to refrain from public attacks on each other until the conciliatory committee reached a verdict.

The truce was short-lived. It was to be officially broken by Bani Sadr, who denounced the government for torture, censorship, and violation of human rights. He questioned the legitimacy of the most cherished institutions of the republic, the Majles and the Guardian Council, and asked Ayatollah Khomeini to abolish them. He even called for a national referendum to settle his dispute with the Islamic Republican Party, a direct challenge to Khomeini.

The Islamic Republican Party was officially silent, but it was tightening the noose around Bani Sadr's neck. His newspaper, *Enqelab-e Islami,* was shut down by the government; sixteen of his close associates were arrested by the Komites; and the ulama were using the mosque network to denounce him.[33]

This animosity in the highest echelons of the government created an opportune moment for the formation of a broad antifundamentalist coalition among Bani Sadr, the nationalists, some orthodox ulama, and the Mojahedin—or at least among some of these groups. The fundamentalists moved to destroy the start of such a coalition by the old but effective strategy of divide and rule.

The National Front had planned a well-advertised, antigovernment, pro–Bani Sadr rally for June 15, 1981. Other groups were invited to join. Ostensibly, the rally was against the Qesas legislation (Islamic retribution laws), which the National Front called inhuman and regressive. Hours before the gathering, Ayatollah Khomeini addressed the nation on national radio and television. The National Front, he declared, had always been more concerned about nationalism than about Islam and, therefore, its opposition to the Qesas legislation was understandable. But how could other Islamic groups and individuals align themselves with the National Front and the Mojahedins? he asked. He was forcing the National Front's potential allies to take sides for or against Islam, thus turning a political issue into a religious one.[34] The policy paid off as Bani Sadr and the Liberation Movement quickly disassociated themselves from the National Front. The rally turned out to be a farce, as the majority of the participants were the

Hezbollah! This symbolized the end of the National Front's open activity in Iran and the defeat of secular/liberal nationalism.

Meanwhile the Students Following the Imam's Line released some Embassy documents that supposedly proved Bani Sadr's connection with the CIA. According to the militant students, a veteran CIA agent, Vernon Cassin, with the code name Guy Rutherford, posed as a U.S. businessman representing a big firm in Pennsylvania. He met Bani Sadr, code name SDLURE/1, in Paris in January 1979. Cassin, whose ostensible goal was to establish business ties with revolutionary Iran, was interested in Bani Sadr's analysis of the political situation in Iran. After Bani Sadr returned to Iran and occupied sensitive posts at the highest echelons of the Islamic Republic, Cassin met him again on at least three different occasions. Bani Sadr was allegedly offered $2,000 for a "half-hour conversation" with Cassin. In one of his reports to the U.S. Embassy in Teheran, Cassin referred to Bani Sadr as "a valuable contact," a reference that the Students Following the Imam's Line interpreted as confirmation that Bani Sadr was collaborating with the CIA. Bani Sadr did not deny meeting Cassin or being offered money by him. But he claimed that he was unaware of Cassin's CIA connection and that he was offered but rejected a $5,000-a-month consulting fee.[35]

The militant students accused Bani Sadr of high treason: "We are one hundred percent, not ninety nine percent, sure that Bani Sadr was cooperating with the CIA. Embassy documents prove that Bani Sadr has committed high treason."[36]

At the same time, the Majles declared Bani Sadr incompetent, paving the way for his impeachment. Ayatollah Khomeini dismissed Bani Sadr as the commander of the armed forces, eliminating the possibility of a pro–Bani Sadr coup. He gave Bani Sadr another chance to repent and stay in office. In a letter to Ayatollah Khomeini, Bani Sadr wrote: "You do not want the Constitution to be implemented. ... You want a weak president, a weak government, an obedient Majles, a judiciary as a vehicle for threatening and destroying your opponents."[37] In return, Ayatollah Khomeini, invoking his constitutional right, dismissed Bani Sadr.[38] In hiding, Bani Sadr called for an uprising against what he called the emerging "mullacracy."

The Lessons of Bani Sadr's Presidency

Bani Sadr's presidency coincided with one of the most tumultuous periods of Iran's recent history. Iran was simultaneously going through four profound crises: the transition from an autocratic monarchy to an Islamic theocracy; the intense interelite rivalry; the war with Iraq; and the hostage crisis. In a period when unity of purpose and action was most needed for Iran, Bani Sadr's presidency brought discord and division. That Bani Sadr's presidency lasted only sixteen months is not surprising; that it lasted that long is.

Many of the factors that rendered Bazargan's provisional government ineffective also worked against Bani Sadr. Like Bazargan before him, he was gradually suffocated by the powerful revolutionary organizations that the fundamentalists controlled. Nor could he control the Students Following the Imam's Line, who were defiant of the president and who, much to his chagrin, determined Iran's foreign policy. Bani Sadr, like Bazargan, was unable to win Khomeini's critical backing in his war against the Islamic Republican Party even though Khomeini called him his "spiritual son." The problem was that the Islamic Republican Party was the incarnation of Khomeini and a reflection of his vision. In fighting it, Bani Sadr, like Bazargan, was fighting Khomeini. Khomeini was cognizant of this and therefore in critical moments sided with the Islamic Republican Party.

Of course, Bani Sadr himself was responsible for some of his misfortunes. He failed both to institutionalize his support and to define clearly the core of his constituency. A loner, he did not, or perhaps could not, create a party. Politically arrogant and ambitious, he conveniently flirted with different groups at different times. He was becoming a man for all seasons. To enlarge his popular base of support among the nationalists, he championed the cause of civil liberty and economic reconstruction. To win the support of the leftists, he favored nationalization of major industries and greater autonomy for minorities. At various times, he aligned himself with the orthodox ulama and with some members of Khomeini's household.

In hard times, however, Bani Sadr was unprepared to defend any of these groups or jeopardize his relations with Khomeini, whom he admired. Thus, when it became clear that his days as president were numbered, he lacked the courage to support the National Front's June 1981 rally against the fundamentalists. When the fundamentalists began their campaign of "cleansing the universities," which were packed with leftists, Bani Sadr triumphantly entered the campus of the University of Teheran to announce the start of the Cultural Revolution. He justified his involvement as a move to deprive the fundamentalists of leadership position in the Cultural Revolution. But once again, he had deceived himself, for it was not he but the fundamentalists who led and managed the Cultural Revolution. Thus, he deprived himself of the consistent support of any one group. This is perhaps why he had little support in the streets.

The closest Bani Sadr came to forming an alliance with any group was his relationship with the Mojahedin, his most powerful supporters. Even in choosing the Mojahedin, he showed little perspicacity. His alliance with them, which he denied during his presidency, was suicidal: It made the fundamentalists more suspicious about his real intentions and isolated him further from the nationalists, who had no desire to watch another Islamic group emerge in the country. Had the alliance resulted in the downfall of the fundamentalists, a very remote possibility, it would have probably ended his presidency too, for the Mojahedin would not have tolerated him any more than the fundamentalists did. After Bani Sadr's dismissal and the bloody confrontation between the Mojahedin and the fundamentalists, both Bani Sadr and Rajavi, the leader of the Mojahedin, went into hiding in Iran, most probably in Kurdistan. When their wishful thinking about a popular uprising did not materialize, they escaped to France in late July 1981, where they formed the National Council of Resistance, a government in exile of sorts, to coordinate their anti-Khomeini activities. The political ties between the two were further tightened when Rajavi married Bani Sadr's daughter. Soon, however, Bani Sadr's tenuous relations with the Mojahedin ended—along with his daughter's marriage to Rajavi—as he defiantly and angrily left the National Council of Resistance.

Bani Sadr, like many other Western-educated intellectuals, suffered from cultural alienation. Ayatollah Khomeini diagnosed this problem well when he told Bani Sadr: "Yes, you are an honest and naive man. But you were not familiar with the situation in Iran. You had come from Europe and did not know the situation; the ulama were shrewd and they took over."[39] His eclectic philosophy, a strange mixture of European social democracy, Marxist dependency theory, and Islam, turned the president into a man everyone, from the fundamentalists to the leftists, loved not to trust.

In retrospect, Bani Sadr tried but failed to create an imperial presidency. His failure was testimony to the effectiveness of the constitutional mechanism devised to contain the power of any president unfriendly to the fundamentalists. But at the same time, his sixteen-month tenure revealed the structural flaw of the constitution, which contained no mechanism to resolve the differences between the president and the prime minister.

Whatever the merits or shortcomings of Bani Sadr's presidency, his ouster removed the fundamentalists' last major hurdle to ruling Iran. But there was still some resistance to their rule. In April 1982, Sadeq Qotbzadeh was arrested and charged with conspiracy to overthrow the government and kill Ayatollah Khomeini.[40] Qotbzadeh, a professional anti-Shah agitator and an adviser to Khomeini in Paris, bravely accepted the charge that he was planning to overthrow the government but insisted that he had no plan to kill Khomeini. Equally intriguing was his confession that Ayatollah Shariatmadari had advance knowledge of the coup plot. Qotbzadeh was found guilty by the Revolutionary Courts and executed. Ayatollah Shariatmadari was strongly condemned and insulted by the fundamentalists and the government. He was put under house arrest until his death in 1986. The government allowed him no public funeral.[41]

The Fundamentalists and the Mojahedin: An Eye for an Eye and More

In the first two years of the Islamic Revolution the fundamentalists had been principally engaged in a bitter but relatively peaceful competition with their rivals, who held powerful positions in the state. Now, after Bani Sadr's removal, they faced a violent threat by the forces that were excluded from any role in the government and were seeking to undermine and overthrow the new Islamic order. The violent confrontation between those forces and the Islamic Republic and the prolongation of the Iraq-Iran war accelerated the Islamic Revolution's drive toward radicalism, which had begun in earnest with the taking of the U.S. hostages in November 1979. The most serious threat to the Islamic Republic was posed by the Mojahedin.

Under the Shah, the Mojahedin had suffered irreparable damage from SAVAK, which had either killed or imprisoned its leaders: Both Mas'ud Rajavi and Mu'sa Khiyabani, two of the organization's top leaders, were released only in the last days of the Shah's rule. With the Shah's collapse, the Mojahedin went into a defensive mobilization mode, rebuilding its shattered organization and recruiting new members. By the end of 1979, it had become a large and powerful party, capable of organizing rallies in major cities attended by as many as 100,000 supporters.

The most serious problem facing the Mojahedin was their ideological competition with the fundamentalists, who mistrusted them and considered their ideology eclectic and tainted with Western influence. Because both the Mojahedin and the fundamentalists claimed to represent the true Islam, the rivalry between the two was intense and bloody.

From the start of the Islamic Revolution, Khomeini refused to recognize the legitimacy of the Mojahedin and excluded them from any decisionmaking role. The Mojahedin's support of the Kurdish rebellion, their opposition to the Velayat-e Faqih, and their boycott of the constitutional referendum in 1979 further strained their fragile relationship with the fundamentalists. Despite their harsh criticism of the fundamentalists in the Islamic Republican Party, the Mojahedin, aware of Khomeini's popularity, refrained from publicly attacking Khomeini, always referring to him as the leader and the founder of the Islamic Republic, even though Khomeini referred to them derogatorily as *monafeqin,* or religious hypocrites.

The question, therefore, was not if the fundamentalists and the Mojahedin would collide, but when and how violently. The inevitable bloody clash erupted during the last days of Bani Sadr's presidency. In the rivalry between the fundamentalists and Bani Sadr, the Mojahedin sided with the president. When they organized a rally against his impeachment in June 1981, some of the Mojahedin were shot to death by the Hezbollah, marking the start of the open armed struggle by the Mojahedin against the Islamic Republic.

On June 28, 1981, the top leadership of the Islamic Republican Party held a conference in Teheran to discuss, among other issues, its strategy in the upcoming presidential election. But the conference ended quickly: A powerful bomb demolished the party's conference room, killing more than seventy persons, including Ayatollah Mohammad Hosseini Beheshti, the party's chairman and president of the Supreme Court, four cabinet ministers, and twenty-five Majles deputies.[42] The bloodiest since the start of the Islamic Revolution, this terrorist act shook the foundations of the Islamic Republic and exposed its vulnerability. Only a few days later, the chief of Teheran's Evin Prison was gunned down, which indicated deep infiltration of the government and the security forces by the opponents of the fundamentalists.

The Islamic Republic blamed the Mojahedin for both actions and interpreted them as a declaration of open war. It moved in two directions. First, it appointed new officials to the vacant positions: Mohammad Javad Bahonar replaced Beheshti as the chairman of the Islamic Republican Party, and Mussavi Ardabilli became the president of the Supreme Court. Despite the Mojahedin's attempt to sabotage the elections, the presidential election was held at the end of July 1981. Raja'i became Iran's second president and named Bahonar the prime minister. Second, the Islamic Republic reacted violently against the Mojahedin, which were identified as enemy number one. Ayatollah Khomeini asked the masses to spy for the government, to report unusual activities in their neighborhoods, and to identify the members of the Mojahedin to the security forces. He ordered an immediate purge of government agencies and of the Pasdaran. Strict preventive security measures for protection of officials and government agencies were imposed. In response, the Mojahedin, and other armed groups, stepped up assassinations of Pasdaran and of Ayatollah Khomeini's representatives in major cities.

For a while Iran looked like the Middle East's new Lebanon, as both the fundamentalists and their armed opponents spoke to each other only in the language of brute violence. In August 1981, the Islamic Republic was once again shaken to its foundations. A powerful bomb exploded at a high-level government meeting, killing, among others, President Raja'i, Prime Minister Bahonar, and the chief of the national police. In response, the fundamentalists quickly filled the vacant government positions and again increased repression.[43] Ayatollah Khomeini appointed Mahdavi Kani as the new prime minister. In the presidential election in October, Ali Khamenei became the third president. His approach to the presidency was harmonious with the spirit of the constitution; throughout his tenure, he remained a weak and uncontroversial president. When asked by his colleagues to accept the nomination for the presidency, he is reported to have said that because of his ill health, he would not be able to spend a great deal of energy as president. "That is why we are offering you the post," they told him.[44] Khamenei was overshadowed by the charismatic personality of Khomeini and by his strong prime minister, Mir Hossein Mussavi, who ran the government and formulated policy.

Now the entire security of the Islamic Republic focused on the Mojahedin threat. The government's campaign against the Mojahedin was effective and furiously brutal. Hundreds of the Mojahedin were killed, poisoned, or forced into exile. Finally, in February 1982, some ten months after the start of their war against the republic, the Mojahedin suffered a disorientating setback: Their main underground hideout in Teheran was discovered by the Pasdaran, who killed Mu'sa Khiyabani, the commander of the Mojahedin in Iran, and at least eight other top leaders.[45] With Rajavi forced out of Iran and Khiyabani killed, many of the Mojahedin joined the Kurdish rebels who were still fighting against the Islamic Republic. Some of them fled to safe sanctuaries in Europe.

In their offensive against the Islamic Republic, the Mojahedin assumed that because they stirred up so much trouble for the late Shah's well-fortified regime, their larger, better-trained, and better-equipped organization should be capable of toppling the yet-to-be-institutionalized Islamic Republic—at war with Iraq and with a weak security force. They followed the strategy of assassinating the key figures of the Islamic Republic in order to shatter the public perception of the Islamic Republic as invincible and in the process to organize the discontented population against the fundamentalists.

But the Mojahedin's calculations were flawed, costing them and the Islamic Republic thousands of innocent lives. First, they underestimated the capacity of the Islamic Republic to withstand the assassination of its leaders, its determination to respond to terror with more raw terror, and its ability to revitalize its security forces. The security forces of the Islamic Republic, inexperienced as they were, were not like SAVAK: They felt no compunction about eradicating their opponents; they were impervious to international condemnation of their use of brute force; and they were ideologically committed and prepared to defend their ideals with their blood.

Second, the Mojahedin underestimated the propaganda capability of the Islamic Republic. The fundamentalists effectively employed both the state-controlled mass media and the mosque network to disparage the Mojahedin as hypocritical atheists clothed in Shi'i garb. Unlike the Shah's government, the Islamic Republic had the religious legitimacy to denounce the Mojahedin as heretics.

Third, the Mojahedin overestimated their own popularity and the appeal of their ideology. Their constituency was confined to the young and a portion of the modern middle class. Their version of Shi'ism, attractive as an ideology of protest against the Shah, could not match the appeal of the fundamentalists' popular Shi'ism.

The Mojahedin's fourth mistake was to consider all opponents of the fundamentalists their potential allies. Many secular and Islamic nationalists and many leftists, discontented as they may have been with the fundamentalists, were not prepared to support a group of young Islamic radicals with no administrative experience whose only credential was the legacy of their anti-Shah adventurism. And those who had not supported the Islamic Republic from the outset were certainly not enthusiastic about helping one Islamic group overthrow another one.

Because of their miscalculations, the Mojahedin's violent encounter with the Islamic Republic produced the exact opposite of what they had hoped to prove: It proved the invulnerability of the Islamic Republic to guerrilla warfare, exposed the weakness of the Mojahedin, invigorated the Islamic Republic's security system, and further solidified the fundamentalists' position.

Since 1983, the Mojahedin have conducted most of their activities in Western Europe, the United States, and Iraq. Because of the pro-Iraqi posture of the Mojahedin and Rajavi's close friendship with Iraq's ruling clique, Bani Sadr withdrew from the National Council of Resistance in 1985. In 1986, the Mojahedin were pressured by the French government to move their headquarters from Paris. Their new headquarters is in Iraq.[46]

Learning the Hard Way:
The Belligerent and the Tamed Marxists
Face the Fundamentalists

The suspicion of and animosity toward the Marxists that the Islamic forces harbor have deep roots in Iran's contemporary history. These roots can be traced to the Jangali Movement in the second decade of the twentieth century when Mirza Kuchak Khan, a devout Moslem and the leader of that movement, was betrayed by his pro-Russian communist allies. The Marxists' anti-Mossadeq policy during the nationalization of the oil industry in the early 1950s and their lack of support for the June Uprising of 1963 only magnified this mistrust. Some of the more cultured leaders of the left, including the Tudeh Party, recognized this justifiable rancor and attempted to rectify it by backing the fundamentalists in the post-revolutionary era. But such support was based more on opportunistic calculation than on sincerity.

Besides the Mojahedin, a number of leftist groups like the Communist League violently challenged the Islamic Republic. Small in size, Maoist in outlook, and unrealistic in political ambition, the Communist League consisted of many Western-educated dissidents and former members of the Confederation of Iranian Students who had returned to Iran during the last days of the Shah's rule.[47]

In January 1982, a few hundred armed members of the Communist League attacked and took over 'Amol, a small city in northern Iran. It was hoped that so inspired a takeover would set off a chain reaction that could precipitate a national uprising against Khomeini. For a brief moment, they controlled the city. But the Communist League, like the Mojahedin, had underestimated the resolve of the fundamentalists. Without any hesitation, the government sent additional forces to the city, quickly recapturing it and killing and arresting the rebels. The government also confiscated sensitive documents about the membership of the league. Using information from the confiscated documents, and perhaps from confessions obtained from the arrested members, the authorities captured most of the league's central committee members. On trial, and according to supporters of the league after being tortured, some of the league's ideologues repented and asked for forgiveness: They glorified Ayatollah Khomeini and the Islamic Republic as a bulwark against imperialism. The fundamentalists showed no mercy: The convicted, tried in Teheran, were taken back to 'Amol and were executed in public at the center of the city. Lucky members and sympathizers, who had escaped arrest, left the country. The Islamic Republic's message was simple: Force will be answered with force.

Two months after the suppression of the 'Amol rebellion, the Islamic Republic scored another victory over the Marxists. For some time, the minority Fada'iyun had been supporting the Kurdish rebellion and building small cells for preparation of the final assault on the Islamic Republic. Although it had drastically reduced the intensity of its armed struggle against the Islamic Republic, its antigovernment publications, its opposition to the Velayat-e Faqih and to the Iraq-Iran war, and its support for Bani Sadr were nuisances to the Islamic authorities. In May 1981, Sa'id Soltanpur, a famous poet and one of the Fada'iyun, was executed by the government. In early 1982, the Fada'iyun's underground publishing facility and a number of underground cells were discovered and some Fada'iyun leaders killed by government agents. After the incident, the Fada'iyun continued its underground agitation against the Islamic Republic, but to no effect.

In the summer of the same year, the Islamic Republic shocked the belligerent Marxists again. A Marxist faction, the Sazman-e Peykar Dar Rah-e Azadi-ye Tabaqe-ye Kargar (the Organization of Struggle in the Path of the Liberation of the Working Class, or Peykar), split from the Mojahedin (Chapter 6). It, too, was critical of the government and of its war policy. In a successful raid on the Peykar's main cell, the government arrested some of its leading ideologues. One of the ideologues, appearing on national television, condemned the Peykar's anti-Khomeini activities, proclaimed the Islamic Republic a progressive, anti-imperialistic government, and urged all Marxists to support the Islamic Republic. After this humiliation, the Peykar, like the Communist League, melted away. Disillusioned and cynical members left the organization, and the more dogmatic members joined the Kurdish rebels.

Not all the Marxists violently opposed the fundamentalists. Amazingly and amusingly, the Tudeh and the majority Fada'iyun, two Persianized Marxist-Leninist parties, tied their fortunes to those of the overtly anticommunist fundamentalists, becoming their volunteer bedfellows and cheerleaders. Their fate, however, was not much happier than that of the belligerent left. The fundamentalists gave these Marxists a dose of their own medicine: They skillfully used them to weaken the nationalists and other rivals and then, by 1983, smashed what little was left of the left.

Despite its small membership, the Tudeh was the most important Marxist party not only because of its support from Moscow but also because it was the ideological innovator of all the Iranian Marxists: They either followed the Tudeh's line or expressed their existence in defiance of or deviation from it.

The Tudeh leadership interpreted the Islamic Revolution as an anti-imperialistic revolution, the first prerequisite to socialist revolution in Iran.[48] Its support of the Islamic Republic had both theoretical and tactical justifications. On the theoretical level, it saw revolutionary Iran as oscillating between the socialist and imperialist camps. By supporting the fundamentalists, and by opposing the pro-Western moderates, like Bazargan and Bani Sadr, the Tudeh hoped to drive Iran closer to the socialist camp.

The Tudeh leadership credulously assumed that with the nationalists eliminated, the fundamentalists, lacking managerial skills, would either have to invite it into a unity government or face a worsening economic crisis, in which case the conditions would be ripe for a coup.

The main pillar of the Tudeh strategy in revolutionary Iran was to provide unconditional support for Khomeini, flattering him rhetorically.[49] The Tudeh leadership justified its support for the fundamentalists because of an alleged ideological harmony between tudehism and fundamentalism: They both favored indiscriminate destruction of all things Pahlavi, promoted egalitarian principles, relied on the support of the toiling masses, and opposed Western imperialism. But they tactically overlooked their profound differences: The fundamentalists endeavored to create a society ruled by the ulama and freed of all non-Islamic influences, whereas the Tudeh extolled socialism. And the fundamentalists' indignation at the West was matched by their contempt of the godless Soviet Union, which the Tudeh glorified. Such incompatible differences made it obvious that supporting Khomeini was merely a tactic, Machiavellianism par excellence.

To improve its tarnished image, the Tudeh deified Khomeini. It unwaveringly claimed that its support for the Imam was strategic and sincere, not tactical and deceptive. Replete with selective quotations from the Imam, Tudeh publications made opposition to Khomeini tantamount to counterrevolution. To cultivate good relations with them, the Tudeh endorsed fundamentalist candidates for various elections.[50]

The Tudeh was a master of Orwellian double-talk. Although the party was to champion the cause of socialism, its publications emphasized that "under present conditions we do not wish to build socialism" while simultaneously distributing some 340,000 copies of the *Communist Manifesto* in the first few months of the revolution.[51] While the same plenum had advocated the creation of a democratic republic, the Tudeh voted for both an Islamic Republic and a constitution that legitimized the ulama's rule.[52] And to display the party's sincerity, Keyanuri falsely declared that the Tudeh "does not have a military wing within the armed forces, nor does it intend to create one."[53]

The fundamentalists were quite aware of the Tudeh's insincerity. But they tolerated the Tudeh because it weakened their opponents, kept the left divided, and improved their relations with Moscow. The Tudeh performed other useful services for the Islamic Republic. It has been alleged that the Tudeh Party and the majority Fada'iyun, which followed the Tudeh religiously, provided critical intelligence to the Islamic government about the whereabouts of the Mojahedin, the Peykar, and the minority Fada'iyun. The Tudeh was also a powerful ideological force whose support of the Islamic Republic kept the left divided and confused. The Tudeh's freedom to conduct its activities in Iran was portrayed by the Islamic Republic both at home and abroad as proof of its political tolerance. As such, the Tudeh was among the few free parties that participated in elections, published newspapers, and expanded its constituency while quietly infiltrating the government and the armed forces.

The government's crackdown on the Tudeh began in 1983. The reasons for and the timing of the government's change of policy toward the Tudeh are not entirely clear. A number of factors, however, could have been instrumental in the decision. First, in June 1982, Vladimir Andreyvich Kuzichkin, a Russian officer in the Soviet Embassy in Teheran, alleged to have been a KGB station chief, had defected to England.[54] He is reported to have given the British some critical information on the Tudeh Party's plan and the names of some 400 Tudeh officials. England is reported to have given the information to the Islamic authorities. What England received from Iran in return is unknown, as is the relationship between Kuzichkin's defection and the arrests of the Tudeh members. Second, in 1983, when Iran had gained the upper hand at the war front, Moscow once again called for an end to the Iraq-Iran war. The Islamic Republic rejected the proposal. The Tudeh's subtle criticism of the Islamic Republic's refusal to sign an "honorable peace treaty" with Iraq and its unconditional support of the Red Army's occupation of Afghanistan provided the Islamic Republic with further rationalization to dismantle the party. And finally, the conservative forces in the Islamic Republic were pressing the government to dismantle the Tudeh.

In its confrontationalist policy toward the Tudeh, the government arrested more than seventy party members, including fourteen from its Central Committee and nine high officials from the armed forces. Among other charges, the government accused the party of spying for the Soviet Union and planning to overthrow the government. Whereas Tudeh ideologues like Ehsan Tabari and Nurredin Keyanuri were imprisoned, the nine army officers, including Amir Afsali, the commander of the navy, were hurriedly tried and executed.

And then, in humiliation, the Tudeh's ideologues appeared on national television and created a fiasco of disproportionate disaster for the Marxists. There were Tabari, the greatest Marxist philosopher of Iran, Keyanuri, a cultured politician, and Behazin (Mahmud E'temadzadeh), a popular writer, begging for forgiveness and mercy. They revered Ayatollah Khomeini, condemned their own past activities, professed that their party had always acted as a spy network for the Soviet Union and as a vehicle to enhance its foreign policy objectives, admitted to their betrayal of Mossadeq's nationalist movement, and concluded that years of research and political activity had finally convinced them that Shi'i Islam was inherently superior to Marxism. They asked the youth to join the Islamic Republic and to abandon Marxism.[55] The stunned cadres of the Tudeh insisted that their leaders had been tortured and drugged to make those confessions. The validity of such charges notwithstanding, some top leaders of the Tudeh Party seemed to have finally realized that their message and the manner in which they had attempted to convey it were unacceptable to the masses, for whose cause they were fighting.

Along with the members of the Tudeh Party, some members of the majority Fada'iyun who had not escaped from Iran were also arrested. It, like its mentor the Tudeh Party, was declared illegal in May 1983. By that time, all political groups, except the Islamic Republican Party and the Liberation Movement, had either been forced underground or demolished by the Islamic Republic. The chaos of the Islamic Revolution was finally giving way to order and tranquility.

Notes

1. Warren Christopher et al., eds., *American Hostages in Iran* (New Haven, 1985), p. 44.

2. For a different interpretation of the documents captured in the Embassy, see John Limbert, "Nest of Spies: Pack of Lies," *Washington Quarterly,* Spring 1992, pp. 75–82.

3. Personal interview with Hojatolislam Khoeiniha, Teheran, August 1983.

4. *Kar,* no. 40, Day 12, 1358/January 3, 1980.

5. The Mojahedin supported the takeover. One of their members who participated in the attack but was purged by the SFLI has written his version of the hostage crisis. See *Majera-ye Poshte-e Parde-ye Gerogangiri* (The Behind-the-Scenes Episode of the Hostage-Taking) (Long Beach, Calif., 1981).

6. *Ettela'at,* Aban 19, 1358/November 10, 1979, p. 2.

7. At the same time, the Islamic Republican Party (IRP) published a series of articles by Hassan Ayat in which the National Front was attacked, giving the impression that many of its leaders were foreign spies. Ayat, for example, claimed that one of the reasons for Ayatollah Kashani's split from Mossadeq was Kashani's belief that Shahpur Bakhtiyar was a British agent (*Jomhuri-ye Islami,* Aban 15, 1358/December 6, 1979, p. 15).

8. Mehdi Bazargan, *Enqelab-e Iran Dar Dau Harekat* (The Iranian Revolution in Two Moves) (Teheran, 1984), pp. 295–296.

9. *Khalq-e Mosalman* (Teheran), no. 11, Mehr 29, 1358/October 21, 1979.

10. *Ettela'at,* Azar 15, 1358/December 6, 1979, p. 1.

11. *Khalq-e Mosalman,* no. 15, Aban 27, 1358/December 18, 1979.

12. *Ettela'at,* Azar 17, 1358/December 9, 1979, p. 2.

13. Ibid., Azar 20, 1358/December 12, 1979, p. 12.

14. Ibid., p. 12.

15. *Majles-e Shura-ye Islami-ye Iran* (The Consultative Islamic Majles of Iran) (Teheran, 1981), p. 199.

16. *Chegunegi-ye Entekhab-e Avalin Nakhost Vazir-e Jomhuri-ye Islami-ye Iran* (The Process of the Selection of the Islamic Republic's First Prime Minister) (Teheran, 1982), pp. 14–15.

17. Abolhassan Bani Sadr. *Khiyanat Be Omid* (Betrayal of Hope) (Paris, 1983), p. 117.

18. *Chegunegi-ye* (1982), pp. 122–124.

19. On the hostage crisis, see Hamilton Jordan, *The Last Year of the Carter Presidency* (New York, 1982); and Pierre Salinger, *America Held Hostage: The Secret Negotiations* (New York, 1981).

20. Bani Sadr suggested that a faction within the U.S. ruling class, one that he did not specify, was consistently moving Khomeini in the direction it wished: "I have said this in my interviews … that fifty Americans are not the hostages, it is our people that have become hostage to the United States."

21. For military dimensions of the rescue, see Paul B. Ryan, *The Iranian Rescue Mission: Why It Failed* (Stanford, 1985), pp. 17–43; Colonel Charles A. Beckwith and Donald Knox, *Delta Force* (New York, 1983); and also Drew Middleton, "Going the Military Route," in Robert McFadden, Joseph Treaster, and Maurice Carroll, eds., *No Hiding Place* (New York, 1981), pp. 215–226.

22. As quoted in Ryan (1985), p. 60.

23. For details see *Koudeta-ye Nozeh* (The Nozeh Coup) (Teheran, 1988).

24. Shaul Bakhash, *The Reign of the Ayatollahs: Iran and the Islamic Revolution* (New York, 1984), pp. 112–113.

25. See R. K. Ramazani, "Who Started the Iraq-Iran War?" *Virginia Journal of International Law,* 33 (Fall 1992), pp. 69–89.

26. Christopher et al. (1985), p. 4.

27. Little is known about the possible contacts between the Reagan election campaign and the Iranian authorities. Flora Lewis quoted Bani Sadr as saying that the fundamentalists "did not want Carter to win the elections." So in October 1980 there were meetings in Paris between their representatives and Reagan's. Lewis indicated that there are no confirmations of such meetings. But she stated that for whatever reason, arms started going to Iran from Israel in the first half of 1981 (Flora Lewis, *New York Times,* August 3, 1987, p. 19); see also Bani Sadr (1983), pp. 156–157.

28. Christopher et al. (1985). The financial aspects of this important treaty have been studied by John Hoffman in Christopher et al. (1985), pp. 235–280. For a more complete version, see Roy Assersohn, *The Biggest Deal: Bankers, the Hostages of Iran* (London, 1982).

29. Bani Sadr (1983), pp. 143–175; and *Mizan*, Esfand 2, 1358/February 21, 1980.

30. Ali Akbar Hashemi Rafsanjani, *Notqha-ye Qabl az Dastur-e Hojatolislam Rafsanjani* (Hojatolislam Rafsanjani's Speeches Before the Official Deliberations of the Majles) (Teheran, 1983), p. 39.

31. Ibid., p. 40.

32. Ibid.

33. *New York Times,* June 3, 1979.

34. Ruhollah Khomeini, *Kalam-e Imam: Goruhhaye Siyasi* (The Imam's Words: The Political Groups) (Teheran, 1984), pp. 264–265.

35. For details see Christos P. Ioannides, *America's Iran* (New York, 1984), pp. 57–68.

36. Ibid., p. 66.

37. Bani Sadr (1983), p. 19.

38. Ayatollah Khomeini's analysis of what Bani Sadr wanted him to do is revealing: "On numerous occasions Bani Sadr told me to remove this government [Raja'i's]; he wanted to make me a dictator, and I would laugh at him and tell him: You have power, do it yourself," (*Kalam-e Imam: Shakhsiyat'ha* [The Imam's Words: Personalities] [Teheran, 1983], p. 81).

39. Bani Sadr (1983), p. 316.

40. *New York Times,* April 4 and 21, 1982.

41. On the government's campaign to discredit this religious figure, see Seyyed Hamid Rauhani, *Shariatmadari dar Dargah-e Tarikh* (Shariatmadari in the Court of History) (Teheran, 1985).

42. *Foreign Broadcast Information Service (FBIS)*, June 29, 1981, vol. 8, pp. I-2 to I-5. The bomb was planted in a school next door to IRP headquarters. The Mojahedin never claimed responsibility for this bombing. A group calling itself the Party of National Equality, however, did claim responsibility. The group claimed to be against "imperialism, Zionism, communism, dictatorship, and fascism, hoping to create a federal system in Iran" (ibid., June 30, 1981, vol. 8, pp. I-5, I-6).

43. The Mojahedin claimed responsibility for the bombing (ibid., August 31, 1981, vol. 8, p. I-9).

44. Personal interview with a member of President Khamenei's administration, Teheran, July 1991.

45. Mohsen Reza'i, the Pasdaran leader, directed the attack. Rajavi's first wife and Khiyabani's wife were killed. Despite this successful raid, Rajavi insisted from Paris that his group would fight until Khomeini was overthrown and that more than 40 percent of the armed forces supported him and only 10 percent supported Khomeini (*FBIS*, February 10, 1982, vol. 8, p. I-1). Radio Free Voice of Iran claimed that the KGB helped the government to track down Khiyabani (ibid.).

46. For a very good discussion of the evolution of the Mojahedin see Ervand Abrahamian, *The Iranian Mojahedin* (London, 1989).

47. See, for example, *Tahlili Az Jonbesh-e Cheriki-ye Iran* (An Analysis of Iran's Guerrilla Movement) (1975).

48. On the Soviet interpretation of the Islamic Revolution, which is essentially the same as that of the Tudeh Party, see Craig Natton, *Soviet Conceptualization of the Iranian Revolution*, Carl Beck Papers in Russian and East European Studies, no. 42, University of Pittsburgh (Pittsburgh, 1985). On Soviet relations with the Shah and with the Islamic Republic, see Aryeh Y. Yodfat, *The Soviet Union and Revolutionary Iran* (London, 1984).

49. *E. Tabari Donya*, Khordad 1357/June 1979.

50. For details see Mohsen M. Milani, "Harvest of Shame: Tudeh and the Bazargan Government," *Middle Eastern Studies*, 29, 2 (April 1993), pp. 307–320.

51. *Mardom*, Esfand 23, 1357/March 15, 1979, p. 6.

52. N. Keyanuri, *Mash-ye Seyasi-ye Hezb-e Tudeh-ye Iran* (Teheran, 1979).

53. *Mardom*, Esfand 28, 1358/March 20, 1979.

54. *FBIS*, May 10, 1983, vol. 8, p. I-2.

55. *Confessions of the Central Cadre of the Tudeh Party* (in English) (Teheran, 1983).

10

Khomeini and the Challenge to Govern

> In revolutions, there are only two sorts of men, those who cause them and those who profit by them.
>
> *Napoleon I, 1804–1815*

> There has been no revolution like ours, with so little destruction and with so many benefits. The result of this revolution was to free [ourselves] from the yoke of the domination of the East and the West, which is no small accomplishment.
>
> *Ayatollah Khomeini, 1983*

By the third year of the Islamic Revolution in 1982, Ayatollah Khomeini and his dedicated supporters were in total control of the state and the revolutionary institutions. For all practical purposes, the opponents of the Islamic Republic had been either silenced, killed, or exiled. Once the task of consolidation was completed, the more challenging business of governance began. The most pressing issues facing Iran's new elites were the fragmentation of the fundamentalist camp, the management of a war-riddled economy, and the war with Iraq.

Factional Politics
Within the Fundamentalist Camp

Like every other revolution, Iran's also created a new political elite, at whose core stood the fundamentalists. Ayatollah Khomeini and his household were at the heart of this new elite structure. Other members included the fundamentalist ulama and the top echelons of the government, the revolutionary institutions, and the armed forces.

Although the fundamentalist camp was not homogeneous from the outset of the Islamic Revolution, it demonstrated a remarkable degree of cohesion when fighting its rivals. More than any other group, the fundamentalists recognized and defended their corporate interests.

The emergence of factions within the fundamentalist camp was inevitable. The polycephalic essence of Shi'ism and the power of the ayatollahs to offer different interpretations of Islam rendered the existence of factions natural in the ulama-dominated politics. It was perfectly normal for those with a common vision to form factions. Moreover, to defeat their opponents, the fundamentalists formed a de facto alliance with segments of the shopkeepers, merchants, and the middle and lower classes. Various factions represented these constituencies, whose interests were sometimes irreconcilable.

The issues that fragmented the fundamentalists revolved around ownership of property, the role of the state, Iran's relations with the West, the nature of the *feqh* (jurisprudence), and the war with Iraq. Divergent views about these issues created three factions, all committed to the principle of the Velayat-e Faqih.[1]

The conservative faction, supported by the rich merchants, landowners, and the high-ranking ulama, were champions of the free enterprise system, stressing the urgency to create a prosperous and expanding economic system. They opposed state ownership and management of the major industries, imposition of any limits on private ownership, nationalization of foreign trade, and land reform. They favored a cautious rapprochement with the West while maintaining close ties with the Islamic nations and free trade with Western Europe, Japan, and other industrialized nations. They also stressed moderation in the export of the Islamic Revolution and a political resolution of the Iraq-Iran war.[2]

Socially, the conservatives supported a strict implementation of the Islamic laws. They were supporters of the traditional *feqh,* according to whose tenets certain Islamic decrees simply transcend "time and space" and therefore are impervious to change and revision by the *faqih* or the ulama.

The crusader faction, supported by the lower middle class, the lower class, the shopkeepers, the middle-rank ulama, and many of the revolutionary organizations, were avid proponents of egalitarianism and self-sufficiency. For them, the economy was not an end in itself, but only a means for achieving the pristine ideal of Islamic justice. To achieve their goals, the crusaders advocated state ownership and management of the major industries and banks, nationalization of foreign trade, imposition of limits on ownership of property, comprehensive land reform, and formation of state cooperatives. In some ways, they espoused a crude form of economic socialism within the parameters of Islam.

In foreign affairs, the crusaders favored an aggressive export of the Islamic Revolution and the prolongation of the war until total victory and the removal of President Saddam Hossein. Hojatolislam Mohammad Khoeiniha, who led the 1979 occupation of the U.S. Embassy in Teheran, summarized the essence of the crusaders' foreign policy when he told me:

We will inevitably have conflict of interests with a world that is under the domination of the West, especially of the U.S. The best alternative [for Iran] is that road which allows Iran to become the standard bearer of an Islamic ideology that can mobilize the Third World and the Islamic world against the West. It is one that would ... allow us to repeat inflicting heavy damage on Western and American interests, that would allow us to keep the Islamic nations awakened from their sleep and would allow us to lead and to mobilize them against the conspiracies of the West.[3]

Oscillating between the conservatives and the crusaders was the pragmatist faction, the weakest faction in Khomeini's Iran. The middle class and the technocrats provided the core support for that faction. Pragmatism is "accepting the world pretty much as it is and working with compromise and caution to move it in incremental steps along a preferred path."[4] The pragmatists were realistic enough to recognize their own limited power to change Iran or the Islamic world. They became the dominant faction in the post-Khomeini era.

The pragmatists' position about the nature of the *feqh* was analogous with that of the crusaders. They were both advocates of a "dynamic *feqh*," according to which time and place are the critical ingredients in making judgments about religious issues. Both factions supported giving the *faqih* extraordinary power to amend old rules and to promulgate new ones. Speaker Rafsanjani maintained that because the exigencies of the modern age are essentially different from the problems of the seventh century, when Prophet Mohammad began his mission, the ulama should now render the *feqh* "compatible with the conditions and necessities of society."[5]

Above the factions stood Khomeini, whose task it was to settle the dispute between them. His modus operandi strengthened factionalism. Mehdi Bazargan told me that "Khomeini's philosophy was based on preventing people from knowing ... how much power they really had so that, if necessary, he could pit one supporter against another."[6] Khomeini also prevented one faction from dominating or eliminating another. This strategy kept his populist appeal intact and precluded the possibility of any one faction getting powerful enough to challenge him. On the issues of nationalizing foreign trade and restricting property ownership, he disappointed the crusaders. To the utter dismay of the conservatives, he issued a series of controversial *fatva*s that allowed the government to set price controls on certain items, permitted the television networks to show Western films in which women appear unveiled, and lifted the ban on the sale of chess sets and some musical instruments.

Khomeini deliberately kept the three factions competitive, giving them much room to maneuver. In few Middle Eastern countries did the elites enjoy as much freedom as those in Iran. With the exception of the Israeli Knesset, the Iranian Majles was probably the most independent parliament in the Middle East. In it, deputies openly and harshly criticized government policies.

At the same time, this interelite competition created a major gridlock and prevented the government from effectively implementing its policy. This gridlock was a main feature of the premiership of Mir Hossein Mussavi, from 1982 to 1988.

During his tenure, the Guardian Council, packed with conservatives, repeatedly rejected bills that were supported by the government and the Majles, both controlled by the crusaders. Most notable among them were the bills to nationalize foreign trade and distribute agricultural lands. To end the gridlock, Khomeini ordered the creation of the Council for the Resolution of Differences in 1988. The council's impact was inconsequential, however.

Differences among the factions and their inability to reach a consensus reached such a critical level that in 1987 Ayatollah Khomeini had to dissolve the Islamic Republican Party, the fundamentalists' only political organization. Its dissolution was the inevitable result of the unbearable pressure that the different constituencies, from the lower class to the rich merchants, brought to bear on the party and on the government.[7]

When it came to Islamizing Iran, however, the only difference among the factions revolved around its rapidity.

Toward Islamizing Iran

When the Islamic Republic was harshly criticized for Iran's deteriorating economic condition in the mid-1980s, Ayatollah Khomeini stated that the Iranian people did not make the revolution to own watermelon. The symbolic reference to watermelon, absurd as it may appear on the surface, underscored Khomeini's rejection of material possessions and comfort as the sine qua non of the Islamic Revolution. He was obsessed with an ideal more precious to him than materialistic issues: the creation of an Islamic society and the making of a new Islamic person with a new mission.

Because Islam is viewed as a set of guidelines encompassing all human activity from birth to death, the fundamentalists have worked hard to implement these godly edicts. Reintroduction of Islamic laws has been the principal pillar of Islamization, which took off with the hostage crisis and reached its zenith just before Khomeini's death in 1989.

In August 1982, all un-Islamic codes and laws adopted since 1907 were declared null by the Supreme Judicial Council. The same body ordered all judges to render their decisions based exclusively on Islamic/Shi'i codified laws and on the *fatvas* by reputable ayatollahs. Secular judges, who controlled the judiciary before the Islamic Revolution, were replaced by the ulama, and the major seminaries, not the Law Department of the University of Teheran, became centers for training the ulama as judges and lawyers.

A body of new Islamic laws became the foundation of the new legal system. The controversial Qesas (retribution) bill was passed by the Majles in August 1983, despite strong opposition by the nationalists and leftists, who condemned it as excessively brutal. The 194-article bill reintroduced such swift punishments as flogging, hand amputation, and stoning.[8]

The Family Protection Law of 1967, which under some circumstances granted women the right to ask for divorce, was declared illegal. Polygamy was legalized. In the past few years, however, some aspects of the Family Protection Law have been restored: Under certain conditions, women are allowed to request a divorce, and the consent of the first wife is needed if a man is to become polygamous.

Islamic laws were introduced to regulate commerce and trade. In August 1983, the Majles passed the Usury-Free Banking Act, which imposed new banking guidelines. Subsequently, thousands of Islamic Interest-Free Funds were created across the country to provide interest-free loans for needy borrowers.

The impact of Islamization on the educational system has been equally momentous. The campaign to change the essence of the educational system began with the launching of the Cultural Revolution in the summer of 1980. At the time, Ayatollah Khomeini urged his followers to cleanse the universities of all elements "who are connected either to the West or the East." If universities can produce only communists and atheists, if they become centers for dissemination of decadent Western ideas and culture, they must be shut down indefinitely, Khomeini declared. He attributed "Iran's backwardness [to] the university intellectuals' lack of proper understanding of Iran's Islamic society and their inability to communicate with the masses."[9]

The campaign to cleanse the universities was also designed to eliminate the leftists who had turned the university campuses into their headquarters for recruiting students. In April 1980, the Council of the Islamic Revolution gave an ultimatum to the leftists to either evacuate the campuses or be prepared to pay a heavy price. The wiser groups left and the defiant ones were beaten and kicked out. In the following month, Khomeini ordered the establishment of the Council of the Cultural Revolution to supervise the restructuring of the educational system. Consisting of seven members, most of them from the Islamic Republican Party, the new council dismissed un-Islamic elements and shut down the universities indefinitely.[10]

Under the rubric of the Cultural Revolution, a new philosophy of teaching and a new code of conduct were introduced. (Much of what was done in the 1980s was still being pursued in 1993.) Teachers, professors, and administrators were required to be the purveyors of the new state ideology or face dismissal. The Islamic student associations created in schools were encouraged by the state to identify defiant teachers and administrators to the authorities. Textbooks were revised to portray the monarchy as a decadent system, kings as criminals, and the ulama as the defenders of justice and national independence. Courses such as history of Islam and of the Islamic Revolution were required at all levels. By the time the first national examination for the entrance to the universities was reinstituted in December 1983, admission requirements were changed. Academic excellence was no longer the only criterion for admission: Also required were ideological commitment to the Islamic Revolution and favorable letters of recommendation from the local clergy.[11] Overall, the quality of education deteriorated as many veteran teachers were forced to retire.

The fundamentalists were also determined to introduce a new system of morality and social behavior. Discos and bars were dismantled, the production and consumption of alcoholic beverages were forbidden, and only traditional music sung by men and martial music were aired on state-controlled radio and television. Western-made films examined for compatibility with Islamic values seldom passed the censors.

But nowhere else has the fundamentalists' obsession with moral purification been as visible as in the forced veiling of women. Women played a significant role in the Shah's overthrow. For many of them, veiling was a symbol of their opposition to the Shah. During the revolutionary movement, however, they enjoyed the choice of whether to wear the veil. In Islamic Iran, this freedom of choice is absent.[12]

Like other aspects of Islamization, compulsory veiling was imposed gradually. It was during Bazargan's tenure that Ayatollah Khomeini, floating one of his usual test balloons, publicly stated that working women should wear the "Islamic form of modest dress." The reaction to the statement was immediate and impressive as thousands of women demonstrated against imposition of any limitation on the way they wished to dress. At this juncture, Bazargan came to the rescue. He condemned the leftists and the counterrevolutionaries for distorting the Ayatollah's position. The Ayatollah, he insisted, rejected compulsory veiling and believed that by proper guidance, not by force, women would freely choose to respect the Islamic standards of dress. The Ayatollah's office chose to keep silent about Bazargan's interpretation.

The period of "guiding the women" was short-lived. In the summer of 1980, veiling became mandatory for those working in government and public offices. This time, when the whole country was frozen in the hysteria of the hostage ordeal and the fundamentalists had launched a major offensive against their opponents, the opposition against veiling was mild, with small sporadic demonstrations here and there. The lack of a decisive response by women emboldened the fundamentalists, who in April 1983 made veiling mandatory for all women in Iran, including non-Moslems and tourists. Thus, what went up by force went down by force: In the 1930s, Reza Shah unveiled women to "modernize" Iran, and in the 1980s Khomeini veiled them to Islamize Iran.

Because of the forced veiling, society has been segregated along gender lines. Coeducation has been eliminated except in universities where female and male students are segregated on different sides of the classroom. In public gatherings and in public buses, the two genders have been physically separated. Women athletes have been barred from participating in international competitions that do not abide by the Islamic dress code.

Veiling, however, should not be confused with forcing women to play their traditional role of staying at home. Although the Islamic Constitution encourages women to preoccupy themselves with the "precious function of motherhood," a higher percentage of women are active in the labor force and attend schools today than under the Shah. Nor has women's participation in politics been reduced, although the new activists do not come from the upper classes, as was the case under the Shah, but from the middle and lower classes. In the Third Majles, four women deputies were elected, and there are eight women in the Fourth Majles (1992–1996). President Rafsanjani has also created the Office of Women's Affairs, which reports to him directly.

From the start, the fundamentalists anticipated some public defiance of their strict moral guidelines and dress code. Thus they created a variety of groups to supervise the activities of the Iranians. The Office for Propagation of Virtues and Prevention of Sins was formed to supervise Islamic morality and behavior. Young zealots, organized in small groups, such as Gasht-e Sarallah, patrolled the streets and arrested those who did not abide by the Islamic dress code and who transgressed Islamic morality.

In Iran, as elsewhere, it has been difficult to legislate morality. Because of the Islamic Republic's strict codes of conduct, a giant gap has been created between the public and the private spheres. Forced veiling and the ban on certain videocassettes and audiocassettes illustrate the point.

Many Iranians find the mandatory veiling acceptable, but many do not. Consequently, those women who oppose veiling pursue a double life: In public they are veiled but at their private gatherings, they dress and behave as they wish. They take advantage of every opportunity to publicly show their disapproval of veiling by wearing colorful scarves and by not completely hiding their hair under the scarf.

Despite the government ban on many Western films, Iranians can obtain just about any Western videocassette or audiocassette through a large underground distribution system. A videocassette released in the United States today, for example, will become available to Iranians next week. The government attempt to destroy this sophisticated distribution system has been futile.

Even Iran's foreign policy was not immune to Islamization, as the fundamentalists dedicated much of their energy to the export of the Islamic Revolution. The creation of the Office of Global Revolution, which linked Iran with Islamic/revolutionary movements all over the world, and Iran's support of the Hezbollah in Lebanon were but a few examples of the interventionist policy of the Islamic Republic.

The Iranian Economy in the 1980s

It is one thing to defeat opponents and an entirely different matter to govern and to manage a modern economy. Although the fundamentalists demonstrated much talent in the former task, their record about the latter in the 1980s was not impressive, to say the least. For much of the decade, with the exception of the period between 1982 and 1984, the Iranian economy remained in a recession.

In the first two years of the Islamic Revolution, the Iranian economy was essentially ignored as powerful forces competed for political hegemony and as the whole political establishment preoccupied itself with the hostage crisis. In this period of economic chaos, the economy suffered its first recession.

The Islamic Republic's first serious attempt to put its economic house in order and reverse its deteriorating economic condition began with the approval of the government's First Development Plan in 1983, proposed by Prime Minister Mussavi in the midst of the Iraq-Iran war. The most essential ingredients of his state-managed development strategy entailed nationalization of the major industries and banks, price regulation on selected items, expensive subsidies, and a restricted trade policy. His First Development Plan contained many popular but unrealistic provisions such as making Iran self-sufficient, ending unemployment, and providing essential social welfare services for the masses. Regrettably, many of the goals set by the First Development Plan were not based on a realistic assessment of Iran's economic capabilities but on ideological considerations.

There is a consensus among most experts that the economic goals of the First Development Plan were not fulfilled. Iran did not even get close to the projected 8 percent annual rate of economic growth. The declining oil revenues and the costs of the war with Iraq forced the state to curtail many of its services: The state's per capita budget decreased by 30 percent in the first decade of the revolution.[13] In fact, Iran was plunged into a recession in 1984 from which it began to gradually recover only after the cease-fire with Iraq in 1988. The living standard of most Iranians was lower in the first decade of the revolution than under the Shah: Between 1978 and 1989, the gross domestic product declined by about 1.5 percent annually, which lowered Iran's real gross per capita income in 1989 "to what it had been a quarter of a century earlier."[14] Major factories were operating far below their normal productive capacity. Low industrial output and excessive governmental regulations, in turn, stifled productivity.

The rate of unemployment did not reach zero, as planned; it progressively increased. High inflation, like government deficits, became a permanent feature of the economy, putting unbearable pressure on the salaried middle class. Rents in the major cities increased faster than the inflation rate, eating away two-thirds of the wage earner's income, which itself continually lagged behind the rate of inflation. The chaotic foreign exchange system was out of control: The official and the black market exchange rates for one U.S. dollar, for example, stood at 76 and between 1,200 and 1,450 rials, respectively, which accelerated the devaluation of the Iranian currency.[15]

Nor did the economy move in the direction of self-sufficiency. The state remained a rentier, receiving an overwhelming amount of its revenues from oil, and Iran continued to import substantial amounts of machinery, consumer goods, and agricultural products.

The revolution did not eradicate poverty or decrease the great disparity between the rich and the poor. Whereas the number of billionaires (in Iranian currency) increased from 100 in the prerevolutionary time to 1,000 in the revolutionary era, so did the proportions of those who could hardly provide the basic necessities of life for themselves. The shantytowns that the revolutionaries viewed as the symbol of the Shah's utter failure did not disappear; in fact, they proliferated.

We should not make a final judgment about the performance of the Iranian economy in the 1980s without considering the inhospitable conditions under which the Islamic Republic operated: The war with Iraq drained the treasury and destroyed a sizable portion of the country's infrastructure; the U.S.-supported trade and credit sanctions deprived the country of much-needed advanced technology and capital; and the decline in the price of oil, coupled with the rapid population growth of about 4 percent annually, meant less oil money for more people. Moreover, the massive exodus of the country's best technocrats along with a huge outflow of funds in the pockets of rich entrepreneurs who had left the country depleted much of the country's skilled manpower pool and some of its wealth. The presence of some 3 to 4 million Afghani, Iraqi, and Kurdish refugees burdened an economy that was already weak. Finally, factionalism prevented the formulation and implementation of a realistic development strategy for the country. The Islamic Republic deserves some credit for preventing the collapse of the economy in the face of such formidable obstacles. To its credit, the Islamic Republic ended the decade without any major foreign debts.

There were some positive developments in the social and economic arenas, however. There was a healthy growth in the small-scale and defense-related industries, a natural reaction to the military sanctions imposed on Iran by the United States and some of its allies. Although the quality of medical care generally declined, a noble attempt was made to provide health care for all Iranians. Thousands of miles of new roads were constructed. There was a substantial increase in electrification of the rural areas. Literacy rates increased, and a higher percentage of Iranian youth were educated than ever before. The book publishing and film industries flourished. More books with larger circulation were published than under the Shah. Despite restrictions, classical Persian music blossomed.

Although the disparity between the rich and the poor was not reduced, a sizable portion of the poor and the lower middle class benefited from the revolution, as they were incorporated into the government payroll. In fact, more Iranians were dependent upon the state's magnanimity than ever before. By 1983, some 68 percent of the total labor force worked for the state sector.[16] In short, the Islamic Revolution strengthened the economic power of the state.

The Iraq-Iran War and the United States

In 1975, the Shah of Iran and Saddam Hossein of Iraq signed the Algiers Treaty, ending years of hostility and border clashes. As a consequence of the treaty, the Shah terminated his military and financial support to the Kurdish rebels inside

Iraq, and Iraq withdrew its claim of sovereignty over the Shatt al-Arab (Arvandan) waterway, agreeing to settle the fluvial dispute over the waterway according to the Thalweg Line (joint sovereignty by Iraq and Iran). Both countries also accepted the inviolability of their established borders and pledged not to interfere in each other's internal affairs. The bilateral relations remained congenial.

With the coming of the Islamic Revolution, relations between Teheran and Baghdad progressively deteriorated as both countries accused each other of irredentist ambitions. Iran accused Iraq of smuggling arms to the Arab dissidents in Khuzestan, permitting the anti-Khomeini forces to establish a radio station on Iraqi territory, and periodic military incursions into Iran. Iraq, for its part, accused Iran of aiding both the Kurdish rebels inside Iraq and the Al-Da'wa Party, an Iraqi revolutionary underground Shi'i group dedicated to the overthrow of the Ba'th Party and the creation of an Islamic republic in Iraq. Clearly, the chiliastic overtones of Shi'ism, coupled with the victory of the fundamentalists in Iran, had energized the discontented Iraqi Shi'ites to become a harbinger of radical change. The Ba'th Party had reasons to fear the Iraqi Shi'ites: Representing the majority, the Shi'ites, who had a lower standard of living than the Sunni minority, had been effectively excluded by the Sunnis from a major share in governmental power.

Iraq was not alone in feeling vulnerable. The gospel of Shi'i fundamentalism was shaking the foundation of the other Arab states in the Persian Gulf, states that were and continue to be fragile, conservative, and repressive. Iran's revolution had truly energized the powerless Arab masses, many of them Shi'ites, in the Persian Gulf region.

The fear shared by all Arab governments in the Persian Gulf that the Islamic Revolution could destabilize the region made President Hossein more belligerent toward Iran. Finally, in mid-September of 1980, in a national television address, Hossein unilaterally abrogated the Algiers Treaty and burned the document to ashes. He defiantly declared that the Shatt al-Arab was an Arab property and that he had signed the 1975 treaty with the Shah under duress. A week later, on September 22, 1980, in the midst of the hostage crisis, Iraq invaded Iran, probably with the blessing of Saudi Arabia, a green light from the United States, and encouragement from some exiled Iranians who allegedly provided Iraq with intelligence on the Iranian army.[17] Thus began one of the bloodiest wars of our century.

Hossein's principal objective was to become the hegemonic force in the Persian Gulf, as the Shah had been in the 1970s, by striking a quick and decisive victory over Iran. He pursued other goals, too: To impose Iraqi sovereignty over the Shatt-al Arab waterway; to destroy the Shi'i fundamentalist movement in Iran and the internal Shi'i opposition to his own rule; to occupy, and if possible annex, the oil-rich Khuzestan province, with its sizable Arab population; to set up a puppet, anti-Khomeini government in the territory he hoped to occupy in order to overthrow Khomeini; and to emerge a great Arab hero of Pan-Arabism who defeated the Persians, on a par with the late president Abdul Naser of Egypt.

President Hossein's invasion was based on his perception of Iran's vulnerabilities. He calculated that Iran's demoralized army, weakened by aborted coups, summary executions of its top echelons, and massive purges, could not withstand Iraq's well-equipped and disciplined army. He assumed that the ongoing rivalry between the fundamentalists and President Bani Sadr would seriously cripple Iran's capacity to unify its forces against Iraq. He was indubitably encouraged by Iran's failure to end the hostage crisis and the animosity it had generated between Iran and the United States, by Iran's international isolation, and by the economic and military sanctions Washington imposed on Iran, which included a ban on sale or delivery of spare parts for Iran's U.S.-equipped armed forces. In short, a chaotic country experiencing a major revolutionary upheaval and at war with itself and with much of the world appeared too tantalizing a prey not to be attacked by the ambitious Saddam Hossein.

But many of Hossein's calculations proved erroneous. This is why he did not achieve any of his goals: After eight years of fighting, the war culminated in a stalemate, economic devastation, and unimaginably staggering loss of life to both sides.

Saddam Hossein was ignorant of the history of revolutions: External aggression has historically contributed to the consolidation of revolutions and to the ascendancy of radical elements. For instance, the invasion of France by the armies of Austria and Prussia in April 1792 not only failed to restore the ancien régime; it actually consolidated the French Revolution. About a year after the invasion, the radical Jacobins defeated the moderate Girondists and imposed the "reign of terror." In Iran, the Iraqi invasion unified the country, consolidated the Islamic Revolution, and undermined the most moderate elements of the revolutionary coalition.

Hossein also misunderstood the policy objectives of the major Western powers, especially the United States, toward Iraq during and after the end of the Iraq-Iran war. After the fall of the Shah in 1979, and especially after the hostage crisis and the Soviet invasion of Afghanistan in December 1979, the United States pursued three objectives in the Persian Gulf: to keep the Soviet Union out of the Persian Gulf, to contain the Islamic Revolution, and to protect the oil fields and assure the free flow of inexpensive oil. So strategic was the Persian Gulf that President Jimmy Carter explicitly stated that the United States would protect its vital interests in the region by all means necessary, including military force (the Carter Doctrine). To put teeth into this declaration, he ordered the formation of the Rapid Deployment Joint Task Force in March 1980. In 1983, this military-planning headquarters evolved into the United States Central Command, which planned and coordinated U.S. military operations in the Persian Gulf during the Iraq-Iran war and afterward.

To achieve these goals, the United States pursued a two-pillar strategy. The first pillar, and the linchpin of that strategy, was to strengthen and fortify Saudi Arabia and to create a regional security structure to contain Iran. Immediately after the outbreak of the war, the United States sent two AWACS aircraft to Saudi Arabia. (In the following year, the Saudis purchased five AWACS.) According to Steven

Emerson, by 1985 Saudi Arabia, a country with a population of about 14 million, had received more than $70 billion worth of military equipment and construction items, becoming the number one buyer of military hardware in the United States, a position Iran had held in 1975 under the Shah.[18] The United States provided the kingdom with the most sophisticated weapons available and built there an electronic communications system that was, according to some experts, equivalent to NATO's. "So, in effect, we had," according to Lawrence Korb, "a replica of U.S. airfields and ports in that part of the world paid for by the Saudis to be used by the United States when and if we had to go over there."[19] Many "surrogate military bases" were constructed that were large enough "to sustain U.S. forces in intensive regional combat."[20] These bases were used against Iraq during the Kuwaiti crisis in 1991.

Four months after the start of the Iraq-Iran war and while the militarization of Saudi Arabia was proceeding quietly, the Gulf Cooperation Council was formed by Saudi Arabia, Kuwait, Bahrain, Qatar, the United Arab Emirates, and Oman. Its main mission was to prevent the spread of the Iraq-Iran war to the entire region. This is why an attack on one was declared to be an attack on all members of the new security pact, a clear signal to Iran to mind its own business.[21]

The second pillar of Washington's strategy of containing Iran was to get closer to Iraq, which at the time had no formal relations with the United States and was still among the State Department's "state sponsors of terrorism." Rapprochement with Iraq, supported by American Arabists, Saudi Arabia, and Kuwait, was viewed as an effective method to neutralize the Islamic Revolution and to bring Iraq back "to the family of nations." Thus, even before the start of the Iraq-Iran war, informal relations between Baghdad and Washington had improved considerably.

The quiet rapprochement toward Iraq perfectly complemented and massaged President Hossein's ambition of becoming a regional superpower. So enthusiastically did he cherish the new U.S. posture that Hossein sought U.S. approval for his invasion of Iran: Washington, according to Kenneth Timmerman, did not oppose the invasion. There is little doubt that the United States had advance knowledge of the invasion. A few weeks before the invasion, Hossein reportedly visited Saudi Arabia, Washington's close ally, and informed the Saudis of his war intentions.[22] Moreover, the sophisticated U.S. satellites could have easily detected Iraq's preparation for the war. The United States had too much at stake not to oppose the Iraqi invasion: Iran was holding U.S. hostages; the Tabas rescue mission to free the U.S. hostages had been aborted; the Nozheh coup had been neutralized by the Islamic Republic; and the Islamic Revolution was becoming more radical. This is perhaps why the United States, which had vociferously condemned the Soviet invasion of Afghanistan, neither condemned the Iraqi aggression of Iran nor identified Iraq as the instigator.[23]

Hossein could not digest one crucial fact: Although the United States had given him the green light to invade Iran and he was being lavishly supported by the West during the course of the war, this was not to make him the hegemonic force in the region, as he so ambitiously hoped. The logic of the U.S. strategy was to permit him to become just strong enough to contain the Islamic Revolution. The objective of Washington during the Iraq-Iran war was to watch the "mutual destruction" of the belligerents, as the British did when Germany fought the Soviet Union in World War II, without permitting either of them to emerge triumphant or, as Kissinger said, to assure that there would be two losers in one war.

In the first month of the war, the Iraqi forces scored a major victory as they occupied more than 14,000 square kilometers (5,400 square miles) of Iranian soil. In the ensuing months, they also captured the port city of Khoramshahr and continued their successful offensive.[24] But Iran was not about to capitulate: A combination of strong religious fervor and passionate nationalism unified the whole country as millions of people volunteered to go to the war fronts.

The first UN resolution, passed in September 1980, called for an immediate cease-fire but did not identify Iraq as the aggressor; nor did it demand the return of the Iraqis to the established international borders. Iran, therefore, rightly rejected the resolution. Nor did Hossein accept it, sensing at the time that he might win the war. So the war continued. With the Iraqis enjoying the upper hand, Washington pursued a "neutral policy" in this phase of the conflict.

It took almost two years for Iran to mobilize its forces. Iran, whose main goal was to expel Iraq from its territory, faced four major difficulties that handicapped its effectiveness on the war front. First, there were rivalries and disputes between the regular army and the Revolutionary Guards about appropriate military strategy. Second, the bitter conflict between President Bani Sadr and the fundamentalists was pushing the infant republic to the brink of collapse. When unity was most needed, discord had become the order of the day. Third, the violent confrontation between the Mojahedin and the Islamic Republic, in which a large number of the government's top leaders were killed, prevented Iran from focusing exclusively on the battle front. And, finally, Washington's refusal to provide spare parts for the Iranian armed forces placed Iran in a militarily disadvantageous position.

By 1982, the war had entered a new phase: Bani Sadr had been forced out of power, the Mojahedin had been eradicated, and the fundamentalists were securely in power. In May of that year, Khoramshahr was taken back and thousands of Iraqi troops surrendered. Following this breakthrough, Iran recovered some of its lost territory and began its successful offensive against Iraq on Iraqi soil. Despite the dedication of thousands of young Iranians who were organized in the so-called human-wave assaults, Iranian offensives failed to assure Iran a decisive victory.

At that juncture, Iran, having the upper hand in the war, had a golden opportunity to end the war from a position of power. But the Islamic Republic, emboldened by its advances, was demanding nothing short of President Hossein's removal from power or total Iraqi capitulation. It was in this spirit of arrogance that Teheran rejected all peace proposals, including the Arab League Peace Plan in 1982, which called for an immediate cease-fire, complete withdrawal of Iraqi troops from Iran, and compensation of some $70 billion to Iran through the Islamic Reconstruction Bank.[25]

As Iran gained the upper hand, the United States abandoned its official policy of neutrality and tilted toward Iraq. In 1984, Washington inaugurated its "Operation Staunch" to stop the flow of arms to Iran. At the same time, Iraq was allowed to arm itself to the teeth, purchasing billions of dollars' worth of armaments. By 1988, Iraq had become the largest importer of arms in the Middle East, accounting for about 31 percent of the region's imports.[26] Greed was a factor in this massive transfer of arms from both the East and the West. The Soviets were the primary provider of weapons, accounting for about 10 percent of the imported arms. France was next, giving Saddam advanced long-range bombers and aircraft. West Germany helped Iraq build chemical and biological weapons. Other Europeans also benefited from Baghdad's lavish expenditures at the arms bazaar.

The United States assisted Saddam both indirectly and directly. Indirectly, Washington approved and encouraged financial contributions to Iraq by Saudi Arabia and Kuwait. These two Arab countries financed the Iraqi war machine to the tune of some $60 billion during the war.[27] The U.S.-managed, Saudi-purchased AWACS planes often provided Iraq with critical intelligence about Iran's military. Moreover, the Saudis transferred, in violation of U.S. law but certainly with the approval of U.S. officials, hundreds of one-ton MK-84 bombs to Iraq.[28] Egypt, another close ally of Washington, sold large quantities of arms to Saddam.

Washington did its share to make life easy for Hossein. It removed Iraq's name from the State Department's list of "sponsors of terrorism" in 1982 and resumed diplomatic relations with Baghdad in 1984. Directly, through the Department of Agriculture's Commodity Credit Corporation, Washington provided Iraq with large amounts of credit, which Iraq used for military purposes. It deliberately closed its eyes to a large network of Iraqi agents who were purchasing modern computers and electronic gadgets to be used for building missiles and atomic bombs.[29] Nor did Washington stop the transfer of some $3 billion in loans to Iraq by the Atlanta branch of Banca Nazionale de Lavoro.

As Iraq was rearmed, it expanded the theater of the war. It took maximum advantage of Iran's vulnerable air defense system and excessive reliance on the Persian Gulf, from which it shipped much of its oil. Thus, Hossein began the "war of the cities" and the "tankers war," which irrevocably changed the calculus of the war and neutralized Iranian ground advances from 1984 to 1987. Iraq began by bombing dozens of Iranian cities, inflicting heavy damage. Iran reciprocated. The world watched silently as thousands of innocent people were killed by these insane and inaccurate bombings. However, once Iraq began the tanker war, that is, once the flow of oil was jeopardized, the world suddenly became concerned about the Iraq-Iran war. By attacking neutral ships, Iranian oil tankers, and Iranian oil facilities, Iraq aimed to deprive Iran of its much-needed oil revenues and to internationalize the conflict.

Iran, however, had no interest in escalating the war because there was little it could do to damage Iraq in the Persian Gulf. Unlike Iran, the Iraqi oil facilities in the Persian Gulf were minimal and Iraq was exporting its oil through the Iraq-Turkey and Iraq-Saudi pipelines. The Iranian strategy was to make shipping inconvenient, if not outright deadly, for everyone in the Persian Gulf and especially for Saudi Arabia and Kuwait, believing that those two main financiers of Iraq would then pressure Hossein to end the tanker war. Had it not been for the direct U.S. intervention, the Iranian strategy could have worked.

Gradually, as Iran was unable to win the war, the division within the fundamentalist camp widened. The crusaders' position was summarized in their slogan displayed in wall graffiti all over the country: "War, War, Until Victory." They sincerely believed that in a war of attrition, Iran would win the war. They, like Saddam Hossein, failed to comprehend that the major powers were determined to preclude such an eventuality. They also underestimated the resilience of the Iraqi army. The pragmatists, in contrast, hoped for a peaceful and honorable resolution of the quagmire, recognizing that Iran would not be able to achieve its ambitious goal of winning the war and overthrowing Saddam Hossein.[30] The crusaders won this round of rivalry, and the war continued unabated.

But what overshadowed the rivalry within the fundamentalist camp and changed the course of the war was the secret dealings between Washington and Teheran, the so-called Iran-Contra or Irangate scandal. The covert operation, which lasted about three years, involved illegal arms sales to Iran, deceptions, negotiations for the release of the U.S. hostages held by the Lebanese Shi'ites, illegal transfers to the Contras of profits from the sale of weapons to Iran, and reliance on dubious middlemen who often pursued their own selfish interests. The entire operation was supervised by the National Security Council and blessed by William Casey's CIA. It was opposed by George Shultz's State Department, whose anti-Iran policy was well known at the time. Despite investigations by the U.S. Congress and by others, the key questions about the scandal have not been satisfactorily answered because some key documents were shredded by Lt. Colonel Oliver North, one of the major players in the drama.[31]

According to the Reagan administration, the operation was designed to create a "strategic opening toward Iran" by strengthening "the moderate elements within and outside the Government of Iran ... in order to enhance the credibility of these elements in their effort to achieve a more pro-U.S. government in Iran."[32] The overture toward Teheran was justified as a strategy to neutralize the Soviet Union's schemes to expand its influence within the Iranian leadership. President Reagan insisted that the operation was not an arms-for-hostage swap and that he was kept out of the loop about the transfer of funds to the Contras. If the objectives were those stated by the Reagan administration, then the Iran initiative was a sound policy with potentially great rewards. The problem was not the nature of the policy but the method used to achieve its goals. The success of such a covert and sensitive operation demanded expertise about Iran and its factions. Those few who orchestrated the operation simply lacked that expertise.

But not everyone accepts this official explanation. According to one theory, Israel, which since the start of the Iraq-Iran war had been selling arms to Iran in the hope of prolonging the conflict, persuaded Washington in 1984 that there was a moderate, pro-Western, anti-Khomeini faction within the Iranian armed forces. An arms sale to such elements, it was argued, would strengthen them and could eventually lead to the overthrow of the Islamic Republic. Robert McFarlane, the national security adviser who supervised the early phase of the operation and secretly visited Teheran in 1986 reportedly carrying a Bible for Ayatollah Khomeini, pointed out "that the Israelis intended to supply arms to certain elements in the Iranian army to overthrow the government."[33] The fact that around 1985 the regular army, not the Revolutionary Guards, was controlling the conduct of the war enticed the Israelis, who had established close relations with the Iranian military establishment during the Shah's years, to contact the so-called pro-Western elements.[34] After Israel's shipment of arms to Iran in 1985, Benjamin Weir was released by the Lebanese Shi'ites, which strengthens the Israeli analysis. Eventually, TOW antitank missiles and HAWK missiles were sold to Iran, both authorized by President Reagan, at inflated prices.

Lt. Colonel Oliver North, whose brilliant performance during the congressional hearings about the Irangate scandal turned him into a national celebrity, bragged about his continuous lies to the Iranians.[35] It is interesting to note that the Iranians who were negotiating with him referred to North as the "brainless colonel" because North, like others who managed the operation, was naively thinking that they were dealing with an anti-Khomeini faction within the Iranian leadership. In Iran, wrote Mansur Farhang, the secret contact with Washington was supervised by no one but Ayatollah Khomeini himself. Iran was in desperate need of arms to conduct its war with Iraq and was prepared to buy them from anyone, including the "Great Satan."

With the new weapons acquired from Washington and Israel, Iran's reinvigorated army made more advances on the ground, capturing the strategic Fao Island in February 1986. It is even suggested that the United States ordered its AWACS "to beam out of the war zone during the Fao campaign ... thereby denying the Iraqi general staff critical intelligence normally passed to them by Riyadh."[36]

Whatever the objectives of both Washington and Iran for entangling themselves in the covert operation, Irangate proved a disaster for Iran and a humiliation for the United States. In November 1986, a Lebanese newspaper revealed that the United States had clandestinely delivered arms to Iran in exchange for Iranian assistance in the release of the U.S. hostages held in Lebanon. The information was allegedly leaked by Mehdi Hashemi, a hard-line crusader who headed the World Organization of Islamic Liberation Movements in Teheran and who eventually was executed by the Islamic Republic in September 1987.[37]

Irangate became a turning point in the U.S. involvement in the war. The revelation about the covert operation was a humiliating crisis for the Reagan administration: While pressuring other countries to cut off arms to Iran (Operation

Staunch), Washington was secretly selling arms to Iran. The scandal decreased Reagan's approval rating by some 21 percent.[38] To appease its domestic critics and befriend its "betrayed" Arab allies, the Reagan administration began an aggressive anti-Iran policy.[39]

In March 1987, House Joint Resolution 216 warned that the continuation of the war could result in an "Iranian breakthrough" that would damage the "strategic interests" of the United States.[40] In November of the same year, a congressional report concluded that "Iraq can lose against Iran."[41] Thus, a campaign began to prevent Iran from winning.

The campaign was conducted on both diplomatic and military fronts. On the diplomatic front, the United States became instrumental in the passage of UN Resolution 598 in July 1987. It called for the cessation of hostilities but failed to address two other issues: the determination of the aggressor in the war and war reparations to Iran. These were two of Iran's main conditions for peace. Knowing that Iran would not accept the resolution, the United States passed it to further isolate Iran and to gather support for an international arms embargo against Iran. Correctly reading Washington's maneuver, Iran neither accepted nor rejected the resolution. Instead, it requested more time to study the resolution while making specific proposals to change its content. Consequently, Iran, with support from China, the Soviet Union, West Germany, and France, prevented Washington from imposing an arms embargo.[42]

But the most critical aspect of the new U.S. policy was direct military intervention in the Iraq-Iran war. The tanker war in the Persian Gulf reached a critical stage when Kuwait sought the support of Moscow and Washington to protect its ships against Iranian attack. First the Soviet Union agreed to lease three tankers to Kuwait and then the United States began reflagging eleven Kuwaiti ships in March 1987.

With the reflagging, the United States became directly involved in the Iraq-Iran war, unequivocally supporting Iraq. Even if more ships were attacked by Iraq than by Iran, Washington condemned only Iran for making navigation in the Persian Gulf dangerous. When in May 1987 Iraq's French-built Excocet missiles hit the USS *Stark* in the Persian Gulf and killed some thirty-seven U.S. sailors, President Reagan blamed Iran.

The reflagging of the Kuwaiti ships coincided with Iran's Karbala V offensive against Iraq. Iran's largest and most carefully planned offensive, Karbala V was designed as a jumping-off point for a march toward the port city of Basra.[43] U.S. involvement in the Persian Gulf contributed to the failure of that offensive, as Iran was forced to allocate a part of its limited resources to confront the U.S. Navy.

The new U.S. policy sparked a debate within Iran's leadership. The crusaders favored confrontation and suicide missions against U.S. ships, believing that after suffering some casualties the United States would leave, as it left Lebanon when the Marine barracks were bombed in 1983. Others, including Rafsanjani, were pessimistic about the consequences of a confrontation with the United States, recommending closer ties with the USSR to neutralize the U.S. influence.[44] They argued that antagonizing the United States would only make it slide further into the Iraqi camp. Khomeini oscillated between these two tendencies. Iran intensified its anti-U.S. propaganda, its navy challenged the United States, and it made enticing gestures to Moscow. But these efforts were too little, too late.

The mighty U.S. Navy quickly demolished at least half of Iran's small navy. The Revolutionary Guards' small speedboats, the subject of sensationalization in the Western media, were more of a nuisance to the U.S. Navy than a serious threat. Without much difficulty, the U.S. Navy did for Iraq what Hossein had attempted but failed to achieve when he began the tanker war: It destroyed some offshore Iranian oil platforms, including the Sirri platform from which Iran exported about 8 percent of its oil. In reality, the U.S. Navy was often used effectively by Iraq as a cover to attack Iranian ships and Iranian oil facilities.

In desperation, Iran began to mine the Persian Gulf, but this proved counterproductive and damaged Iran's diplomatic efforts to win international support for its position. Leading European nations condemned Iran for its mining activities.

Meanwhile, Iraq gradually gained the upper hand in the war. Having acquired new weapons, including the long-range missiles from Moscow, Iraq restarted "the war of the cities" in early 1988. In a few weeks it fired more than 180 SCUD missiles at Teheran and other cities, inflicting devastating economic and psychological damage.[45] Benefiting from U.S. intelligence, Iraq recaptured the strategic Fao Island in April 1988. Most tragically, Iraq, in blatant violation of international law, used chemical weapons against Iranian soldiers and Kurds. In the Kurdish village of Halabja, whose inhabitants Hossein accused of collaboration with Iran, some 5,000 innocent men, women, and children were gassed to death while the world watched in cynical silence. The United States prevented the UN from intervening to halt the war of the cities or from condemning Iraq's unconscionable use of chemical weapons.[46]

At the same time, popular support for the war was waning in Iran. The sharp decline in the price of oil, which had started in 1985, had deepened recession; the death and injury of hundreds of thousands of Iranians had worn out the population; and the open siding of the United States with Iraq had convinced many people that Iran could never win the war. It was in July 1988, during these trying times, that the USS *Vincennes* downed a commercial Iranian aircraft and killed all of its 290 passengers. Many in Iran considered the tragic event as a deliberate signal that the United States would apply brute force to end the war. Internationally isolated, unable to gather much international support to condemn the *Vincennes* incident, and militarily under pressure from the United States and Iraq, Iran accepted the UN resolution on July 18, 1988.[47]

Khomeini's surprising announcement of a cease-fire wreaked havoc among Iranian soldiers in the battlefield. The Iraqis took advantage of the confusion and recaptured a small portion of Iranian territory, but Baghdad was quick to accept the UN-sponsored cease-fire. Meanwhile, the Mojahedin, who were stationed in

Iraq, began their infamous military attack on Iran, the so-called Eternal Light. Having argued that unless the war continued Khomeini's regime would collapse, the Mojahedin hoped to capitalize on the confusion of the Iranian army by capturing small cities and then marching toward Teheran. Once again, the fundamentalists punished the Mojahedin as hundreds, if not thousands, of their armed men were annihilated by the Islamic Republic.

The eight-year Iraq-Iran war was certainly one of the bloodiest and most expensive wars of our century. In many ways, Kissinger's wish of having two losers in that war was realized. According to a United Nations team, the damage to Iran alone was about $97 billion.[48] It is estimated that the cost of the war to both belligerents exceeded both nations' total oil revenues in this century.[49]

The insane war between the two Islamic nations that share more historical and cultural commonalities than any other two nations in the Middle East depleted their precious resources, devastated much of their economies and infrastructures, caused the death of at least 300,000 men, injured millions of people, inflicted pain on millions more who became homeless and hopeless, and left deep scars in the psyche of the two neighbors. There is much wisdom in what Charles C. Colton once said of wars: "War is a game in which princes seldom win; the people never."

Notes

1. For an analysis of elite factionalism, see Shahrough Akhavi, "Elite Factionalism in the Islamic Republic of Iran," *Middle East Journal*, 41, 2 (Spring 1987), pp. 181–202.

2. For a perceptive discussion of the economic position of factions, see Hooshang Amirahmadi, *Revolution and Economic Transition* (Albany, N.Y., 1990), pp. 114–131.

3. Personal interview with Hojatolislam Khoeiniha, Teheran, August 1991.

4. Richard Barnet, "Reflections: The Disorder of Peace," *New Yorker*, January 20, 1992, p. 74.

5. *Iran Times*, October 14, 1988. See also Mohsen Milani, "The Ascendance of Shi'i Fundamentalism in Revolutionary Iran," *Journal of South Asian and Middle Eastern Studies* 8, 1 and 2 (Fall/Winter 1989), pp. 5–28.

6. Personal interview with Mehdi Bazargan, Teheran, July 1991.

7. Gregory Rose, "Factional Alignment in the Central Council of the Islamic Republican Party of Iran: A Preliminary Taxonomy," in Nikki Keddie and Eric Hooglund, eds., *The Iranian Revolution and the Islamic Republic* (Washington, D.C., 1982), pp. 45–55.

8. "The Qisas Bil," trans. Mahmud Da'wati in *Al-Tawhid*, 1, 4 (July 1984), pp. 136–165.

9. Ruhollah Khomeini, *Kalam-e Imam: Daneshgah Va Enqelab-e Farhangi* (Imam's Words: University and the Cultural Revolution) (Teheran, 1983), pp. 208–209.

10. See Khomeini (1983), p. 219.

11. On the fundamentalists' interpretation of the Cultural Revolution, see Seyyed Mohammad Hosseini Beheshti, "The Divine Cultural Revolution," *Al Tawhid*, 1, Muhram 1404/(1984); and Mohammad Javad Bahonar, "The Goals of Islamic Education," *Al Tawhid*, 2, 2, January 1985, pp. 93–107.

12. See Farzaneh Milani, *Veils and Words* (Syracuse, N.Y., 1992), pp. 19–45.

13. Amirahmadi (1990), p. 292.

14. Ibid.

15. For a good study of the Iranian economy, see Jahangir Amuzegar, "The Iranian Economy Before and After Revolution," *Middle East Journal*, 8, 3 (Summer 1992) pp. 413–425. Much of the information in this section is derived from this article and Amirahmadi's book (1990).

16. Djavad Salehi-Isphahani, "The Iranian Economy Since the Revolution," in S. Hunter, ed., *Internal Developments in Iran* (Washington, D.C., 1982), pp. 25–48.

17. On how the war started, see Nita Renfrew, "Who Started the War?" *Foreign Policy*, 66 (Spring 1987), pp. 98–108. For a recent and comprehensive analysis, see R. K. Ramazani, *Revolutionary Iran: Challenge and Response in the Middle East* (Baltimore, Md., 1986), esp. chaps. 4 and 5; Anthony H. Cordesman, *The Gulf and the Search for Strategic Stability* (Boulder, Colo., 1984), pp. 725–771; and Liesl Graz, *The Turbulent Gulf* (London, 1990).

18. *Frontline*, February 16, 1993 (transcripts), p. 2.

19. Ibid., p. 3.

20. Ibid., p. 4.

21. See Joseph Kechichian, "The Gulf Cooperation Council: Containing the Iranian Revolution," *Journal of South Asian and Middle Eastern Studies*, 8, 1 and 2 (Fall/Winter 1989), pp. 146–165.

22. *Frontline* (1993), p. 5.

23. Ibid., p. 4.

24. For a comprehensive analysis of the war, see Christopher C. Joyner, ed., *The Persian Gulf War* (New York, 1990).

25. As quoted in Amirahmadi (1990), p. 53.

26. Quoted in Simon Henderson, *Instant Empire* (San Francisco, 1991), pp. 172–176.

27. This is an estimate by James Akins, former U.S. ambassador to Saudi Arabia from 1973–1975. See *Frontline* (1993), p. 5.

28. *L.A. Times*, April 2, 1992.

29. For the list of the U.S. companies that helped Iraqi nuclear technology, see *New York Times*, April 24, 1992, p. A-15.

30. Personal interview with Dr. Kamal Kharrazi, Iran's ambassador to the United Nations, New York, May 1991.

31. For details, see *The Chronology: The Documented Day-by-Day Account of the Secret Military Assistance to Iran and the Contras*, L. Chang et al., eds. (New York, 1987); John Tower, Edmund Muskie, and Brent Scowcroft, *The Tower Commission Report* (New York, 1987).

32. See Mansour Farhang, "U.S. Policy Toward the Islamic Republic of Iran: A Case of Misperception and Reactive Behavior," in H. Amirahmadi, ed., *The United States and the Middle East* (Albany, N.Y., 1993), p. 165.

33. Ibid., p. 166.

34. See Stuart Schaar, "Irangate: The Middle Eastern Connections," in Amirahmadi (1993), p. 182.

35. See Oliver North, *Taking the Stand: The Testimony of Lieutenant Colonel Oliver L. North* (New York, 1987).

36. Schaar (1993), p. 183.

37. See Mohammad Rayshahri, *Khaterat-e Rayshahri* (Rayshahri's Memories), (Teheran, 1989). Rayshahri prosecuted Hashemi. His discussion of the events is fascinating and revealing.

38. Cynthia J. Arnson, *Cross-Roads: Congress, the Reagan Administration, and Central America* (New York, 1989).

39. See Eric Hooglund, "Reagan's Iran: Factions Behind U.S. Policy in the Gulf," *Middle East Report*, no. 151 (March–April 1988).

40. H.J. Res. 216, 100th Congress, "Overview of the Situation in the Persian Gulf," *Hearings and Markup Before the Committee on Foreign Affairs* (Washington, D.C., 1987), p. 302.

41. Ibid., p. 25. Also see *War in the Persian Gulf: The U.S. Takes Sides*, A Staff Report to the Committee on Foreign Relations, U.S. Senate, Washington, D.C., November 1987.

42. See Anthony C. Arend, "The Role of the United Nations in the Iran-Iraq War," in C. Joyner (1990), pp. 191–208.

43. For a military perspective, see S. Pelletiore and D. Johnson III, *Lessons Learned: The Iran Iraq War* (Carlisle Barracks, Penn., 1991), especially Appendix X, pp. 83–93.

44. Personal interview with Dr. Kamal Kharrazi, Iran's ambassador to the United Nations, New York, May 1991.

45. *Washington Post*, April 23, 1988.

46. Gary Sick, "Does the U.S. Really Want Peace in the Gulf?" *Washington Post National Weekly Edition*, February 2, 1988, pp. 21–22.

47. Personal interview with Dr. Kamal Kharrazi.

48. UN Security Council, S/23322, December 24, 1991, as quoted in Amuzegar (1992), p. 422.

49. Kerman Mofid, *The Economic Consequences of the Gulf War* (New York, 1990), p. 147.

11

The Drive Toward Moderation: Iran Under Khamenei and Rafsanjani

We must stop making enemies.

President Ali Akbar Hashemi Rafsanjani, Teheran, 1989

The radical of one century is the conservative of the next.

Mark Twain, Notebook, *1935*

In June 1989, Ayatollah Ruhollah Mussavi Khomeini died. With the exception of Mozaffar ad-din Shah Qajar, Khomeini was the first Iranian leader of the past one-and-a-half centuries to die while ruling the country. All the other rulers were forced into exile, where they eventually died; Naser ad-din Shah Qajar was assassinated.

Since the Ayatollah's death, the pragmatic faction within the fundamentalist camp has gained the upper hand in the Byzantine politics of postrevolutionary Iran. The pragmatic leadership of the Islamic Republic has steered Iran toward moderation. Using the jargon in the study of revolutions, we can state that the Islamic Revolution is now experiencing the Thermidorian stage of its evolution. This moderation has come to fruition because of the domestic and international pressures exerted on the Islamic Republic during the past fourteen years and because of the belated but welcomed realization by the Islamic Republic that its ability to change Iran or the Islamic world is limited indeed. In this last chapter, we will examine the tensions and contradictions of this drive toward moderation in the post-Khomeini era.

Succession to Khomeini

For as long as he was alive, Khomeini was the Islamic Revolution and the Islamic Revolution was Khomeini. The fundamentalists realized that Khomeini was irreplaceable and that a smooth transition of power to his successor was indispensable for the survival of the infant republic. This is why while Khomeini was still alive, the Council of Experts, whose eighty or so members were all clerics, chose Ayatollah Hossein Ali Montazeri as Khomeini's heir apparent in 1985, even if he was recognized for that role long before his official anointment.

Hossein Ali Montazeri was born in Nejafabad in 1914. A student of Khomeini, he was jailed for his anti-Shah activity by SAVAK in 1965 after Khomeini was exiled to Turkey. From that time until 1978, he was a frequent guest in SAVAK's prisons. In the secret network that Khomeini had established in Iran during his exile, Montazeri was undoubtedly a key player. He was respected for his relentless struggle against the Shah and for his authorship of a two-volume book in Arabic about the Velayat-e Faqih.[1]

As the designated successor to Khomeini, Montazeri controlled a relatively large network because he made hundreds of appointments, especially in the judiciary. As chairman of the assembly that wrote the Islamic Constitution in 1979, he was an outspoken proponent of theocracy with a powerful *faqih* at its helm. His portrait appeared everywhere, always next to Khomeini's. But in 1986 his fortune suddenly began to reverse.

In November of that year, a Lebanese newspaper publicized the secret dealings between Washington and Teheran. (For details of the Iran-Contra affair, see Chapter 10.) The information was allegedly leaked to the Lebanese paper by Mehdi Hashemi. Hashemi's execution in September 1987 and the arrest of his brother, Montazeri's son-in-law, infuriated Montazeri.[2] Although Montazeri was not implicated in the Hashemi conspiracy, he was pressured to denounce Hashemi and his own staff. But he was in no mood to compromise and began to publicly lambast the government for violating human rights and mismanaging the economy. Such provocative criticism was a heavy blow to Khomeini, one he could not tolerate. Even before Montazeri had begun his venomous diatribe against the Islamic Republic, Sheikholislam Ahmad Khomeini, Khomeini's son, had privately warned the heir apparent that he was surrounded by a group of "hypocrites and selfish staff" that needed to be purged. Gradually, the government's denunciation of Montazeri became public. His leadership capability was questioned, and he was accused of having developed congenial relations with "liberal circles," an unambiguous reference to Bazargan's Liberation Movement.

Finally, in a letter to Ayatollah Khomeini, Montazeri submitted his resignation and declared his loyalty to both the Islamic Revolution and Khomeini. Khomeini happily accepted the resignation and admitted that he had committed an egregious error in judgment by supporting Montazeri as his successor.

With Montazeri out of the picture, the succession issue once again began to haunt the Islamic Republic. What confounded the situation was the inability of the Council of Experts to select, and Khomeini's refusal to appoint, a successor. Khomeini was well aware that his successor must be both a capable manager and a popular *marja* accepted and respected by the majority of the people, as the Islamic Constitution stipulated. There were many candidates with one of these qualifications, but no one with both who was also acceptable to Khomeini. The great majority of the leading ayatollahs were old, conservative, and ideologically incompatible with the relatively young elite of the Islamic Republic.

One logical way to solve the riddle was to change the constitutional qualifications of the *faqih*. With that goal in mind, in 1989 Khomeini ordered the formation of the Assembly for Reconsideration of the Constitution. It quickly removed the clause that required the *faqih* to be a popular *marja,* rendering it possible for a younger fundamentalist to succeed Khomeini.

After Khomeini's death, it took eight hours of deliberation before the all-male Assembly of Experts selected the new *faqih*. Khamenei was selected, with sixty votes in favor and fourteen against.[3] Ironically, Khamenei, who was not a *marja,* was selected before the Assembly for Reconsideration of the Constitution could vote to eliminate the *marjaeyat* clause. Therefore, the Council of Experts announced that Khamenei was selected temporarily. Once the revised constitution was ratified, his selection became permanent.

Revising the Constitution

When he ordered the formation of the Assembly for Reconsideration of the Constitution, Khomeini admitted that he had been aware of the constitution's deficiencies but had chosen to remain silent in order to focus on the war with Iraq.[4] Selecting twenty of the twenty-five members, he identified the exact areas in which the new assembly was to revise the constitution. Without offering any specifics, he ordered that power in the executive branch be centralized and that the *marjaeyat* clause be removed.

The conditions under which the constitution was being revised in 1989 were radically different from those when the constitution was written in 1979. When the war with Iraq ended in July 1988, the Islamic Republic entered a critical phase in its turbulent evolution. After eight years of war, the weary population, disgusted at losing its youth on the battlefield, was expecting to receive a "peace dividend." But the Iranian economy was in shambles and the standard of living for many Iranians was lower than it had been under the Shah. Therefore, improving the economy was critical for an enduring stability, which in turn required that the constitutional gridlock be eliminated.

The political landscape was also drastically different. Although the opponents of the Islamic Republic were either forcibly silenced or exiled by the government, intraelite rivalry between the three factions had intensified. With the deterioration of Khomeini's health, rivalry among the factions intensified because they all recognized that the new *faqih* could play a major role in determining Iran's future. In short, the constitutional revisions must be understood in the context of the ongoing factional struggle, the deteriorating socioeconomic conditions, and the uncertainties about Khomeini's succession.

The most profound revisions in the constitution relate to the qualifications of the *faqih* and the powers of the president.

Before he died, Khomeini stated in a letter to the deputies that he had never believed that the *marjaeyat* must be a qualification for the *faqih* and that "it is sufficient to have a just *mujtahed* who is selected by the Council of Experts."[5] His orders were obeyed.

There was virtual unanimity of opinion about removing the clause that required the *faqih* to be accepted by the majority of the people. The deputies recognized that no such leader could be found in post-Khomeini Iran. In 1979, Khomeini's popularity had justified granting him excessive powers, but now the fundamentalists, reversing their position, argued that because the *faqih* would be selected by the Assembly of Experts, whose members were popularly elected, the *faqih* would be indirectly recognized by the people.[6]

There were, however, some deputies who feared that the separation of the *marjaeyat* from the political leadership could lead to the separation of the state from religion or even the collapse of the Islamic Republic.[7] But most delegates foresaw no dangers in the proposed revision.[8] Khamenei, unaware that he would soon become the new *faqih,* rejected the notion that the key to Khomeini's success was his *marja* status: Khomeini succeeded, Khamenei said, because he was both a qualified *marja* and a gifted political leader.[9] Rafsanjani, supporting Khamenei, maintained that by the time someone becomes a *marja,* he is usually old and devoid of enough energy to manage the country,[10] which requires a different kind of temperament and skills than being a *marja.*[11]

While all the deputies supported granting the *faqih* sweeping powers, some of them tried in vain to establish mechanisms of accountability. In addition to the powers delegated to him in the original constitution, the *faqih* now has the authority to decide the general policy of the Islamic Republic, in consultation with the Assembly to Determine the Interests of the Republic, whose members he appoints.[12] He also appoints the head of the radio and television networks and calls for referenda. Rafsanjani pleaded that the *faqih* should not be allowed to decide policy because that would render the executive and legislative branches superfluous.[13] He also proposed setting a ten-year limit on the *faqih*'s rule.[14] Most deputies opposed this proposal. One said, "We cannot say that the *Faqih* is the Representative of the Hidden Imam only for 10 years."[15]

The constitutional revisions within the executive branch were also significant. The original design of a divided executive and weak presidency reflected the fundamentalists' goals of monopolizing power and precluding the possibility that a strong president might challenge them later. That configuration protected the fundamentalists but also created an ineffective government that was often in gridlock.

Although there was no quarrel about centralizing power in the executive branch, there was considerable disagreement about the methodology of achieving that goal. Mir Hossein Mussavi, Iran's prime minister, was the spokesman for the crusader faction and favored keeping the presidency weak and the divided executive intact. He warned everyone about the possibility of "presidential dictatorship" and the gullibility of the masses who could be deceived by a demagogic president.[16]

The main architects of a strong presidency were Hojatolislam Ali Akbar Hashemi Rafsanjani, who was himself a presidential candidate, and President Khamenei. Admitting that the original framers, of whom he was one, lacked the necessary "administrative skills"[17] to design a smooth and effective government, he identified two major flaws in the executive branch: the decentralized nature of power and the conspicuous absence of a system of accountability. As a remedy to these dual problems, he advocated a strong presidential system in which the president is chiefly responsible for governmental policy.

Rafsanjani, supporting Khamenei, reminded the deputies that Iran's economic and social problems would not be resolved with a divided executive.[18] He found the fear of dictatorship utterly unfounded: Because the *faqih* is the commander of the armed forces, no president could impose himself as a dictator.

In the revised constitution, the office of the prime minister was eliminated, and all his powers were transferred to the president, who now determines government policies. The president also selects and dismisses ministers, who must be confirmed by the Majles. His power to conduct economic and foreign policies was substantially increased by placing him directly in charge of the Planning and Budget Organization and the Supreme Council of National Security, which coordinates the activities related to defense, intelligence, and foreign policy. And a new council was created to resolve institutional conflicts between the Majles/government and the Guardian Council.

The new conception of executive power has striking similarities with the 1906 constitution. In both documents, there is a powerful and bigger-than-life figure who stands above the government. The center of power and the heart of the system, he is called shah in one system and *faqih* in the other.

Khamenei as the New "Faqih"

The problem with Khamenei's controversial selection was that he enjoyed neither Khomeini's popularity nor his status as a grand ayatollah: He was a *hojatolislam,* which in the Shi'i hierarchy ranks a level below the ayatollah. The challenge for the Islamic Republic, therefore, was to legitimize his selection not only to the population at large but also to the clerical establishment.[19]

The legitimization campaign consisted of both persuasion and tough warnings to potential critics. At least publicly, the elites of the Islamic Republic collectively endorsed the selection. The mass media cleverly implied that before his death, Khomeini had in fact endorsed Khamenei. In his congratulatory letter to Khamenei, Ahmad Khomeini wrote: "The Imam [Khomeini] consistently spoke of you as a qualified *mujtahed,* and regarded you as the most qualified leader for the Islamic Republic."[20] Rafsanjani declared that it was incumbent upon all Moslems to obey the new *faqih* and that disobedience would not be tolerated.[21]

As the legitimization campaign was proceeding, Khamenei moved cautiously to consolidate his position. He faced major difficulties because he lacked either a popular base of support or a nationwide network of supporters. As president (1981–1989), his role was ceremonial and he thus made few appointments. Perhaps his lack of an independent base of support was the critical factor in his selection as the *faqih*; he did not seem threatening to the rival factions.

Aware of his shortcomings, Khamenei in the early stage of his rule stayed above factions, as Khomeini had done earlier. Stressing the need for unity, he warned the ulama of a conspiracy to divide their ranks and assured them that he would do everything possible to increase their participation in politics. Most important, he sought to capture the control of Khomeini's vast personal networks by not removing Khomeini's many appointees. He promised to carry on Khomeini's torch to the very end. Thus, he refused to rescind Khomeini's *fatva* against Salman Rushdie for writing *The Satanic Verses* and denounced the "Great Satan" as the enemy of the Islamic Revolution.

It took about six months for Khamenei to consolidate power. Secure in his new position, he declared that "I am the successor of that great personality [Khomeini]. With all my power I will defend the *Velayat-e Faqih* doctrine ... [and] will not tolerate any attempt to weaken this divine doctrine, which is tantamount to weakening our entire Islamic order."[22] To demonstrate that he meant business, Khamenei declared that resumption of relations with Washington, the most sensitive issue of the post-Khomeini era, could proceed only with his consent.

Rafsanjani's election as Iran's fourth president in July 1989 also helped Khamenei to consolidate power more quickly. The close collaboration between the two men goes back to the early 1960s when they were a part of Khomeini's small network in Iran. They were both associated with the United Islamic Societies, formed when a few small Islamic groups were unified by Khomeini's order in early 1960.[23] On the important issues, which I will discuss in the following section, Khamenei and Rafsanjani were on the same side. In fact, as he felt more secure in his position, Khamenei seemed to lean more toward the pragmatists.

Although in the post-Khomeini era religious power has somewhat shifted from the institution of the Velayat-e Faqih to the main Shi'i seminaries and to the leading ayatollahs, Khamenei's religious authority has also gradually increased. In March 1992, he issued his first *fatva* in response to a question by the minister of health about the permissibility of transplanting an organ from an individual whose heart beats but whose brain is functionally dead. Khamenei declared that if such a transplant will save a life, it is religiously permissible. The significance of this *fatva* was not its content but what it symbolized: Khamenei's determination to emerge as a religious authority.

Today, the Velayat-e Faqih is far from dead. It is active and relatively powerful, but it plays a different role from that under Ayatollah Khomeini.

In their evolutionary process, revolutions grow gradually, going through different stages and temperaments. Each phase demands a particular type of leadership and a particular type of institutional configuration. The transformation in the Velayat-e Faqih reflected two interrelated phenomena: the transition from the consolidation phase to the reconstruction phase of the Islamic Revolution and the reemergence of the state as the central player on the Iranian political scene. In its original shape, the Velayat-e Faqih rule was a necessity if the Islamic Revolution was to be consolidated and if the ulama were to emerge as the new elite of Iran. Actual power, therefore, was shifted away from government to revolutionary institutions, the most powerful of which was the Velayat-e Faqih. Because the *faqih* was also a *marja,* religious power also shifted to the Velayat-e Faqih institution, making it the predominant force in the country.

By the time Ayatollah Khomeini died, the Islamic Revolution was consolidated and had entered into the Thermidorian, or moderate, phase of its evolution. In that phase, the main agenda item has been the reconstruction of a war-ravaged country. By its very nature, the Velayat-e Faqih cannot manage the implementation of this imperative. Only the executive branch can; hence the gradual reemergence of the state as the central political player.

The changes in the Velayat-e Faqih should be attributed to one other equally important factor. The new *faqih* has neither Khomeini's phenomenal popularity nor his religious credentials. Khomeini, a unique product of unique historical circumstances, is simply irreplaceable. It was Khomeini who made the institution of the Velayat-e Faqih powerful, not the other way around. His immense power was not based on the constitution, as Khamenei's is, but on his charismatic leadership, his status as a *marja,* and his undisputed role as the leader of the Islamic Revolution.

Rafsanjani and the Shah's Regime

Ali Akbar Hashemi Rafsanjani was born in 1935 into a petit-landowning family in the small village of Bahrman in the province of Kerman in central Iran.[24] The young Ali Akbar went to a local *maktab* (traditional school) to learn the basics of the Quran and Islamic jurisprudence. In 1948, when he was thirteen, he left Bahrman for Qom, where he completed his advanced Islamic studies under Ayatollahs Hossein Borujerdi, 'Alame Tabataba'i, and Hossein Ali Montazeri. For seven years, he also studied under Ayatollah Khomeini, with whom he developed a special relationship that lasted for decades.

Like his mentor Khomeini, the young Rafsanjani was intensely interested in politics, whose separation from Islam he did not accept. In Qom, his political views were influenced by the activities of the Fada'iyun-e Islam, the most active group in the city, and to a lesser extent by the popular movement to nationalize the oil industry.

At an early stage, Rafsanjani and his colleagues, especially Mohammad Javad Bahonar, who later became prime minister of the Islamic Republic in 1981, published a journal called *Maktab-e Tushuy'yu*. At the time of its publication, Rafsanjani recalled, the prevailing attitude among the ulama was not to get involved in politics and instead to focus on religious issues: "Many young *tollab* [students] did not even read ordinary newspapers. Therefore, we decided to publish a journal that covered serious contemporary issues, a journal that was compatible with the revolutionary spirit of some of the younger students."[25]

From his formative years in Qom, Rafsanjani was a pragmatist. This is how Mehdi Bazargan, certainly not a supporter of President Rafsanjani, described his first encounter with Rafsanjani in the early 1960s:

> Among Ayatollah Khomeini's supporters, [Rafsanjani] was effective. He did not display much fanaticism and was capable of communicating with intellectuals. He did not have the fanaticism the *akhund*s usually have. Any time we had a conversation with the Khomeini camp, Mr. Hashemi Rafsanjani was present in those meetings. It was easy to reach an understanding with him. He is pragmatic. ... He is a moderate, very knowledgeable, and a clever man. He is well-informed and has good instincts for politics.[26]

Rafsanjani's political career against the Shah began in 1962, when, in retaliation to Khomeini's agitation against the Shah, the government suddenly changed its policy and enlisted religious students for military service. One of those recruited for military service was the young Rafsanjani. Having served for only two months, he did not return to the barracks after the June Uprising of 1963. At the same time, because the Shah's government relaxed its policy of recruiting religious students, Rafsanjani was not punished for his escape.

Rafsanjani divided his time and energy between supporting his family of five children, writing, and engaging in anti-Shah political activities. That he also managed his own small pistachio business certainly influenced Rafsanjani's liberal views about the economy and the free enterprise system.

The list of Rafsanjani's writings includes an unpublished novel, a series of articles he wrote about the Quran while he was serving in jail, and three books. He translated one book from Arabic about Palestine and coauthored another with Mohammad Javad Bahonar about the socioeconomic and political conditions of the major world powers before the rise of Islam in the seventh century. His most serious piece of scholarship is *Amir Kabir*, an interesting book about Iran's strong prime minister around the middle of the nineteenth century. The selection of Amir Kabir as the focus of research is itself revealing. Rafsanjani wrote the book because "from an Islamic perspective, Amir Kabir seemed interesting to me, and because as a nationalist he initiated moves and rendered services that were compatible with my own Islamic views."[27] This subtle recognition that Iranian nationalism and Islam are not necessarily incompatible distinguishes Rafsanjani from many other figures in the Islamic Republic.

Rafsanjani's anti-Shah activities, which intensified after the crushing of the June Uprising in 1963, consisted of preaching, helping the families of political prisoners, and, most important, acting as one liaison between Khomeini and the many small, Islamic, anti-Shah groups, which included the Mojahedin-e Khalq-e Iran. He was one of the main elements of the secret network Khomeini created in Iran (see Chapters 3 and 8).

Rafsanjani was arrested by SAVAK on several occasions. In 1965, a few months after Ayatollah Khomeini's exile to Turkey and then to Iraq, he was imprisoned and charged with the publication of a book without government approval and with involvement in the assassination of Prime Minister Hassan Ali Mansur. He rejected the latter charge but had no quarrel with the former, arguing that he was unaware that publishing a book required government permission. The book he had translated from Arabic to Farsi was about Palestine and was written by Akram Zeytar, who at the time was the Jordanian ambassador to Iran. Since there was no evidence implicating Rafsanjani in Mansur's assassination, he was, like most other political prisoners, tortured and then released.

Before the Shah's coronation in 1967, Rafsanjani was again arrested by SAVAK for his alleged subversive activities. But he was soon released. Rafsanjani was cunning enough not to commit any illegal action that would justify his indefinite imprisonment. He legally but effectively used the pulpit to communicate with his receptive audience. He regularly lectured to a number of Islamic associations, some with as many as 1,000 members, always lamenting Iran's social and cultural ills and always offering the return to Islam as the incontrovertible solution for the country's problems. He was restrained enough not to directly attack the monarchy but articulate enough to convey his gospel of change.

After 1967, Rafsanjani was incarcerated three more times. Once he was charged with collaborating with the Mojahedin Khalq and once with distributing funds to the families of political prisoners. Finally in 1976, after his return from a trip to Europe, the United States, and Lebanon, he was jailed, not to be released until the midst of the revolutionary movement in 1978.

Upon his release from the Shah's prison, Rafsanjani joined the revolutionary movement. Ever since, he has been one of the central figures of the Islamic Revolution. He has certainly defied the cliché that "revolution devours its children." He has escaped two assassination attempts and was one of the few who remained dear and near to Khomeini until Khomeini died. He was one of the first appointed by Khomeini to settle the oil strike when the Shah was still in Iran. Khomeini also appointed him to the secret Council of the Islamic Revolution. It was Rafsanjani who read Khomeini's official decree appointing Bazargan as the prime minister of the provisional government. He was one of the founders of the Islamic Republican Party; Khomeini's representative in, and the spokesman for, the High Council of Defense; commander of the armed forces in 1988; and speaker of the Majles from the dawn of the Islamic Revolution until 1989 when he became president.

The Domestic Challenge
to President Rafsanjani

In July 1989, Rafsanjani was elected Iran's fourth president. The problems he faced were colossal: a weak, cash-hungry economy with a devastated infrastructure; a huge and inefficient state bureaucracy with too few good managers and a strong instinct to meddle in every conceivable social and economic issue; a weary population; international isolation; U.S.-supported economic sanctions; a relatively powerful crusader faction sworn to prevent any major changes in the country's domestic and foreign postures; and a strange system that was based on dualism of power and tension between the revolutionary institutions/private foundations and the regular state.

Against such horrendous obstacles, Rafsanjani promoted his "new thinking" in Iranian foreign policy and a "new realism" in dealing with the country's economic malaise, a policy orientation quantitatively different from that of Prime Minister Musavi. The foundation of Rafsanjani's strategy has been the reconstruction of the war-shattered economy. In foreign affairs, an extension of this domestic agenda, he has maneuvered to end Iran's costly isolation by pursuing a cautious rapprochement with the West and improving relations with Iran's neighbors.[28]

Toward these goals, Rafsanjani has attempted to centralize political and economic power, an awesome task that has thus far had limited success. When inaugurated, he had to confront the crusaders, who were still a formidable force. They controlled not only some of the revolutionary organizations but the Majles too. Rafsanjani, therefore, moved cautiously, so as not to alienate them completely. First, to deprive the crusaders of the ability to criticize him from a religious perspective, he emphasized that his policies were a logical extension of the Imam's thoughts. The new *faqih* certainly helped him in this legitimizing campaign. Second, while depriving some crusaders of real power, he gave others ceremonial positions. While Mir Hossein Musavi, the former prime minister, became an adviser to the president and Hojatolislam Khoeiniha was funded to operate a small think tank in northern Teheran, Ayatollah Sadeq Khalkhali, known in the West as the "hanging judge," lost his chairmanship of the Majles Committee on Foreign Affairs and Hojatolislam Ali Akbar Mohtashami, one of the most radical members of the Musavi cabinet, was not named to the new cabinet, despite a plea by 138 Majles deputies to retain him.[29]

Rafsanjani has succeeded in diminishing, albeit not significantly, the autonomy of some of the revolutionary organizations, some of which are still controlled by the crusaders. The Komites, the gendarmerie, and the police have been integrated to create the new Security Forces under one central command structure. The Armed Forces and the Revolutionary Guards were integrated to establish the General Staff (Setad-e Koll-e Niruha-ye Mosallah) under a single leader.

The increasing power of the pragmatists has recently forced the crusaders into a defensive posture. In 1992, for example, Khamenei endorsed a new law that required all candidates for the Guardian Council to pass an examination on Islamic jurisprudence. The law was strongly condemned by the crusaders: Some prominent crusaders failed the exam and others refused to take it.[30]

The crusaders received another blow in the Majles election. In 1992, candidates from the pragmatic, crusader, and conservative factions competed in the parliamentary elections, the fourth since the Iranian Revolution in 1979. Although the elections were free, the nominating process was controlled. The Guardian Council, dominated by the conservatives, examined the credentials of more than 3,000 candidates and disqualified more than 1,000 of them, including a number of crusaders—an action endorsed by Ayatollah Khamenei. The result of the elections proved that even without the screening by the Guardian Council, the crusaders would not have fared well. Of the 230 seats (to which 9 women were elected), they won only 50, with much of their strength coming from the provincial cities. The three most prominent crusaders, Hojatolislams Mehdi Karrubi, Mohammad Mussavi Khoeiniha, and Ali Akbar Mohtashami, all running from Teheran, were soundly defeated.[31]

Despite the crusaders' defeat in the 1992 parliamentary elections, and despite Rafsanjani's policy of integrating the revolutionary organizations with the regular state, the crusaders continue to exercise a considerable degree of influence in the judiciary and in the revolutionary organizations. A number of financially powerful *bonyad* (foundations) remain outside government's jurisdiction. They have become a mini-state with substantial power. The Fifteenth Khordad Foundation, run by Ayatollah Hassan Sanei, is one of the richest of these foundations. It operates many hospitals, schools, factories, charitable organizations, housing units, and other organizations. There is little, if any, government control over its finances and activities. Recently, for example, the foundation single-handedly increased the bounty for the murder of Salman Rushdie, thus increasing tensions between the Iranian government and a host of European states and damaging Rafsanjani's somewhat successful public relations campaign to portray Iran as a responsible member of the international community.

Despite strong opposition by the conservatives and the crusaders, the Rafsanjani administration has followed a social and cultural policy that is more moderate than Khomeini's. The enforcement of veiling is not as strict as before, although to appease its critics the government occasionally initiates a harsh campaign to penalize the violators of the Islamic dress code. Women are allowed to publicly play classical Persian music for an all-female audience. The Teheran Symphony Orchestra periodically performs Western classical music for the public. The government is displaying the Royal Jewels, the very symbol of the grandeur of Imperial Iran, and has increased funding for the protection and maintenance of the historical monuments, many of them from the pre-Islamic era.

For better or worse, Iran has historically experienced stability and economic growth only when the central government has been centralized and powerful. For the first time since the Shah's fall in 1979, the government has now become relatively centralized and powerful, more so than any other time since the dawn of the Islamic Revolution.

Although power has been somewhat centralized, the opposition to Rafsanjani's policies has not disappeared. The crusader faction, with its control of some of Iran's most popular dailies such as *Salam,* has relentlessly criticized the government for its reform policies and conciliatory approach toward the West.

The government has also faced violent opposition to some of its policies. In May 1992, protestors rioted in the cities of Mashhad and Arak over government efforts to evict squatters and raze slums. Small areas of the Teheran bazaar were set ablaze by arsonists. Decisively, the government executed at least eight "antirevolutionary hooligans and riff-raff" for these incidents, which were more of a nuisance than a threat to the stability of Rafsanjani's government.

Confounding these problems has been the challenge by the Mojahedin and Bazargan's Liberation Movement. After signing a disparaging open letter to the president in which the government's major policies were strongly condemned, some members of the Liberation Movement were imprisoned by the government. Since then, relations between the government and the Liberation Movement have remained quarrelsome.

Because the Liberation Movement is not armed and does not seek to overthrow the government, it poses no fatal threat to the Islamic Republic. The armed Mojahedin does. Although the Islamic Republic claims to have eradicated it inside Iran, the Mojahedin, to Teheran's dismay, continue to receive substantial support from the Iraqi regime and some support from Washington. The Mojahedin are the most organized opponents of the Islamic Republic outside of Iran. They operate an effective network of professional activists in the Western nations. In the past few years, the Mojahedin has persuaded the European Parliament and many members of the U.S. Congress to condemn the Islamic Republic for its human rights violations.

Several assassinations of exiled leaders have also undermined the government's attempt to improve Iran's international image. The Islamic Republic has categorically denied any involvement in these violent acts. The most notorious of these was the assassination of former Prime Minister Bakhtiyar in Paris in 1992. The incident resulted in President François Mitterrand canceling his scheduled trip to Iran, which would have been the first official trip to Iran by the head of a major Western government since 1979.

The alleged assassination of the exiled leaders by the Islamic Republic is one reason why the international human rights agencies have consistently condemned Iran. The Islamic Republic has persistently rejected such charges as vacuous and a smear tactic designed to undermine the Islamic Republic and denigrate the Islamic Revolution.

Rafsanjani's Economic Policy

Although Rafsanjani has been somewhat accommodating toward those who control the revolutionary organizations and the private foundations, he has been remarkably tenacious and uncompromising about the urgency of reconstructing Iran's war-damaged economy. In his inaugural address to the Majles in 1989, he admonished his rivals "to forego their extremism" to allow for Iran's speedy reconstruction.[32] The composition of his new cabinet was one reflection of his new approach: It consisted of only four clerics and a large number of Western-educated technocrats.[33]

The Rafsanjani administration's economic philosophy and goals are accurately reflected in the Five-Year Development Plan, which was readily approved by the Majles in 1990. The total cost was estimated at around $390 billion, about $27 billion above projected government revenues, to be raised from foreign credits and investments.[34]

The Rafsanjani administration's most urgent task was to invigorate the oil industry, Iran's main source of revenue. Iran's oil industry, second only in export capability to that of Saudi Arabia, has been revitalized since its wartime devastation. The major refineries and oil platforms are being repaired, with European assistance. In 1992, Iran was producing some 4 million barrels of oil a day (up from a wartime low of 2 million), 75 percent of which was exported, mainly to Japan and Western Europe. Although oil revenues surged—1992 income from oil reached about $20 billion—price stability in the international oil market frustrated Iran's pursuit of additional oil revenues.

Because of Rafsanjani's new economic policy, there has been a gradual shift away from state ownership of the major industries, price regulation, expensive subsidies, and closing of Iranian markets to foreign products and toward a more market-regulated economy, privatization of nonstrategic industries, reduced subsidies, and opening of Iranian markets to foreign products and investments. The government has identified some 500 industrial units to be sold to the private sector, and a few have been privatized. The government has offered some incentives for the return from the West to Iran of the former owners of the expropriated enterprises and the technocrats of the Shah's bureaucracy. For the first time since 1979, the ban on importing foreign automobiles has been lifted, and Iran has provided lucrative concessions to foreign investors, especially in the two free-trade zones it has established in the Qeshm and Kish islands in the Persian Gulf. The Iranian Tobacco Company has recently signed an exclusive import deal with R. J. Reynolds Company, manufacturer of Winston cigarettes.[35] R. J. Reynolds will reportedly manufacture a new brand of cigarette, Bistoon, in the Khorasan province. Iran's relations with the major international financial institutions have also improved. In 1993, the World Bank agreed to lend Iran some $463 million for developmental projects.[36] The decision was made despite Washington's vehement opposition.

Perhaps the most symbolic manifestation of the new economic realism is that the revolutionary graffiti written on the walls are gradually being replaced with billboards advertising European and Japanese products.

Despite the serious problems Iran inherited from the Mussavi administration (see Chapter 10) and the eight-year war with Iraq, and despite a worldwide recession, in the past three years Iran has experienced a modest economic recovery as its gross national product grew slightly and its overall economic health did not deteriorate. But the problems the country faces today remain potentially calamitous. Inflation is rampant and seemingly uncontrollable. Rents in the major cities are rising even faster than the rapacious rate of inflation. Industrial output remains low. Excessive governmental regulations stifle productivity. The government is unable to stabilize the chaotic foreign exchange system that continuously devalues Iranian currency. The government has not been able to attract as many foreign investors as it had hoped. And the U.S. sanctions are depriving Iran of access to some of the most modern technologies.

Rafsanjani's New Thinking
in Foreign Policy
and the Crisis in Kuwait

Under Rafsanjani, Iranian foreign policy has moved further away from adventurism toward pragmatism. The three main pillars of this new thinking are the acceptance of Iran's very limited ability to change the political landscape of the Islamic world, a gradual rapprochement with the West, and improved relations with Iran's neighbors.[37]

Iran, Rafsanjani has repeatedly said, must "stop making enemies." In that spirit, he has improved relations with Iran's neighbors. Under both presidents Gorbachev and Yeltsin, Teheran and Moscow have solidified their friendly relations. Since the breakup of the Soviet Union, Iran has become one of Russia's most important buyers of arms. Thus, despite Washington's strong opposition, Russia sold Teheran three diesel-fueled, Kilo-class submarines. In 1993, Russian foreign minister Andrei Kozyrev met President Rafsanjani and agreed to sell Iran three nuclear reactors. He also reiterated Russia's goal of improving trade with Iran.[38]

Iran has also solidified its linguistic, cultural, historic, and commercial ties with the newly formed independent republics in Transcaucasia and Central Asia. These new republics provide lucrative markets for Iranian goods. They also have become an enticing arms bazaar from which Iran has purchased some military equipment. That President Rafsanjani attended the first summit meeting of the Central Asian republics in May 1992 shows how vital this region is to Iran and how important Iran is to that region. Iran has signed contracts for some twenty economic projects with these republics.

Iran also acted to mediate the conflict between Armenians and Azerbaijanis over the Nagorno-Karabakh region. In March 1992, their representatives met in Teheran and agreed to resolve their conflict, which of course they failed to do. Iran's mediation was a sign of both its growing importance in the region and its desire to see stability there.[39]

Iran's relations with the European Community have also improved, although Iran's continuing refusal to revoke Khomeini's alleged *fatva* to kill Salman Rushdie, the author of *The Satanic Verses,* has generated some tension. Despite this, Iran's trade with Britain exceeded $1 billion in 1992, and its trade with France increased sixfold in 1991–1993. And Germany has remained Iran's number one trade partner.

It is in the Persian Gulf, however, that the essence of Rafsanjani's new thinking becomes most visible.[40] The jugular of the Iranian economy is the Persian Gulf, where the government generates more than 90 percent of its revenues and where Iranian and Western interests historically have collided.

In 1980, Iraq invaded Iran and started a stunningly bloody war, which ended in 1988. A decade later, Iraq invaded Kuwait. President Saddam Hossein gambled big, and Iraq lost big: When it was expelled from Kuwait in February 1991, Iraq, according to a UN report, was "relegated to a preindustrial age."[41]

Even before the invasion of Kuwait, Iranian policy in the Persian Gulf had undergone a transformation: Iran's goal was no longer exporting its revolution but improving relations with Iraq and with the littoral states of the Gulf Cooperation Council (GCC). In that spirit, Iran resumed relations with Kuwait, started a dialogue with Saudi Arabia, and concentrated on peace negotiations with Iraq. Economically, Teheran solidified its ties with the GCC members (with the exception of Saudi Arabia) and encouraged the rich sheikhdoms to invest in Iran. Through quiet diplomacy, Iran was trying to influence the gulf oil policy by demanding lower production levels and higher prices. In short, Iran's objective was to reduce tension in the region. Was this posture tactical? The Kuwaiti crisis proved it was not.

Why did Iraq invade Kuwait? Part of the answer may be found in the way the Iraq-Iran war ended. During the Iraq-Iran war, Iraq, "the lesser of the two evils," was armed to the teeth. Over the previous decade, it had purchased at least $80 billion worth of armaments. Iraq ended the war with a massive arsenal of weapons of mass destruction and with between $80 and 120 billion in foreign loans.[42] Iraq also needed to give a peace dividend to its tired population and to begin reconstruction.[43] Iraq's financial crisis was so severe that it defaulted on its loans to France and some other Western powers. Saddam needed help: either higher oil revenues, some kind of restructuring or forgiveness of Iraq's loans, outside (Arab) aid, or demilitarization.

To alleviate Iraq's economic problems, Saddam pressured OPEC to increase oil prices. But his "friends of convenience," Saudi Arabia, Kuwait, and the United Arab Emirates, opposed higher prices. The latter two went even further and violated OPEC's production quotas in order to keep the prices depressed. To Saddam, this was "a deliberate plan" backed by the CIA to wage "another war on Iraq."[44]

Saddam's Western and Arab financiers were not eager to forfeit their loans. Nor were his rich Arab brothers prepared to finance an "Arab Marshall plan" for Iraq's reconstruction. Saddam told the U.S. ambassador, April C. Glaspie, that "our war [against Iran] also amounted to their defense. Therefore, the aid they gave us should not be regarded as a debt."[45] It was painful to Saddam to accept that he had been used as a "useful idiot" by the rich Arabs.

Pressured to repay his debts, unable to increase his revenues, and unwilling to slow down Iraq's militarization, Saddam resorted to conquest. Kuwait thus became another victim to the process of containing the Islamic Revolution: To contain the revolution, Iraq invaded Iran; to prevent Iraq from losing, Iraq was militarized; militarization led to borrowing, which led to the financial crisis of the state, which pressured Saddam to attack Kuwait.

The "trap theory" blames the United States for inciting Iraq to invade Kuwait to justify its destruction of the Iraqi military, which had become a menace to Israel.[46] However, it appears that before the start of the war the Bush administration went out of its way to build bridges with Baghdad, although it was somewhat concerned about Iraq's militarization. For example, National Security Directive 26, signed by President Bush in November 1989, regarded Iran and the Soviet Union, not Iraq, as the main threat to U.S. interests.[47]

In reality, Saddam was trapped by his feeling of grandiosity and by his miscalculations. He had many opportunities to withdraw unilaterally but did not. Pandered to by both Washington and Moscow, he exaggerated Iraq's strategic significance and underestimated U.S. resolve to defend its interests.[48] Thus, he probably ruled out the prospect of an all-out war. In such a case, he was counting on support from Moscow, a dying power that was moving closer to Washington than Saddam had realized.

Whatever its reasons, Iraq invaded Kuwait in August 1990. Iran was the first country in the Persian Gulf and the second in the Islamic world, following Algeria, to officially demand that Iraq withdraw from Kuwait.[49] Saddam's conquest of Kuwait would have given Iraq about 20 percent of the world's petroleum reserves, turning it into a regional superpower that Iran could not tolerate.

In the early stage of the crisis, there was unanimity of opinion between the crusader and the pragmatist factions. Both hated Saddam with equal intensity and denounced him for his aggression. The introduction of U.S. forces in the region, however, became a source of factional friction. Neither faction took seriously Washington's announcement that it did not intend to permanently station troops in the area.[50] Teheran, therefore, denounced the U.S. intervention.

Determined to get Iraq out of Kuwait without a U.S. military presence in the region, Iranian diplomats moved in two directions. On the regional level, two days after the invasion, the Iranian foreign minister, Ali Akbar Velayati, traveled to Bahrain, Qatar, and the United Arab Emirates to convince them not to request assistance from Washington, offering them Iranian protection against external threats.[51] On the international level, Iran emphasized that the conflict must be resolved through the United Nations.

As the United States formed an international coalition against Saddam, and as Iran failed to prevent the introduction of U.S. forces, Rafsanjani decided not to allow the crisis to reverse his rapprochement with the West and the Gulf Cooperation Council. Thus, he opted for a policy of neutrality.

Whereas the Allies were gratified by Iran's neutrality, Iraq worked indefatigably to entice Iran to come to its support. Saddam's strategy toward Iran was similar in some ways to his strategy toward other Islamic nations. He wrapped his irredentist ambitions in an Islamic and Palestinian robe. At once, he managed a personal metamorphosis, from a secular Ba'thist to a devout Moslem and to an Abdul Naser dressed as Robin Hood. First, Iraq's National Assembly declared that if Iraq were to be attacked, all Moslems were obligated to engage in a *jihad* (holy war) against the United States.[52] Symbolically, Iraq inscribed "Allah Is Great" on its flag. Then, Saddam linked his Kuwaiti policies with Israeli withdrawal from the occupied territories. He promised to share the spoils of his conquest with all Arabs. "All Arabs are one nation," his foreign minister, Tariq Aziz, wrote to the Arab League, "and what belongs to one of them should belong to all and benefit all."[53]

Saddam's strategy generated favorable sentiment in the streets of the Moslem world. In non-Arab Iran, this strategy had some effect only after Iraq offered Teheran a major concession.

In the month preceding his invasion of Kuwait, Saddam wrote three conciliatory letters to Rafsanjani. In the first two, he warned of a foreign conspiracy to ignite another war between the two nations and proposed a meeting between the two presidents. As Saddam was still occupying some Iranian soil, perhaps he was hoping to sign a peace treaty with Iran from a position of strength, which would then allow him to concentrate on his plan to invade Kuwait.

A day after invading Kuwait, Saddam wrote to Rafsanjani again, reiterating his old proposals but reminding him that what had happened in Kuwait was an "Arab problem" and that any Iranian involvement in it would jeopardize the peace process with Iraq.[54]

A week later, Rafsanjani finally responded to the letters. Rejecting the urgency of a meeting between the two presidents and in an unmistakenly nationalistic tone, he discarded Saddam's contention that the Kuwaiti crisis was an "Arab problem."[55] He made it clear that although Iran "does not seek to exploit the crisis," it would protect its own interests. The invasion, he wrote Saddam, "could weaken our trust and create serious doubts about the motives of the past few months' talks." He explicitly stated that the 1975 Algiers Treaty was the only basis for peace.

One week after these subtle warnings from Rafsanjani, Saddam did what Rafsanjani had asked him to do. To assure that Iran did not open a front while he was moving thirty divisions of his army from the Iranian border to Kuwait, Saddam accepted the Algiers Treaty. "Now that you have gotten everything you have asked for," he wrote to Rafsanjani, "we must work together to expel the foreign troops." Accepting the peace offer, Rafsanjani remained silent on Saddam's request to "expel the foreign troops," giving a signal to all parties that Iran could not be ignored or marginalized. Moreover, Rafsanjani rejected any linkage between peace with Iraq and the Kuwaiti crisis. Thus, Iran became the first winner of the conflict as all of its terms for peace were unconditionally accepted.

Only after this major concession did the crusaders begin their rumblings about the tilt toward Iraq. The Militant Clerics Association declared that Iran should not tolerate the U.S. presence and that the Saudi request for help from the United States was more "shameful" than the invasion of Kuwait.[56] And Ayatollah Sadeq Khalkhali condemned the United States as "the number one aggressor of our era," calling for the formation of an anti-U.S./Israel coalition.[57] Hojatolislam Ahmad Khomeini suggested that the government should take a more anti-U.S. stance,[58] and Mohtashemi and Khalkhali argued that cooperation with Iraq would serve the interests of Islam.[59] But the crusaders were unable to reverse Iran's policy of active neutrality.

Throughout the crisis, Ayatollah Khamenei, who remained an ally of Rafsanjani, was in charge of the ideological blitz against the United States. His occasional condemnation of the United States was a double-edged sword: It was a genuine reflection of Iran's concerns about the permanent presence of U.S. forces in the region as well as an effective weapon to deprive the crusaders of reasons to denigrate the government for any complacency toward the Allies.

Ultimately, Saddam's strategy of manipulating the elite rivalry in Iran proved futile. He had overestimated the power of the crusaders. Excluded from the corridors of power, they had in fact no effective institutional base from which to change policy. Saddam also misread the political climate in Iran. Still fresh in the people's minds was Saddam's attempt to turn the Iraq-Iran war into an ethnic war between the Arabs and the Persians. And they still had their somber memories of defenseless civilian populations showered by SCUD missiles, of the unconscionable use of chemical weapons against Iranians and Kurds, and of the incalculable pains he inflicted on millions of people who lost their loved ones and homes during the Iraq-Iran war. Rafsanjani's government rode on such pervasive feelings toward Iraq to gain support for its neutrality and to checkmate the crusaders.

Iran's main concern throughout the crisis was the United States. Domestic considerations precluded the possibility of direct talks with Washington. When a few months prior to the Kuwaiti crisis Vice-President Ata'ollah Mohajerani had proposed such talks, the crusaders condemned him, Khamenei rejected his idea, and Rafsanjani distanced himself from the proposal.[60] Thus, Secretary of State Baker admitted, the United States had to approach Iran through intermediaries, which included Syria and Turkey.[61]

Clearly, Washington was aware that Iran could play the role of spoiler and change the regional balance of power. When Saddam made his peace overtures to Iran, the prospect of a military alliance between Iraq and Iran became more probable, although Washington correctly viewed this as unlikely.[62]

Despite their varied strategies, Washington and Teheran had many common goals. Both sought to expel Iraq from Kuwait, both opposed any alterations in the region's political map, both wanted to see Iraq militarily weakened, both supported the UN trade embargoes on Iraq, and both opposed the Lebanonization (fragmentation) of Iraq. Aware that it shared so many goals with Washington and cognizant of its inability to achieve those goals single-handedly, Iran shrewdly stayed on the sidelines, did not antagonize the United States, and in the end shared the many spoils of the liberation of Kuwait.

Washington's objective was to keep Iran neutral by rewarding it. Iran's long-term goals were to have its assets in the United States unfrozen and to forestall the permanent presence of the United States in the region.

Iran did stay neutral. Although Rafsanjani consistently opposed the U.S. presence, he explicitly stated that Moslems would drive U.S. forces out of the region if "they tried to make their stay in Saudi Arabia a *permanent* one" (my emphasis).[63] When Iraqi jets sought sanctuary in Iran in January 1991, Iran impounded them for the duration of the war. Shortly before the start of the air strike, Velayati stated that in the event of war, Iran would remain neutral.[64] And there were no attacks against U.S. interests by radical Islamic groups sympathetic to Iran.

Washington reciprocated. It paid Iran $200 million in September 1990 for undelivered weapons Iran had purchased under the Shah. In December 1990, President Bush authorized U.S. oil companies to import about 200,000 barrels of Iranian oil.[65] Nor did Washington oppose Iran's request for foreign loans from the World Bank, the International Monetary Fund, and Japan. Secretary of State Baker declared that Iran was abiding by the UN trade embargo and that Iran would have a positive role to play in any future security arrangements in the region.[66]

Having reached an understanding with Washington through intermediaries, Iran reached out to the GCC. Its goal was to demonstrate the Islamic Republic's goodwill and to better position itself for the post–Kuwait War period. Relations were already improving with the GCC before the invasion of Kuwait. Three short weeks before the invasion, Iran restored diplomatic relations with Kuwait. After the invasion, the trend toward better neighborly relations continued. In October, for the second time, the foreign ministers of the GCC met with Velayati in New York, stressing the need for greater cooperation.[67] As the end of the crisis approached, Iran announced its readiness to sign a nonaggression pact with the GCC members.

Iran's relations with Iraq were cautiously warm as diplomatic relations were restored. High-ranking Iraqi officials often met with their Iranian counterparts in Teheran. And during the air war when the Allies had complete control of Iraq's airspace, Iran allowed Iraqi officials to travel to the Soviet Union through Iran.

Once the air war began, the conflict between the crusaders and the pragmatists intensified. The crusaders strongly denounced the bombing of the civilian population and pleaded that Iran assist Iraq. But when only a few thousand demonstrators participated in a Teheran rally the crusaders had organized to condemn the air war, it became abundantly clear that their views enjoyed little popular backing.[68]

With the start of the air strike, Iran's concerns were the future of Iraq and its own future role in the Persian Gulf. Neutrality did not mean indifference to the fate of Iraq and its large Shi'ite population. Although Iran was quietly celebrating the diminishing power of the Iraqi military, devastation in Iraq could pave the way for the Balkanization of Iraq and the potential creation of an independent Kurdistan, which would have incited the other ethnic groups in Iran to demand autonomy. Like the crusaders, the pragmatists denounced the United States for its bombing of the civilian population. But such denunciations were never translated into concrete actions against the Allies.[69]

To demonstrate its new role as a peacemaker, Iran proposed a peace plan in February 1991. Rafsanjani's offer to mediate between Washington and Baghdad must be understood in the context of his unspoken desire to improve relations with Washington and to emerge as a stabilizing force in the region. His seven-point plan was a combination of some unrealistic but popular public relations moves and some genuine proposals. It realistically called for an Iraqi withdrawal, the signing of a nonaggression pact between Iran and the GCC, and the establishment of a regional mechanism to foster economic, political, and security cooperation among the gulf states. It unrealistically proposed that after an Iraqi withdrawal, Rafsanjani or Khamenei, along with the leaders of Malaysia, Indonesia, Pakistan, Algeria, Jordan, Sudan, and Yemen, would go to Baghdad to appeal to the Allies to withdraw their forces, so they could be replaced with an Islamic force.[70] It called for the formation of a committee composed of the Persian Gulf states and other Islamic nations to discuss the region's problems and of an Islamic Bank to rebuild Kuwait and Iraq.

Although the proposal generated enthusiasm among some Europeans and the Soviet Union, it proved inconsequential. Having spent billions of dollars, Washington was not about to bestow on Iran the role of peacemaker. After all, the United States had intervened militarily to impose its own agenda, not Iran's.

Iran's peace proposal, and many other proposals, bore no fruit. What had begun with a military conquest ended with a military defeat. The Allies routed the Iraqi forces in a war that took only 100 hours. Kuwait was freed at last.

A defeated Saddam was then confronted with a major uprising by the Kurds in the north and the Shi'ites in the south. The rebels scored major victories against Saddam. Having been promised support by the Allies if they rose against Saddam, the Kurds and the Shi'ites soon found themselves defenseless against Saddam's defeated but angry Republican Guards. The atrocities committed by the

Iraqi army against the Kurds and the Shi'ites were no less shocking than those inflicted on the Kuwaiti population during the occupation.

Perhaps the most revealing aspect of Iranian policy after the Iraqi defeat was Teheran's silence about the civil war in Iraq. Although Rafsanjani called for Saddam's resignation, and although Iran supported various plans by Saddam's opponents to form a government in exile, the Islamic Republic still was remarkably passive during the civil war, another example of Iran's moderation in the conduct of its foreign policy.

It is ironic how the misfortunes of one country can catalyze the resurgence of another. Consider the case of Iran. The aggression against Kuwait set into motion a series of chain reactions that have changed the landscape of the Persian Gulf region for decades to come. Kuwait itself was pillaged and ruined. The region's environment was seriously damaged. Thousands of people were killed and millions more were forced to leave their homes. And Iraq's military and economic infrastructures, the product of decades of hard work and investment, were demolished.

The military cost of freeing Kuwait was staggering, about $60 billion, most of it contributed by Kuwait and Saudi Arabia, the same two countries whose magnanimous contributions had kept Saddam's war machine lubricated during the Iraq-Iran war.

But Iran has been different from other countries in the Persian Gulf: It has emerged out of the Kuwaiti crisis politically and economically more stable than before. Iran benefited enormously from increased oil prices, somewhere between $3 and $5 billion. It improved its ties with the major international financial institutions, such as the IMF, and with the United Nations. Some of its frozen assets were unfrozen in the United States. It moved forward in its rapprochement with the West and the Arab nations of the gulf. Iran's image improved. Iraq accepted all of Iran's conditions for peace. And the invading Iraqi army freed from the Kuwaiti jails the fifteen Lebanese Shi'i prisoners convicted of bombing the French and U.S. embassies in Kuwait in 1983 and turned them over to Iran, making it possible to resolve the issue of the Western hostages in Lebanon.

With its military capability seriously damaged, Iraq is not likely to dominate the region for years to come. Saudi Arabia, with its small population, small armed forces, and fragile political system, is incapable of dominating the area. Other gulf states are too small to play any major role in securing stability. Nor can Syria or Egypt safeguard tranquility. Their interests are economic, and their military presence will be accompanied by political ideologies that will threaten the conservative sheikdom of the region.

How, then, can security be maintained in the region? The Second Persian Gulf War was a resource war, a war over an essential commodity, oil. Had Kuwait been an exporter of bananas, the world would have tolerated Saddam's aggression. With the end of the Cold War, we have entered into a new and yet undefined world order. It appears that in the new world order, there will be only one military superpower, the United States, but multiple economic superpowers, namely Japan, Germany, and perhaps even a United Europe. Multipolarity in the economic sphere, in turn, will only increase the strategic significance of the Persian Gulf: With its control of Persian Gulf oil, the United States will be able to exercise a profound influence on the economies of its main competitors, Japan and Europe, which rely heavily on gulf oil. The long-term stability of the region, therefore, is of vital concern to the United States.

Since the end of the war, the United States has not defined how it seeks to secure stability in the Persian Gulf. It is clear that the United States intends to stay in the region for a while; it has already established some bases and has signed a number of military pacts with the members of the GCC.

In many ways, the Kuwaiti War was the outcome of the U.S. tilt toward Iraq during the Iraq-Iran war, a tilt that helped Saddam build his aggressive military machine. Today, some policymakers are advocating that Iran be ignored or marginalized in future security arrangements for the region.[71] If their advice is taken seriously, we should anticipate more turmoil in that volatile region of the world.

The experience of the past decades has proven that no security arrangement can assure stability in the region without Iranian participation. Iran must accept that Washington has vital interests in the region for which it is prepared to go to war. Furthermore, Iran must accept that the United States has become its latest southern neighbor, at least for a while. The United States is also well advised to recognize the legitimate interests of Iran in the region.[72] Both Washington and Teheran should remember the maxim, "Nations do not have friends; they only have interests."

Notes

1. For the Persian translation of Ayatollah Montazeri's book, see Mahmood Salavati, *Mabani-ye Feqhi-ye Hokumat-e Islami* (The Jurisprudential Bases of the Islamic Government) (Teheran, 1367/1988).

2. See Mohammad Rayshahri, *Khaterat-e Rayshahri* (Rayshahri's Memories), (Teheran, 1989).

3. *Iran Times*, June 23, 1989.

4. Ibid., April 20, 1989.

5. *Surat-e Mashruh-e Mozakerat-e Shora-ye Baznegari-ye Qanoun-e Asasi-ye Jumhuri-ye Islami-ye Iran* (The Proceeding of the Council to Reconsider the Constitution of the Islamic Republic of Iran) (Teheran, 1989), vol. 1, p. 174 (hereafter referred to as *Surat*).

6. Ibid., vol. 1, p. 192, and vol. 3, p. 1256.

7. Ibid., vol. 1, p. 196.

8. Ibid.

9. Ibid., pp. 193–194.

10. Ibid., pp. 196–197.

11. Ibid., p. 197.

12. The Constitution of the Islamic Republic of Iran (Teheran, 1990), p. 62–64.

13. *Surat,* vol. 2, p. 679.

14. Ibid., vol. 1, pp. 196–197.

15. Ibid., vol. 3, pp. 1210–1211.

16. Ibid., vol. 1, p. 269.

17. Ibid., pp. 1, 12.

18. Ibid., p. 249.

19. *Iran Times,* June 23, 1989.

20. Ibid., June 16, 1989.

21. Ibid., June 23, 1989.

22. Ibid., June 12, 1990.

23. Personal interview with Fazlollah Tavakoli Bina, adviser to the president for economic affairs and trade unions, Teheran, July 1991. Tavakoli was one of the founding members of this organization. Personal interview with Ayatollah Anvari, Teheran, July 1991. Anvari was jailed by the Shah's regime for having issued the *fatva* to assassinate Mansur. He denied issuing such a *fatva.*

24. The information about President Rafsanjani in this section was gathered from a number of interviews with individuals who have worked very closely with him. It is also based on some documents released by the president's office.

25. Interview with President Rafsanjani, Teheran, August 1991.

26. Personal interview with Mehdi Bazargan, Teheran, July 1991.

27. Interview with President Rafsanjani, Teheran, August 1991.

28. For details, see Shireen Hunter, *Iran After Khomeini* (New York, 1992).

29. *Foreign Broadcast Information Service* (hereafter referred to as *FBIS*), August 21, 1990.

30. *Iran Times,* October 26, 1990. Karubi was not even elected in the recent Majles election in 1992.

31. Bahman Bakhtiari, "Elections in Iran," *Washington Report on the Middle East,* July 1990, pp. 42–44.

32. *Washington Post,* August 18, 1989.

33. *Political Handbook of the World, 1990–91* (New York, 1991), the chapter on Iran.

34. *Iran Times,* January 29, 1993.

35. Ibid.

36. Ibid., February 2, 1993.

37. R. K. Ramazani, "Iran's Foreign Policy: Both North and South," *Middle East Journal,* 393 (Summer 1992), pp. 393–412.

38. *Iran Times,* April 2, 1993.

39. Ibid., March 26, 1993.

40. An example of this new thinking can be found in Mohammad Masjed Jame'i's *Iran Va Khaleej-e Fars* (Iran and the Persian Gulf), (Teheran, 1989).

41. *Report to the Secretary-General on Humanitarian Needs in Kuwait and Iraq,* prepared by Martti Athisaari, March 20, 1991, p. 5.

42. Sciolino estimated the total loans to be about $80 billion. See Eliane Sciolino, *The Outlaw State* (New York, 1991), p. 188. Saddam's own estimate is about $40 billion, which, he told Glaspie, does not include what he had borrowed from the Arab nations of the Persian Gulf. See the text of his conversation with April Glaspie in ibid., p. 273.

43. Kerman Mofid, *The Economic Consequences of the Gulf War* (New York, 1990), p. 145. He claims that the cost of the Iraq-Iran war was about $1,097 billion, which exceeds the two nations' total oil revenues in this century (p. 147).

44. See the text of Saddam's conversation with Glaspie in Sciolino (1991), pp. 273–278.

45. Ibid., p. 281.

46. See Michael Massing, "The Way to War," *New York Review of Books,* March 28, 1991. For a different view, see Tom Tsutomu Kone, "Road to the Invasion" *American-Arab Affairs,* nos. 3 and 4 (Fall 1990), pp. 29–45.

47. Quoted in Sciolino (1991), p. 173.

48. See Bahman Bakhtiari, "Iranian Foreign Policy in the Persian Gulf," in H. Amirahmadi, ed. *The United States and the Middle East* (Albany, 1993); Hooshing Amirahmadi, "Global Restructuring: The Persian Gulf War and the United States Quest for World Leadership," in Amirahmadi (1993); Shahram Chubin, "Iran and the Gulf Crisis," *Middle East Insight,* 7, no. 4, pp. 34–35, and Said Amir Arjomand, "A Victory for the Pragmatists," in James Piscatori, ed., *Islamic Fundamentalisms and the Gulf Crisis* (Chicago, 1991), pp. 52–69.

49. *FBIS* (South Asia), August 6, 1990.

50. *Washington Post,* July 10, 1990.

51. *Financial Times,* August 13, 1990.

52. *FBIS* (SA), August 11, 1990.

53. For the contents of the letter, see Pierre Salinger and Eric Laurent, *Secret Dossier* (New York, 1991), pp. 223–235.

54. President Saddam Hossein's letter to President Rafsanjani, August 3, 1990.

55. President Rafsanjani's letter to President Saddam Hossein, August 8, 1990. The letter is translated by the Islamic Republic. The quotations in this section are all from this letter.

56. *FBIS* (SA), August 15, 1990.

57. *Abrar* (an Iranian newspaper), August 17, 1990.

58. *FBIS* (SA), December 2, 1990.

59. *Resa'lat,* January 23, 1991.

60. *FBIS,* April 27, 1990.

61. *Washington Post,* September 11, 1990.

62. John Kelly, assistant secretary of state, made the prediction. *The Persian Gulf Crisis, Joint Hearings of the Committee on Foreign Affairs and the Joint Economic Committee* (Washington, D.C., 1991), p. 125.

63. *Financial Times,* September 8, 1990.

64. *FBIS* (SA), January 2, 1991.

65. *Washington Post,* December 23, 1990.

66. *New York Times,* November 3, 1991.

67. *FBIS,* October 10, 1990.

68. Ibid., January 3, 1991.

69. Personal interview with a member of Iran's Foreign Ministry, Teheran, July 9, 1991.

70. *The Persian Gulf Crisis: Relevant Documents, Correspondence, Reports,* Prepared by the Sub-committee on Arms Control, International Security and Services, Washington, D.C., 1991, p. 204.

71. See James Bill, 'The Persian Gulf Crisis: An Analysis of Diplomacy and War," The Committee on Armed Services U.S. House of Representatives, December 6, 1990. I am grateful to Professor Bill for sending me a copy of his testimony, which still has much relevance to the present situation in the region.

72. See R. K. Ramazani, "Future Security in the Persian Gulf: American Role," *Middle East Insight,* Special Report, Policy Review, no. 2, 1991.

Conclusion

Before the dawn of the Islamic Revolution in Iran, it was fashionable in the West to ignore Islam as an irrelevant or peripheral force in politics. Today, Islam can no longer be ignored because it has become the most powerful ideology in the Islamic world. In fact, we are witnessing a powerful revival of Islam that is unprecedented in modern times. Nowadays, it has become fashionable to exaggerate the "threat" of Islam. Why this exaggeration?

The collapse of the former Soviet Union has created an intellectual and geopolitical crisis for the United States and for some of its Middle Eastern allies. For four decades, U.S. policy was based on a Manichaean division of the world into two rival camps of good and evil: the former represented by the Soviet Union and its allies and the latter by the United States and its allies. With the collapse of the Soviet Union, that Manichaean paradigm has become obsolete. We need to develop a new paradigm that corresponds to the realities of the emerging new world order, one that demands revisions of some of our dearly held assumptions.

Clearly, there is a great deal of intellectual resistance to develop this much-needed new paradigm. Regrettably, there is a powerful constituency in the United States, supported by some Middle Eastern countries, that is sworn to resuscitate the corpse of the old paradigm by creating a new enemy. The Islamic Republic of Iran and Islam have been conveniently chosen, perhaps for the lack of any better alternatives, to replace the Soviet Union and communism, respectively. For obvious reasons, Iran is no Soviet Union and Islam is not communism.

For decades, many U.S. allies in the Middle East, including the Shah, received generous U.S. support because of their strategic value as bastions against Soviet communism. Thus, they got away with much that should not have been tolerated, such as corruption and despotism. With the end of the Cold War, some of these countries have lost their strategic value. They may regain that lost value only if they can become bastions against a new threat. The Iranian-inspired, Islamic fundamentalist movements have become that new threat.

In 1993, for example, President Hosni Mubarak of Egypt claimed that Iran was behind the resurgence of a popular Islamic movement in his country that was threatening his regime. History, it is said, repeats itself twice: the first time as a tragedy and the second time as a farce. About thirty years ago, when the Shah was in power, Khomeini began his crusade against the Pahlavis, which culminated in the June Uprising of 1963. When hundreds of pro-Khomeini zealots were killed by the government, the Shah blamed the Egyptians for the turmoil in Iran. He claimed that Khomeini had received lavish financial support from a certain Egyptian, who was identified as an intelligence officer for the Egyptian security forces. President Abdul Naser denied this absurd charge. What the Shah failed to recognize was that his own policies had caused the June Uprising. The failure to grasp that critical fact eventually cost him the Peacock Throne. President Mubarak is making the same mistake the Shah made in 1964. His fate might not be much happier than the Shah's.

But we need not make the same mistake. Although Teheran has been support-ive of all Islamic movements, even to the detriment of its national interests, Iran is not the cause of the Islamic resurgence. Its roots are the popular belief in Islam as a religion of justice and salvation, the prevailing corruption and poverty, the inability of such ideologies as socialism and secular nationalism to offer accept-able solutions to the people's pressing problems, increased Western encroach-ment, and the utter failure of the despotic governments to democratize the politi-cal system and to improve the people's living conditions. As was the case in Iran, Islamic fundamentalism is, more than anything else, the political manifestation of the desire of the deprived segments of the population to participate in the po-litical process and to rebuild a new society and state. Rather than trying to sup-press them or identifying them as the enemy, which could very well evolve into a devastating religious war between Islam and Christianity, the major powers are well advised to either help counteract the conditions that nourish and sustain the Islamic movements or to recognize the basic right of the people to live the way they want.

Many of the conditions that paved the way for the Islamic Revolution in Iran exist in most Islamic nations today. By learning about Iran, we can better appreci-ate the nature of the Islamic movements in other countries. And it is to the Ira-nian experience that once again we must turn.

The Islamic Revolution in 1979 ended a cycle in Iran's long history, one that be-gan with the Constitutional Movement of 1905–1911. During that cycle, but espe-cially under Mohammad Reza Shah's rule, the Iranian economy, which was pre-dominantly agrarian at the turn of the century, was somewhat modernized. The political system, however, remained archaic, autocratic, and unresponsive to the demands of the masses who sought to participate in the political process. By de-nying participation to all but those few who obediently followed his directions, the Shah isolated his regime from the bulk of the population and failed to build durable political institutions. Consequently, a gap was created between the institution-building capacity of the Shah's regime and the growing productive forces of the society. This gap ruptured and evolved into a revolution in Iran for two reasons: (1) the coincidence of an economic contraction following a period of stupendous economic expansion with the liberalization of the polity after years of repression and (2) the prevalent perception in Iran of the weakening of the "support linkage" between Washington and Teheran.

The system the Shah had created appeared powerful from outside but was in fact infested with the fatal virus of autocracy. It was a one-man show, a highly centralized system, and when the apex of that system was overcome by a paralysis of will, the entire system quickly crumbled even before the revolutionaries took over. The state managers were no more than paper tigers—insecure about their legitimacy and unwilling to fight for the survival of a system that had so lavishly enriched them.

Thus, the Islamic Revolution was the explosion of pent-up frustrations and grievances of a population against the consequences of radical change imposed on them by the Pahlavis—change they neither understood nor supported. A large portion of the population, coming from diverse socioeconomic backgrounds, supported the revolution; hence its multiclass character. Therefore, all endeavors to attribute the victory of the revolution to a single group or ideology are misleading.

Once the Shah was dethroned, fierce competition for control of the state began. The nationalists, the Mojahedin, and the leftists contend that the fundamentalist ulama "hijacked" the revolution, but this contention is more an accurate reflection of their delusion about their own popularity and their frustration with the outcome of the revolution than it is a fair analysis of the political situation in the aftermath of the collapse of the ancien régime.

Immediately after the Shah's overthrow, the nationalists, both Islamic and secular, found themselves lacking a charismatic leader who could unify them and rally the masses behind their cause. Victims of the misguided belief that the ulama would not and could not take over the government, the nationalists had a reformist agenda for a country that was desperately searching for a revolutionary solution. They had good ideas and ideals that were unsuited for the time. Nor could they communicate with the lower classes, which constituted the largest block of the urban population and which the revolution had politicized.

The fate of the Mojahedin was no happier than that of the nationalists. In the first few months of the revolution, they were preoccupied with rebuilding their shattered organization, which had been almost demolished by SAVAK. Once they revitalized their organization, the Mojahedin, whose constituency was limited to the young, tried to do the impossible: to defeat the established Shi'i hierarchy, the ulama, as the champion of the true Islam. They eventually placed their destiny with President Bani Sadr against the fundamentalists. It was a big gamble, and they lost. Frustrated, they resorted to violence. But their violence was answered by the even more raw violence of the fundamentalists.

The leftists were in an even worse position than the Mojahedin or the nationalists. Their constituency was small and their ambition large. They too failed to unify their forces and to win the allegiance of the lower classes for whose cause they were fighting but with whom they could hardly communicate. A good portion of the leftists, especially the Tudeh and the majority Fadae'iyun, pursued a suicidal strategy reminiscent of the deadly game their counterparts had earlier played in Germany, not that I intend any comparison between fascism and fundamentalism. German communists campaigned indefatigably to weaken the Social Democrats, who were considered their greatest enemy. This facilitated the rise of Adolf Hitler, who decimated the Social Democrats, the communists, and millions of innocent people, including the Jews. In Iran, the leftists, intoxicated with the illusion of eventually ruling Iran, opposed the nationalists, whom they saw as agents of imperialism. Eventually, the shrewd fundamentalists gave the leftists a bit of their own medicine: They sat on the sidelines and jubilantly watched the leftists weakening the nationalists and defaming each other. At the opportune moment, the fundamentalists dismantled the leftist organizations and discredited their leaders.

The fundamentalists' Pyrrhic victory became possible first and foremost because Ayatollah Khomeini had emerged as the leader of the revolution before the Shah was overthrown. Khomeini then used this leadership status, along with his immense popularity, to create an Islamic republic. Complementing his broad popularity and his skill to communicate with the masses, he received aggressive support from his antinomian protagonists, whose devotion to him was largely independent of any material benefits they may have received. Their invisible bond of loyalty to him was mystical in essence: No other leader in revolutionary Iran had his extraordinary power to conquer the people's mind.

Nations, like individuals, each have a consciousness. They go through occasional periods of self-examination, introspection, and soul-searching. With the monarchy dismantled, many Iranians resorted to a revolutionary interpretation of Shi'ism to get them through this difficult process. Shi'ism, with its apocalyptic overtones, its emphasis on spiritual purification, its insistence on equality before God, and its deep-seated roots in the Iranian culture and psyche, became attractive to millions of Iranians. Khomeini capitalized on this and energized a populist movement that surfaced in the first year of the Islamic Revolution. The main base of support for that movement was the shopkeepers and the lower classes. That movement's goal of revolutionizing the society by indiscriminate destruction of all things Pahlavi was harmonious with the revolutionary extremism that the Iranian Revolution, like all other revolutions, had generated.

The fundamentalists' victory was also a function of several other factors: their fortitude and singleness of purpose; their competence as institution builders who created a state within the state; their creation of their own militia; excellence as mass psychologists whose sensitive antennae guided them to move smoothly along with popular demands of the day and to strengthen their links with the dispossessed and displaced; their exploitation of anti-Americanism to increase their popularity; and their lack of compunction to apply force to suppress their opponents.

Thus, by the third anniversary of the Islamic Revolution, the fundamentalists were securely at the helm of the state. The Islamic Republic under Ayatollah Khomeini managed to survive, despite economic hardship and stagnation (which was the result of the inexperience and flawed policies of the officials of the Islamic Republic), strong internal and external opposition, a devastating war with Iraq, and Washington's open hostility toward the fundamentalists. The ideological regime that Khomeini founded, unlike the Shah's, suffered from no inferiority complex toward the West and in fact regarded its ideology and mission as divinely inspired and therefore superior to the human-formulated ideology of the West.

With the death of Ayatollah Khomeini in 1989, intraelite rivalry between factions has intensified. Because of this competition, the Iranian elites, not the masses, have much room to maneuver to express their views: The lively debates in the Majles and publication of daily newspapers that are highly critical of Rafsanjani are examples of this new political atmosphere. The challenge for all democrats is to push the Islamic Republic to expand this freedom to all segments of the population.

Thus far, the pragmatic faction has been on the ascendance in the Byzantine politics of revolutionary Iran. The pragmatic leadership has steered Iran toward moderation. Using jargon from the study of revolutions, we can state that the Islamic Revolution is now experiencing the Thermidorian stage of its evolution. This new posture is not, as some experts claim, merely tactical or deceptive. It is real. This moderation has come to fruition because of the domestic and international pressures exerted on the Islamic Republic during the past fourteen years and because of the belated but welcomed realization by a good portion of Iran's ruling elite that the ability of the Islamic Republic to change Iran or the Islamic world is limited indeed. Examples of this moderation include President Rafsanjani's economic policy of curtailing state subsidies and moving Iran away from a crude form of socialism toward a free enterprise system; Iran's help in the release of the U.S. hostages in Lebanon; Iran's 1992 signing in Paris of the international treaty to ban chemical and biological weapons; and Iran's neutrality during the Second Persian Gulf War and its remarkable silence during the Iraqi Civil War, when the Islamic Republic did not fully support the Shi'ites in southern Iraq.

That the pragmatists are in control today does not mean that their victory is irreversible. Today, the crusader faction has become considerably weaker than it was under Khomeini. But it is still a powerful force that cannot be ignored. Not only are the crusaders powerful within various governmental agencies and the Revolutionary Guards; they also exercise considerable influence within the economically powerful *bonyad*s, or foundations.

Nor does the ascendance of the moderate faction mean that Iran no longer faces serious social and political problems. Far from it. Certain policies are making the government more distanced from the masses. There is also considerable tension between the regular state that Rafsanjani heads and the many powerful revolutionary organizations created after the revolution. Although these organizations were instrumental in the victory of the fundamentalists, they have now become a major hindrance to policy implementation and to Rafsanjani's centralization of power.

But the greatest challenge facing the Islamic Republic today is reconstructing Iran's war-damaged economy. There is a growing demand by all segments of the population for improvements in their living condition, which is poorer than it was under the Shah. This imperative for reconstruction and economic development has placed the Islamic Republic at a dangerous crossroads: The successful undertaking of such a task requires not only a rapprochement with the West but also the active participation of the professional middle class, which means democratization of the political process. The dilemmas for the new elite are these: Can they retain the Islamic character of the state while engineering a rapprochement with the West? Can they win the allegiance of the modern middle class, whose ideology is not always compatible with strict codes of the Islamic Republic, such as the veiling of women and harsh punishment for the violators of the Islamic morality?

The new Islamic elites are learning that the art of winning a revolution, which they knew well, is quantitatively different from the art of governing a complicated society like Iran, which they have not yet mastered. To remain in power, they must quickly master that precious art of statecraft, the essence of which is learning how to compromise.

Select Bibliography

Theories of Revolution

Adelman, J. R., ed. *Revolutions and Superpowers.* New York: Praeger, 1986.

Anderson, Perry. *Lineages of the Absolutist State.* Norfolk, Va.: Verso, 1979.

Arendt, Hannah. *On Revolution.* New York: Penguin, 1965.

Brinton, Crane. *The Anatomy of Revolution.* London: Jonathan Cape, 1953.

Burke, Edmund. *Reflections on the Revolution in France.* New York: Penguin, 1979. Reprint.

Chorley, Katherine. *Armies and the Art of Revolution.* London: Faber and Faber, 1973.

Davies, James. "The J-Curve of Rising and Declining Satisfactions as a Cause of Some Great Revolutions and a Contained Revolution." In *Violence in America,* Hugh Davis Graham and Ted Robert Gurr, eds. New York: Signet Books, 1969. Pp. 671–709.

de Tocqueville, Alexis. *The Old Regime and the French Revolution.* Trans. from the French by Stuart Gilbert. New York: Doubleday Anarcher, 1955.

Fanon, Frantz. *The Wretched of the Earth.* Trans. Constance Farrington. New York: Grove Press, 1963.

Goldstone, Jack, Ted Robert Gurr, and Farrokh Moshiri, eds., *Revolutions of the Late Twentieth Century.* Boulder, Colo.: Westview Press, 1991.

Greene, Thomas. *Comparative Revolutionary Movements.* Englewood Cliffs, N.J.: Prentice-Hall, 1990.

Gurr, Ted. *Why Men Rebel.* Princeton: Princeton University Press, 1970.

Hobsbawm, Eric. *Primitive Rebels.* Manchester: Manchester University Press, 1959.

Hoffer, Eric. *The Ordeal of Change.* New York: Harper and Row, 1952.

Huntington, Samuel. *Political Order in Changing Societies.* New Haven: Yale University Press, 1968.

Kelley, George, and Clifford Brown, Jr., eds. *Struggles in the State: Sources and Patterns of World Revolutions.* New York: John Wiley, 1970.

Marx, Karl. *The Class Struggles in France (1848–1850).* New York: International, 1964.

Moore, Barrington, Jr. *Injustice: The Social Basis of Obedience and Revolt.* New York: M. E. Sharpe, 1978.

―――― . *Social Origins of Dictatorship and Democracy.* Boston: Beacon Press, 1966.

Oberschall, Anthony. *Social Conflict and Social Movements.* Englewood Cliffs, N.J.: Prentice-Hall, 1973.

Skocpol, Theda. *States and Social Revolutions: A Comparative Analysis of France, Russia and China.* New York: Cambridge University Press, 1979.

Stavarianos, L. S. *Global Rift: The Third World Comes of Age.* New York: William Morrow, 1981.

Tilly, Charles. *From Mobilization to Revolution.* Reading, Mass.: Addison-Wesley, 1978.

Wolf, Eric. *Peasant Wars of the 20th Century.* New York: Harper and Row, 1963.

English Sources on the Islamic Revolution and Revolutionary Iran

Abrahamian, Ervand. *Iran Between Two Revolutions.* Princeton: Princeton University Press, 1982.

_____ . *Khomeinism.* Berkeley: University of California Press, 1993.

Afkhami, Gholam Resa. *The Iranian Revolution: Thanatos on a National Scale.* Washington, D.C.: Middle East Institute, 1985.

Afshar, Haleh, ed. *Iran: A Revolution in Turmoil.* London: Macmillan, 1985.

Akhavi, Shahrough. *Religion and Politics in Contemporary Iran: Clergy-State Relations in the Pahlavi Period.* Albany: State University of New York, 1980.

Alexander, Yonah, and Allan Nanes, eds. *The United States and Iran: A Documentary History.* Frederick, Md.: University Publications of America, 1980.

Algar, Hamid. *Religion and State in Iran, 1785–1906: The Role of the Ulama in the Qajar Period.* Berkeley: University of California Press, 1969.

Amirahmadi, Hooshang. *Revolution and Economic Transition.* Albany: State University of New York Press, 1990.

_____ , ed. *The United States and the Middle East.* Albany: State University of New York Press, 1993.

Amuzegar, Jahangir. *The Dynamics of the Iranian Revolution.* Albany: State University of New York Press, 1991.

Arjoamand, Said Amir. *The Shadow of God and the Hidden Imam.* Chicago: University of Chicago Press, 1984.

_____ . *The Turban for the Crown.* New York: Oxford University Press, 1988.

Ashraf, Ahmad. "Theocracy and Charisma: New Men of Power in Iran," *International Journal of Politics and Society,* 4, 1 (1990): 43–52.

Ashraf, Ahmad, and Ali Banuazizi. "The State, Classes and Modes of Mobilization in the Iranian Revolution," *State, Culture and Society,* 1:3 (Spring 1985): 3–39.

Bakhash, Shaul. *The Reign of the Ayatollahs: Iran and the Islamic Revolution.* New York: Basic Books, 1984.

Baktiari, Bahman. "International Law: Observations and Violations." In *The Iran-Iraq War,* Farhang Rajaee, ed. Gainesville: University Press of Florida, 1993. Pp. 152–166.

_____ . "The Leftist Challenge: The Mojahedin-e Khalq and the Tudeh Party," *Journal of South Asian and Middle Eastern Studies,* 13, 1 and 2 (Fall/Winter 1989): 29–51.

_____ . "Revolutionary Iran's Persian Gulf Policy: The Quest for Regional Supremacy." In *Iran and the Arab World,* H. Amirahmadi and N. Entessar, eds. New York: St. Martin's Press, 1993. Pp. 69–93.

Banuazizi, Ali. "Iran's Revolution Reappraised," *Third World Quarterly,* 10, 2 (April 1988): 1041–1047.

Banuazizi, Ali, and M. Weiner, eds. *The State, Religion, and Ethnic Politics: Afghanistan, Iran, and Pakistan.* Syracuse, N.Y.: Syracuse University Press, 1986.

Beeman, William. *Language, Status, and Power in Iran*. Bloomington: Indiana University Press, 1986.

Benard, Cheryl, and Zalmay Khalilzad. *The Government of God*. New York: Columbia University Press, 1984.

Bharier, Julian. *Economic Development in Iran, 1900–1970*. London: Oxford University Press, 1971.

Bill, James. *The Eagle and the Lion: America and Iran*. New Haven: Yale University Press, 1988.

——— . "The New Iran: Relations with Its Neighbors and the United States," *Asian Update* (1991).

Chehabi, H. E., *Iranian Politics and Religious Modernism*. Ithaca: Cornell University Press, 1990.

——— . "Religion and Politics in Iran: How Theocratic Is the Islamic Republic?" *Daedelus*, 120, 3 (Summer 1991): 69–91.

Christopher, Warren, et al., eds. *American Hostages in Iran*. New Haven: Yale University Press, 1985.

Cottam, Richard. *Iran and the United States*. Pittsburgh: University of Pittsburgh Press, 1988.

——— . *Nationalism in Iran*. Pittsburgh: University of Pittsburgh Press, 1979. Reprint.

Debashi, Hamid. *Ideology and Discontent: The Ideological Foundation of the Islamic Revolution in Iran*. New York: New York University Press, 1993.

Dorraj, Manochehr. *From Zarathustra to Khomeini*. Boulder, Colo.: Lynne Rienner, 1990.

Enayat, Hamid. *Modern Islamic Political Thought*. Austin: University of Texas Press, 1982.

Espesito, John, ed. *The Islamic Revolution: Its Global Impact*. Miami: Florida International University Press, 1990.

——— . *Voices of Resurgent Islam*. New York: Oxford University Press, 1983.

Farazmand, Ali. *The State, Bureaucracy, and Revolution in Iran*. New York: Praeger, 1989.

Fischer, Michael. *Iran: From Religious Dispute to Revolution*. Cambridge: Harvard University Press, 1980.

Fuller, Graham. *The Center of the Universe*. Boulder, Colo.: Westview Press, 1991.

Gasiorowski, Mark. *U.S. Foreign Policy and the Shah: Building a Client State in Iran*. Ithaca: Cornell University Press, 1991.

Green, Jerrold. *Revolution in Iran: The Politics of Countermobilization*. New York: Praeger, 1982.

Hickman, William F. "Ravaged and Reborn: The Iranian Army, 1982." Staff paper. Washington, D.C.: Brookings Institution, 1982. Pp. 1–33.

Hoogland, Eric. *Land and Revolution in Iran, 1960–1980*. Austin: University of Texas Press, 1982.

Hunter, Shireen. *Iran After Khomeini*. New York: Praeger, 1992.

——— . *Iran and the World*. Bloomington: Indiana University Press, 1990.

Huyser, Robert. *Mission to Tehran*. New York: Harper & Row, 1986.

Irani, Manuchehr. *King of the Benighted*. Transl. Abbas M. Milani. Washington, D.C.: Mage Publisher, 1990.

Joyner, Christopher, ed. *The Persian Gulf War*. New York: Greenwood Press, 1990.

Kapuseinski, Ryszard. *Shah of Shahs*. New York: Helen and Kurt Wolff Books, 1982.

Karshenas, Massoud. *Oil, State, and Industrialization in Iran*. New York: Cambridge University Press, 1990.

Katouzian, Homa. *The Political Economy of Modern Iran: Despotism and Pseudo Modernism, 1926–1979.* New York: New York University Press, 1981.
Kazemi, Farhad. *Politics and Culture in Iran.* Ann Arbor, Mich.: Center for Political Studies, 1988.
_____ . *Poverty and Revolution in Iran.* New York: New York University Press, 1980.
Keddie, Nikki, and with a section by Yann Richards. *Roots of Revolution: An Interpretive History of Modern Iran.* New Haven: Yale University Press, 1981.
Keddie, Nikki, and Mark Gariorowski. *Neither East Nor West.* New Haven: Yale University Press, 1990.
Kellner, Douglas. *The Persian Gulf T.V. War.* Boulder, Colo.: Westview Press, 1992.
Khomeini, Ruhollah. *Islam and Revolution: Writings and Declarations of Imam Khomeini.* Trans. and annotated by Hamid Algar. Berkeley, Calif.: Mizan Press, 1981.
Koury, Enver, and Charles MacDonald, eds. *Revolution in Iran: A Reappraisal.* Hyattsville, Md.: Institute of Middle Eastern and North African Affairs, 1982.
Ladjevardi, Habib. *Labor Unions and Autocracy in Iran.* Syracuse, N.Y.: Syracuse University Press, 1985.
Lambton, Ann K.S. *The Persian Land Reform, 1962–1966.* Oxford: Clarendon Press, 1969.
Lenczowski, George, ed. *Iran Under the Pahlavis.* Stanford, Calif.: Hoover Institution Press, 1978.
Looney, Robert. *Economic Origins of the Iranian Revolution.* New York: Pergamon Press, 1982.
Menashiri, David. *Iran: A Decade of War and Revolution.* New York: Holmes and Meier, 1990.
Milani, Abbas, and Manoucher Ganji. "Iran: Development During the Last Fifty Years." In *Iran: Past, Present and Future,* Jane Jacqz, ed. Aspen, Colo.: Aspen Institute for Humanities Studies, 1976. Pp. 129–140.
Milani, Farzaneh. *Veils and Words: The Emerging Voices of Iranian Writers.* New York: Syracuse University Press, 1992.
Milani, Mohsen M. "Harvest of Shame: Tudeh and the Bazargan Government," *Middle Eastern Studies,* 29, 2 (April 1993): 307–320.
_____ . "Iran's Active Neutrality During the Kuwaiti Crisis: Causes and Consequences," *New Political Science,* 21 and 22 (Summer 1992): 41–60.
_____ . "Shi'ism and the State in the Constitution of the Islamic Republic of Iran." In S. K. Farsoun and M. Mashayekhi, ed., *Political Culture of the Islamic Republic.* London: Routledge, 1992. Pp. 135–161.
_____ . "The Transformation of the Velayat-e Faqih Institution: From Khomeini to Khamanei" *Moslem World,* 82, 3–4 (July–October 1992): 175–190.
Mottahedeh, Roy. *The Mantle of the Prophet.* New York: Pantheon Books, 1985.
Najmabadi, Afsaneh. *Land Reform and Social Change in Rural Iran.* Salt Lake City: University of Utah Press, 1988.
Pahlavi, Mohammad Reza. *Answer to History.* New York: Stein and Day, 1980.
Parsons, Anthony. *The Pride and the Fall: Iran, 1974–79.* London: Jonathan Cape, 1984.
Rajaee, Farhang. *Islamic Values and World View: Khomayni on Man, the State and International Politics.* Lanham, Md.: University Publications of America, 1983.
Ramazani, R. K. "Iran's Foreign Policy: Both North and South," *Middle East Journal,* 393 (Summer 1992): 393–412.

_____ . *Revolutionary Iran: Challenge and Response in the Middle East.* Baltimore, Md.: Johns Hopkins University Press, 1986.

_____ . *The United States and Iran: The Patterns of Influence.* New York: Praeger, 1982.

_____ . "Who Started the Iraq-Iran War?" *Virginia Journal of International Law,* 33, 1 (Fall 1992), pp. 69–89.

Roosevelt, Kermit. *Counter Coup: The Struggle for the Control of Iran.* New York: McGraw-Hill, 1979.

Rosen, Barry M., ed. *Iran Since the Revolution.* New York: Brooklyn College Program on Society in Change, 1985.

Rubin, Barry. *Paved with Good Intentions: The American Experience in Iran.* New York: Oxford University Press, 1980.

Shawcross, William. *The Shah's Last Ride.* New York: Touchstone, 1988.

Sick, Gary. *All Fall Down: America's Tragic Encounters with Iran.* New York: Random House, 1985.

_____ . *The October Surprise.* New York: Random House, 1991.

Sullivan, William. *Mission to Iran.* New York: Norton, 1981.

Wright, Robin B., *In the Name of God.* New York: Simon and Schuster, 1989.

Zabih, Sepehr. *The Communist Movement in Iran.* Berkeley: University of California Press, 1966.

Zonis, Marvin. *Majestic Failure: The Fall of the Shah.* Chicago: University of Chicago Press, 1991.

Persian Language Sources on the Islamic Revolution

Asnad-e Lane-ye Jasusi (Documents of the Spy Nest). Teheran: Daftar-e Entesharat-e Islami. Various volumes.

Asnad-e Nehzat-e Azadi-ye Iran: Rahandazi-ye Naft va Tanzim-e E'tesabat (Documents of the Freedom Movement of Iran: Resumption of Oil and Coordination of Strikes). Teheran: Daftar-e Nehzat-e Azadi-ye Iran. Various volumes.

Bahsi Dar Bare-ye Marja'iyat Va Rauhaniyat (A Discussion on Marja'iyat and Rauhaniyat). Teheran: Enteshar, 1963.

Bakhtiyar, Shahpur. *Sio Haft Ruz Pas Az Sio Haft Sal* (Thirty-Seven Days After Thirty-Seven Years). Paris: Entesharat-e Radio Iran, 1981.

Bani Sadr, Abolhassan. *Khiyanat Be Omid* (Betrayal of Hope). Paris: n.p., 1983.

_____ . *Osul-e Paye Va Zavabet-e Hokumat-e Islami* (Fundamentals and Regulations of the Islamic Government). Teheran: n.p., 1979.

Bazargan, Mehdi. *Enqelab-e Iran Dar Dau Harekat* (The Iranian Revolution in Two Moves). Teheran: Daftar-e Nehzat-e Azadi-ye Iran, 1984.

_____ . *Shura-ye Enqelab Va Daulat-e Movaqat* (The Islamic Revolutionary Council and the Provisional Government). Teheran: Nehzat-e Azadi-ye Iran, 1983.

Chegunegi-ye Entekhab-e Avalin Nakhost Vazir-e Jomhuri-ye Islami-ye Iran (The Process of the Selection of the Islamic Republic's First Prime Minister). Teheran: Ravabet-e Omumi-ye Nakhost Vaziri, 1992.

Dahnavi. *Qiyam-e Khunin-e Panzdah-e Khordad-e Chehel-o Dau* (The Bloody Uprising of June 5, 1963). Teheran: Rasa, 1984.

Homayoun, Darioush. *Diruz Va Farda: Se Goftar Dar Bare-ye Iran-e-Enqelabi* (Yesterday and Tomorrow: Three Talks About Revolutionary Iran). Los Angeles: n.p., 1981.

Keyanuri, Nuredin. *Khaterat-e Nuredin Keyanuri* (Keyanuri's Memoirs). Teheran, 1992.

Khomeini, Ruhollah. *Hokumat-e Islami Ya Velayat-e Faqih* (The Islamic Government or Velayat-e Faqih). Najaf: Adab Press, 1969.

———— . *Kashfol Asrar* (Secrets Discovered). Teheran: n.p., n.d.

Koudeta-ye Nozeh. (The Nozeh Coup). Teheran: Center for Political Research, 1988.

Mavaz'e Ma (Our Positions). Teheran: Islamic Republican Party, n.d.

Mesl-e Barf Ab Khahim Shod: Mozakerat-e Shura-ye Farmandehan-e Artesh (Like Snow We Will Melt: Negotiations of the Council of the Commanders of the Army). Teheran: Nashrani, 1983.

Moqttar, Mohammad. "Barresi-ye Sho'arha-ye Dauran-e Enqelab" (Review of the Slogans of the Revolutionary Period), *Ketab-e Jom'e, 13, 20, and 21 (Teheran, 1979).*

Motahhari, Morteza. *Piramun-e Enqelab-e Islami* (On the Islamic Revolution). Teheran: Sephehr, 1981.

Najafabadi, Salehi. *Velayat-e Faqih, Hokumat-e Salehin* (The Guardianship of the Jurisconsult: The Rule of the Righteous Ones). Teheran: Rasa, 1984.

Qarabaghi, Abbas. *Haqayeq Dar Bare-ye Bohran-e Iran* (Truth About the Crisis in Iran). Paris: Soheyal, 1982.

Qiyam-e Hemaseh Afarinan-e Qom Va Tabriz (The Heroic Uprising of Qom and Tabriz). 3 volumes. Teheran: Nehzat-e Azadi-ye Iran, 1981.

Rafsanjani, Ali Akbar Hashemi. *Enqelab Va Defa-ye Moqaddas* (Revolution and the Holy Defense) Teheran: Amir Kabir, 1988.

———— . *Enqelab Ya Be'sat-e Jadid* (Revolution or a New Mission). Teheran: Yaser, 1985.

———— . *Notqha-ye Qabl Az Dastur-e Hojatolislam Rafsanjani* (Hojatolislam Rafsanjani's Speeches Before the Official Deliberations of the Majles). Teheran: Majles, 1983.

Rauhani, Seyyed Hamid. *Barresi Va Tahlili Az Nehzat-e Imam Khomeini* (Review and Analysis of Imam Khomeini's Movement). 11th ed. Teheran: Entesharat-e Islami, 1982.

———— . *Shariatmadari dar Dargah-e Tarikh* (Shariatmadari in the Court of History). Teheran: Entesharat-e Islami, 1985.

Shadman Valavi, Seyyed Fakhreddin. *Taskhir-e Tamaddon-e Farangi* (The Conquest of Foreign Civilization). Teheran: Zandi, 1948.

Shari'ati, Ali. *Islam Shenasi* (Islamology). Teheran: Ershad, n.d.

———— . *Shahadat* (Martyrdom). Teheran: Ershad, 1971.

Tabari, Ehsan. *Barkhi Masa'el-e Had-e Enqelab-e Iran* (Some Significant Issues of the Iranian Revolution). Teheran: Tudeh, 1980.

Taleqani, Mohmood. *Az Azadi ta Shahadat* (From Freedom to Martyrdom). Teheran: Entesharat-e Abuzar, 1980.

Yazdi, Ebrahim. *Akharin Talashha Dar Akharin Ruzha* (The Last Efforts in the Last Days). Teheran: Qalam, 1984.

———— . *Barresi-ye Safar-e Huyser Be Iran* (Investigation of Huyser's Trip to Iran). Teheran: Nehzat-e Azadi-ye Iran, 1984.

Zanjani, 'Amid. *Mabani-ye Feqhi-ye Qanun-e Asasi-ye Iran* (The Jurisprudential Foundation of the Islamic Republic of Iran). Teheran: Daftar-e Markazi-ye Jahad-e Daneshgahi, n.d.

About the Book and Author

In this fully revised and expanded second edition, Dr. Milani offers new insights into the causes and profound consequences of Iran's Islamic Revolution. Drawing on dozens of personal interviews with the officials of the Islamic Republic and on recently released documents, he presents a provocative analysis of the dynamics and characteristics of factional politics in Islamic Iran. Among the new issues covered are the events leading up to the Teheran hostage crisis, Ayatollah Khomeini's life and writings, President Rafsanjani's activities against the Shah, Rafsanjani's recent reforms, Iran's involvement in the Kuwaiti crisis, and the domestic and foreign policy challenges facing Iran in the post–Cold War era.

The second edition is specifically revised for use as a text for courses dealing with Iran, the Middle East, and revolutionary movements.

Mohsen M. Milani is associate professor of politics, Department of Government and International Affairs, University of South Florida in Tampa.

Index